Forging an Integrated Europe

Michigan Studies in International Political Economy

SERIES EDITORS: Edward Mansfield and Lisa Martin

Michael J. Gilligan
Empowering Exporters: Reciprocity, Delegation, and Collective Action in American Trade Policy

Barry Eichengreen and Jeffry Frieden, Editors
Forging an Integrated Europe

Thomas H. Oatley
Monetary Politics: Exchange Rate Cooperation in the European Union

Robert Pahre
Leading Questions: How Hegemony Affects the International Political Economy

Forging an Integrated Europe

BARRY EICHENGREEN

AND

JEFFRY FRIEDEN,

EDITORS

Ann Arbor

THE UNIVERSITY OF MICHIGAN PRESS

First paperback edition 1999
Copyright © by the University of Michigan 1998
All rights reserved
Published in the United States of America by
The University of Michigan Press
Manufactured in the United States of America
⊖ Printed on acid-free paper

2002   2001   2000   1999   5   4   3   2

A CIP catalog record for this book is available from the British Library.

Library of Congress Cataloging-in-Publication Data

Forging an integrated Europe / Barry Eichengreen and Jeffry Frieden, editors.
    p.   cm. — (Michigan studies in international political economy)
    Includes bibliographical references and index.
    ISBN 0-472-10840-9 (alk. paper)
    1. Europe—Economic integration.   2. Monetary unions—European Union countries.   3. European Union countries—Politics and government.   I. Eichengreen, Barry J.   II. Frieden, Jeffry A. III. Series.
    HC240.F62   1997
    337.1′42—dc21   97-36700
                                                     CIP

ISBN 0-472-08610-3 (pbk. : alk. paper)

Contents

1. Introduction   1
    Barry Eichengreen and Jeffry Frieden

Part 1. Economic and Monetary Union

2. The Transition to Economic and Monetary Union   21
    Geoffrey Garrett

3. The Political Economy of French Economic Policy in the
    Perspective of EMU   49
    Christian de Boissieu and Jean Pisani-Ferry

4. Macroeconomic Stabilization with a Common Currency:
    Does European Monetary Unification Create a Need for
    Fiscal Insurance or Federalism?   91
    Kenneth M. Kletzer

Part 2. Political Institutions

5. Economic and Political Integration: Institutional Challenge
    and Response   129
    Lisa L. Martin

6. Banking Regulation with Variable Geometry   159
    Jürgen von Hagen and Michele Fratianni

7. The Impact of Economic Integration on European Wage-
    Setting Institutions   185
    Michael Wallerstein

Part 3. Enlargement

8. Nordic Accession: An Analysis of the EU Referendums   211
    Jonathon W. Moses and Anders Todal Jenssen

9. Alpine Contrasts: Swiss and Austrian Responses to the EU   247
    Sven W. Arndt

10. The Political Economy of Eastern Enlargement   273
    Peter Bofinger

Contributors   327

Index   329

CHAPTER 1

Introduction

Barry Eichengreen and Jeffry Frieden

European integration is an increasingly delicate balancing act. The three principal items on the European agenda—Economic and Monetary Union, the reform of political institutions, and enlargement—are all difficult and contentious. Indeed, some aspects of the three may be mutually contradictory.

Monetary union is a core goal, but whether it will be achieved remains uncertain. Most of Europe could have a single currency and central bank by the middle of the next decade, but plans for monetary union could also collapse before the end of the century and bring the entire structure of European integration tumbling down.

Discussions of Economic and Monetary Union (EMU) take place against the backdrop of dissatisfaction with the structure and operation of the European Union's (EU) political institutions. In many quarters, EU institutions are regarded as opaque, undemocratic, and inefficient. Such concerns about governance and accountability acquire immediacy insofar as some believe that bringing EMU to its logical conclusion requires political integration.

Concern about EU political institutions is given further urgency in the context of EU enlargement. The Union currently faces demands for accession from a score of countries in Central and Eastern Europe, the Middle East, and North Africa. The member states are considering whether to move toward an EU of 25 or even 35 members over the coming decades. Inevitably, it will be necessary to restructure political institutions to cope with an expanding membership.

These three issues—economic and monetary union, the reform of political institutions, and enlargement—pose major challenges to the process of European integration. Comprehending their implications is itself a challenge for policymakers and academics. Meeting that challenge means grasping the interplay of domestic and international politics.[1] It means synthesizing research from the disparate fields of economics and political science.

This volume attempts to do just that. It contains analyses by economists and political scientists concerned with the domestic and international and economic and political dimensions of the integration process. It is the product of an interdisciplinary group conducting research on the political economy of European integration that has met since 1991 under the auspices of the Center for German and European Studies at the University of California.[2] The book is divided into three parts, corresponding to the three issues identified previously as central to the integration process.

Like other attempts to analyze the political economy of European integration, the studies in this volume have to grapple with the interplay of different arenas in which which political and economic factors come together to affect European outcomes. European integration implicates and grows out of interests and institutions at both the national and European levels. Scholarship has long debated the relative importance of these different influences on European integration, although most recognize that these are not mutually exclusive. It is useful to begin by summarizing the principal levels of analysis on which explanation has been based.

I.   Levels of Analysis

I.I.   Domestic Interests

For social scientists, and for economists in particular, seeking to trace the progress of European integration, a natural point of departure is socioeconomic interest groups. Each country possesses its own constellation of interest groups, whose makeup reflects the economy's factor endowment and comparative advantage. Some groups see free trade, unrestricted capital mobility, and other forms of integration as in their economic self-interest and lobby accordingly. Others oppose the same on equally selfish grounds. The Heckscher-Ohlin model of international trade predicts, for example, that a country's abundant factors of production will favor unrestricted trade and capital movements; this will be capital's preference in capital-abundant countries and labor's preference in countries where capital is scarce. Other models provide somewhat different predictions, but the general approach—tracing policies to interests and interests to underlying structure—is fundamentally the same.

Thus, many attempts to understand the EU's development focus on big business and finance as catalysts for integration and on agriculture as a protectionist lobby to be overcome. They attribute the progress of integration to the ascendancy of integrationist lobbies and to the waning influence of declining sectors, both of which reflect the changing sectoral structure of the European economy.

A problem with this approach is that it cannot explain why European integration appears to proceed in fits and starts. The structure of the economy, and the interest group pressures emanating from it, evolve gradually and incrementally, but policy repeatedly appears to reverse itself. For example, there was no obvious change in the balance of special interest influence between 1985 and 1987, when the Single Act was passed, or between 1990 and 1992, when the Maastricht Treaty was signed. It is hard to explain pivotal events in the evolution of the European Union in terms of the interest group model strictly construed. In addition, it is generally accepted that similar confluences of interests can give rise to a variety of different policy outcomes; the structure of interests rarely provides sufficient information to predict policy.

1.2. National Institutions

For interests to affect policy, they must be channeled through social and political institutions. Institutions amplify the influence of some interest groups and dissipate the influence of others. Institutions are often seen as restricting the number of possible policies that a set of interests might achieve, thus providing a crucial mediating link between interests and outcomes.

Many (but not all) of the relevant institutions are national. Thus, labor's concern about policies toward unemployment tends to have more impact in countries with powerful and cohesively organized national labor unions and working-class political parties. Electoral institutions, the partisan orientation of governments, and the influence of national bureaucracies and technocrats similarly amplify or mute the influence of different interest groups. Some would go further, arguing that bureaucratic institutions themselves often come to have an independent or autonomous impact on policy—as is commonly asserted about central banks, the courts, and regulatory agencies. It follows that national institutions can exercise a powerful impact on the progress of integration. Such factors have been invoked to explain why countries' policies toward European integration vary and why those policies differ across issue areas.

In principle, sociopolitical institutions have the capacity to magnify the impact on policy of small changes in economic structure and special interest lobbying, mitigating one of the shortcomings of the simple interest group approach. In the European context, analysts often point to domestic political institutions to explain how and why national policies toward European integration are adopted in the absence of clear societal demands for them—and sometimes in the presence of societal opposition. Common interpretations of EMU include the assertion that, in some countries at least, the commitment to monetary union has been taken by independent executives in the face of broad popular skepticism.

One problem with this approach is that it often seems to allow independent institutional actors to do just about anything. This is incompatible with the equilibrium selection story, in which political institutions restrict the range of feasible policies. If political institutions effectively shelter policy from social pressures, it is hard to know what the sources of policy might be other than policymakers' particularistic biases. Another problem is that the focus on national political institutions seems to provide little or no obvious avenue through which events abroad can affect domestic policies.

1.3. Intergovernmentalism

In fact, few who suggest that domestic political institutions mediate interest group politics so as to produce a national policy stance would really assert that the foreign policy positions taken by governments are independent of their foreign counterparts. How hard governments push for a particular objective may depend on how hard their foreign counterparts push back. Bargaining among nation-states is unquestionably important, in other words.

Analyses of such bargaining typically use game-theoretic tools. These techniques help to clarify how governments arrive at the strategies they use. Systematically modeling this interaction forces one to think hard about the likely reaction of other states (and nonstate actors). This approach is known as "intergovernmentalism" in the literature of the European Union because of its emphasis on the interaction of member states as prime movers.

A problem with intergovernmentalism, as with game-theoretic approaches more generally, is that they admit of a multiplicity of outcomes. Especially when governments interact repeatedly over time, there is more than one sustainable outcome to the policy game, and arbitrary assumptions must be added to select an equilibrium. This is reminiscent of the problem with domestic interest group analysis, in that many possible outcomes are consistent with the same configuration of national interests. In addition, the rich analysis of interests and institutions that is used to analyze the politics of European policy at the national level tends to drop from sight when attention turns to the strategic interaction of governments.

1.4. Transnational Institutions and Interests

As at the domestic level, it would be desirable to introduce a role for transnational—in the European context, trans-European—institutions to select among possible interstate bargaining equilibria. At the same time, there is little question that the European Union is more than a simple alliance of independent national states, a coalition of countries seeking to achieve a cooperative solution. Just as domestic institutions work to amplify certain interests, mute the voices of others, and allow technocrats to advance agendas of their own, EU institutions can have an independent effect on EU policy outcomes. The Council of Ministers, it is true, is largely a venue for national government influence. But the European Commission and the European Court of Justice have considerable independence from the governments of member states (although their precise degree of independence is a subject of scholarly debate). Experience has made clear that the institutions of European integration profoundly influence the outcomes of intergovernmental debates.

Something analogous is true of interests. The integration of markets for merchandise and factors of production—incomplete as it may remain—has helped to create Europe-wide interest groups. Pan-European industry and trade organizations are now active in policy debates—witness the role of lobbies like the Association for the Monetary Union of Europe in the EMU debate. As anticipated by the "neofunctionalists" of the 1950s and 1960s, integration has given rise to cohesive pan-European interests within both national and EU bureaucracies.[3]

One problem with transnational analysis is that of measurement: analysts are unable to agree on the political influence of European, as opposed to nationally bound, interests and institutions. It is even more true at the international than at the domestic level that it is often difficult to identify the independent explanatory impact of institutions and in particular to distinguish their effects from the impact of the interests that led to their creation. And, if European institutions are asserted to be independent of national governments, there seems to be little basis on which to predict the policies they will pursue.

2. The Dynamics of European Integration

This set of analytical distinctions helps organize our thinking about the political economy of European integration by clarifying the different factors at play. Domestic interest group and other pressures are transmitted through political institutions to national foreign policies. Member states with varied foreign policy goals interact with each other at the European level within the context of European institutions, sometimes of trans-European interests.

There are also identifiable empirical tensions related to these levels of analysis that have been present throughout the history of the European Communities and remain very visible today. Thus, while the factors considered in section 1 are analytical—aimed at helping us to better understand European integration—we can also point to a second and related set of empirical regularities that have run through debates over the past and future of European integration.

We point to four tensions whose push and pull shape the dynamics of European integration. Like a set of tightly coiled springs, these four tensions are capable of generating highly nonlinear effects. When analyzed at the levels identified previously, they may hold the key to understanding the dynamics of the integration project.

2.1.   Tensions between Domestic and International Commitments

As integration unfolds, the concessions made by member states in the interest of the European enterprise can become disruptive of the domestic economic and political status quo. For many years the focus of European integration was the removal of trade barriers. While the creation of a customs union raised contentious issues, its domestic impact was limited. This is no longer true of today's integration agenda. Items on that agenda include not just trade liberalization but the creation of a single European currency, allowing the free movement of persons throughout the EU, subjecting national judiciaries to the dictates of the European Court of Justice, harmonizing social policies and labor relations, and transforming the nation-state's regulatory capabilities. It is hard to imagine any socioeconomic group whose vital interests are unaffected. In this sense, European commitments can challenge the political balance within national societies.

However, European commitments can also help alleviate domestic political tensions. Central to the European enterprise is the creation of encompassing institutions providing scope for cross-issue trades.[4] Imagine, for instance, that a government (say, that of Germany) might be prepared to agree to monetary unification, which it would normally resist owing to domestic opposition, in return for a security agreement that it and its constituents favor but which they would otherwise be unable to secure.[5] But, according to the Maastricht timetable, monetary union will precede political union and the creation of an effective EU foreign policy within which Germany can project influence abroad. (This sequencing presumably reflects the different amounts of time required to build policy-making institutions in the two domains.) If this permits France to first secure German support for completing the monetary union, a step that will prove permanent or at least very costly to reverse, what then will prevent Paris from reneging on its commitment to pursue political integration when the time comes to take steps in that direction? One answer is the institutions and procedures of the European Union, which can be understood as a commitment mechanism that reins in the temptation to renege on the bargain.

Linkage politics, as this phenomenon is known, can provide gains from political trade domestically as well as internationally. An international agreement can alter the domestic balance of power by "bundling" issues, allowing policy changes that render the majority of domestic interests better off—that free them from the tyranny of small blocking coalitions, in other words. An international dimension to policy can thus smooth the way for politically desirable domestic adjustments.

The interplay of domestic and international commitments figures in several of the chapters in this volume. Christian de Boissieu and Jean Pisani-Ferry show how French government strategies have been shaped since the 1970s by the need to harmonize monetary policy with that of France's EU partners, surmounting domestic opposition to costly and unpopular measures. The monetary and fiscal provisions of the Maastricht Treaty, which are the subject of the chapters by Geoffrey Garrett and Kenneth Kletzer, are by their nature at the juncture of domestic and international commitments. The chapters by Jonathon Moses and Anders Todal Jenssen and by Sven Arndt on the accession of the Nordic and Alpine countries are concerned with how domestic constituencies weigh the costs and benefits of international commitments. Peter Bofinger's chapter on enlargement to the East documents the influence of domestic interests over a venture that responds to broad foreign policy and security concerns.

At the same time, conflict between national and international objectives can exert countervailing pressures on domestic political institutions. It is common to hear arguments that European commitments challenge the authority of national policymakers and national policy in ways neither envisioned nor desired. Lisa Martin suggests that there is some truth to this assertion. However, she also holds that national political institutions can be a significant source of national political autonomy and that they continue to shape the course of European integration.

In analogous ways, Michael Wallerstein's chapter argues that, despite common complaints about the impact of European integration on the labor relations of most European countries, the social partners have retained some capacity to tailor those arrangements to national conditions. Still, integration is ongoing, and its logic implies that intrusions on domestic economic and political arrangements may grow over time.

2.2. Tensions between Authority and Accountability

No European policy can be effective unless a European body can enforce compliance with EU directives. It may be possible to implement policies at the national level, but some supranational power must possess final say. Whether this authority is vested in the European Parliament, the Commission, the Council, or the Court, the European entity in question must have the power to override national officials when the latter countermand EU directives.[6] It must be able to surmount the opposition of countries, factions within countries, and interest groups whose membership transcends national borders.[7]

Those who unsuccessfully resist EU decisions will insist that institutional arrangements provide an inadequate voice. In a sense, of course, it is inevitable that EU institutions will not be equally responsive to all governments and interest groups; were they to attempt to do so, they would be incapable of all but the most trivial actions. If their endeavors are meaningful, they will be controversial, and controversy will center on the EU's responsiveness to its diverse constituencies.

This division between authoritative policy making and indirect representation poses an obvious dilemma. It may not be feasible to ask the citizens of a European country lacking direct access to the European policy-making apparatus to obey dictates over whose formulation they have little influence. This may indeed be a violation of democratic principles. If European policymakers are not selected by the European citizenry and cannot be made answerable to it, it is hard to see how they can claim legitimate authority. On the other hand, states have long had the ability to conclude international agreements that bind their citizens.

The chapters by Jürgen von Hagen and Michele Fratianni and by Lisa Martin address this tension between political authority and political accountability. Von Hagen and Fratianni describe various proposals to combine or divide authority over issue areas, applying their findings to financial regulation. Martin considers complaints about the inadequate democratic accountability of European institutions and points out that these complaints are not without foundation. She suggests how national political institutions have acted to counter these complaints and on this basis suggests how the democratic deficit might be reduced.

2.3. Tensions between Consolidation and Extension

Far-reaching as European integration has been, its achievements have disappointed its more ardent supporters. Even the most optimistic plans for monetary union before the end of the century now encompass only a subset of member states, for example. Some EU members surely will not satisfy the preconditions for monetary union when the decision is taken to proceed. The United Kingdom and Denmark are likely to exercise their right not to participate. Other countries have the right to opt out of EU policies on everything from social policy to snuff.

Even where there is agreement on a common policy, implementation remains a problem. The free movement of individuals as mandated by the Single Act is still years from being realized. Even among the members of the Schengen Group (Belgium, France, Germany, Luxembourg, the Netherlands, Portugal, and Spain), progress toward the removal of border controls has been halting. Thus, even where there exist formal agreements and binding treaties, additional measures are still needed to render policy truly European in scope.

Many would argue that existing agreements are still inadequate to secure the full benefits of European integration. They insist, for example, that only if EMU encompasses all member states can it eliminate the transaction costs and uncertainties associated with separate national currencies and solidify the operation of the Single Market. They invoke the 1992–93 EMS crisis, in whose wake member states engaged in devaluations that undermined support for open markets.

Taken to an extreme, this implies that completing the Single Market requires a level of policy harmonization commonly associated with unitary states, encompassing technical standards, health and safety regulations, labor relations, and social policy. To those eager to construct a federal or quasi-federal union, anything less is capitulation to insularity and nostalgia.

But if existing agreements have been controversial their extension to new realms will be more so. Either members will focus on applying the *acquis communautaire* throughout the Union or they will expand the competency of EU decision making in a subset of member states. Either they will march forward in lockstep, to invoke a not altogether attractive martial metaphor, or they will divide into ranks prepared to advance more and less quickly. The chapter by von Hagen and Fratianni suggests different ways of accommodating alternative conceptions of varying levels of member state interest in common policies. Unfortunately, none of the proposed solutions overcomes the inherent fact that there is a tension between the desire to move forward together and the equally powerful requirement not to force countries to move more quickly than they are able.

It seems unlikely, in light of the debate over the Maastricht Treaty, that countries will allow themselves to be dragged, kicking and screaming, to a significantly higher level of policy harmonization. But tensions remain, and uncertainty continues to complicate the EU's marching orders.

2.4. Tensions between Deepening and Widening

Throughout its history, the EU has been forced to strike a balance between expanding its membership and more fully integrating the existing members.[8] This problem acquired new urgency with the collapse of the Soviet Union, economic transformation in Eastern Europe, and rising immigration from North Africa. Commitments to incorporate new members already exist, like that reached at the Copenhagen Summit to work toward the accession of Eastern European countries. But, given the EU's limited management resources, honoring them may require putting deepening on hold until an EU of 20 or 25 countries is in place. The alternative would be to put enlargement on hold until the EU of 15 member states has been consolidated. It is inconceivable that either strategy will be agreed upon without a fight.

In a sense, the problem is deciding how much attention to devote to the EU's internal and external peripheries. Germany's priority is integrating countries on the EU's eastern border. France's is stabilizing relations with the African countries on the southern rim of the Mediterranean. Thus, the two countries that traditionally comprise the driving force for a more deeply integrated Europe are increasingly preoccupied with the EU's external periphery. For other members, it is more important to address the economic problems of the EU's internal periphery—the low-income states and regions that are the traditional recipients of transfers from the Structural Funds and the hard core of long-term unemployed in high-income EU countries.

This volume's three chapters on accession and enlargement address aspects of these issues. In addition, von Hagen and Fratianni's discussion of variable geometry and financial regulation is closely tied to evaluations of the feasibility of enlargement.

3.   The Structure of the Book

The different analytical perspectives and empirical tensions outlined previously are elaborated in the three sections of this book, respectively organized around the three policy problems identified at the beginning of our introduction. The first of these problems, economic and monetary union, requires national governments to subjugate macroeconomic policy to international commitments. It raises the question of how the EU's political institutions must be altered to make monetary union work. It highlights the conflict between consolidating policies already agreed upon and expanding the EU's competence.

Chapters 1 through 3 address these issues. Geoffrey Garrett considers the political economy of monetary union. Garrett seeks to identify which member states will gain and lose from a single currency. He considers standard factors employed to analyze the desirability of currency union, especially the degree of economic integration with potential partners and the extent to which macroeconomic shocks are correlated among potential currency partners. But Garrett goes beyond this to suggest that the domestic impact of monetary union can be thought of analogous to increasing central bank independence by transferring monetary authority to the European Central Bank. In this way the national impact of EMU will depend on how independent the existing national central bank is and importantly on the nature of labor market institutions. Previous analyses have considered these factors in isolation; Garrett shows how they interact. He concludes that Germany, Austria, and the Benelux countries would experience the fewest dislocations, while the United Kingdom will face the most difficult adjustment. He finds that Denmark, France, and Ireland are countries for which the transition to EMU will be relatively smooth, while Southern Europe, Finland, and Sweden will find it most difficult.[9]

France is in the middle of Garrett's ranking. This reinforces the notion that France's ability to meet the preconditions for EMU is critical for the project's success. It provides a natural introduction to Christian de Boissieu and Jean Pisani-Ferry's chapter on the political economy of French economic policy. De Boissieu and Pisani-Ferry argue that French interest groups are divided over the merits of monetary integration but the institutions of French policy making insulate the European agenda from domestic politics. This has allowed French officials to repeatedly invoke the deus ex machina of European integration when formulating macroeconomic policy. While this has begun to change due to the invasiveness of the Maastricht Treaty, the imperatives of integration continue to dominate French macroeconomic policy, a state of affairs that de Boissieu and Pisani-Ferry ascribe to the inability of opponents to articulate a viable alternative.

One can imagine that once monetary union commences French macroeconomic policy will not be constrained to the same extent. Although France will lack an independent monetary policy, the existence of a European Central

Bank with an unquestioned commitment to price stability will allow France to adjust fiscal policy in response to business cycle disturbances without engendering inflationary fears. At the same time, there are those—German Finance Minister Theo Waigel among them—who argue that restraints on fiscal policy even stricter than those in the Maastricht Treaty should be applied to the governments of countries that participate in EMU.

In his chapter, Kenneth Kletzer addresses these and other questions associated with the relationship between EMU and fiscal policy. Kletzer argues that there is little need to constrain national fiscal autonomy once monetary union has commenced. Nor is it essential that participating countries construct institutions of fiscal federalism at the EU level. National fiscal policymakers, left to their own devices, can provide the requisite macroeconomic stabilization. There is scope for some cooperative provision of fiscal insurance at the European level, but there is no purely economic need for the sorts of plans for fiscal harmonization that have been the focus of such controversy since the late 1980s. This suggests that we need to look more closely at European political interests and institutions to understand current debates over fiscal convergence.

The same is true in the ongoing controversy over the harmonization of policies associated with political union. This debate raises questions about the relationship between national polities and the EU and about how national and Europe-wide constituencies are represented in EU decision making more directly. It is to the question of how European institutions affect and are affected by national interests and institutions, and what this means for the future of the EU's institutional structure, that the next three chapters turn.

Lisa Martin's chapter addresses the character and implications of Europe's political institutions. She argues that we need to acknowledge the legitimacy of complaints about the inadequate accountability of EU institutions. Martin shows that piecemeal reform will not suffice; rather, it will be necessary to alter systematically how EU institutions interact and to enhance the monitoring and surveillance mechanisms of national political bodies. Martin's chapter also demonstrates, however, that national political actors can and do have an impact on European decision making that is greater than that often pointed to in debates over the democratic deficit. At least some of the institutional reforms necessary to avoid ever greater conflict over accountability can and should be implemented at the national level.

In addition to reforming European institutions, concerns about their inadequate responsiveness can be addressed by allowing member states to opt out of programs that are unresponsive to their needs. The reluctance of member states to embrace enthusiastically all of the EU's integration initiatives has given a name to this option: variable geometry. Jürgen von Hagen and Michele Fratianni distinguish two variants of this approach. The first, which they call "concentric circles" and associate with the German government's view, anticipates that a core of countries participates in all integration initiatives but the rest subscribe only to a subset. The second, "excentric circles," is closer to the French government position and foresees that countries could opt out of individual programs at will. Using financial regulation as a case study, they show that a common policy embracing all member states maximizes economic efficiency but also heightens the risk that no common policy will result. Less encompassing forms of variable geometry, in contrast, allow for less efficiency-enhancing alternatives which are more likely to be viable politically.

Michael Wallerstein's chapter shifts the focus to labor market institutions. It is commonly argued that European integration will undermine centralized bargaining at the national level. Wallerstein challenges this presumption. Insofar as the objective of centralized bargaining has been to encourage wage restraint, he suggests that the more competitive labor market produced by intra-European factor mobility may actually increase the demand for institutions that can meet that goal. He therefore questions whether mobility will undermine the traditional European pattern of strong and relatively centralized labor market institutions and national wage bargaining. Where centralized bargaining is in decline, Wallerstein concludes, this reflects domestic factors, not pan-European influences.

Tensions at the domestic and international levels also dominate discussions over the enlargement of the European Union, both in countries that have recently joined or considered joining and within long-time member states. Voting and procedural arrangements already strained by 15 members might break down with 25, rendering increased reliance on some form of majority voting all but inevitable. Enlargement would bring in countries less developed than the poorest incumbents, further straining the operation of the economic and monetary union.

EU enlargement is thus a complex problem, involving controversy among both existing and prospective members. Jonathon Moses and Anders Todal Jenssen open the last section of the book with a detailed analysis of the referendums for EU membership in the three Nordic countries. They start with an interest-group model in which individuals favor or oppose integration depending on its impact on the sector or industry to which their livelihoods are tied. Their model, which distinguishes traded from nontraded goods and manufactures from services, goes a long way toward explaining electoral outcomes. While voting is also affected by individual attitudes that depend on a variety of noneconomic factors, these cancel out at higher levels of aggregation.

Sven Arndt provides matched case studies of Austria and Switzerland, whose referendums on EU membership yielded opposing results. Arndt identifies several straightforward explanations for the contrast. For example, while Switzerland stands to gain from its stature as a global (not merely a European) financial center, Austria aspires to be the EU's gateway to Eastern Europe. Like Moses and Jenssen, Ardnt argues that such aspects of economic structure played a part in the different referendum outcomes, although he also argues for a role for language, political institutions, and the Swiss tradition of neutrality.

The final chapter, by Peter Bofinger, considers enlargement to the east from the perspectives of both Western and Eastern Europe. He emphasizes that different Eastern European countries have very different prospects for accession; in particular, the Visegrad 4 (the Czech Republic, Hungary, Poland, and Slovakia) have much better chances than the eastern and southern tiers of transition economies. Bofinger explores the degree to which political economy models can be used to predict how interest groups in the various Eastern European states will be affected by imperatives of accession and in particular by the need to conform to the dictates of the Maastricht Treaty. This effort is made difficult, Bofinger argues, by the great uncertainties of local economic conditions. He concludes, though, that throughout Eastern Europe the effort to qualify for EU membership is likely to strengthen the position of consumers and exporters relative to large enterprises that produce for the domestic market. In Western Europe, the principal resistance to enlargement will come not from manufacturing industries but from farmers, German taxpayers, and Southern European member states that are presently the main beneficiaries of the Structural Funds. Bofinger also addresses the problems associated with potential expansion to the east and the domestic and regional obstacles to the degree of harmonization implied by drawing the countries of Eastern and Central Europe into the European Union.

4. Conclusion

No one claimed that creating an integrated Europe would be easy. But the tension between national sovereignty and transnationality simmered on the back burner as long as the European Community was preoccupied with creating a Common Market free of barriers to merchandise trade. Although national governments bridled at their loss of tariff-setting power, they retained room for maneuver on the domestic front. The Single European Act and the Maastricht Treaty, by making integration deeper and more invasive, turned up the heat. It was no longer possible to ignore the tension between national autonomy and EU authority.

That tension is especially prominent in the debate over monetary union for real and symbolic reasons. The reasons are real because monetary union implies a sacrifice of monetary prerogatives and the Maastricht Treaty imposes restrictions of fiscal policy as well. The reasons are symbolic because little better symbolizes a country's sovereignty than its currency. The same tension between domestic and international prerogatives arises in connection with enlargement because the larger the number of member states the greater the need to stream-line EU institutions and potentially override national concerns. But the scalpel of streamlining can cut two ways: while majority voting can raise the danger that countries in the minority will feel trampled upon, it might also provide an opportunity to give domestic constituencies greater voice in EU decision mak-ing. However that scalpel is wielded, it is clear that the EU's political institu-tions have in store a radical face-lift.

Thus, the three issues on which this volume focuses—economic and mon-etary union, the reform of European political institutions, and enlargement—open illuminating windows on the future of the European Union. Studying them is a useful way, we believe, of anticipating the challenges ahead.

NOTES

1. For expositional reasons, we include in this introduction under the heading "international" commitments among EU member states that might more precisely fall under the heading "regional."

2. Early versions of the contents of the present volume were presented at a con-ference in Berkeley in 1995, also sponsored by the Center for German and European Studies. The Center is supported by a Center for Excellence grant from the Federal Republic of Germany. Its director, Gerald Feldman, provided generous support for the conference, as he has for the ongoing activities of the Political Economy of European Integration program. Previous publications of the program include Eichengreen and Frieden 1994 and Eichengreen, Frieden, and von Hagen (1995a, 1995b).

3. For presentations and discussions of the neofunctionalist literature, see Pent-land 1973, especially 100–146; Webb 1983; George 1985, especially 16–35; and Keohane and Hoffmann 1991.

4. This point, associated with the literature on neofunctionalism, has been at the center of analyses of European integration that emphasize linkage or spillover effects.

5. On this process, see Garrett 1994, Woolley 1994, and Martin 1994. National governments can also invoke international agreements as scapegoats for unpopular policies. They can plead that they are being forced to take unpopular steps by the imperatives of European integration. Admittedly, the viability of this strategy rests on broad-based, if incompletely informed, support for the European enterprise. And it requires at least limited public ignorance of the policy options in question. Such ignorance may be rational, given the high costs of obtaining information about issues that are technically complex. But its persistence depends on no opposition politician or other Eurosceptic challenging the argument that "there is no alternative." These questions are explored in the contributions in Evans, Jacobson, and Putnam 1993.

6. While EU regulations automatically apply to member states, directives must be implemented through national legislation. Martin (this volume) reports statistical evidence on the implementation shortfall.

7. The influence of this last class of actors is increasingly important. The prohibition of barriers to trade in particular products affects all European producers and consumers of the goods in question, for example, irrespective of their country of residence. EU financial regulations similarly enrich or impoverish bankers, lenders, and borrowers in every member state. Many of these transnational interest groups constitute powerful lobbies at the EU level.

8. This was true in the 1960s and 1970s, when membership was enlarged from six to nine, and again in the 1980s when Greece, Portugal, and Spain were admitted. The deepening versus widening conflict was somewhat less prominent in the most recent episode of enlargement, perhaps because the new members were high-income countries. It did rear its head in the form of opposition in the Nordic and Alpine countries to monetary unification and the harmonization of social policies.

9. At the time of writing, Ireland has reaffirmed its commitment to go ahead with monetary union, while Sweden has restated its reluctance. These contrasting attitudes, which might otherwise appear perplexing, are readily explicable in terms of Garrett's analysis.

REFERENCES

Eichengreen, Barry, and Jeffry Frieden, eds. 1994. *The Political Economy of European Monetary Unification.* Boulder: Westview.
Eichengreen, Barry, Jeffry Frieden, and Jürgen von Hagen, eds. 1995a. *Politics and Institutions in an Integrated Europe.* Berlin: Springer.
————. 1995b. *Monetary and Fiscal Policies in an Integrated Europe.* Berlin: Springer.
Evans, Peter, Harold Jacobson, and Robert Putnam, eds. 1993. *Double-Edged Diplomacy.* Berkeley: University of California Press.
Garrett, Geoffrey. 1994. "The Politics of Maastricht." In *The Political Economy of European Monetary Integration,* edited by Barry Eichengreen and Jeffry Frieden, 47–66. Boulder: Westview.

George, Stephen. 1985. *Politics and Policy in the European Community.* Oxford: Clarendon.

Keohane, Robert, and Stanley Hoffmann. 1991. "Institutional Change and Europe in the 1980s." In *The New European Community: Decisionmaking and Institutional Change,* edited by Robert Keohane and Stanley Hoffmann, 1–39. Boulder: Westview.

Martin, Lisa L. 1994. "International and Domestic Institutions in the EMU Process." In *The Political Economy of European Monetary Integration,* edited by Barry Eichengreen and Jeffry Frieden, 87–106. Boulder: Westview.

Pentland, Charles. 1973. *International Theory and European Integration.* London: Faber and Faber.

Webb, Carole. 1983. "Theoretical Perspectives and Problems." In *Policymaking in the European Community,* edited by Helen Wallace, William Wallace, and Carole Webb, 1–41. 2d ed. New York: Wiley.

Woolley, John T. 1994. "Linking Political and Monetary Union: The Maastricht Agenda and German Domestic Politics." In *The Political Economy of European Monetary Integration,* edited by Barry Eichengreen and Jeffry Frieden, 67–86. Boulder: Westview.

Part I
Economic and Monetary Union

CHAPTER 2

The Transition to Economic and Monetary Union

Geoffrey Garrett

I. Introduction

The critical issue concerning the immediate future of economic and monetary union (EMU) is which countries will be members by around the year 2000. Focusing on the convergence criteria laid down in the Treaty on European Union (the Maastricht Treaty), particularly fiscal policy, prospects are dim for a broad monetary union matching the size of the European Union's (EU) internal market.[1] According to Organization for Economic Cooperation and Development (OECD) projections for 1997 (on the basis of which the earliest possible membership decisions would be made), only tiny Luxembourg is expected to meet the government deficit and debt targets laid out at Maastricht (see table 2.1).[2] Even if one were to forgive annual deficits in 1997 of more than 3 percent of gross domestic product (GDP) as long as accumulated public debt were below the 60 percent threshold, only France and the United Kingdom could join Luxembourg in a monetary union. Few Europeans would cherish the prospect of this minimal EMU, excluding the entire deutsche mark (DM) zone, as the final product of the Maastricht process.

The convergence criteria, however, are not hard and fast rules for membership in EMU. The Maastricht Treaty clearly states that members of the EU that have made substantial progress or good faith efforts toward meeting the criteria should be eligible. Furthermore, admission decisions will be made using the EU's qualified majority voting rule, which stops individual countries (in fact, any two countries) from vetoing potential members (Garrett 1993). Thus, it seems certain that some countries that do not satisfy the convergence criteria will nonetheless be part of EMU. The question is, which ones?

TABLE 2.1. EMU Convergence Criteria, 1997 (OECD projections)

	Budget Deficit (% GDP)	Public Debt (% GDP)
Austria	3.2	73.9
Belgium	3.7	131.1
Denmark	0.8[a]	70.9
Finland	1.2[a]	61.0
France	3.7	56.9[b]
Germany	3.6	62.4
Greece	6.8	107.3
Ireland	2.6[a]	80.3
Italy	6.4	124.8
Netherlands	2.7[a]	78.2
Portugal	4.2	72.5
Spain	4.7	70.7
Sweden	3.1	79.8
United Kingdom	3.7	58.7[b]

Source: OECD 1996, 13.
[a]Would satisfy the Maastricht criterion of 3.0 percent of GDP.
[b]Would satisfy the Maastricht criterion of 60.0 percent of GDP.

This essay speculates about the likely membership of Europe's monetary union. It does so by analyzing the likely macroeconomic benefits and costs for different countries of participation. I then work backward to consider which countries will want to join EMU, focusing on the bargaining game among them that will ultimately determine membership. My analysis is based on four variables. The first two are common in studies of monetary union—the integration of national economies into the EU's regional economy and the symmetry of macroeconomic shocks across countries. More integrated economies will receive more benefits (both static and dynamic) from membership, while the costs of participation increase with the extent to which shocks to specific national economies are out of step with the rest of the monetary union.

In addition, however, I also argue that the greater the implicit increase in the autonomy from political tampering of monetary policy-making associated with participation in EMU, the greater the short-run adjustment costs of membership (in terms of the dislocations associated with pursuing a "hard money" policy) will be.[3] This perspective stands in marked contrast to the credibility literature, which contends that countries with histories of "soft money" policies have the most to gain from joining EMU. The credibility approach may make sense over the long run. However, it overlooks the short-run costs of adjusting to EMU for erstwhile soft money countries, which are likely to be critical to politically charged membership decisions.

The second distinctive element of my analysis concerns the relationship between national labor market institutions and the monetary policy regime. I argue that the more "encompassing" labor market institutions are (i.e., the greater the portion of the work force that is organized and the more concentrated authority is within the organized labor movement), the better the likely macroeconomic effects of EMU membership will be. Encompassment facilitates the regulation of economywide wage growth in accordance with the dictates of the prevailing monetary regime.

Taking into account each of these four variables, my analysis suggests that if EMU is to be governed by a "textbook" independent central bank (the European System of Central Banks, ESCB) that pursues price stability come what may, only six of the EU's current 15 member states would unquestionably benefit from participation—Austria, Belgium, Denmark, Germany, Luxembourg, and the Netherlands. Austria, Germany, Luxembourg, and the Netherlands will undoubtedly be at the "core" of EMU. However, Denmark's participation must be in doubt because of continued domestic opposition to the monetary union project. Furthermore, Belgium's participation in EMU is deeply problematic. The core countries wish to have Belgium in monetary union with them notwithstanding its massive public debt overhang. But this would make it considerably more difficult for these countries to argue against the membership of any other EU state wishing to join (all of which have smaller public debt levels than Belgium does).

More importantly, the group of EMU "winners" in my analysis does not include France, even though successive French governments have gone to great lengths in the last decade to meet the convergence criteria (through the franc fort and fiscal consolidation; see Pisani-Ferry and Boissieu in this volume). One reason for France's EMU enthusiasm is clearly geopolitical—French leaders view participation in monetary union as essential to broader objectives regarding European integration. But the French government may also believe that EMU, in practice, will not be all-constraining on its policy autonomy.

My analysis up to this point has assumed that the ESCB will focus myopically on the pursuit of price stability in setting EMU's monetary policy. But, whether the ESCB in practice will behave as a textbook independent central bank is open to question. The Maastricht Treaty laid down decision-making rules that conflict with the commitment to price stability. Decisions in the Governing Council of the ESCB will be taken by a simple majority of its members. The bigger the monetary union the more the Governing Council will be dominated by central bank governors from member states. If enough national governors believe that loose monetary policy is sometimes justified—for example, to try to stimulate output or employment—this would become ESCB policy notwithstanding resistance from the Executive Board of the ESCB.

Thus, whether price stability *über alles* will rule EMU will largely depend on its size. The larger the monetary union, the greater the number of participants that would lose economically from the textbook ESCB, and hence the more likely that they would form a majority in the ESCB to loosen monetary policy. In turn, expectations about the size of EMU will influence who wants to join in the first place and how other countries will react to various applications. To reiterate, while there will be some constraints imposed on membership by the convergence criteria, there is enough ambiguity in the Maastricht Treaty to render membership decisions far from automatic and consensual.

The specter of a broad EMU sacrificing price stability in the name of short-term employment and output goals is at the heart of the Bundesbank's insistence on rigid adherence to the Maastricht convergence criteria for admission. This possibility is also critical to German Finance Minister Theo Waigel's "stability pact" for placing even tighter fiscal constraints on members of the monetary union. Conversely, the vision of a kinder, gentler EMU no doubt is a major factor behind the EMU enthusiasm of a number of countries. Most importantly, once the goal of cementing EMU as a centerpiece of the European integration project is achieved, French leaders may well become considerably more responsive to domestic demands to loosen macroeconomic conditions. The prospect of a "loose money" coalition headed by France is the Bundesbank's nightmare, and hence it can be expected to fight hard to restrict EMU membership. But a more encompassing EMU (certainly one that contains France) is central to German Chancellor Helmut Kohl's vision of Europe's future. Who wins this battle inside Germany will have a marked bearing on EMU and the European integration project more generally.

The remainder of the chapter is divided into six sections. Sections 2 and 3 briefly rehearse analyses of the likely costs and benefits of EMU based on cross-national differences in the extent of market integration and the symmetry of business cycles. Respectively, section 4 explores the implications of historical differences in monetary regimes among member states. Section 5 analyzes the macroeconomic effects of the interaction between national labor market institutions and different monetary regimes. Section 6 synthesizes the preceding sections by assessing the likely aggregate effects for different countries of participating in a monetary union whose sole objective is price stability. By way of conclusion, in section 7 I speculate about the conditions under which EMU might operate in this textbook fashion and about likely developments in the transition to monetary union in the next few years.

2. Intra-EU Trade and the Benefits of EMU

The EU Commission (1990) has argued that the move to monetary union is essential to realizing the full benefits of the internal market program. There are clear static gains from eliminating the transaction costs associated with exchanging national currencies. Moreover, the dynamic gains from monetary union are potentially much greater—stimulating investment and trade by stabilizing exchange rate expectations. While there is reason to doubt the Commission's optimistic forecasts (Eichengreen 1992a), it seems reasonable to conclude that EMU would somewhat improve the functioning of the internal market. From this perspective, the benefits accruing to different countries would vary with the importance to their economies of intra-EU trade.[4] Countries that are more trade integrated into Europe are likely to benefit more from participation in EMU.[5]

The first column of table 2.2 reports the portion of a country's total trade with other members of the EU. Intra-EU trade constitutes substantially more than half of the trade done by all member states. But there is considerable variation in the importance of total trade to total economic activity among EU members. Exports plus imports constitute well over 100 percent of GDP in Belgium; the comparable figure is under 40 percent for Italy and Spain. The second column of table 2.2 shows that there are marked cross-national differences in the size of EU trade relative to GDP. Intra-EU trade is larger than Belgian GDP. At the other end of the scale, EU trade constitutes less than one-third of GDP for Finland, France, Italy, Spain, and the United Kingdom.

When considering intra-European economic integration in the context of EMU, trade relations with Germany are likely to be of greatest importance. In some cases, these data (reported in the third and fourth columns of table 2.2) are very different from those for intra-EU trade as a whole. For example, Ireland and to a lesser extent Portugal are much less dependent on trade with Germany than their EU trade numbers would suggest. Nonetheless, the countries at the top of the trade-with-Germany standings are the same as those at the top of the intra-EU standings—Austria, Belgium, and the Netherlands. So, too, are the five countries at the bottom of both lists.

Aggregating the data in table 2.2, there are clear differences among EU members in the potential benefits of participation in EMU as a means to

TABLE 2.2. Intra–European Union Trade, 1992

	Trade with the EU		Trade with Germany		Trade Integration Rank
	% Total Trade	% GDP	% Total Trade	% GDP	
Germany	54.1	34.9	—	—	—
Belgium	74.8	106.7	23.4	33.4	1
Netherlands	75.4	84.3	26.3	29.4	2
Austria	66.1	52.5	41.5	33.0	3
Ireland	74.2	86.7	10.8	12.6	4
Portugal	80.9	65.6	16.4	13.3	5
Denmark	54.5	33.5	22.6	13.9	6
Greece	64.2	35.9	21.4	12.0	7
Sweden	55.8	35.6	16.6	10.6	8
France	63.0	31.3	18.2	9.0	9
United Kingdom	55.5	29.1	13.9	7.3	10
Finland	53.2	26.1	15.9	7.8	11
Italy	57.7	22.3	21.2	8.2	12
Spain	66.3	25.0	16.1	6.1	13

Source: Data from *Eurostat* (1994) and OECD, *Statistics of Foreign Trade* (1994).

Note: The trade integration ranks are based on the sum of standardized scores for EU trade/GDP and German trade/GDP.

maximizing gains from the internal market. The likely benefits are greatest for Austria and the Benelux countries. There is a considerable gap to the next tier of countries—Denmark, Greece, Ireland, Portugal, and Sweden. Finally, the potential benefits of EMU as a stimulus for trade and investment in Europe are smallest for Finland, France, Italy, Spain, and the United Kingdom. Germany would also be included in the last group on the basis of the relative importance to the German economy of its trade with other EU member states.

3. Europe's Optimum Currency Area and the Costs of EMU

There is a large literature applying the theory of optimum currency areas, or OCA (Mundell 1961), to EMU. OCA theory suggests that countries will be able to reap the benefits of monetary union (such as those outlined in the previous section) without incurring significant costs if the business cycles of all countries are highly symmetric. Under these circumstances, there is a common monetary policy that suits all member economies. If countries face asymmetric economic shocks, however, a common monetary policy can only be pursued without deleterious consequences if wages are highly flexible, if labor is highly mobile, or if there is a system of fiscal transfers in place ("fiscal federalism") that redistributes money from countries that are experiencing buoyant macroeconomic conditions to those that are in recession.

None of the factors that might mitigate the costs of a monetary union is satisfied in Europe. Wages are less flexible in Europe than they are in North America (Bruno and Sachs 1985). Labor is not very mobile within European countries, let alone among them (Eichengreen 1992b). Finally, the EU's budget is tiny in terms of the Union's total economic output, and hence its ability to redistribute wealth from boom to bust regions is very limited.

Thus, participation in EMU only makes sense from an OCA perspective if macroeconomic disturbances among members are highly correlated. There is broad consensus among economists that the EU–15 is not an optimum currency area, but a subgrouping of countries might well benefit from sharing a common monetary policy (Bayoumi and Eichengreen 1993; Neumann and von Hagen 1991; de Grauwe and Vanhaverbake 1991).[6] I will not present the complex analyses employed in these studies because the thrust of the results can be captured more simply.

Table 2.3 presents correlations over time among annual rates of GDP growth as a basic indicator of the symmetry of business cycles in Europe. National growth rates are correlated both with EU averages and those of Germany. Belgium, Austria, and the Netherlands are not only countries that might benefit substantially from EMU because of their EU trade integration. The costs of giving up monetary policy autonomy would also be low for these countries because their business cycles are symmetric both with those of the EU as a whole and with Germany. At the other end of the spectrum, Finland and the United Kingdom are peripheral in terms of both trade and their business cycles.

The relative positions of some other countries, however, change considerably from table 2.2 to table 2.3. European trade is vital to the Irish economy, but its business cycle is clearly out of kilter with those of its European partners. Conversely, even though intra-EU trade is relatively unimportant to the French economy, its business cycle has been closely correlated with that of the whole EU and with Germany in particular.[7]

In sum, conventional macroeconomic accounts of the costs and benefits of EMU suggest that participation in monetary union makes sense for four countries—Austria, Belgium, Germany, and the Netherlands. Luxembourg undoubtedly also belongs in this group. For these countries, the economic benefits of stabilizing exchange rates are high while little is lost from pursuing a common monetary policy. It is not surprising, therefore, that these countries

TABLE 2.3.   The Symmetry of Business Cycles in the European Union, 1965–92

	Correlation between National EU Average Growth Rate	GDP Growth Rate and German Growth Rate	Symmetry Rank
Germany	0.81		1
France	0.91	0.70	2
Belgium	0.88	0.71	3
Netherlands	0.82	0.76	4
Austria	0.78	0.69	5
Spain	0.82	0.61	6
Italy	0.83	0.59	7
Greece	0.69	0.62	8
Portugal	0.74	0.52	9
Denmark	0.63	0.58	10
Sweden	0.67	0.43	11
Finland	0.66	0.36	12
United Kingdom	0.56	0.38	13
Ireland	0.36	0.30	14

Source: OECD Economic Outlook—Historical Statistics (various issues) and OECD 1996, A4.

already form an effective DM zone in Europe. At the other extreme, the analysis points to another four countries for which the internal market benefits of a common currency would be small and the costs of giving up monetary autonomy would be high—Finland, Greece, Sweden, and the United Kingdom. For the remaining six EU members, including three of the five largest countries in the Union—France, Italy, and Spain—it is more difficult to draw strong conclusions about the appropriateness of monetary union.

4.   Transition Costs of Moving to EMU

The analyses in the preceding two sections treated the institutions that determine monetary policy within countries and in monetary unions as "black boxes." In the context of EMU, this means assuming that the domestic consequences of delegating monetary policy authority to the European level will be affected neither by differences in preexisting policy regimes in individual member states nor by the institutional rules governing the operation of the ESCB. In the remainder of the chapter, I augment this approach through a political economic analysis that is sensitive to the details of institutional arrangements within countries and at the EU level.

Let us begin by surveying the theoretical and empirical terrain concerning the macroeconomic effects of central banking arrangements (be they at the national or regional level).[8] The basic thrust of the "credibility" approach is that delegating monetary authority to a central bank that is independent of political manipulation will lower rates of inflation without adversely affecting real aggregates.[9] The reasoning is well known. Governments are plagued by a "time inconsistency" problem. They have strong electoral incentives to inflate more than is justified on macroeconomic grounds during downturns in the business cycle and before elections. But economic actors know this, and thus they build inflationary expectations into their behavior. As a result, expansionary macroeconomic policies are deemed unable to stimulate the real economy; they can only lead to higher inflation. This inflation bias can be reduced by ceding control over monetary policy to an institution that is credibly committed to price stability (by the "conservative" disposition of office holders, by statute, or both).

Assume for the moment that the credibility account is accurate. Countries with independent central banks (or with stable exchange rate pegs to countries with independent central banks, such as Germany) have lower inflation rates than those in which monetary policy is controlled by elected officials, and this has no impact on growth and unemployment. It simply does not follow that countries with dependent central banks would incur no costs in delegating monetary authority to an institution committed to price stability.[10] Among other things, voters used to expansionary monetary policies during recessions or before elections cannot be expected immediately to accept the news that this has been rejected in favor of price stability. Moreover, it is implausible that economic actors will immediately understand and fully take into account the implications of the newly found credibility of the central bank. New Zealand's experience in the late 1980s—when its central bank was transformed from one of the least insulated from political pressures to one of the most—bears ample testimony to the short-term economic and political costs of hard money (Castles, Gerritson, and Vowles 1996).

Now consider the transition costs of moving to EMU. If joining Europe's monetary union is akin to delegating monetary authority to an inflation-averse central bank, one would expect that the transition costs will be higher for countries that, before the Maastricht Treaty was signed, either had dependent central banks or were not stable members of credible fixed exchange rate regimes (the narrow band of the pre-1993 EMS or stable bilateral pegs to the DM).[11]

Measuring central bank independence (CBI) is not easy. The literature is replete with behavioral and legal definitions of the autonomy of monetary authorities. Behavioral approaches are appealing because they are sensitive to issues beyond the purview of legal definitions (such as the personalities of policymakers, historical settings, and informal norms), but they are inherently tautological: central banks that behave autonomously are deemed independent. I thus rely on legal definitions of CBI and more specifically on the two most comprehensive empirical studies—Cukierman 1992; and Grilli, Masciandaro, and Tabellini 1994 (hereafter GMT). Both take into account the primary factors that heighten the autonomy of the central bank: the laws governing the appointment, dismissal, and terms of office of the bank's CEO and board; laws defining responsibility for the running of monetary policy; statutes establishing the primacy of price stability as a policy goal; and legal restrictions on the ability of governments to borrow from the bank.

Table 2.4 ranks EU members according to their combined scores on the Cukierman and GMT indices for the late 1980s. I also have coded the ESCB using the same criteria. Some EU members have recently increased the independence of their central banks pursuant to the Maastricht Treaty—most notably France and Spain (EMI 1994). Nonetheless, for the purposes of my analysis it is better to use the late 1980s as a benchmark since subsequent changes in national arrangements should be considered part of the transition to EMU.

On these legal definitions, the ESCB will be marginally more independent than the German Bundesbank. Thus, the transition costs of EMU would be very small for Germany. Nor would the move to monetary union entail a substantial increase in the independence of monetary policy setting for Austria, Denmark, and the Netherlands. The Greek and Irish central banks rank as the next most independent in Europe, above those of France and the United Kingdom.[12] At the other end of the scale, central banks were least independent before the Maastricht Treaty in the Mediterranean and Nordic countries. Among the founding members of the European Community, the Belgian central bank was the least independent of political control.

It is perhaps not surprising that those countries that rank highest on central bank independence also tend to have been stable participants in fixed exchange rate regimes in Europe—Denmark, Germany, Ireland, and the Netherlands in the EMS, and Austria by virtue of its bilateral peg to the DM. But some countries with relatively dependent central banks in the latter 1980s, most notably Belgium and France, were also stable members of the EMS.

In sum, these data suggest that for about half the members of the EU— Austria, Belgium, Denmark, France, Germany, Ireland, the Netherlands (and Luxembourg)—the transition costs of moving to EMU would be relatively small because these countries have already adopted monetary regimes in which government control over policy is limited. On legal definitions of central bank

TABLE 2.4.   The Independence of Central Banks in the European Union

	Central Bank Independence			Credible Commitment to a Fixed Exchange Rate[d]
	Cukierman[a]	GMT[b]	CBI Rank[c]	
European system of central banks[e]	.68	13	1	—
Germany	.66	13	2	yes
Austria[f]	.58	9	3	yes
Netherlands	.42	10	4	yes
Denmark	.47	8	5	yes
Ireland	.39	7	6	yes
Greece	.51	4	7	no
France	.28	7	8	yes
United Kingdom	.31	6	9	no
Belgium	.19	7	10	yes
Finland	.27	—	11	no
Italy	.22	5	12	no
Sweden	.27	4	13	no
Spain	.21	5	14	no
Portugal	—	3	15	no

Note: The central bank data do not take into account reforms undertaken after the signing of the Treaty of European Union in 1992.

[a]Cukierman's (1992, 381) legal independence measure for the 1980s.

[b]The sum of Grilli, Masciandaro, and Tabellini's (1994, 368–69) economic and political independence measures.

[c]The sum of standardized scores for the Cukierman and GMT indices (Cukierman minus GMT).

[d]Stable participation in +/− 2.25 percent band of the EMS, except where otherwise stated.

[e]The ESCB value was calculated using Cukierman's and GMT's criteria.

[f]Stable peg with DM.

independence, Greece might possibly be added to this group. For the remaining six members of the EU, however, the transition costs of participation in EMU are likely to be substantial.

5.   Labor Market Institutions and Monetary Regimes

The previous section assumed that while significant transition costs may be associated with changing regimes, countries that credibly delegate monetary authority to an independent institution committed to price stability will, in equilibrium, have lower inflation rates but not lower growth rates or higher unemployment rates. In this section, I join recent skeptics in economics who have questioned whether central bank independence always provides a macroeconomic "free lunch" of costless reductions in the inflation rate.[13] I argue that the real effects of delegating monetary authority to an independent institution (be it the national central bank, the Bundesbank, or the ESCB) are significantly influenced by the type of labor market institutions in a given country. I contend that "hard money" regimes are less costly in a macroeconomic sense where labor market institutions are sufficiently "encompassing" to tailor wage growth to the low-inflation monetary regime.[14]

One of the central results of cross-national research on the macroeconomic effects of labor market institutions is that encompassing organizations that can coordinate the behavior of most of the labor force tend to be associated with both lower inflation rates and lower unemployment rates (Calmfors and Driffill 1988; Cameron 1984; Golden 1993). The thrust of these studies is that encompassing organizations internalize the externalities associated with wage push by small groups of organized workers. The logic underpinning this argument can be explained briefly.

Workers suffer from a pervasive collective action problem (Olson 1982). All would benefit from a situation in which the cumulative result of wage bargains throughout the economy maximizes real wages and total employment. For any well-organized group of workers that has the capacity to extract wage settlements from employers that exceed productivity growth (the normal definition of labor "power"), however, the rational strategy is to use their organizational power to maximize their nominal wage increases—irrespective of the effects on inflation and unemployment in the whole economy. Since each isolated subgroup of workers can reasonably anticipate that its wage militancy will have little impact on price rises throughout the economy, each believes it can increase its real wage through nominal wage militancy. Moreover, to do otherwise would be to risk being "suckered" into having the group's real income eroded by wage militancy in other parts of the economy.

Encompassing organization provides an institutional solution to this collective action problem. The negative externalities usually associated with labor power—wage-push inflation coupled with lower aggregate levels of economic activity and employment—can be mitigated where the labor market is highly organized (through high levels of union density or the extension of collective bargaining agreements to nonunionized workers) and authority is highly centralized within the organized labor movement (e.g., in a single umbrella confederation with few constituent unions). In such cases, labor leaders have powerful incentives to internalize the externalities of wage militancy. They know that efforts to push wages beyond productivity growth will only lead to higher inflation, which in turn will constrain economic growth and ultimately reduce the real wages and employment prospects of all workers.

This line of argument has important implications for the economic effects of delegating monetary authority to an institution committed to price stability. Consider first the calculations of the leaders of an encompassing set of labor market institutions. In attempting to maximize economywide real wages and employment, they will take into account the likely reactions of all other relevant actors, be they firms or public officials. With respect to the public realm, the leaders of encompassing labor organizations know that wage push will be neutralized by higher interest rates where monetary authority has been delegated to an independent institution committed to price stability.[15] If wage push is 5 percent and price stability can only be achieved by raising interest rates, say, by five points, this is how an independent monetary authority will behave—regardless of the contractionary real effects of the interest rate hike. Of course, this argument holds irrespective of the impact of interest rate increases on inflation. I use this simple one-to-one relationship merely for simplicity in calculations.

Understanding the structure of the monetary regime, the rational strategy for the leaders of encompassing labor market institutions is to minimize nominal wage push, ex ante—because they know that militancy cannot have any real benefits for the welfare of workers. Thus, the monetary authority would not have to raise interest rates, ex post, and price stability would be achieved without putting a brake on output and employment. This scenario is exactly that envisaged in the credibility literature. The credibility of the monetary authority's threat to raise interest rates means that it doesn't have to be used, and the whole economy benefits.

The situation is very different where individual trade unions are strong but their behavior is not coordinated by a powerful central authority.[16] The leaders of individual unions know that the central bank will use its interest rate weapon to maintain economywide price stability. But they also know that this is a very blunt weapon. Higher interest rates cannot be targeted solely on that portion of the economy in which their workers are employed. The leaders of one union are now considering whether to push for a 5 percent wage increase. Using the simple relationship just outlined, the union's leaders reason that this might push up inflation in the economy as a whole by one point, and they know that the monetary authority will respond by increasing interest rates by one point to counteract this pressure. Clearly, the union would decide to push up its own nominal wages in this case because the only cost to it would be the adverse demand effects of the small interest rate increase in its part of the economy.

Of course, it is rational for all individually powerful but centrally uncoordinated unions to act in this way. The result would be that the monetary authority would have to counteract a 5 percent wage push throughout the economy with a five-point increase in the interest rate—a major brake on real economic activity. In this case, it is irrelevant that the monetary authority's threat to raise interest rates to maintain price stability is credible. As long as it cannot target specific sources of wage push, there will always be incentives for individual unions to push up their own nominal wages.

Whether or not the monetary authority is committed to price stability does not affect the impact of labor market institutions on wage behavior. Encompassing labor movements will always think about the externalities of wage push; decentralized labor movements never will. Neither the presence of an independent central bank, commitment to a fixed exchange rate, nor participation in a monetary union can solve this problem alone. Hard money regimes increase the macroeconomic benefits of encompassing labor market institutions, and heighten the costs of uncoordinated labor markets. Put differently, "sacrifice ratios" (how much unemployment is needed to achieve a given cut in inflation) in hard money regimes will be lower the more encompassing are labor market institutions.

Let us now apply this argument specifically to the case of EMU. The macroeconomic benefits of delegating control over monetary policy to the ESCB will depend on the extent to which national labor market institutions can internalize the externalities of wage militancy. When this is not the case, participation in EMU should not be expected to constrain overall wage militancy.

Operationalizing the encompassment of labor market institutions is notoriously difficult. In recent years, however, new data have been gathered that facilitate the generation of sophisticated encompassment indices. In this essay, I use two measures to capture the portion of the labor market that is organized—Visser's (1991) data on trade union density (union members as a percentage of total labor) and Traxler's (1994) study of the portion of the work force that is covered by collective bargaining agreements—and two indicators of the concentration of authority within national labor movements derived from Golden and Wallerstein's (1995) data on the size and composition of labor confederations.

Table 2.5 breaks EU members into two groups in terms of the breadth of organized labor movements and the concentration of authority within them.[17] National labor market institutions are considered more encompassing the higher union density is, the greater the coverage of collective bargaining, the greater the portion of union members in a single umbrella union confedera-

TABLE 2.5. Labor Market Institutions among EU Members, 1990

	Breadth		Concentration of Authority		
	Union Members/Total Labor Force (%)	Workers Covered by Collective Bargaining Agreements/Total Labor Force (%)	Concentration of Authority across Labor Confederations	Number of Unions in Largest Confederation	Encompassment of Labor Market Institutions
Austria	46	98	1	15	high
Belgium	55	90	.44	22	high
Denmark	74	—	.47	30	high
Finland	72	95	.38	24	high
Germany	32	90	.70	16	high
Netherlands	23	71	.56	15	high
Sweden	83	83	.45	23	high
France	11	92	.22	—	low
Greece[a]	30	—	.03	—	low
Ireland[b]	34	—	.86	54	low
Italy	34	—	.39	20	low
Portugal	35	79	.45[c]	140[c]	low
Spain	15	68	.25[d]	—	low
United Kingdom	38	47	.72	76	low

Sources: The data on union membership are from Visser 1991. The data for the coverage of collective bargaining are from Traxler 1994. The data on the concentration of union authority are from Golden and Wallerstein 1995.

[a]Data from Kritsantonis 1992.
[b]Data from von Prondzynski 1992.
[c]Data from Barreto 1992.
[d]Data from Lucio 1992.

tion, and the fewer individual unions comprise that confederation. These data on labor market institutions tell a familiar story. Institutions are considerably more encompassing in northern Europe than elsewhere.

Given the arguments in this section, table 2.5 suggests that participation in EMU would be considerably more costly for France, Ireland, the Mediterranean countries, and the United Kingdom than for the northern European members of the EU. These conclusions are supported by a recent article in which Christopher Way and I estimated the interactive effects on macroeconomic performance of variations in central bank independence and the encompassment of labor market institutions (Garrett and Way 1996). The study is based on the period 1968–92 and comprises the largest sample of OECD countries for which all the relevant data are available.[18]

Our results (summarized in table 2.6) demonstrate that it is the combination of independent monetary institutions and encompassing labor market institutions (LMI), rather than monetary independence on its own, that lowers the "misery index"—the combined rates of inflation and unemployment. Indeed, at low levels of labor market encompassment, monetary independence is associated with poorer macroeconomic outcomes. The key to understanding this table is that the coefficients for the central bank independence variable are positive and relatively small in both equations, whereas the parameter estimates for the LMI*CBI multiplicative interaction term are negative and considerably larger. For example, where the value of LMI is less than about .4, central bank independence is associated with higher rates of inflation. But above this value delegating monetary authority to an independent institution is expected to lower inflation. The cut point in the unemployment equation is higher, about .6 for LMI, but the basic pattern of relationships is the same.

Now let us apply these estimates to the transition to EMU (viewed as an increase in implicit monetary autonomy from the prevailing national regime). Consider the cases of Austria and Spain. Austria is a country with an independent central bank, a stable peg to the DM, and highly encompassing labor market institutions. Let us assume that the implicit increase in monetary independence associated with participation in EMU for Austria is .10 (.68 to .58 on Cukierman's index; see table 2.4). Austria's labor market institutions index in 1990 was .88 (the highest in the Garrett-Way sample). Using the relevant coefficients from table 2.6, we can thus estimate the following macroeconomic consequences were Austria to join EMU: the equilibrium inflation would be cut by 0.7 percentage points; and unemployment would be reduced by 0.1 points. These are not large benefits, and they might be further reduced if one considers the DM-Schilling peg to be completely credible (and hence the in-

TABLE 2.6.   The Interactive Effects of Monetary Regimes and Labor Market Institutions, 1968–92

Independent Variables	Inflation	Unemployment
Lagged dependent variable	0.39	0.88
	(0.13)	(0.08)
1968–72	−0.70	−0.61
	(2.24)	(0.96)
1973–77	3.96	0.49
	(2.31)	(1.01)
1978–82	−0.36	0.54
	(2.43)	(0.99)
1983–87	−4.09	0.64
	(2.38)	(0.98)
1988–92	−1.99	−1.54
	(2.27)	(0.94)
OECD GDP growth	−0.007	−0.001
	(0.006)	(0.006)
Trade/GDP	−0.004	−0.001
	(0.003)	(0.002)
Participation in the narrow band of the EMS	−0.117	1.26
	(0.628)	(0.50)
Encompassment of labor market institutions	13.08	2.69
	(3.80)	(1.85)
Central bank independence	6.41	2.57
	(3.21)	(1.72)
LMI*CBI	−15.36	−4.38
	(4.85)	(2.49)
Observations	65	65
Adjusted R^2	0.68	0.83
F-statistic	77.19	98.28

Source: The central bank independence index is Cukierman's (see table 2.4). The regression equation is from Garrett and Way 1996.

Note: Panel-robust standard errors are in parentheses. The labor market institutions index sums standardized scores for the breadth of organized labor movements and concentration of authority within them (see table 2.5).

crease in the independence of monetary authority associated with EMU participation to be even smaller). Nonetheless, given Austria's encompassing labor market institutions, table 2.6 implies that membership cannot be costly to Austria in macroeconomic terms.

The counterfactual estimates of the effects of joining EMU are very different for Spain. The central bank is highly politicized (.21 on Cukierman's index), and Spain was never part of the narrow band of the EMS. Thus, the move to EMU would entail an enormous increase in the independence of the monetary regime. While the data are not complete, it seems reasonable to conclude that Spanish labor market institutions are no more encompassing than those in Canada and the United States (around .30 on the Garrett-Way index). Using the parameter estimates in table 2.6 for the effects of different combinations of monetary regime and labor market institutions, we can project the following macroeconomic effects of joining EMU for Spain: an increase of 0.8 percentage points in the steady state inflation rate and a 0.6 point increase in the unemployment rate. Of course, it might be unrealistic to expect Spanish inflation to rise within EMU. But my analysis suggests that avoiding this increase in domestic inflation would require a further increase in the unemployment rate (how much would depend upon the elasticities of the short-term Phillips curve). Either way, participation in EMU is expected to be quite costly for Spain given the decentralized nature of its labor market institutions.

In closing, it is important to note that cases such as Spain's—a costly mismatch between the monetary regime and labor market institutions—are relatively rare. There is a strong correlation between the encompassment of labor market institutions and countries' histories with hard money regimes (through either independent national central banks or fixed exchange rates). Finland and Sweden are the only cases of encompassing labor market institutions that historically have not been committed to hard money. Conversely, France and Ireland are the only hard money countries with less encompassing labor market institutions. Thus, most countries have reconciled their monetary regimes with prevailing domestic labor market institutions.

As the estimates given earlier suggest, however, EMU threatens to disrupt this coherence for a number of countries with decentralized labor movements and histories of loose monetary regimes. As the data in tables 2.4 and 2.5 show, this is largely a Mediterranean problem, affecting, to somewhat different degrees, Greece, Italy, Portugal, and Spain.

6. A Benefit-Cost Analysis of EMU Membership

The preceding four sections can now be synthesized with respect to the likely overall macroeconomic consequences of participation in EMU—assuming that monetary policy will be determined by an independent ESCB solely targeting price stability. I have argued that the net effects of membership in such an EMU would be better for a given member state: the more integrated its economy is in the EU's internal market and the more symmetrical its business cycle is with those of other EU members, the smaller is the increase in monetary independence implied by participation in EMU and the more encompassing are its labor market institutions.

Table 2.7 divides EU members into five groups based on these criteria. There are four countries for which the decision to accept an invitation to join the textbook EMU would be easy—Austria, Belgium, Germany, and the Netherlands (Luxembourg no doubt also belongs in this group). The group is not surprising—it contains Germany and the countries that are stable members of the DM zone. These countries are tightly interconnected through trade. If EMU allows them fully to reap the benefits of the internal market, this could only be to their advantage. These countries have highly symmetric business cycles. It thus makes sense for them to share a common monetary policy. All of these countries except Belgium have independent national central banks, but Belgium has compensated for this by effectively pegging its franc to the DM. The transition costs of moving to EMU would thus be quite small. Finally, all of these countries have relatively encompassing labor market institutions that are capable of tailoring wage growth to the dictates of a hard money regime.

The United Kingdom stands out at the other end of the spectrum. It is the one EU member state for which participation in EMU seems most unwise on purely economic grounds. The British economy is poorly integrated into Europe—in terms of both trade patterns and business cycles. The behavior of the Bank of England continues to be heavily influenced by the government even afer the 1997 reforms, and sterling has not been part of Europe's efforts to fix exchange rates in the post–Bretton Woods era. British labor market institutions have always been very fragmented, and individual trade unions remain quite powerful. Thus, while British concerns about the impact of EMU on its sovereignty are no doubt real, there is clearly an economic justification for the unpopularity of EMU.

The remaining countries lie between these two extremes. Denmark would seem quite well suited to participation in EMU, although its business cycle is not particularly symmetric with those of the EMU core (table 2.7, group 1). On the other hand, there are more minuses and pluses to membership for the Mediterranean and Nordic countries (group 4), even though each country has one characteristic that is compatible with participation in EMU.

Finally, France and Ireland lie in the middle of the EU, countries for which the EMU membership decision could go either way on economic grounds. Ireland is a large EU trader that participated stably in the narrow band of the EMS. But its labor market institutions are not very encompassing and its business cycles are sufficiently out of alignment with the EMU core that adopting a common monetary policy with them could be a real mistake. Turning to

TABLE 2.7. Expected Economic Consequences of EMU Participation

	Market Integration[a]	Symmetry of Business Cycles[b]	Credible Delegation of Monetary Authority to an Independent Institution[c]	Labor Market Institutions[d]
Group 1				
Austria	high	high	high	high
Belgium	high	high	high	high
Germany	high	high	high	high
Netherlands	high	high	high	high
Group 2				
Denmark	high	low	high	high
Group 3				
France	low	high	high	low
Ireland	high	low	high	low
Group 4				
Finland	low	low	low	high
Greece	low	low	high	low
Italy	low	high	low	low
Portugal	high	low	low	low
Spain	low	high	low	low
Sweden	low	low	low	high
Group 5				
United Kingdom	low	low	low	low

[a]The seven countries for which intra-EU trade was most important were coded "high"; the others were coded "low" (see table 2.2).

[b]The seven countries with the most symmetrical business cycles were coded "high"; the others were coded "low" (see table 2.3).

[c]The eight countries with histories of stable commitments to fixed exchange rate regimes (most of which also ranked at the top of the national central bank independence indices) were coded "high"; the others were coded "low" (see table 2.4).

[d]The seven countries with the most encompassing labor market institutions were coded "high"; the others were coded "low" (see table 2.5).

France, the argument in favor of EMU would concentrate on the symmetry of the French business cycle with the rest of the EU and with Germany's in particular. Moreover, the franc fort policy has been maintained for more than a decade. But, on the other hand, French labor market institutions are among the least encompassing in Europe and intra-EU trade is not particularly important to the French economy.

This macroeconomic balance sheet in table 2.7 makes for an interesting comparison with predictions about how close countries will come to meeting the Maastricht convergence criteria in 1997 (see table 2.1). There are some marked disjunctures between the two tables. On the one hand, the United Kingdom's fiscal record is projected to be among the best in the EU in 1997, but its political economic structure suggests that it should not exercise the option to join if the EMU operates in textbook fashion. On the other hand, Belgium is one of the countries that would likely do very well from participation in the textbook EMU, but its public debt poses a considerable obstacle to its admission. Moreover, the debt ceiling for participation in EMU would have to be raised to 80 percent of GDP for Austria, Germany, and the Netherlands to be allowed to join—even though these countries should form the core of the monetary union in any reasonable analysis.

The simple point of this comparison—as others have observed—is that there is little correlation between the current fiscal predicaments of EU members and the likely macroeconomic consequences of their joining EMU (Buiter, Corsetti and Roubini 1993). Less prosaically, the convergence criteria make little economic sense (de Grauwe 1996).

7. A Politicized EMU?

Let us now analyze the EMU membership endgame in the light of the evidence presented in this chapter. Monetary union without Germany is inconceivable, and with German membership will likely come Austria, Luxembourg, and the Netherlands—even if this entails adding 20 points to the accumulated public debt threshold for membership and overlooking deficits under 4 percent (see table 2.1). The Franco-German alliance has always been at the core of the monetary union project. Following the sacrifices successive French governments have been willing to make in terms of the franc fort and fiscal consolidation, French participation in EMU must be almost certain. Most agree that this is the minimal monetary union that would be both economically and politically meaningful: Germany and France, with Austria, Luxembourg, and the Netherlands as acolytes.

But what about the other 10 members of the EU? Let us play out some different scenarios. On most indicators, Belgium is part of the EU's core. If, as seems plausible, France and Germany would like Belgium to be a member in spite of its enormous accumulated public debt, how easy would it be for the EMU core to oppose the inclusion of other countries with smaller debt burdens? After all, Portugal and Spain both wish to join EMU, and they would be eligible under a de facto 80 percent debt threshold. So, too, would Finland and Sweden, but it is less likely that governments in these countries would wish to join. Italy's public debt is smaller than Belgium's. How could Belgium be admitted if Italy is not?

The reason there is so much speculation about the size of EMU is that this will have a dramatic impact on how European monetary policy is set. The ESCB can only be expected to operate as a textbook independent central bank pursuing price stability *über alles* if its membership is limited to countries for which such a policy makes economic and political sense. Although it is reasonable to characterize the ESCB as a "super-Bundesbank" under legal definitions of central bank independence, even the Bundesbank is not immune to political pressures to pursue more lax monetary policies (Hall 1994; Lohmann 1995). In the German case, this has not been a problem (or was not a problem until unification) because of the broad societal consensus as to the importance of price stability given the history of the 1920s and 1930s. But one might be more skeptical about EMU.

Decisions in the ESCB will be made by a simple majority of members of its Governing Council. If all EU members participated in the EMU, there would be 21 votes in total. Six would come from the Executive Board of the European Central Bank. Assume that they would act as classically conservative central bankers, pursuing price stability come what may. The central bank governors from members of the monetary union would each have one of the remaining 15 votes. Even though the Maastricht Treaty mandates reforms to national central banks designed to render their governors just as insulated from political pressures as the Executive Board, it seems plausible that under some conditions many national governors would put the interests of their countries over those of the monetary union.

Consider a scenario in which all countries participate in EMU under the types of macroeconomic conditions that have obtained in the 1990s. The national central bank governors from Austria, Germany, Luxembourg, and the Netherlands vote as a bloc with the Governing Council of the ESCB to maintain price stability in Europe. The hard money coalition would thus have 10 votes (one short of a majority). But what if the other members of the EU are in varying forms of recession, have high structural unemployment rates, or have fiscal problems that might be alleviated by looser European monetary policy? It is unlikely that the Mediterranean countries would vote with the core, nor should one necessarily expect solidarity from Finland and Sweden.

If Denmark and the United Kingdom were to join EMU, this might swing the ESCB in favor of hard money. But whether any Danish government could generate enough domestic support to join EMU is doubtful. Moreover, the United Kingdom will only join under a Labour government, and there must remain doubts about Labour's commitment to price stability. What about Belgium and France? There would be great temptations for the Belgian central bank governor to vote for loose European monetary policies to lessen the real value of Belgium's debt. Similarly, given the price that French governments have had to pay for the franc fort, and given the magnitude and entrenchment of the French welfare state, French central bankers would be sorely tempted to allow an easing of European monetary policy.

It is the fear that there would not be a stable winning "hard money" coalition inside a large EMU that has motivated pronouncements by the Bundesbank and Theo Waigel about the importance of adhering to the Maastricht convergence criteria and imposing even stricter limits on national fiscal policy inside EMU than those laid down in the treaty. But their views are counterbalanced by Helmut Kohl's desire to ensure that the transition to monetary union goes smoothly and EMU endures as a lasting legacy of his more than 15 years as a pro-European chancellor.

Ultimately, however, membership in EMU will be determined by a qualified majority vote, and Germany has no institutional capacity to block the admission of loose money countries. Germany could probably rely on Austria, Luxembourg, and the Netherlands voting with it against the admission of Spain or even Italy. But it would require the participation of Belgium in this coalition to generate enough votes to block the admission of these countries under qualified majority voting. Belgium's support could only be expected if it were voted into EMU—but this could only happen by turning a blind eye to the convergence criteria.

There is a further, potentially more important problem lurking for Germany. Would the German government, let alone those from the Benelux countries, be prepared to vote against the participation of France—even if they thought there was some chance that France would galvanize a loose money coalition? This is difficult to envisage given the centrality of French-German cooperation to every major move toward European integration since the early 1950s.

But let us leave aside these strategic calculations. Consider what might transpire were the Council of Ministers to vote in 1999 on membership in terms of a loosened set of convergence criteria and only three countries clearly were ineligible (Belgium, Greece, and Italy). We might also reasonably assume that the United Kingdom and Denmark would exercise their "opt outs" and choose not to join. What would the German government choose to do when confronted with the option of whether to participate in a monetary union with, among others, Portugal, Spain, and Sweden? The domestic cries to keep the sanctity of the DM would no doubt be very loud. If German political leaders were prepared to sacrifice the DM in the name of EMU, this would be the ultimate testament to the Kohl government's commitment to European integration.

The primary lesson to be drawn from this analysis is clear. There is little relationship between the extent to which countries are likely to get close to the Maastricht convergence criteria and the probable macroeconomic consequences of membership in EMU for them. Assuming that the strict letter of the convergence criteria is violated, which the Maastricht Treaty explicitly allows, it quickly becomes very difficult to generate conditions for membership that will be consensually supported by all member states. Moreover, the size of EMU will have a marked bearing on the types of monetary policies it produces— again, the Maastricht Treaty made this possible. Thus, European monetary politics in the run-up to the establishment of monetary union can only be expected to get ever more contentious. The stakes are high, and the rules of the game are uncertain. This is a potentially volatile cocktail.

NOTES

I would like to thank Matthew Canzoneri for helpful comments on an earlier version of this chapter. Barry Eichengreen and Jeffry Frieden deserve special thanks for their tireless efforts to help me improve the essay. This research was supported by the Reginald Jones Center, the Wharton School of the University of Pennsylvania.

1. Greece is the only country whose inflation and interest rates are radically out of line with the convergence criteria.

2. Given data limitations and the unique nature of the Luxembourg economy, the rest of the chapter will not include this country in the analysis. However, it is safe to assume that any EMU that forms in Europe will contain Luxembourg.

3. Changes in national central banking arrangements prompted by the Maastricht Treaty should thus be considered the first step toward participating in EMU.

4. Over time, the internal market–monetary union combination may, of course, result in some convergence in trade patterns.

5. Intra-European trade integration was a powerful predictor of stable membership in the "snake" and the narrow band of the EMS throughout the 1970s and 1980s (Frieden 1996).

6. Again, this does not mean that, over time, participation in EMU might not reduce asymmetries among members' business cycles (Frankel and Rose 1996).

7. In this context, it should be remembered that the mismatch between an overheating German economy (at least in the Bundesbank's view) and recession in France in the 1990s—which has heightened political and economic problems in Europe since Maastricht—is aberrant from a historical perspective.

8. This analysis is based on the simplifying assumption that the domestic consequences of delegating monetary authority to an independent national central bank are

very similar to participating in a credible fixed exchange rate regime—such as EMU, the EMS in the post-capital-controls era, and bilateral pegs to the DM (again with no capital controls). Where differences in the level at which monetary policy is set matter, these are discussed explicitly in the text.

9. Much of the major research on independent central banks is collected in Persson and Tabellini 1994.

10. From a credibility perspective, of course, it is precisely those countries without histories of price stability that "need" independent central banks.

11. The credibility of the EMS, of course, can be debated (Eichengreen and Wyplosz 1993; Weber 1991).

12. One might question the placement of the Greek central bank, however, given the de facto control of government over its behavior.

13. The empirical validity of this approach has been questioned in recent years (Ball 1993; Debelle and Fischer 1994; Walsh 1995). Most importantly, critics contend that while inflation rates may be lower in countries with independent central banks a significant price must be paid for price stability in terms of slower growth and higher unemployment.

14. Franzese (1996) and Hall (1994) come to a similar conclusion. For a different approach to the labor market institutions–monetary regime interaction, see Iversen 1996.

15. This is less certain if monetary policy is set by the government, especially one dominated by left-of-center parties.

16. There is a third theoretical category in which labor is effectively unorganized. Perhaps the United States is an example. In Europe, however, there are no cases that come at all close to the "free" labor market ideal type.

17. For more complete discussion of these indices, see Garrett and Way 1996.

18. The sample includes seven members of the EU—Austria, Finland, France, Germany, the Netherlands, Sweden, and the United Kingdom—and Australia, Canada, Japan, Norway, Switzerland, and the United States.

REFERENCES

Ball, Laurence. 1993. "What Determines the Sacrifice Ratio?" Princeton University. Typescript.

Barreto, José. 1991. "Portugal: Industrial Relations under Democracy." In *Industrial Relations in the New Europe,* edited by Anthony Kerner and Richard Hyman. Oxford: Blackwell.

Bayoumi, Tamim, and Barry Eichengreen. 1993. "Shocking Aspects of European Monetary Unification." In *Transition to Economic and Monetary Union in Europe,* edited by Francisco Torres and Francesco Giavazzi. New York: Cambridge University Press.

Bruno, Michael, and Jeffrey Sachs. 1985. *The Economics of Worldwide Stagflation.* Cambridge, Mass.: Harvard University Press.

Buiter, Willem, Giancarlo Corsetti, and Nouriel Roubini. 1993. "Maastricht's Fiscal Rules." *Economic Policy* 16:57–100.

Calmfors, Lars, and John Driffill. 1988. "Bargaining Structure, Corporatism, and Macroeconomic Performance." *Economic Policy* 6:13–61.

Cameron, David R. 1984. "Social Democracy, Corporatism, Labour Quiescence, and the Representation of Economic Interest in Advanced Capitalist Society." In *Order and Conflict in Contemporary Capitalism,* edited by John H. Goldthorpe. Oxford: Oxford University Press.

Castles, Francis, Rolf Gerritson, and Jack Vowles, eds. 1996. *The Great Experiment: Labour Parties and Public Policy Transformation in Australia and New Zealand.* Sydney: Allen and Unwin.

Commission of the European Union. 1990. "One Market, One Money." *The European Economy* 44, special issue.

Cukierman, Alex. 1992. *Central Bank Strategy, Credibility, and Independence: Theory and Evidence.* Cambridge: The MIT Press.

Debelle, Guy, and Stanley Fischer. 1994. "How Independent Should a Central Bank Be?" Paper presented at the CEPR/Federal Reserve Bank of San Francisco conference, Monetary Policy in a Low Inflation Regime.

de Grauwe, Paul. 1996. "Monetary Union and Convergence Economics." *European Economic Review* 40:1091–1101.

de Grauwe, Paul, and Wilhelm Vanhaverbeke. 1991. "Is Europe an Optimum Currency Area?" CEPR Discussion Papers, no. 555. London: CEPR.

Eichengreen, Barry. 1992a. "Should the Maastricht Treaty Be Saved?" Princeton Studies in International Finance, no. 74. Princeton: International Finance Section, Department of Economics, Princeton University.

———. 1992b. "Labor Markets and European Monetary Unification." In *Policy Issues in the Design of Monetary Unions,* edited by Paul Masson and Mark Taylor. Cambridge: Cambridge University Press.

Eichengreen, Barry, and Charles Wyplosz. 1993. "The Unstable EMS." *Brookings Papers on Economic Activity* 1:51–143.

EMI. 1994. *Annual Report of the European Monetary Institute.* Frankfurt: European Monetary Institute.

Frankel, Jeffrey, and Andrew Rose. 1996. "The Endogeneity of the Optimum Currency Area Criterion." University of California, Berkeley. Typescript.

Franzese, Robert. 1994. "Central Bank Independence, Sectoral Interest, and the Wage Bargain." Harvard University. Typescript.

Frieden, Jeffry. 1996. "The Impact of Goods and Capital Market Integration on European Monetary Politics." *Comparative Political Studies* 29:193–222.

Garrett, Geoffrey. 1993. "The Politics of Maastricht." *Economics and Politics* 5:105–24.

Garrett, Geoffrey, and Christopher Way. 1996. "Labor Market Institutions and the

Economic Consequences of Central Bank Independence." University of Pennsylvania. Typescript.

Golden, Miriam. 1993. "The Dynamics of Trade Unionism and National Economic Performance." *American Political Science Review* 87:439–54.

Golden, Miriam, and Michael Wallerstein. 1995. "Unions, Employers, and Collective Bargaining: A Report on Data for 16 Countries from 1950 to 1990." Paper presented at the annual meetings of the Midwest Political Science Association, Chicago, April 6–8.

Grilli, Vittorio, Donato Masciandaro, and Guido Tabellini. 1994. "Political and Monetary Institutions and Public Financial Policies in the Industrial Countries." In *Monetary and Fiscal Policy*, edited by Torsten Persson and Guido Tabellini. Cambridge: The MIT Press.

Hall, Peter A. 1994. "Central Bank Independence and Coordinated Wage Bargaining: Their Interaction in Germany and Europe." *German Politics and Society* 31:1–23.

Iversen, Torben. 1996. "The Real Effects of Money." Harvard University. Typescript.

Kritsantonis, Nicos. 1992. "Greece: From State Authoritarianism to Modernization." In *Industrial Relations in the New Europe*, edited by Anthony Ferner and Richard Hyman. Cambridge, Mass.: Blackwell.

Lohmann, Susanne. 1995. "Federalism and Central Bank Autonomy." UCLA. Typescript.

Lucid, Miguel. 1992. "Spain: Constructing Institutions and Actors in the Context of Change." In *Industrial Relations in the New Europe*, edited by Anthony Ferner and Richard Hyman. Cambridge, Mass.: Blackwell.

Mundell, Robert. 1961. "A Theory of Optimum Currency Areas." *American Economic Review* 51:657–65.

Neumann, M., and Jürgen von Hagen. 1991. "Real Exchange Rates within and between Currency Areas: How Far Away Is EMU?" Indiana University. Typescript.

OECD. 1996. *OECD Economic Outlook. 59.* Paris: OECD.

Olson, Mancur. 1992. *The Rise and Decline of Nations.* New Haven: Yale University Press.

Traxler, Franz. 1994. "Collective Bargaining: Levels and Coverage." In *OECD Employment Outlook.* Paris: OECD.

Visser, Jelle. 1991. "Trends in Trade Union Membership." In *OECD Employment Outlook.* Paris: OECD.

Von Prondzynski, Ferdinand. 1992. "Ireland: Between Centralization and the Market." In *Industrial Relations in the New Europe*, edited by Anthony Ferner and Richard Hyman. Cambridge, Mass.: Blackwell.

Walsh, Carl. 1995. "Central Bank Independence and the Short-Run Output-Inflation Trade-Off in the European Community." In *Monetary and Fiscal Policy in an Integrated Europe*, edited by Barry Eichengreen, Jeffry Frieden, and Jürgen von Hagen. New York: Springer.

Weber, Axel. 1991. "Reputation and Credibility in the European Monetary System." *Economic Policy* 12:57–102.

CHAPTER 3

The Political Economy of French Economic Policy in the Perspective of EMU

Christian de Boissieu and Jean Pisani-Ferry

I. Introduction

For nearly two decades, from the creation of the European Monetary System to the Maastricht Treaty and the discussions concerning its implementation, France has been a driving force for European monetary integration. This goal has been consistently pursued by governments of different political affiliations, and domestic economic priorities have been set accordingly. When a conflict arose between domestic and European objectives, in 1982–83, 1992–93, and 1995, for example, priority was given to the European commitment.

The extent to which this objective has shaped French economic policy can hardly be overestimated. In large part, the major changes in the framework for economic policy that have taken place in the 1980s and 1990s can be attributed to it. Having committed itself to exchange rate stability and being aware of the conditions the country had to meet in order to be eligible for shared leadership in European monetary affairs, French governments from the Left and the Right undertook sustained efforts in order to adapt the country and redefine the implicit or explicit rules of economic policy: during the 1980s, disinflation was consistently pursued in spite of its short-run macroeconomic costs and a policy of nominal exchange rate stability was initiated; in the mid-1980s, credit markets were liberalized and the traditional modus operandi of monetary policy through credit ceilings was abandoned; capital controls were progressively lifted from 1986 to 1990; in 1993, the institutional framework of economic

49

policy itself was rewritten with the granting of independence to the central bank (actually, this reform required a constitutional amendment); between 1992 and 1995, despite repeated speculative attacks, monetary policy was assigned to maintaining a fixed exchange rate; and from 1995 on, notwithstanding its political cost, fiscal retrenchment was carried out in order to meet the Maastricht criteria. France therefore offers the rare example of a medium-sized, nonhegemonic country the domestic policy choices of which seem to have been shaped by an external agenda.

From 1982–83, when the debate over *l'autre politique* was first settled, to 1992–93, when it arose again, this policy was fairly consensual, although a consistent minority on both the right and left opposed it. Controversies began to reemerge in the early 1990s, as the French economy suffered from keeping the Fr-DM exchange rate fixed in spite of German unification. They became more or less permanent in 1993–96 as the short-term costs of the macroeconomic strategy became visible against the background of mediocre growth and employment performance. More generally, public discontent vis-à-vis the process of European integration expressed itself in the 1992 referendum on the ratification of the Maastricht Treaty, in the elections for the European Parliament of 1994, and in the winter strikes of 1995.

European integration thus became the center of major policy controversies. However, in spite of two changes of parliamentary majority in 1993 and 1997 and a presidential election in 1995 (after which a new prime minister was appointed), macroeconomic policy remained oriented toward qualifying France for membership in Economic and Monetary Union. No political realignment occurred, and heated debates within each party did not prevent successive governments from following a continuous line. This raises major questions as regards the political economy of European monetary integration. However, there is, paradoxically, very little available research on this issue in France. This was understandable as long as the goals of achieving exchange rate stability and building a monetary union were pursued by the government with the (mostly silent) consent of the public. Yet, after events revealed that public support for the project was in fact limited, it became urgent to clarify the politics of monetary unification.

This chapter is an attempt to analyze these issues. It consists of four parts. Part 2 presents an overview of French economic policy since the late 1970s and a short assessment of its results. Part 3 discusses the political and the economic logic of policy choices from the point of view of policymakers. Part 4 analyzes the positions of the various categories of agents vis-à-vis EMU. Conclusions are drawn in part 5.

2.   French Economic Policy since the 1970s

2.1.   Major Macroeconomic Developments

Reflation and Adjustment, 1974–80
The first oil shock brought to an end the continuous expansion that the French economy had been experiencing since the 1950s (fig. 3.1). In 1975, Prime Minister Jacques Chirac decided to boost the economy by implementing an expansionary monetary-fiscal mix. France thus reacted to the supply shock by giving preference to reflation over inflation control and accommodated it through inflation, nominal depreciation, and an increase in the wage share in national income (see fig. 3.2).

It was only a few years later that the negative consequences of this choice became obvious. After 1976, the government of Raymond Barre attempted to give priority to disinflation, external balance, and nominal exchange rate stability—a goal he reached with the creation of the EMS in 1979. This early attempt met with opposition from the unions and was not supported by the employers, for which memory of the successful devaluations of 1958 and 1969 was still present. It was still widely accepted that changes in the nominal exchange rate would, ex post, offset any inflation differential vis-à-vis the country's main trading partners.

This experiment was significant but unsuccessful. The Plan Barre was crucial for the evolution of French economic policy thinking because it prepared the field for the 1982–83 turning point, but its record was deceptive: disinflation was not achieved, and a significant gap remained between the appeal to wage moderation and the drop in the profit share in total value added (fig. 3.2). The disinflation effort was not only limited, but it was probably also unsustainable because it relied on an excessive reduction in the profit share.

"Relance" and "Rigueur," 1981–92
The initial reaction to the second oil shock was similar to that of 1974–75. At the beginning of the first Mitterrand presidency, the Mauroy government launched a Keynesian reflation program, whose impact on growth and employment soon proved deceptive while its consequences for inflation, the current

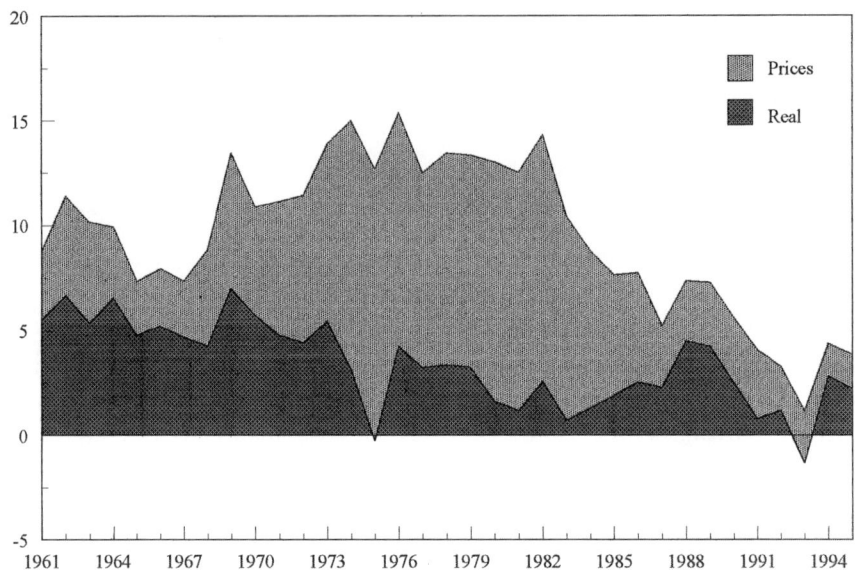

Fig. 3.1. Nominal and real GDP growth, 1961–95. (Data from INSEE.)

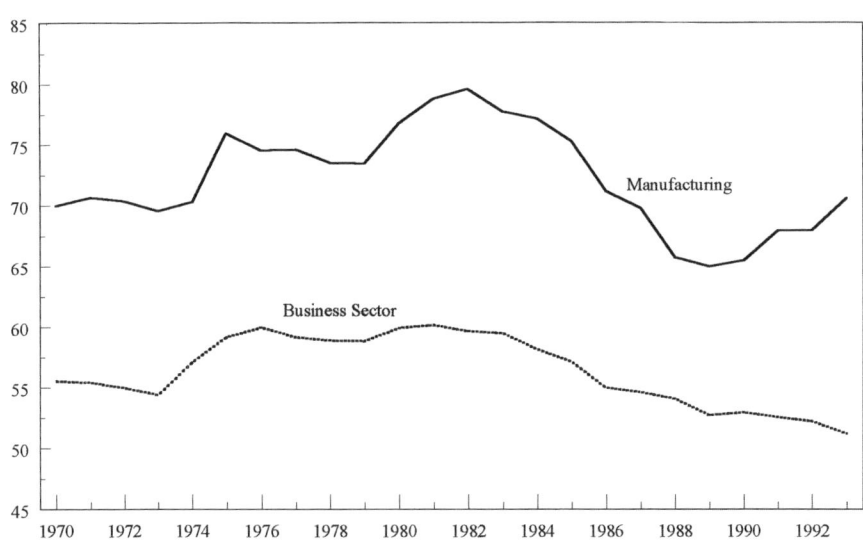

Fig. 3.2. Share of wages in value added, 1970–93. (Data from CEPII and OFCE.)

account, and external debt were clearly negative. The current account deficit exceeded 2 percent of GDP in 1982, a level that was considered excessive. Furthermore, this policy was at odds with that of France's main trading partners which were implementing a restrictive monetary-fiscal mix in order to limit the inflationary consequences of the second oil shock.[1] The franc was devalued three times, in 1981, 1982, and 1983. This led to much debate within the government and to the formulation of new policy objectives, which were implemented by Jacques Delors, then minister of finance:

1. Disinflation was officially recognized as an overriding priority. The full indexation of nominal wages was abandoned, as, according to the "Delors rule" for the public sector—de facto extended to most of the private sector—nominal wages were indexed to a target rate of inflation.
2. The pegging of the French franc to the mark was reasserted.
3. Fiscal retrenchment was undertaken.

This restrictive economic policy was presented as a necessary response to the "external constraint." The meaning of this expression, which had become prominent in the economic policy debate under Raymond Barre, was not entirely clear (Cooper 1983). Literally, it referred to the current account balance, a policy target that played a major role in the 1980s, especially since the oil shocks worsened the trade balance and the capital account had not been liberalized. It was widely accepted because of its merely accounting character. But more broadly it was a reference to the need for French policymakers and private agents to open up to the external environment and adapt to the constraints arising from European integration.

This policy philosophy was continuously followed in the 1980s and the early 1990s. The French franc was not devalued until the two realignments within the Exchange Rate Mechanism (ERM) in 1986 and 1987 (fig. 3.3), and from 1987 on the nominal exchange rate vis-à-vis the DM remained stable.[2] Disinflation was achieved by 1986–87 (fig. 3.4), and, as several other ERM members were less successful in their disinflation effort, the French real exchange rate vis-à-vis the rest of the European Community (EC) appreciated only slightly in 1983–86 and began to depreciate again in 1987. Disinflation was translated into competitiveness gains, an evolution that accelerated after the German economy began to experience the inflationary consequences of the reunification shock.

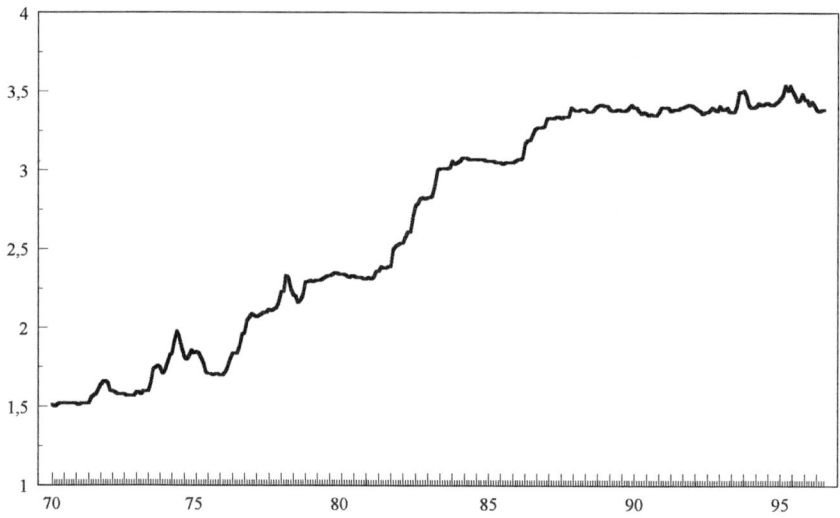

Fig. 3.3. The franc-mark exchange rate, 1970–96. (Data from FERI/ Deutsche Bundesbank.)

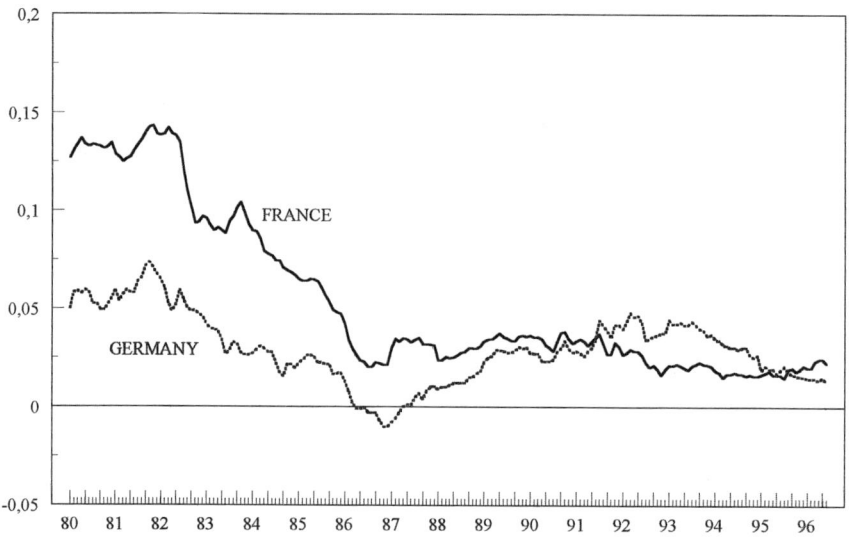

Fig. 3.4. Year-by-year inflation in France and Germany, 1980–96. (Data from the IMF.)

Exchange Market Tensions and Recession, 1992–96

For the French economy, however, German unification was only briefly a blessing. From 1991 on, tensions increased between the German Bundesbank and the governments of partner countries. The French government is widely reported to have opposed a revaluation of the deutsche mark within the ERM because this would have weakened the credibility of its exchange rate policy. Other testimonies report that France would have accepted a revaluation of the mark, but not a devaluation of the franc vis-à-vis the Dutch guilder and the Belgian franc, because in this case the French franc would have been associated with the weak ERM currencies. These disagreements resulted in collective inflexibility in the management of the ERM, which led to crisis.

Beginning in September 1992, the ERM was subject to speculative attacks. In September-October 1992, the franc was not the main target of speculation, but in July 1993 it became the target of attacks, as many market participants perceived the *franc fort* policy as unsustainable in the long run against the background of rising unemployment. Throughout this period, the government and the central bank gave priority to maintaining the fixed Fr-DM link and increased short-term interest rates whenever it was necessary for that purpose.

In August 1993, the move to a large-band ERM (±15 percent with respect to the central rate) was a last-minute solution that was adopted after Belgium and the Netherlands opposed letting the DM float vis-à-vis other ERM currencies, but it helped ease the tensions. In this context, the central bank attempted to maintain the franc in the neighborhood of this central rate vis-à-vis the mark but without trying to stick to the former narrow band of ±2.25 percent. Monetary policy was eased and followed that of the Bundesbank until early March 1995, when short-term rates were raised by 200 basis points as renewed tensions arose in the run-up to the presidential elections. Thereafter the central bank remained cautious, and the monetary loosening only accelerated after President Chirac announced in October 1995 that priority was to be given to fiscal adjustment.

The recession of 1991–93 was both long and severe. In spite of the slow-down in real activity and the rise of the unemployment rate (OECD definition) from 8.9 percent in 1989 to 12.5 percent in 1994, monetary policy remained devoted to the exchange rate target, while fiscal policy turned expansionary as the general government deficit increased from 1.2 percent of GDP in 1989 to 6 percent of GDP in 1994. France therefore faced the prospect of not being able to meet the Maastricht deficit criterion of 3 percent of GDP. One of the first initiatives of the Chirac administration was therefore to propose postponing the beginning of Stage 3 of EMU until 1999, a proposal that was endorsed by the European Council in June 1995. But commitment to the single currency was emphasized in the autumn of 1995, and the preparation of the 1996 budget signaled that priority was effectively being given to meeting the announced budgetary target. Cuts in the social insurance budget and accompanying structural reforms prompted major strikes in December 1995, which were soon labeled "strikes against Maastricht." However, the government essentially stuck to its objective in spite of rising unpopularity and a sharp slowdown in growth in 1995–96. Eventually, President Chirac called a snap general election in June 1997, but the majority in Parliament switched again to a left-wing coalition. A new government was appointed under Prime Minister Lionel Jospin, which soon reaffirmed French commitment to monetary union.

2.2. Structural Changes

During the last two decades, the French economy has undergone sweeping structural changes that have been, at least in part, the result of European policy initiatives. At the beginning of the 1980s, France was still a highly regulated economy in which the state had direct or indirect control over a significant portion of private sector decisions. In fact, intervention had increased as a result of the socialist government's first initiatives, especially the nationalization of five industrial groups and most of the banks (the largest of which had already been nationalized in the aftermath of World War II). At the time, nationalized firms accounted for one-fourth of the turnover in French industry. Virtually all the energy, public utility, and telecommunications sectors were in public hands, and banks were overwhelmingly owned by the state. Furthermore, the government exerted influence on private sector decisions through subsidies, product and labor market regulations, and the distribution of credit. Although the effectiveness of industrial policy was already much weaker than some of its proponents suggested, few executives from major companies could avoid devoting considerable energy to lobbying for favorable government decisions. Furthermore, foreign trade was only partially liberalized and capital controls remained prevalent, including those on inward and outward foreign direct investment.

Within a decade, this landscape was transformed by a series of policy initiatives:

1. In 1986–87 and after 1993, right-wing governments privatized most of the industrial and financial sectors, including firms that had been nationalized in the 1940s.

2. Financial liberalization was initiated in the mid-1980s under Finance Minister Bérégovoy and pursued by his successor Balladur. As a result, credit and capital controls were eliminated and financial innovation led to sweeping changes in the financing of the French economy.
3. Many product markets regulations, some of which acted as trade barriers, were lifted or harmonized at the European level within the context of the Single Market.
4. The macroeconomic policy framework was transformed by the independence of the Banque de France. As required by the Maastricht Treaty, it was implemented in January 1994 at the beginning of Stage 2 of EMU.

Although some of these initiatives, such as privatization, were primarily the result of domestic political choices, a significant part of the transformation of the French economy during the 1980s and the 1990s can be attributed to European integration. Both the Single Market and EMU required French policymakers to abandon interventionist powers over the economy. As argued by Schmidt (1996), European integration has thus decreased the authority of the French state, while it has increased the independence of business from government decisions. Although France remains interventionist and regulated in comparison with the United States and Britain, the extent to which the domestic relations between interest groups and public authorities have been transformed should not be underestimated.

2.3. Assessing the Results

Successful Disinflation under Fixed Exchange Rates
France is one of the few European countries that successfully achieved disinflation under a fixed exchange rate regime. This experience contrasts with that of other ERM members and shadow members like Italy, Spain, and Sweden. As argued by Alberto Giovannini (1995), putting economic policy on automatic pilot via an exchange rate commitment generally failed to produce sustainable disinflation. Eventually, the real exchange rate became overvalued, markets became skeptical of the sustainability of the exchange rate commitment, and an exchange crisis occurred.

Why was France different? A first factor was that, although the commitment to exchange rate stability was instrumental in ensuring price discipline, the profitability of the tradable goods sector did not suffer excessively: as shown in figure 3.5, the Fr-DM exchange rate constantly remained above its

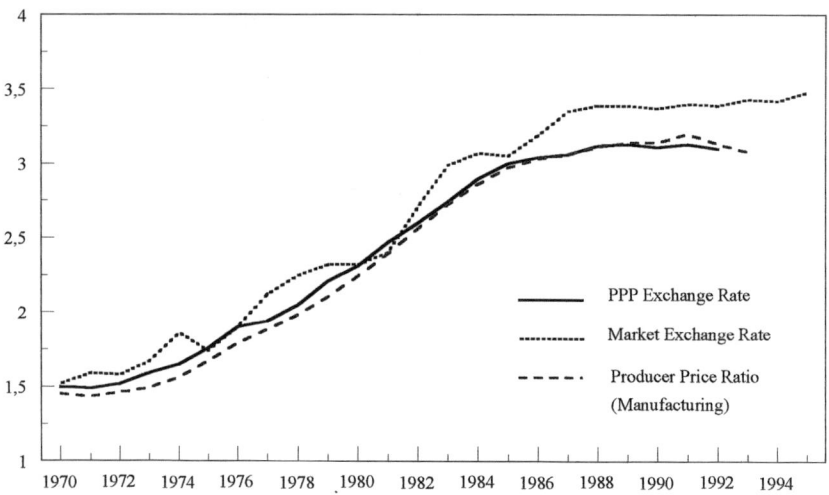

Fig. 3.5. Market and PPP Fr-DM exchange rates, 1970–95. (Data from Freudenberg and Ünal-Kescenci 1995 and FERI/Deutsche Bundesbank.)

purchasing power parity (PPP) level[3] and the share of profits in value added actually increased during the disinflation period. After the initial sharp devaluations of 1981, 1982, and 1983, this was obtained through a combination of small realignments and incomes policy. Ironically, the concept of incomes policy had almost disappeared from the policy agenda, but it became reality in the early 1980s as deindexation sped up disinflation and ensured an increase in the share of profits in value added after its drop in the early 1980s. Econometric estimates confirm that incomes policy was decisively effective in 1982–83.

A second factor behind the success of disinflation was fiscal policy. Throughout the disinflation period, fiscal policy remained tightly under control, and the structural deficit moved from 3.2 percent of GDP in 1982 to 0.7 percent in 1987 (it increased again thereafter). Thus, unlike the Italian, the French economy was not subject to contradictory macroeconomic impulses.

Finally, the timing of disinflation was especially opportune. It began while the recovery in Europe was under way, benefited from the effects of the drop in oil prices of 1986–87, and translated early on into real exchange rate depreciation vis-à-vis the less successful European partners (and eventually Germany). Thanks to the widespread confidence of market participants in the "new ERM"

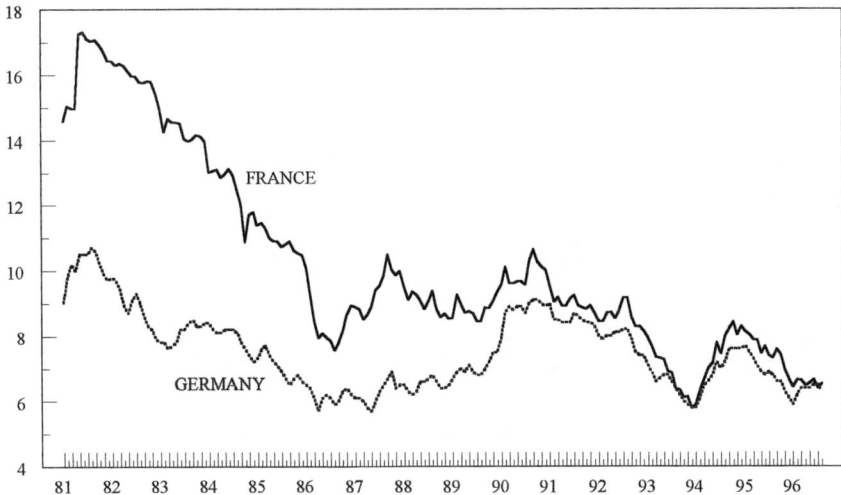

Fig. 3.6. Long-term interest rates in France and Germany, 1980–96. (Data from FERI/Banque de France and Deutsche Bundesbank.)

of the late 1980s, credibility also was achieved in the early 1990s, as is indicated by the sharp narrowing of the Fr-DM bond spread (fig. 3.6).

Careful evaluations of this strategy (Blanchard and Muet 1993) indicate that in spite of the credibility gains that were expected from the country's participation in the ERM it was not successful in reducing the unemployment cost of disinflation. After controlling for the effects of the 1983–84 wage policy, standard wage equations are stable over the 1970–90 period; that is, credibility effects are not discernible. Furthermore, Blanchard and Muet have pointed out that competitiveness through disinflation is a slow process: starting from an initial situation of high inflation, pegging the exchange rate eventually succeeds in bringing inflation down but at the cost of an increase in unemployment that may last for several years. It is therefore little wonder that rough comparisons of the sacrifice ratio (de Grauwe 1989) exhibit a high disinflation cost in France compared to non-ERM OECD countries.

Exchange rate discipline was instrumental in fostering adjustment in manufacturing industry. Exchange rate overvaluation was avoided, but the message to manufacturing was that it could not count on another round of devaluation to solve its competitiveness problems. Plant closures and layoffs in traditional sectors such as steel and metalworking, which had long been delayed, accelerated significantly after 1982–83. The process was painful, and French manufacturing output declined from some 62 percent of that of Germany in the early 1980s to 56 percent in 1992 (Freudenberg and Ünal-Kesenci 1994). Even taking into account the effects of German unification, this was a significant drop.

It is apparent that the costs of disinflation were overwhelmingly borne by wage earners. Between 1983 and 1990, a period in which growth was buoyant in the EC, the unemployment rate (OECD definition) remained above 9 percent (fig. 3.7) while the share of profits in value added rose continuously (see fig. 3.2).

Costs and Benefits of the Franc Fort Policy

Disinflation was achieved at the end of the 1980s. In the 1990s, the exchange rate ceased being an intermediate target and became an objective in its own right. Against the background of repeated attacks on the currency, extraordinary efforts were made to keep the franc close to its central DM rate within the ERM.

The rationale for this behavior was rarely spelled out. In 1992 and early 1993, policymakers were genuinely convinced that, unlike the lira or the pound sterling, the franc was not overvalued and the attacks would eventually subside. It was also widely believed that devaluation would not result in lasting real exchange rate depreciations. Even after policy discussions and a new generation of formal models had lent support to the idea that speculation could be based on the assessment that French monetary policy was at odds with the fundamentals (Ozkan and Sutherland 1995; Masson 1995), French attitudes did not change. An important test came in the second half of 1993 after ERM discipline had ceased to be binding. German inflation was still higher than French inflation (fig. 3.4), and the Bundesbank's monetary policy was still restrictive. Although many economists called for making use of wide bands and adopting new monetary targets, exchange rate targeting de facto remained the overriding monetary policy objective.

This decision had far-reaching consequences. It indicated that the credibility of monetary policy was to remain invested in keeping the DM exchange rate in the neighborhood of its ERM central rate. The rationale for adopting this strategy blended conservatism (embracing a new monetary strategy would have involved risks, especially as the Banque de France was to be given independence on January 1, 1994, and could expect to be tested by market participants) with the aim of acquiring credibility and genuine commitment to exchange rate stability in the perspective of EMU. Political considerations probably inter-

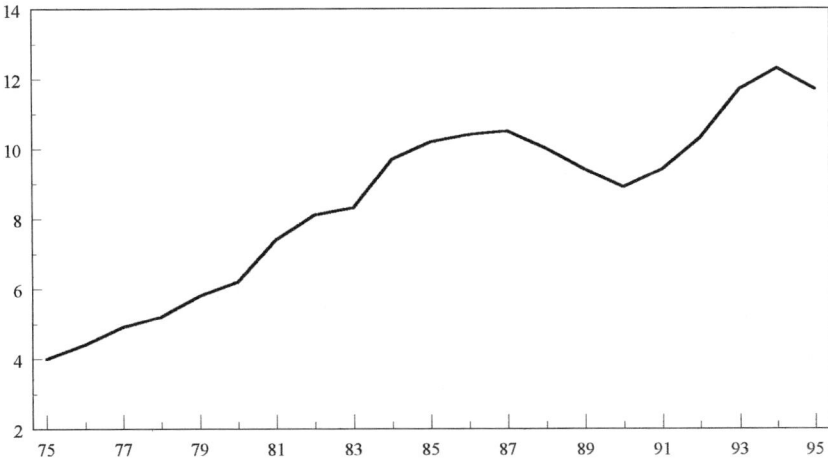

Fig. 3.7. French unemployment rate, 1975–95. (Data from OECD.)

vened also (devaluation was still unpopular and Balladur did not want to run for president as the man who had devalued the currency). Whatever the reasons, France de facto remained in a fixed exchange rate regime and interest rates were assigned to defending the currency.

The economic implications of this choice can be assessed by comparing short-term interest rates with a normative benchmark like the Taylor rule, as has been done by Goldman Sachs (1996). From 1990 until 1996, short-term interest rates remained above the level implied by the Taylor rule. Even excluding interest rate hikes, the spreads vis-à-vis the Taylor rule frequently exceeded 300 basis points.

A Closer Look at Fiscal Policy
Postwar France has a tradition of fiscal discipline, and from 1974 until the early 1990s the general government deficit exceeded 3 percent of GDP only in 1983, when it reached 3.2 percent. From the standpoint of fiscal rectitude, this was the best performance among the G–7 countries. Fiscal policy went through successive periods of expansion (1974–75, 1981–82) and retrenchment (1976–80, 1983–87), but both the structural and actual general government deficits remained within narrow margins.[4] In the late 1980s, however, a combination of tax cuts and expenditure increases resulted in a deteriorating

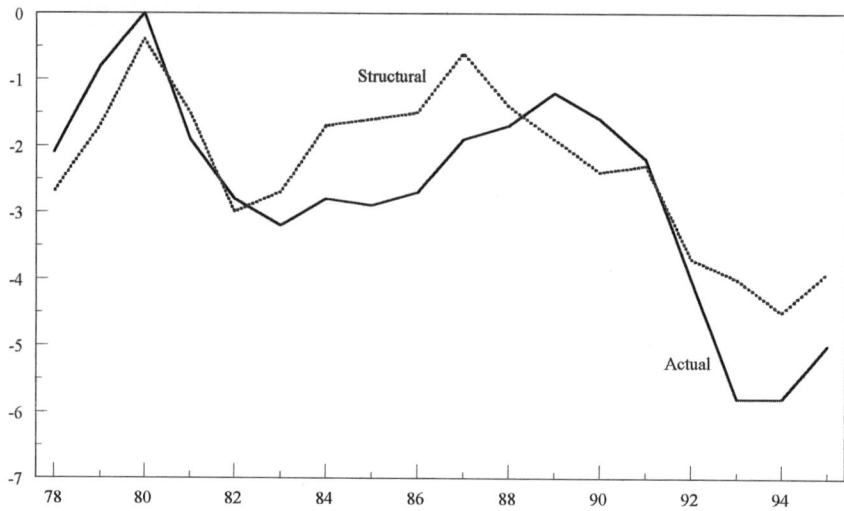

Fig. 3.8. Actual and structural general government deficits, 1978–95. (Data from OECD.)

structural deficit in spite of buoyant growth (fig. 3.8).[5] This was to a certain extent due to the acceleration of growth that occurred in the late 1980s, which was perceived as more permanent than it turned out to be. Therefore, policy-makers considered fiscal policy on track as long as the actual deficit was falling, and they underestimated the extent of the actual deterioration, which became evident only with the recession of 1993.

Once the actual deficit deteriorated, however, fiscal tightening was delayed until 1995–96, while in most European countries it began in 1993 or 1994. In 1992–94, fiscal policy was used as a substitute for monetary policy because the latter was assigned to targeting the exchange rate. The governments of Bé-régovoy and Balladur chose to smooth out the recession through the use of automatic stabilizers and a limited discretionary reflation. The policy mix was therefore characterized by a tight monetary policy and a relatively lax fiscal policy.

The legacy of the 1988–94 period was therefore a fiscal problem of unprecedented magnitude (by French standards), which was a problem in its own right (because French public deficits and debt were not sustainable in the medium run and had to be corrected) and a very significant hurdle to

EMU. Fiscal retrenchment only began with the autumn 1995 deficit-cutting measures that prompted the strikes of late 1995. In order to meet the Maastricht deficit criterion in 1997, the Juppé government sought to reduce the deficit from close to 6 percent of GDP in 1994 to 5 percent in 1995, 4 percent in 1996, and 3 percent in 1997. Although creative accounting contributed to approaching this goal, this was nonetheless a very significant shift in the policy.

To some extent, French policymakers thus succeeded in reducing the short-term macroeconomic costs arising from the choice to stick with the DM exchange rate target through fiscal policy. But this cost was merely postponed, as fiscal adjustment had to be carried out in 1995–96 in the context of slow growth at home and in continental Europe.

3.   The Logic of the Policy

3.1.   European Politics and Domestic Economic Policy

Understanding the logic of these policy choices requires tracing their origins. In post–World War II Europe, economic policy priorities were largely shaped by the diagnosis of prewar failures. The main economic lesson that the French elite drew from the interwar period was that growth, and therefore modernization, had to be given absolute priority if France was to regain its prewar status. *Modernisation ou décadence* was the motto.[6] Price stability per se was not an overriding objective. To the contrary, French policymakers recalled the failure of the deflation experiment of the early 1930s, when the Laval government attempted to restore a competitive real exchange rate by lowering prices and wages, which resulted in aggravating the decline in real activity.[7] A policy of monetary stringency therefore had little support within French society and even within the ruling elite.[8] In contrast with Germany, the focus was much more on low interest rates (actually negative in real terms) and a competitive real exchange rate.[9]

Still, once the Bretton Woods System broke down and Europeans began to envisage monetary arrangements of their own, French policymakers became more conscious of the importance of price stability. There were two rationales for this, one political and one economic. The political logic was that only a low-inflation, stable-currency France could pretend to leadership in Europe. In the same way that after the war industrial growth had been considered essential to maintaining the country's rank, macroeconomic discipline (or *rigueur*, as it was termed in the early 1980s) was a precondition for maintaining France's status within the EC and the so-called French-German couple. Only on the basis of such a policy record could France expect to participate in European monetary decision making and so become the coleader of the EC and one of its agenda shapers.

This link between France's ambitions within the EC and its macro-economic performance has been repeatedly noted. Reflecting on his experience as prime minister in 1976–81, Raymond Barre, for example, emphasized that "France had to be able to play an eminent role in the EC and in international affairs. She could not fulfill it without an economy able to sustain competition and without a solid and stable currency."[10] It may be surprising, especially in light of the U.S. case, that foreign policy considerations could receive such priority over domestic economic concerns. But it should be remembered that in the institutional structure of the French government, the prime minister, who is in charge of economic policy, reports to the president, who has a prominent role in foreign policy and whose seven-year term favors giving priority to long-term goals. This institutional structure gives disproportionate weight to foreign policy.

President Mitterrand's priorities during his two seven-year terms conformed perfectly to the logic of the country's political institutions. His initial priorities were essentially domestic and mostly economic. Yet, after he made the choice of giving priority to France's European commitments over his own economic program in 1983, European integration gained weight in the policy agenda until it became the number-one objective of his 1988–95 term. In the same vein, EMU was primarily endorsed on political grounds.[11] It is not an exaggeration to say that economic and monetary policies became instruments serving the political goal of creating an integrated Europe of which France could be coleader.

President Chirac followed the same logic. Although the basis for his election was his emphasis on domestic concerns and his call for new policy objectives, it was only a few months before the European agenda was given priority and economic policy was assigned the goal of ensuring French participation in EMU. This sharp reorientation, whose domestic political cost was high, can be explained by the harshness of the dilemma Chirac had to face. Only a quick move could give France a chance to participate in the single currency. And failure to achieve fiscal discipline at home would have resulted in France (and its president) being held responsible for the breakdown of the monetary union project.

3.2. Economic Rationales for Price Stability

Monetary rectitude was obviously not given priority for political reasons only. But economic rationales for price stability also involved external considerations.

There can be different economic rationales for price stability, which link domestic and international considerations in different ways. Low inflation may be pursued because private agents express a preference for stable prices, as in Germany, or because policymakers consider that it is conducive to allocative efficiency and growth, as Robert Barro (1995) recently attempted to demonstrate.[12] In such cases, disinflation is domestically grounded. Exchange rate arrangements only play the role of a "commitment technology," a way for the government to surmount the time inconsistency problem and "tie its hands" as well as those of its successors (Giavazzi and Pagano 1988). This view is consistent with the standard approach to the ERM as an instrument for borrowing credibility from the Bundesbank. According to this view, exchange rate stability within the ERM was only an intermediate objective, while price stability was the final objective.

There is, however, an alternate view of the logic of disinflation, which attaches importance to the exchange rate stability commitment. If governments do have a preference for exchange rate stability per se and come to realize that it is incompatible with higher inflation than that of the partner countries, then exchange rate stability acquires the status of a final objective and disinflation becomes the intermediate objective.

This second approach to disinflation deserves serious discussion in the French case. For a long time, France has expressed a strong preference for exchange rate stability. In the early 1970s, French governments attempted to resist the move to floating exchange rates. Since then they have taken every occasion to emphasize the link between trade liberalization and international monetary reform and to advocate a return to some form of international monetary order (Landau 1994). This emphasis on exchange rate stability is specific to France among the G–7 countries, and it has been a major objective of French international economic diplomacy at both the regional and global levels. French insistence encountered some success at both levels, temporarily at least, with the creation of the European Monetary System in 1979 and the G–7 Louvre agreement of 1987.

It is not obvious why France has given such priority to nominal exchange rate stability. One explanation is that, in accordance with de Gaulle's criticism of the U.S. attitude during the Bretton Woods era (Jeanneney 1994), the establishment of international rules of the game was seen as a way of putting constraints on the policies of the global and regional hegemons, the United States and Germany. More generally, it was seen as necessary to foster cooperation: like other Europeans, postwar French policymakers remembered the experience of the 1920s and 1930s when beggar-thy-neighbor exchange rate policies contributed to the deterioration of international relations. A second explanation is that because of its intellectual background the French elite was less inclined to a laissez-faire attitude than that of the United States and has always been doubtful of the ability of floating exchange rates to deliver "fair" equilibrium real exchange rates. Support for floating exchange rates has always been weak in France, both within academic circles and in the enterprise sector. Hence, there has been constant advocacy of fixed nominal exchange rates as a way of achieving real exchange rate stability. Finally, the choice of a fixed exchange rate system at the European level was consistent with the operation of the Common Agricultural Policy and the EC budget (Giavazzi and Giovannini 1989). Whatever the reason, it is clear that the return to a fixed exchange rate regime implied price stability as a major domestic policy objective.

This is not to say that an alternative logic has not been at work as well. Policymakers who considered low inflation a goal in its own right knew that companies, labor unions, and the public could only be convinced of the merits of disinflation to the extent that it was conducive to the attainment of "real" objectives. Therefore, disinflation was essentially presented as a policy whose benefits would show up in the form of improved competitiveness, employment, growth, and the achievement of external balance.[13] In the eyes of the public it was a derived objective. Germany was admired not because of its success in mastering inflation but because stable prices appeared to be a key component of its industrial and commercial successes.

There is little evidence, however, that the view of exchange rate arrangements as commitment technologies was widespread among policymakers, while from the aftermath of the first oil shock until the 1990s the alternative reasoning is apparent in a very large body of policy papers, including the successive medium-term plans, as shown in table 3.1.[14] In virtually all this literature, the inflation objective was (1) formulated in comparison with the other countries' performance rather than in an absolute manner and (2) was directly related to the growth perspectives through price competitiveness vis-à-vis other European countries.[15] The implicit framework

TABLE 3.1.   Medium-Term Inflation and Exchange Rate Targets, 1981–93

Period	Reference	Inflation Target
1981–85	Report for the Eighth Plan[b]	"inflation rate [at least] below the [OECD] partners' average"
1981–85	Eighth Plan[a]	"continue disinflation"
1981–83	Two-Year Plan[a]	"a progressive decrease in the inflation rate"
1984–88	Ninth Plan[a]	"stabilise inflation at the level of the [OECD] competitors"
1989–92	Report for the Tenth Plan[b]	"convergence of French inflation towards the EMS average"
1989–92	Tenth Plan[a]	"best European performance"
1993–97	Report for the Eleventh Plan[b]	"maintain one of the best inflation performances among EC members"

Source: Commissariat Général du Plan.
[a]Official policy document of the government.
[b]Macroeconomic experts' group's report.

was therefore a neo-Keynesian model in which disinflation automatically translates into real exchange rate depreciation, gains in market share, and growth.[16]

The logic of disinflation under fixed exchange rates was first pushed to its ultimate conclusion in an article by Jean-Baptiste de Foucauld (a former aide to Finance Minister Delors who later became the head of planning), who in 1986 coined the expression *désinflation compétitive* and proposed to adopt zero inflation as a policy target.[17] His article makes only brief reference to the standard microbenefits of stable prices but argues that zero inflation would improve French competitiveness vis-à-vis Germany and be conducive to maintaining the country's rank as a great power. In 1992, this objective was made official policy philosophy by Jean-Claude Trichet (then director of the Treasury). Trichet, upon becoming governor of the central bank in 1993, argued that "*if competitive devaluation is not considered acceptable* [in a fixed exchange rate regime], the only remaining competitiveness strategy at the disposal of economic policymakers is competitive disinflation" (Trichet 1992; emphasis added).[18]

However, the noncooperative character of this doctrine, in which gains mainly arise at the expense of trading partners, was not seriously discussed until the early 1990s. It only became obvious when some of France's partners left the ERM (or devalued their currency). French policy thinking lost one of its pillars, and, more importantly, public support for price stability weakened, as it could no longer be presented as conducive to exchange rate stability or as giving rise to immediate real gains.

3.3.   EMU as a Culmination

From the outset, EMU was conceived as the culmination of the drive for price stability. Accordingly, the ranking of its potential benefits in the view of French policymakers was different from that of their counterparts in other European countries. The chief benefits expected from the creation of a single currency were: (1) equal participation in monetary decision making; (2) a softening of the current account constraint, which had been perceived as a major obstacle to growth;[19] (3) emergence of the euro as a world currency that could challenge the dominance of the U.S. dollar; (4) elimination of the expected depreciation and risk premiums affecting French interest rates; and (5) further competitiveness gains through the continuation of the *désinflation compétitive*.

As it was conducive to the achievement of long-standing diplomatic as well as economic objectives, France accepted the need to build its monetary institutions on the model of Germany's, even though this was a significant departure from its own tradition: as documented by Garrett (chap. 2 of this volume), France was among the countries for which the change was significant. The adoption of the German model was initially at least not considered to be a benefit in its own right but a price to be paid for the achievement of France's European goals.[20] A significant illustration of this attitude was provided by the way in which central bank independence was legislated. As this independence necessitated a constitutional amendment (because the constitution states that the government "determines and conducts the policy of the Nation"), the choice was made to draft this amendment in such a way that the bank's new status was explicitly linked to the building of EMU. In fact, because the Parliament passed the law granting independence to the central bank in 1993, before the ratification of the Maastricht Treaty had been completed by all twelve nations, the constitutional court ruled that the law could only enter into force after the completion of the ratification process.[21]

Another indication of French reluctance to forsake its policy-making model is the emphasis that was put in the Maastricht negotiations on creating an "economic government" that could serve as a counterweight to the European Central Bank. As France was at the same time reluctant to adopt a federalist agenda, this could only be achieved by coordinating national economic policies within the framework of the Council of Ministers of Economy and Finance (ECOFIN). French negotiators encountered limited success in this regard, however, since the Maastricht Treaty only envisages very general provisions for policy coordination (Art. 103) and puts considerable limits on the ability of the Council to constrain the central bank through formulating guidelines for exchange rate policy toward third currencies (Art. 109).

Summing up, in the 1980s and early 1990s external motives very significantly influenced the domestic economic policy agenda. This does not mean that economic policy has been detrimental to domestic objectives (few economists would dispute that disinflation was necessary) but rather that both the ranking of objectives and their formulation have not been derived from domestic priorities.

4. Interest Groups, Monetary Policy, and EMU

4.1. Agents' Views on European Monetary Integration

An agenda dominated by external commitments can only be pursued as long as it does not conflict with domestic priorities. From 1992 on, a conflict of priorities arose between domestic concerns and the external agenda: disinflation cum European integration stopped being a consensual objective, and policy debates became increasingly acrimonious, both among political parties and within them, as internal discussions increasingly reflected tensions between the private agents and the policy elite.

An obvious difficulty in studying the political economy of European monetary integration is that it involves several different channels of influence on the welfare of interest groups. Among the most significant effects are:

1. Central bank independence and low inflation
2. The loss of interest rate autonomy
3. The loss of the exchange rate as a policy instrument
4. The end of nominal exchange rate uncertainty and transaction costs
5. European integration more broadly

Furthermore, additional channels have to be considered in relation to the costs and benefits of the transition to EMU. These are:

6. Costs of budgetary convergence toward the Maastricht objectives
7. Transition costs associated with the introduction of a single currency

These channels are obviously not independent, but when turning to the political economy of monetary integration there are two reasons for considering them separately. First, the relative significance of each channel varies over time. For example, the gains from eliminating exchange rate uncertainty were significantly increased by the post-1992 return to exchange rate variability in Europe. Second, divisions within sectors and coalitions across sectors (e.g., tradable vs. nontradable sectors, banks vs. nonfinancial industries, small vs. large enterprises, and wage earners vs. the business sector) depend on the channel under consideration. Exchange rate effects discriminate between enterprises depending on their positions in product markets (i.e., by industry), while interest rate effects discriminate between them depending on their reliance on short- versus long-term borrowing (i.e., their position in credit markets). Constituencies for or against European monetary integration are therefore based upon linkage politics[22] and may not be stable over time.

Furthermore, EMU is a complex undertaking whose effects are not observable in advance and are by nature uncertain. The economics profession is divided on the relative significance of its macro- and microeconomic effects, and, in contrast to what happened when the Single Market Program was launched, no one has been able to provide a definitive assessment of its consequences. As agents try to assess the costs and benefits of EMU, two consequences can be expected.

The first one is a status-quo bias in the spirit of Fernandez and Rodrik (1991), who pointed out that uncertainty regarding the distribution of the costs and benefits of efficiency-enhancing reform may lead a majority to oppose it even if the losers are expected to be a minority. This is because all those who face the risk of ending up as losers may expect the winners to block a redistribution of the gains from the reform. This kind of effect should be especially relevant for a policy reform whose benefits are likely to be concentrated (among individuals and firms that are engaged in transactions with the rest of the EU), while its costs—for example, those arising from the loss of monetary autonomy in the presence of an asymmetric shock—are likely to be more evenly distributed.

The second effect is that the agent's own weighting of the various channels can be expected to be affected by uncertainty. This is bound to affect choices for or against EMU according to simple decision rules, for example, on the basis of one's attitude toward European integration in general or toward the experience with the ERM and disinflation. It can also be expected that agents will attach great weight to any information that may signal what the real effects of EMU will be. Evidence of this was widespread when voters were asked to voice their opinions in the Maastricht referendum. People who were mostly ignorant about monetary affairs desperately sought any piece of information that would allow them to make an "informed" decision.

4.2. The Policy Debates

France's participation in the ERM was initially fairly consensual. But exchange rate policy was thereafter the focus of two cathartic debates. The first one took place in 1982–83, when the Mauroy government had to choose between leaving the ERM and undertaking disinflation. In technical terms, it was a debate about the exchange rate regime and the choice between nominal and real exchange rate stability (interest rates were not the focus of discussion because at that time they were disconnected from foreign rates by capital controls). Politically, it was a debate between the supporters of *l'autre politique*—those within the ruling Socialist Party who gave priority to the Left's domestic agenda (fiscal reflation, growth, and employment) and therefore advocated letting the exchange rate float—and those who refused to break away from the ERM and considered that *l'autre politique* was an illusion. After the choice was made, disinflation was pursued by five successive governments.

Over time, its benefits began to emerge. However, these benefits were called into question by the German unification shock, as the cost of a fixed exchange rate regime manifested itself. The breakdown of the ERM also meant that the "virtuous" link between disinflation and competitiveness was ruptured.

The second cathartic debate about monetary and exchange rate policy began in 1992–93, during the Maastricht referendum campaign and its aftermath, and became more or less permanent: it was still going on when this chapter was completed. *L'autre politique* reemerged, but the essential difference with 1982–83 was that in 1992–95 its proponents could make a more credible economic case for changing the course of monetary policy. This was because, in a stagnation context, pursuing a tight interest rate policy was not warranted on domestic economic grounds and could be portrayed as obsessive (Fitoussi 1995).

Discussion of the *franc fort* has been going on since 1992. During the 1994–95 recovery, the debate over interest rates lost intensity (except for periods of money market rate hikes), but exchange rate issues became the subject of increasing controversy with the depreciation of the lira and the peseta. The presidential election of 1995 did not give rise to a debate about Europe or about monetary policy, but the victory of Jacques Chirac was built upon his commitment to consider employment as the overriding objective of economic policy. As he later gave priority to meeting the Maastricht fiscal criteria, debates intensified in 1995–96 in the context of a significant economic weakening. Politicians from within the parliamentary majority, industrialists, and economists publicly called for a much looser monetary policy and for abandoning the Fr-DM link.

Why did policy remain constant despite the intensity of the debate? One explanation, at least from 1994 on, is the independence of the central bank and its search for credibility. But the Banque de France is not in charge of exchange rate policy. In the event of a disagreement, the government could have made use of its legal responsibility for formulating exchange rate policy to constrain the central bank's behavior. As already argued, a deeper reason for the continuity is that the economic policy debate is dominated by the wider issue of France's European strategy. In that respect, proponents of alternative policies have not spelled out what they would propose in lieu of the present policy if France were to forsake EMU and therefore scale down its ambitions as regards European integration. Even some of the staunchest critics of the *franc fort* policy (Fitoussi 1995) fully support monetary union and even propose accelerating it. Furthermore, for reasons mentioned earlier, the British alternative (i.e., the deliberate choice of floating the exchange rate and adopting a "small open economy" strategy) does not appeal to French politicians.

4.3. Public Opinion

The referendum on Maastricht that took place in September 1992 came at a crucial juncture. Growth had been slowing for more than a year but had not yet bottomed out. Unemployment was on the rise, but the recession was still expected to be mild. The EMS was in turmoil and Britain had been forced to exit the ERM a few days earlier, but the general public was not yet aware of the depth of the crisis. Yet the result of the referendum was unexpectedly close: "yes" won by a very narrow margin—50.8 to 49.2 percent. This was surprising because for years French voters had routinely expressed support for the single European currency in opinion polls[23] and virtually the entire political establishment supported the Maastricht Treaty. Only the fringes—the Communists and the nationalistic Right—and a few political dissidents were clearly opposed.

The treaty became a best-seller, and at the grassroots level European integration was for the first time the subject of intense discussion. As the campaign developed, voters became increasingly skeptical of the virtues of the Maastricht Treaty, and polls conducted afterward indicated that the trend did not reverse on September 20. The *Eurobarometer* survey regularly conducted by the EC Commission shows that the margin between the proportion of Frenchmen believing that France has benefited from participation in the EU and those believing that it has not benefited dropped from 30 percent in 1990, to 20 percent in 1992, to zero in 1994.[24]

It is not clear to what extent EMU was prominent among the voters' concerns. Opposition to the loss of monetary autonomy, to the independence of the central bank, and to fiscal austerity was clearly expressed by the leaders of the "no" camp (Séguin 1992), but motives indicated by the voters in exit polls were rather general. "Yes" voters mentioned peace (89 percent), the building of Europe (88 percent), and the need to be able to withstand competition from Japan and the United States (83 percent). "No" voters were no more specific: they gave sovereignty (75 percent), the Brussels technocrats (74 percent), and German dominance (71 percent) as the main reasons for opposing the treaty.[25] The fear of austerity policies (69 percent) ranked only fifth in the voters' explicit concerns. Analyses of the determinants of the voters' choices reveal the interplay of several factors including political affiliations and preferences but overwhelmingly indicate that the main determinants were sociological. The referendum was the occasion for a divide between the rich and the poor, the educated and the noneducated, the winners and the losers (table 3.2).

These results should obviously be read in the light of previous observations about the distributional effects of the disinflation effort. Socialist governments under President Mitterrand relied on the support of wage earners and labor unions to bring about the disinflation and restoration of profits that the center-right governments under Giscard d'Estaing had not been able to achieve. Labor unions were generally critical of this policy, at least the Confédération Générale du Travail (CGT) and Force Ouvrière (FO) confederations (the Confédération Française Démocratique du Travail [CFDT] was more supportive) but did not oppose it in a frontal way. They were also critical of the process of European integration (the CFDT again being more supportive) but did not attempt to organize opposition within the working class. As disinflation was pursued in the name of Europe, the "losers" in the process, (i.e., the working class and the unemployed) grew skeptical of the benefits of European

TABLE 3.2. Proportion of "Yes" Votes in the Referendum on Maastricht

Overall	51
Political preference (a)	
Extreme left	46
Left	75
Center	51
Right	43
Extreme right	7
Monthly income in U.S. dollars (a)	
Less than 1,000	43
1,000–1,500	46
1,500–2,000	49
2,000–3,000	52
3,000–4,000	62
More than 4,000	64
Age at end of education (b)	
14 or less	46
15 to 16	47
17 to 18	43
19 to 21	51
22 or more	65
Still in education	61
Profession (a)	
Farmer	29
Entrepreneur	44
Manager, higher intellectual profession	70
Intermediate profession	57
Employee	44
Production worker	42
Inactive	55
Opinion on the working of democracy in France (b)	
Works very well	81
Works well	68
Does not work well	28
Works very badly	13
Confidence in one's professional and personal future (b)	
Very confident	78
Rather confident	76
Rather worried	39
Very worried	17

Source: (a) SOFRES exit poll in SOFRES 1993; (b) BVA exit poll.

integration. Their skepticism merged with that of other groups that had become reluctant to support European integration, either because of their experience with the implementation of the Single Market or, in the case of farmers, because they had been affected by the unrelated, but quasi-simultaneous, reform of the Common Agricultural Policy (CAP).[26]

The referendum was a shock in both sociological and political terms. Revelation of a split between the France of the winners and that of the losers contradicted the view that class struggle was over and France had been gently moving in the same direction as other industrial countries, namely, toward the formation of a large middle class with an elite above and an underclass below. The referendum, and the results of the elections for the European Parliament of June 1994, in which mainstream parties favoring European integration attracted only 40 percent of the vote,[27] gave rise to a new paradigm, that of two Frances (Todd 1994). According to this view, the split in public opinion over European integration revealed a deeper sociological divide. This analysis was reflected in the electoral campaign of candidate Chirac, who repeatedly mentioned the threat of a *fracture sociale* and the need to rebuild France's social fabric.

In analytical terms, there is no clear evidence that inequalities and divisions within French society can be specifically attributed to *European* integration. The debate on the effects of international trade on the labor market has focused more on the consequences of industrial relocation in, or trade with, low-wage countries. However, European integration is frequently seen by those who oppose opening the French economy as a symbol of globalization. Specific concerns relate to the elimination of public service monopolies (in utilities, telecommunications, and railroad and air transportation), sectors which are more unionized than is the private sector. Threats to the French model of providing public services receive a larger echo because this model, which in part originates in the compromise reached at the end of World War II between the government of General de Gaulle and the Communist Party, epitomizes the postwar modernization alliance between labor and technocrats. More generally, European integration is perceived as limiting redistributive policies and policies aiming at the integration of recent immigrants into French society.[28] Although fiscal adjustment would be needed independent of the Maastricht criteria, it is widely considered the product of European constraints. Such concerns were clearly present in the winter 1995 strikes.

Even those who do not endorse this view acknowledge that there is now a *perceived* conflict between pursuing the goal of European integration and restoring social cohesion in a society that has suffered the effects of industrial restructuring, urban decay, tensions between natives and immigrants, and the rise in long-term unemployment and whose cohesion has traditionally rested on the integrating role of government institutions. One may dispute the existence of such a conflict in the long run, as the authors of this chapter do, yet it is indisputable that it arises in the short term, if only because of the budgetary requirements of the Maastricht Treaty.

4.4. The Corporate Sector

Analyses of monetary and exchange rate policies have highlighted the interplay between economic structures, private sector preferences, and public institutions in shaping the political economy of monetary and exchange rate policy. Frieden (1994) emphasizes the divisions between producers of tradables and nontradables vis-à-vis the level of the exchange rate and between internationally and domestically oriented producers and investors as regards its variability. In his study of the United States, Germany, and Japan, Henning (1994) argues that since banks tend to be agnostic on exchange rate issues, the emergence of a homogeneous private sector view on exchange rate policy depends on the degree of bank participation in industrial shareholding and on industry's reliance on bank credit for financing. According to this thesis, the United States' neglect of exchange rate issues is rooted in the almost complete separation of banking and manufacturing that characterizes the country. This kind of reasoning should not be applied mechanically to a country like France in which, according to a recent study (Bauer and Bertin-Mourot 1995), 47 percent of the top executives of major corporations are former civil servants. Nevertheless, analysis reveals interesting transformations.

From the 1950s to the 1990s, French enterprises experienced dramatic changes in their relationship with the rest of the world. In the 1950s, French industry was heavily protected and traded less with the future EC than with the colonies. The employers' association Conseil National du Patronat Français (CNPF) opposed the European Coal and Steel Community in 1951 and only accepted with reluctance the establishment of the Common Market in 1957. It was skeptical about the merits of foreign trade liberalization and until the 1980s routinely called for devaluation in order to restore profit margins and maintain domestic and foreign market shares. By and large, however,

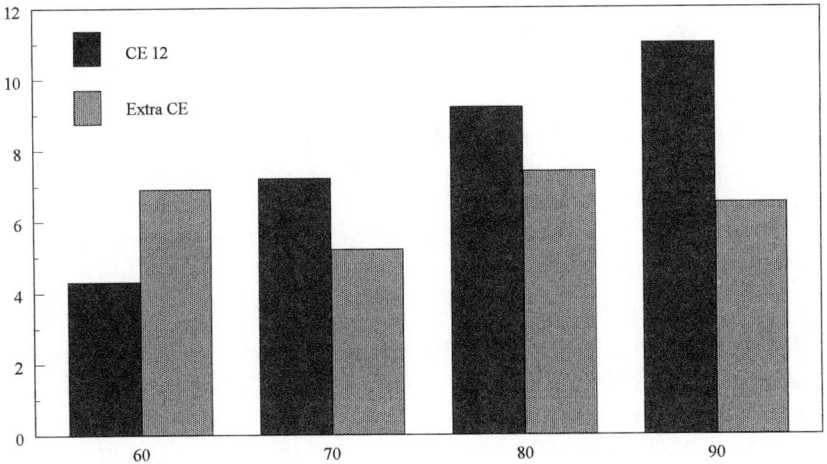

Fig. 3.9. French exports by destination, 1960–90. (Data from the European Commission.)

French companies' experience with European integration has been a success. Catastrophes have not taken place, and France has been able to meet or even anticipate the liberalization deadlines. Over the last decades, changes in economic structure have transformed the companies' involvement in European integration. The Community has become the major market for French producers (fig. 3.9). The establishment of the Single Market has prompted new efforts to devise European marketing strategies, especially by small and medium-sized enterprises, significantly enhancing their exports to the EC.

The launching of the Single Market and the liberalization of the capital account led larger industrial and financial companies to embark on ambitious foreign investment and acquisition programs, mainly in other EC countries. Outward FDI grew from Fr 20 billion per year in 1985–86 to Fr 150 billion in 1990 (the flow thereafter decreased to Fr 70 billion in 1993), and according to the Banque de France, the stock of French FDI increased from Fr 276 billion to Fr 774 billion between 1987 and 1992. Most of this increase was due to intra-EC FDI, and at the end of 1992 the EC represented 58 percent of the total stock of FDI abroad. This proportion was even higher in sectors like banking (68 percent) and insurance, which essentially started developing abroad with the launching of the Single Market. Data on mergers and acquisitions point in the same direction, as they indicate that French firms were the most actively engaged in intra-European deals.[29] French capitalism now has a stake in European integration as a result of FDI and mergers and acquisitions. The trend continues with the increasing involvement of transport, telecommunications, and utilities in the Single Market.

To what extent does this increased involvement in European affairs translate into support for monetary integration? Until the exchange crises of 1992–93, French firms were generally supportive of monetary union, although support was weaker than for the Single Market (AMUE 1990; Coutu et al. 1993). EMU was perceived as a positive addition to the Single Market but not an essential one. Until September 1992, exchange rate stability was taken for granted, and as long as high-inflation countries like Italy and Spain were experiencing real appreciation within the ERM, French enterprises benefited from a steady improvement in their competitiveness. When this process came to an end in September 1992, the emergence of misalignments within the Community tested the compatibility of the Single Market with floating exchange rates. This unprecedented experience (unprecedented because the creation of the Single Market had removed all remaining safeguards against "unfair" competition as well as the possibility for a government to subsidize loss-making enterprises) provoked French business to react against "unfair" competition from Italy and Spain.

This new situation may significantly affect companies' attitudes toward EMU. According to "one market, one money" logic, it could trigger demands for monetary union as a way to avoid misalignments. A number of declarations to this effect have been made by industrialists and representatives of the agricultural sector. Yet, as monetary integration will certainly be of a two-speed variety, EMU is unlikely to bring a full solution to the problem. To the contrary, the formation of a core EMU between Germany, Denmark, France, and the Benelux countries could be seen as offering those outside the core a golden opportunity to pursue noncooperative exchange rate policies. This concern has been repeatedly expressed by French industrialists and politicians as well as by Jean Gandois, the chairman of the employers' association, when he stated that enterprises "want neither a free-trade area without a single currency nor a Europe divided in two by the currency."[30] Resentment against competitive devaluations is especially widespread in traditional sectors and among smaller companies which tend to be more affected by competition from low-cost producers. But it is by no means confined to small and medium-sized enterprises (SMEs) and declining industries: the automobile sector, for example, is also highly attentive to the exchange rate of the lira. Similar attitudes prevail in sectors like aerospace, the profitability of which is sensitive to the

TABLE 3.3. Borrowing Practices in France, Germany, and the United Kingdom (percentage of total borrowing of each sector)

	France	Germany	United Kingdom
Households			
Short term and adjustable medium and long term	13	36	90
Fixed long term	87	64	10
Business sector			
Short term and adjustable medium and long term	56	40	48
Fixed long term	44	60	52

Source: Borio 1995.

exchange rate of the dollar. Business leaders in this sector tend to be agnostic, as their attitude toward the single currency will essentially depend on the exchange rate of the euro vis-à-vis the dollar.[31] An early appreciation of the euro vis-à-vis the dollar would no doubt prompt strong reactions within the company sector.

A second significant factor shaping companies' attitudes toward EMU is their dependence on short-term interest rates. The British experience of 1991–92 demonstrates that extensive reliance on financing indexed to short-term rates can be incompatible with the maintenance of a fixed exchange rate. In France, opposition to the franc fort was especially vocal in sectors with significant dependence on short-term rates. It has been suggested by some observers that asymmetries in the borrowing structure between France and Germany could be an obstacle to monetary integration.

When borrowing is primarily linked to bond rates, private agents should favor a stability-oriented policy like that of the Bundesbank. When they rely more on short-term rates, borrowers are likely to be critical of a monetary policy that may imply short-term rate hikes. A study by the Bank for International Settlements (BIS) (Borio 1995) confirms that both France and Germany differ from the United Kingdom in the extent of fixed-term lending to households, but it also indicates that French firms rely more on short-term or adjustable rate credit than do German firms (table 3.3). There is therefore a rationale for the differences between French and German reactions to interest rate hikes.[32]

Furthermore, there is a significant difference between large firms, which rely more on self-financing and borrowing in the bond market, and SMEs, which depend more on short-term bank credit, the cost of which is indexed to money market rates (table 3.4).[33] SMEs were therefore more exposed to the upward shift in short-term rates and to the inversion of the yield curve that

TABLE 3.4. Financing of French Companies, 1992–93 (percentage of total resources)

	Small and Medium-sized Firms		Large Firms	
	1992	1993	1992	1993
Self-financing	75.1	77.1	83.3	83.7
Debt	24.9	22.9	16.7	16.3
Bond financing	0.6	0.8	2.5	3.7
Short-term bank credit	9.7	8.7	4.6	3.9

Source: Banque de France.

occurred in the early 1990s and might give preference to a policy of low real money market rates rather than one of low nominal bond rates.

Thus there is now a strong constituency for European integration in the corporate sector (a much stronger one than 10 years ago), but support for European integration does not automatically translate into support for EMU. A majority of companies remain supportive of monetary integration, but attitudes are diverse and there are rationales for this diversity. This is a very significant difference from the Single Market Program, which attracted opposition but was soon perceived by companies as beneficial for business.

4.5. The Banking Sector

The banks' attitude toward European monetary integration differs depending on their involvement in international transactions, but they have generally been supportive of the process. Although they are bound to lose from the elimination of some exchange market operations, their attitude is understandable in view of the benefits they would draw from the merging of national financial markets. In contrast to German banks, French banks are also less engaged in long-term relationships with companies, and, as shown in table 3.5, France has been moving quite rapidly away from the German model and the direction of the Anglo-Saxon one: the two intermediation ratios calculated by the Conseil National du Crédit both indicate a dramatic extension of disintermediation during the period 1982–86 that resumed in the 1990s after having been interrupted by the October 1987 stock market crash. The banks' views on monetary integration are therefore increasingly independent of those held by companies.

Unlike other sectors, which at that time were still considering their options, French banks began concrete preparation for the changeover to the euro

TABLE 3.5. Intermediation Ratios, 1983–95

	1983	1984	1985	1986	1987	1988	1989	1990	1991	1992	1993	1994	1995
Demand approach[a]	0.66	0.58	0.57	0.34	0.55	0.63	0.55	0.58	0.48	0.28	0.0[b]	0.0[b]	0.19
Supply approach[c]	0.76	0.74	0.74	0.58	0.68	0.73	0.65	0.67	0.56	0.51	0.37	0.51	0.62

Source: Banque de France.

[a]Ratio defined as net bank credit to nonfinancial agents (households, firms) over the overall net financing of nonfinancial agents (annual flows).

[b]Not significantly different from zero.

[c]Ratio defined as net bank financing to nonfinancial agents (through various channels: credit, the purchase of securities, etc.) over the overall net financing of nonfinancial agents (annual flows).

immediately after the European Council of Madrid confirmed the 1999 and 2002 deadlines. The year 1996 was therefore a turning point, as the banking sector realized that in order to be ready it had to begin investing without delay in the transformation of computer and payment systems. Although the cost of this transformation is nontrivial (estimates available in the mid-1990s were on the order of Fr 15 billion, some 0.2 percent of GDP), by mid-1996 banks were moving ahead. A major reason for this attitude was the perception that German banks were already putting resources into preparation and that failure to follow suit would prevent French banks from meeting German competition in the future banking market. In the second half of the 1980s, this is what led many European companies to invest in anticipation of the Single Market, thereby adding to the momentum toward the 1992 objective. To a more limited extent, a similar logic is now at work in the banking sector.

Furthermore, French banks and financial companies see monetary union as an occasion to enhance their position in the competition with British financial institutions. If Britain does not participate in the single currency, French banks could derive some advantage from their participation in the monetary core in euro-denominated credit markets. They are therefore opposed to giving access to the ESCB's refinancing facilities to the banks of the countries not belonging to the euro core, including doing so on an intraday basis.[34]

Divisions may arise, nevertheless, as there are both potential winners and losers in the transition to EMU. Since the rapid introduction of euro banknotes is technically infeasible, and since the main political cost arising from the transition to a single currency will certainly be that of introducing the euro at the retail level, governments may be tempted to delay it. In this case, the costs of maintaining a dual currency system will accrue to the banks. A possible strategy for the introduction of the euro at the retail level might even be to leave it in the hands of the banks. Since they would collectively profit from the elimination of national currencies, there would be an incentive for the banking system to price its services differently for euro and national currency operations. However, the adoption of such a strategy would significantly affect the expected gains from EMU for the banks, and it might affect their attitudes. This again illustrates the instability of constituencies for and against EMU.

Summing up, there is no evidence of strong private sector preferences in favor of or against EMU. Wage earners appear to be divided between the "losers" and the "winners," a division that is disturbing both for the political parties and for a country as a whole, and, although polls indicate that support for monetary union remains strong, opinions seem to be moving in the direction of opposing it as citizens experience the short-term costs of tight fiscal and monetary policies. Companies are more favorable to European integration than in the past and generally support EMU, though with qualifications. Finally, banks are more favorable to monetary integration, although they are also concerned about the possible costs of introducing the single currency. Attitudes toward monetary union will therefore depend on its effects along the transition path.

5. Conclusions

For many years, the French attitudes toward European economic and monetary integration have been driven by the political and technocratic elites' views of the country's long-term interests. French leaders' commitment to the goal of European integration has been a powerful force triggering major changes in the economy, at both the macro- and microlevels. These changes in attitudes toward price and exchange rate stability, as well as liberalization, have been accepted by private agents in the name of European integration rather than for their own merits. In short, Europe has been, at least for the last 15 years, a driving force for modernization and economic reform.

The dominance of this external political and economic agenda was made possible by a number of factors. Some, like the president's role in shaping foreign policy, are institutional. But the dynamics of French integration was sustainable because its successes gave rise to the building of constituencies: companies' initial reluctance gave way to support as their involvement in cross-border goods and asset transactions increased, and disinflation was supported because under a fixed exchange rate regime it delivered competitiveness. Opposition to the process existed because there were losers along the way but remained divided and unable to find political expression.

The Treaty of Maastricht was conceived as the culmination of this process, the achievement of a goal already implicit in the creation of the EMS. It was a clear expression of the strategy of reform throughout Europe, and the changes it introduced, especially the independence of the central bank, were of a quasi-constitutional nature. By the time it had to pass the test of a popular vote, however, the balance of costs and benefits from participating in a fixed exchange rate regime had deteriorated sharply as a consequence of recession and German unification. Opponents to the treaty were able to build on the frustration accumulated among the losers to almost form a winning coalition. This event demonstrated that French society was deeply divided and generally much more reluctant about European integration than had been thought.

Maastricht could have been expected to trigger a realignment in French politics. It did not. Analysis of the debates and the preferences of the private sector helps us to understand why: divisions on European matters between the losers and the winners in the integration process are widespread and run deep through each party and each category of agents. Furthermore, opponents of the European strategy have made a case against the economic consequences of the ERM, but they have had difficulty articulating an alternative strategy of modernization and internationalization.

Continuity has therefore prevailed. But the malaise has not vanished. Instead of a realignment, the debate over Europe that emerged in the early 1990s has given rise to the perception of a conflict of priorities between domestic concerns and European objectives. Since the 1992 referendum, this conflict of priorities has continued to haunt French politics.

NOTES

This is a revised and updated version of a paper initially presented at the conference on the Political Economy of European Integration: The Challenges Ahead, held at the University of California, Berkeley, on April 20–21, 1995, and released by the Centre d'études prospectives et d'informations internationales as CEPII Working Paper no. 1995–09 in October 1995. We are grateful to Manuel Lafont for research assistance; to Paul Adler, Jean-Michel Charpin, Stefan Collignon, Barry Eichengreen, Jeffry Frieden, Pierre Jaillet, Miles Kahler, Peter Lange, Claire Lefebvre, Armand Lepas, and Didier Maillard for discussions; and to anonymous referees for comments. We also wish to thank the Centre d'étude de la vie politique française for granting us access to its documentation. Opinions expressed are those of the authors and do not represent the views of the institutions to which they belong.

1. For a detailed account of this period, see Fonteneau and Muet 1985.

2. For most of the 1987–92 period, exchange rate policy was decided upon by Pierre Bérégovoy, who was successively minister of finance and prime minister and remained totally committed to exchange rate stability.

3. This obviously depends on the measurement of PPP exchange rates, which are open to criticism.

4. Recent research has made use of a periodization of fiscal policy into large-scale expansions and adjustments and standard policy episodes. Until the mid-1990s, France was one of the very few OECD countries that did not alternate between such episodes (see Cour et al. 1996).

5. The decomposition of deficit changes into discretionary and cyclical components has to be taken with caution, since the calculation of structural deficits remains open to debate.

6. As documented by Stanley Hoffmann (1963) and Richard Kuisel (1984), a key motive was the search for international prestige and power.

7. In 1996, numerous references to this experience were made in economic policy debates.

8. This is documented in several studies of French post–World War II history. See, for example, Kuisel 1984 and Zysman 1983. A firsthand account of this period is also given in Bloch-Lainé and Bouvier 1986.

9. It is significant that in 1945 the French government had to make a choice between monetary reform intended to eliminate the monetary overhang (as advocated by the socialist Pierre Mendès-France) and acceptance of a price surge in response to the lifting of rationing (as advocated by the centrist René Pleven). The latter thesis prevailed, and Mendès resigned from the government.

10. Raymond Barre, interview with François Furet, *Le débat*, September 1983, 21.

11. There was almost no French ex-ante evaluation of the effects of EMU, and the debate among economists did not really begin until the referendum on the Maastricht Treaty.

12. Preferences may change over time because agents and policymakers learn from experience or under the influence of exogenous factors (e.g., changes in the size and structure of public debt or in the distribution of wealth and the asset composition of private portfolios).

13. One might be surprised that external balance is mentioned as a "real objectives." Yet external balance played a disproportionate role in the French policy debates of the 1970s and 1980s. As France began to experience moderate current account deficits, policymakers made major (and successful) efforts to convince the public that these deficits had to be eliminated. The external balance was thus taken as a benchmark for the observance of the open economy's constraints. Richard Cooper (1983) has argued convincingly that the stringency of this constraint may have been overestimated.

14. In the early 1980s, the importance of planning had already diminished very significantly. Nevertheless, medium-term plans still represented official policy targets as well as collective preferences.

15. Note that in the 1980s economic policy evaluations relied heavily on policy simulations of macroeconomic models. As all French models were run under fixed exchange rates, disinflation automatically yielded benefits in the form of improved competitiveness.

16. As is illustrated in table 3.1, the objective was initially formulated in a "soft" manner: until the late 1980s. There was a debate between those who argued that France should aim at an inflation rate close to the OECD or EC average performance and those who favored the more ambitious objective of converging to the German level.

17. See Jean-Baptiste de Foucauld, "Une occasion à saisir: l'inflation zéro," *Le Monde,* April 8, 1986.

18. This logic was perceived by Herbert Giersch, who as early as 1979 envisaged that "a disguised form of support for real growth in West Germany [might] arise from the EMS . . . if German labor unions accept a major responsibility for price level stability . . . and exchange rate adjustments within the EMS are delayed so that unit labor costs in Germany are artificially reduced most of the time, making locations in Germany again more attractive . . . " (Giersch 1979).

19. As explained, the external constraint played a major role in the formulation of economic policy in the 1970s and the 1980s. It is hardly relevant in 1997, as France now exhibits a current account surplus, but it was important when the EMU project was launched.

20. For example, P. Duquesne (1994), then a high-level Treasury official, considered that: "The European Central Bank's independence is not primarily the result of an efficiency constraint (some 'dependent' central banks, such as that of Japan, are at least as efficient as the independent central banks). Its independence results from an institutional choice. In general, the independent central banks have been put together by 'federal' or 'confederal' types of States. . . . This is naturally the construction chosen for the European framework" (70).

21. Décision du Conseil Constitutionnel, August 3, 1993.

22. For a discussion of linkage politics, see Eichengreen and Frieden 1994.

23. For example, in May 1989, 60 percent of French voters were in favor of replacing the franc with a European currency, while 33 percent were opposed. (Société Française d'Etudes et de Sondages [SOFRES] poll, cited in SOFRES 1990).

24. EC Commission, *Eurobarometer,* July 1994.

25. BVA Exit polls.

26. Table 3.2 also provides striking evidence of the status-quo bias effect, since the single most important factor accounting for voters' choices appears to be their opinion of their own future. To the extent that views on the working of democracy represent opinions on the ability of a democratic regime to ensure equity, they could be interpreted in the same way.

27. Not all the nonmainstream parties were opposed to European integration.

28. This concern was expressed bluntly by Emmanuel Todd (the author of the "two Frances" paradigm) after the June 1995 local elections in which the extreme right made further progress. According to him, "there is an easy recipe for stopping the growth of the National Front [the far Right]: declare that European construction is over" (interview, *Liberation,* June 21, 1995).

29. According to the EC Commission (1994), French firms were bidders in 27.6 percent of intra-EC cross-border acquisitions in 1990–92, a share significantly above France's share of EC GDP.

30. The statement is by Jean Gandois on the occasion of the presentation of his institution's view on the single currency, March 20, 1996 (*Les Echos,* March 21).

31. It is not clear why French industrialists seem to be much more sensitive to exchange rate fluctuations than German ones. Detailed analysis of foreign trade structures (Freudenberg and Müller 1994) suggest that German enterprises more frequently specialize in "niches" and more generally that vertical differentiation is more prevalent in German foreign trade than in French trade, but econometric estimates do not confirm a higher price elasticity of French foreign trade in comparison with Germany.

32. In table 3.4, borrowing by French firms includes bonds, which account for some 15 percent of total borrowing (Grunspan 1995). It should be kept in mind that only a few companies issue bonds and most of them belong to the state sector.

33. In addition, the cost of credit depends on firm size. A task force of the Conseil National du Crédit conducted an empirical investigation in the course of 1988 concerning possible discrimination between large and small firms as regards lending rates. The conclusions were straightforward: during the period 1977–87, there was a systematic spread, the magnitude of which depended on the type of credit. It was around 150 basis points for discounting facilities, 200 to 250 for overdrafts, and so on.

34. See the report of the working groups set up by the central bank and the banking community, *Passage à la monnaie unique,* July 1996.

REFERENCES

AMUE. 1990. *A Strategy for the Ecu.* London: Kagen Page.
Barro, R. 1995. "Inflation and Economic Growth." *Bank of England Quarterly Bulletin,* 35, no. 2 (May 1995): 166–76.
Bauer, M., and B. Bertin-Mourot. 1995. *L'accès au sommet des entreprises françaises.* Paris: Cabinet Boyden.
Bénassy, A., A. Italianer, and J. Pisani-Ferry. 1994. "The External Implications of the Single Currency." *Economie et Statistique,* special issue, pp. 9–22. Paris: INSEE.
Blanchard, O., and P. A. Muet. 1993. "Competitiveness through Disinflation: An Assessment of the French Macroeconomic Strategy." *Economic Policy* 16 (April): 11–56.
Boissieu, C. de, ed. 1990. *Banking in France.* London and New York: Routledge.
Borio, C. 1995. "The Structure of Credit to the Non-Government Sector and the Transmission Mechanism of Monetary Policy: A Cross-Country Comparison." In *Financial Structure and the Monetary Transmission Mechanism.* Basel: Bank for International Settlements.
Boutillier, M., and J. Cordier. 1994. "L'adaptation de l'intermédiation financière française aux nouvelles modalités de gestion du change." *Cahiers Economiques et Monétaires de la Banque de France,* no. 43, 247–76. Paris.
Conseil National du Crédit. *Annual Reports.* Paris.
———. 1988. *Le coût du crédit aux entreprises selon leur taille.* Paris.

Cooper, R. 1983. "External Constraints on European Growth." In *Barriers to European Growth,* edited by R. Lawrence and C. Schultze. Washington, D.C.: Brookings Institution.

Cour, P., E. Dubois, S. Mahfouz, and J. Pisani-Ferry. 1996. "The Cost of Fiscal Retrenchment Revisited: How Strong Is the Evidence?" CEPII Working Paper no. 96-16, Paris.

Coutu, D., K. Hladik, D. Meen, and D. Turcq. 1993. "Views of the Business Community on Post-1992 Integration in Europe." In *The European Challenges Post-1992,* edited by A. Jacquemin and D. Wright. Edward Elgar.

Duquesne, P. 1994. "EMU: Institutional Aspects and Main Stages." In *Economie et Statistique,* special issue. Paris: Insee.

Dutailly, J. C. 1984. "Aides aux Entreprises." *Economie et Statistique* (September).

Eichengreen, B., and J. Frieden. 1994. "The Political Economy of European Monetary Unification: An Analytical Introduction." In *The Political Economy of European Monetary Unification,* edited by B. Eichengreen and J. Frieden. Boulder: Westview Press.

European Commission. 1994. "Competition and Integration." *European Economy,* no. 57 (special issue).

Fernandez, R., and D. Rodrik. 1991. "Resistance to Reform: Status Quo Bias in the Presence of Individual-Specific Uncertainty." *American Economic Review* (December): 1146–55.

Fitoussi, J.-P. 1995. *Le débat interdit.* Paris: Arléa.

Fonteneau, A., and P.-A. Muet. 1985. *La gauche face à la crise.* Paris: Presses de la FNSP.

Freudenberg, M., and D. Ünal-Kesenci. 1994. "France-Allemagne: prix et productivité dans le secteur manufacturier." *Economie internationale,* no. 60: 33–70.

Frieden, J. 1994. "Exchange Rate Politics: Contemporary Lessons from American History." *Review of International Political Economy* (Spring): 81–103.

Giavazzi, F., and A. Giovannini. 1989. *Limiting Exchange Rate Flexibility: The European Monetary System.* Cambridge: MIT Press.

Giavazzi, F., and M. Pagano. 1988. "The Advantage of Tying One's Hands." *European Economic Review* (June): 1055–75.

Giersch, Herbert. 1979. "Aspects of Growth, Structural Change, and Employment: A Schumpeterian Perspective." *Weltwirtschaftliches Archiv* 115:629–52.

Giovannini, A. 1995. "A Note on the Politics of EMU in Italy." Mimeo.

Goldman Sachs. 1996. "The Taylor Rule for the G7." *The International Economic Analyst* (June): vii–xviii.

De Grauwe, P. 1989. "The Cost of Disinflation and the EMS." CEPR Discussion Papers, no. 326, London.

Grunspan, T. 1995. "Le rôle respectif des taux à court terme et des taux à long terme dans le financement de l'économie." *Bulletin de la Banque de France,* no. 20: 113–22.

Henning, C. R. 1994. *Currencies and Politics in the United States, Germany, and Japan.* Washington, D.C.: Institute for International Economics.

Hoffmann S. 1963. *In Search for France.* Cambridge: Cambridge University Press.

Holcblat, N., and J. L. Tavernier. 1989. "Entre 1979 et 1986: la France a perdu des parts de marché industriel." *Economie et Statistique* (January–February): 37–50.

Jeanneney, J.-M. 1994. "De Bretton Woods à la Jamaïque: contestations françaises." *Economie internationale,* no. 59 (July): 55–70.

Kuisel, R. F. 1984. *Le capitalisme et l'Etat en France.* Paris: Gallimard.

Landau, J.-P. 1994. "Système monétaire international et libre-échange." In *Bretton Woods: Mélanges pour un cinquantenaire,* edited by T. Walrafen. Paris: Association d'Économie Financière.

Maas, C. 1995. "The Preparation of the Changeover to the Single European Currency." Interim Report to the European Commission, January. Mimeo.

Masson, P. 1995. "Gaining and Losing ERM Credibility: The Case of the United Kingdom." In *European Currency Crises and After,* edited by C. Bordes, E. Girardin, and J. Melitz. Manchester: Manchester University Press.

Ozkan, G., and A. Sutherland. 1995. "A Currency Crisis Model with an Optimizing Policy Maker." In *European Currency Crises and After,* edited by C. Bordes, E. Girardin, and J. Melitz. Manchester: Manchester University Press.

Pébereau, M. 1985–90. *La politique économique de la France.* Vol. 1, *Les instruments.* Vol. 2, *Les objectifs.* Vol. 3, *Les relations economiques financières et monétaires internationales.* Paris: Armand Colin.

Pisani-Ferry, J. 1994. "Union monétaire et convergence: qu'avons-nous appris?" *Document de travail CEPII,* no. 94-14 (December).

Séguin, P. 1992. *Discours pour la France.* Paris: Grasset.

Sicsic, P., and C. Wyplosz. 1994. "French Post-War Growth: From (Indicative) Planning to (Administered) Market." CEPR Discussion Papers no. 1023 (September), London.

SOFRES. 1990. *L'Etat de l'opinion, 1990.* Paris: Seuil.

———. 1993. *L'Etat de l'opinion, 1992.* Paris: Seuil.

Todd, E. 1994. "Aux origines du malaise politique français." *Notes de la fondation Saint-Simon* (November), Paris.

Trichet, J.-C. 1992. "Dix ans de désinflation compétitive en France." *Les notes bleues de Bercy,* October 16, Paris.

CHAPTER 4

Macroeconomic Stabilization with a Common Currency: Does European Monetary Unification Create a Need for Fiscal Insurance or Federalism?

Kenneth M. Kletzer

I. Introduction

The prospects for European monetary integration have focused the attention of policymakers and economists on the implications of monetary unification for the role of fiscal policy. The loss of independent monetary policies for member states and the proposed creation of a European Central Bank should increase the importance of autonomous national, or regional, fiscal policies for aggregate demand management in the face of national, or regional, macroeconomic shocks. They have also raised the perceived need for fiscal policy coordination in the European Union and for restrictions on the fiscal actions of member countries. This chapter addresses the fiscal consequences of monetary unification in Europe and critically discusses the literature concerning the implications of a common currency for macroeconomic stabilization in the European Union.

Much of the policy debate over the adoption of a common currency concentrates on the ability of national fiscal policy instruments to replace autonomous monetary policies and flexible exchange rates. A primary question in this debate is whether a system of fiscal federalism that implements temporary fiscal transfers across members or regions, similar to that practiced by the

United States and Canada, is necessary to assure stabilization against idiosyncratic regional aggregate supply and demand shocks.

One of the primary objectives of this chapter is to reexamine the argument, originating with Ingram (1959), that a system of fiscal transfers between states can partially replace nominal exchange rate flexibility under monetary union. I argue, on the basis of a macroeconomic model incorporating savings and investment behavior by rational households and firms, that fiscal transfers between the member states of a monetary union do little or nothing to increase the set of fiscal instruments available to separate national authorities for replacing the role of autonomous monetary policies. This statement holds as long as the set of fiscal and financial tools available to national authorities is not restricted and money is neutral in the long run. In particular, if national fiscal authorities retain the capacity to run budget deficits and issue public debt, then adding temporary fiscal transfers does not necessarily add to the capacity of the fiscal policies at hand for short-run stabilization. It does not say that a system of international fiscal insurance is not beneficial; such a system can and will increase the capacity of governments to smooth national purchasing power and stabilize real output, employment, and investment in the face of asymmetric national disturbances to real supplies and demands. This result has two implications. One is that restrictions on public sector debts and deficits imposed with monetary union may create their own need for fiscal federalism. The other is that there are efficiency-based arguments for international fiscal insurance schemes, so that these may be observed in national monetary unions, such as the United States, because political union allows the nation to take advantage of them.

A second objective is to address the issue of whether political union is necessary to sustain a system of fiscal insurance between member states. I argue that if policy makers act on long horizons then some degree of international fiscal insurance for stabilizing real incomes across idiosyncratic temporary supply and demand shocks is sustainable for sovereign states. There are further gains from a more extensive fiscal transfer scheme that requires external enforcement to be viable. Political unification would allow these additional gains from fiscal insurance to be realized. Together these arguments about the role of fiscal federalism and its sustainability without external state power suggest that monetary integration does not necessitate political unification. The arguments here complement those given by Eichengreen (1996) to make the same point.

This essay discusses the role of fiscal policy in a monetary union. The discussion of the consequences of a common currency and a single central bank is separated between issues that arise when all prices and wages are perfectly flexible and the problem of macroeconomic stabilization in the presence of nominal price or wage rigidities. The next section reviews the effect of monetary union on the budgetary instruments and policies of national fiscal authorities without price or wage stickiness. The review is brief, but it provides definitions used later and discusses issues related to the argument that political union need not be necessary for monetary union.

The third section turns to macroeconomic stabilization in the presence of wage and price rigidities. It critically reviews the empirical findings and theoretical arguments used by others to suggest that fiscal federalism may be needed to realize gains from monetary integration. Section 4 discusses how fiscal insurance schemes augment the set of instruments available to national authorities for stabilization in the presence of asymmetric national disturbances. The possibility of international fiscal insurance schemes without political unification and the gains from political union are taken up in section 5. The last section concludes.

2. Fiscal Implications of Monetary Union without Nominal Rigidities

This section touches on two topics concerning how monetary unification, independent of the integration of markets, affects the fiscal policy choices of national governments. Monetary union has budgetary implications for member states by eliminating national control over the monetization of public sector budget deficits. The reduction of the set of fiscal instruments available to member states by the adoption of a common currency is reviewed first. Monetary unification also can change the incentives for fiscal discipline by national authorities because the social costs of monetization by a single central bank are spread across all other members of the union. Fears that the proposed European Central Bank will not be able to resist pressure for monetary expansion in the face of a fiscal crisis for an enterprise as large as a member state have given birth to restrictions on public sector debt and deficits in the Treaty of Maastricht and a subsequent German proposal. A number of critiques of these restrictions are already available,[1] so the discussion is brief and focuses on the underlying issue of whether monetary unification for Europe really changes the problem of fiscal discipline.

2.1.   Budgetary Consequences of a Common Currency

The right to issue an intrinsically valueless money useful as a medium of exchange allows a government to appropriate real resources from the private economy. By maintaining a national currency, a national government can use seignorage revenues and inflation taxes to help finance public expenditures. Exchange rate flexibility allows individual national governments to use these instruments independently of each other. Monetary union eliminates the ability of governments to pursue independent monetary policies, restricting the use of these fiscal policy instruments by national governments. Under a permanently fixed exchange rate, the equilibrium rate of inflation of the prices of traded goods is the same across borders and equilibrium rates of inflation in nontraded goods' prices differ to the extent that national productivity growth rate differentials between traded goods and nontraded goods diverge. With the adoption of a common currency, seignorage revenues must accrue to the single central bank to be allocated across members or, equivalently, to be divided between the member banks of a system of central banks according to a prescribed scheme.

Seignorage and the inflation tax are related but readily confused concepts. Seignorage is defined as the resources raised by the government through an expansion of the monetary base. Seignorage as a fraction of nominal GDP, $P_t Y_t$, in period t is given by

$$\sigma_t \equiv \frac{\Delta H_{t+1}}{P_t Y_t}, \tag{1}$$

where H_t is the nominal quantity of base money at the beginning of period t and $\Delta H_{t+1} \equiv H_{t+1} - H_t$. The inflation tax is defined as the reduction in the real value of the monetary base due to increases in the price level. Inflation tax revenues are the proportionate rate of increase in the price level times the real monetary base. As a fraction of GDP, the inflation tax rate is given by

$$\tau_t \equiv \frac{1}{Y_t}\left[\frac{\Delta P_{t+1}}{P_t}\right]\left[\frac{H_{t+1}}{P_{t+1}}\right] = \pi_{t+1}\frac{Y_{t+1}}{Y_t}h_{t+1}, \tag{2}$$

where $\Delta P_{t+1} \equiv P_{t+1} - P_t$, $\pi_{t+1} \equiv \Delta P_{t+1}/P_t$ is the inflation rate and $h_{t+1} \equiv H_{t+1}/[Y_{t+1}P_{t+1}]$ is the base money to GDP ratio.

A little algebra shows that the inflation tax and seignorage are related by the identity

$$\sigma_t = \tau_t + g_{t+1}h_{t+1} + (h_{t+1} - h_t),\tag{3}$$

where g_{t+1} is the growth rate of real GDP. This says that seignorage exceeds the inflation tax by the amount that real demand for money increases due to economic growth (the term g_{t+1}, h_{t+1}) and to changes in the demand for base money (the term $h_{t+1} - h_t$).[2] In a growing economy, the government collects seignorage revenues by issuing additional base money to meet the increasing real demand for liquidity.

The inflation tax defined in equation (2) is more accurately described as the *anticipated* inflation tax. *Unanticipated* inflation reduces the real value of outstanding nominally indexed fixed rate public debt. The longer the maturity of a given quantity of debt, the larger is this effect for a given increase in current and future inflation. The rate of interest on new public debt issues will take account of expected inflation and may include a risk premium reflecting possible unanticipated inflation. Countries with histories of low inflation tend to be most able to use unanticipated inflation tax levies to reduce the real burden of their national debts. A reputation for low inflation allows a government to issue longer maturity fixed interest rate debt on more favorable interest terms to a larger number of creditors. Unanticipated inflation tax levies on the national debt have been the primary means used by the governments of the United States and the United Kingdom to appropriate real resources through inflation. An unanticipated increase in the price level, in contrast to an increase in the rate of change of the price level, will reduce the real value of both fixed and variable rate debt denominated in national currency. This can be achieved by an unanticipated discrete devaluation.

Monetary unification implies that national governments lose the capacity to impose differential anticipated and unanticipated inflation taxes. The inflation tax is a distortionary tax whenever money demand responds to the expected rate of inflation. Public finance theory implies that an optimal fiscal policy would include seignorage collection and inflation taxation when no nondistortionary tax instruments are available (a realistic presumption). It seems natural to think that national governments seeking to maximize social welfare would choose different inflation rates as their tax bases and costs of tax collection and administration vary, so that welfare gains are possible by maintaining national currencies and exchange rate flexibility. Mankiw (1987) demonstrates this in an ad hoc economic model, and Buiter (1995) shows that identical inflation tax rates should be chosen by different countries in a simple model based on optimizing behavior, so that the theoretical case for divergent optimal inflation taxes is not strong.

At a practical level, seignorage and the inflation tax have been of little importance for members of the European Union in recent years, with the exceptions of Spain, Italy, Greece, and Portugal. Excluding these countries, the highest average inflation tax rate for the other 11 members during 1990–94 was 0.34 percent, shared by Germany and Sweden. The highest inflation tax and seignorage rates over the period for all 15 were 2.90 percent and 2.93 percent, respectively, both achieved by Portugal in 1990–92.[3] The imposition of a common low rate of inflation is unlikely to increase the excess burden of taxation in any significant way for the European Union. However, the distribution of seignorage revenue from a common central bank or system of banks undoubtedly will differ from the status quo ante. This will affect the use of seignorage as a contingent source of revenue.

Monetary unification may increase the importance of seignorage as a source of public revenue for the European Union as a whole. It is likely that a single European currency will compete with the U.S. dollar as an international vehicle and reserve currency, so that total demand for base money issued by the European Union membership will increase. If it does, then the capacity for earning seignorage revenues and for transferring real resources from other nations will increase. Because estimates indicate that a majority of the currency of the United States circulates outside the country, this increase could represent a significant amount of resources. A single currency could generate greater opportunities for using the inflation tax depending on the anti-inflationary credibility of the European Central Bank.

2.2. Budget Deficits and Fiscal Discipline under a Common Currency

The problem that has dominated the debate over monetary unification in Europe since the signing of the Treaty of Maastricht is that a common currency may lead to an erosion of fiscal discipline by national governments. One argument is that with a common monetary policy individual member states have a greater incentive to accumulate public debt if they expect future monetization. The entire community shares the social costs of monetizing national deficits more with a single currency than with autonomous monetary policies and flexible nominal exchange rates. The treaty addresses this problem by forbidding the European Central Bank to finance public sector budget deficits and also forbidding bailouts of member governments by the European Union. It goes further, specifying the excessive deficit procedure requiring member states to keep deficits and debt below 3 percent and 60 percent of GDP, respectively, and setting forth a process for sanctioning states exceeding the reference value. Many authors have noted that the additional procedure seems excessive or redundant.[4] The recent proposal of the Ministry of Finance of Germany goes further, setting a standard for deficits at 1 percent of GDP under unexceptional circumstances and requiring deposits equal to 0.25 percent of GDP for countries violating the 3 percent limit.

The fear that national fiscal authorities left to manage deficits by themselves might imperil the stability of the common currency must follow from the presumption that the European Central Bank will be unable to resist bailing out governments in financial distress. If the central bank is expected to monetize large levels of debt, then fiscal authorities have an incentive to incur excessive deficits. This problem of the time inconsistency of a central bank's pledge to not monetize the treasury's deficits arises as well for single countries with national currencies. The natural and common answer is to establish an independent central bank, as envisioned in the treaty, although a de jure independent central bank does not necessarily translate into a de facto independent central bank.[5] At issue is whether these problems are different for a monetary union than for nations with individual currencies.

Buiter and Kletzer (1991a) and Eichengreen and von Hagen (1995) argue that there is no reason that the public debts of individual member states should not remain the responsibility of those states under monetary union as long as national governments do not give up tax instruments to a supranational authority. Eichengreen and von Hagen show that the likelihood of a federal bailout of a lower fiscal jurisdiction in fiscal federations depends on the proportion of total tax revenue collected at the federal level. They also show that the adoption of restrictions on state and local government indebtedness by the states of the United States[6] was unrelated to monetary unification in the United States and find that restrictions on debt issuance by subnational (state, provincial, or local) levels of government are unrelated to federal structure in a large cross section of countries. Eichengreen and von Hagen do find that fiscal restraints on lower jurisdictions are negatively correlated with the share of subcentral government expenditures financed by tax revenues generated at the same level of government. They draw the conclusion that if, as anticipated, the majority of tax revenues continue to be collected by national governments, the member states will have the fiscal capacity to service their own public debts so that the commitment by the European Central Bank to the no-bailout provision can be credible without fiscal restraints imposed by a higher level of government.

Because monetary union eliminates control by national authorities of seignorage and unanticipated inflation levies on holders of nominally indexed debt, the set of fiscal instruments available to national governments facing a potential fiscal crisis is reduced. If the fiscal and monetary bailout provisions are credible, then the only recourse for a government that is insolvent given its share of unionwide seignorage revenues is default. As the probability of sovereign default rises, the risk premium demanded by debt holders (and incorporated into the real interest rate) should increase. In the extreme, the public sector solvency constraint binds and no more public debt can be issued at any rate of interest. If financial markets are complete and not subject to preexisting distortions, the equilibrium risk premium reflects the full costs of default risk, so that these would be borne entirely by bond issuers and bondholders. The social costs of possible default are internalized fully by willing bondholders and by the households and firms subject to taxation by the concerned state and enjoying the benefits of its public spending. In that case, a bailout by other member states can only serve to redistribute income and wealth between the residents of member states and toward the debtor's creditors. An efficiency-based argument for an ex post bailout requires that insolvency by one member has external effects.

The assumption that financial markets are complete is unrealistic. It rules out contagion effects in financial markets that can arise if they are incomplete. One example of contagion is that sovereign default by one member government negatively affects the borrowing opportunities of others. Another important possibility is that public sector default leads to a monetary contraction through the workings of the banking system, initiating a liquidity and financial crisis. Financial market imperfections allow insolvency for one member government to create financial distress with consequences for real economic activity throughout the community. More generally, the presence of other preexisting distortions, such as distortionary policy instruments and effective demand failures of a Keynesian variety, implies that the market interest terms and risk premiums on national government debt will not reflect the full social costs of public sector borrowing.[7]

In the case of the European Union, however, the benefits of a bailout may be unaffected by monetary unification. With the very high degree of financial capital mobility already achieved in Europe, it is difficult to see why monetary union would increase the costs or likelihood of a financial crisis spreading across member states. If national treasuries are able to generate the same primary surpluses after monetary union as before, then they can make the same real repayments to holders of public debt. Since inflation tax revenues are relatively unimportant in the budgets of European Union members and the primary responsibility for other taxes is expected to remain with national authorities, member states should not have a greater incentive to bail out one another with monetary unification than without.

3. Nominal Rigidities and the Consequences of Monetary Union

A major concern in the analysis of monetary unification in Europe is that the loss of nominal exchange rate flexibility reduces the capacity of fiscal and monetary authorities to promote macroeconomic adjustment to supply and demand disturbances that are asymmetric across nations or regions. The theory of optimum currency areas is taken as the starting point by most of the literature on the stabilization problem.[8] According to the definition of Mundell (1961), an optimum currency area exists if permanently fixing the exchange rate has no consequences for economic performance.[9] This will be the case if all relative prices are flexible or if factors are perfectly mobile across countries even though prices and wages adjust sluggishly. If all relative prices are flexible, then the choice of exchange rate regime has no effect on economic performance, so that the only real effects of a common currency are the efficiency gains from the adoption of a common medium of exchange and means of payment. Under perfect international factor mobility, exchange rate flexibility is superfluous for the allocation of resources; labor and capital move freely in response to asymmetric supply and demand shocks to maintain productive efficiency. With nominal rigidities and imperfect labor mobility, monetary authorities can pursue independent monetary policies if exchange rates are flexible so as to reduce the costs of adjustment to idiosyncratic real shocks. With a system of irrevocably fixed exchange rates, the common monetary policy and national fiscal policies need to bear the burden of adjustment that was previously borne by the combination of independent national monetary and fiscal policies.

It is conceivable that monetary policies have both short-run and long-run effects on the economy. The exchange rate regime can only matter in the long run in the event of long-run monetary nonneutrality. For example, if the natural rate of unemployment depends on past actual unemployment, then temporary shocks to employment can have permanent effects on real output and incomes, so that the short-run nonneutrality of money leads to long-run nonneutrality. But significant evidence of hysteresis in natural rates of unemployment for members of the European Union is lacking, so long-run monetary neutrality would seem to be a reasonable hypothesis to maintain for the analysis of monetary unification.[10]

When money is nonneutral in the short run, exchange rate flexibility allows national monetary policies to influence economic performance temporarily. Transitory adjustment to real or nominal shocks is possible through monetary management, while permanent adjustment can be achieved only through changes in relative prices or production and consumption. By joining a monetary union, a country loses its ability to use monetary policy to respond to internal and external shocks that are transitory in nature or to adjust temporarily to permanent shocks. Nominal exchange rate flexibility adds to the temporary capacity of a national government to influence its real exchange rate, output growth, employment, and other important measures of economic performance in response to supply or demand shocks. Permanently fixing nominal exchange rates in the presence of sluggish price adjustment with money neutral in the long run, therefore, does not reduce the capacity of the government to adjust to permanent shocks but can affect the short-run costs of adjustment.

Nominal rigidities also allow nominal disturbances to affect economic performance, even when such shocks are unrelated to economic fundamentals. Indeed, a primary motivation for European monetary unification is that exchange rate volatility may reflect financial market noise and speculative capital flows to such an extent that exchange rate flexibility contributes more to the creation than to the mitigation of shocks. Fluctuations of asset prices on financial markets can be caused by intrinsic noise due to the trading activity of agents who are less informed than others about the fundamental determinants of asset values and who use the prices themselves to infer these values. Financial markets can also be subject to extrinsic, or sunspot, noise which arises when traders believe that information unrelated to fundamentals affects asset prices. Since nominal exchange rate volatility translates into real exchange rate volatility with price and wage stickiness, the possibility that intrinsic or extrinsic noise induces exchange rate fluctuations implies that a fixed exchange rate could promote welfare.[11]

The accumulating evidence that much of exchange rate volatility and speculative trading on exchange markets is unrelated to fundamentals adds to the usefulness of monetary unification for minimizing the international transmission of shocks to national money demands and supplies with integrated international financial markets. However, the costs of foregoing nominal exchange adjustment as a tool for temporary stabilization in the face of asymmetric national or regional real shocks must be weighed against the benefits of reducing financial and other nominal shocks.

3.1. Empirical Analysis of Adjustment to Shocks

Building on the theory of optimum currency areas, the recent literature on monetary unification emphasizes the relative importance of asymmetric and symmetric supply and demand shocks as a critical determinant of the net benefits of a common currency. A common approach used in the literature is to compare the incidence of macroeconomic shocks and adjustment to them between the European Union and the United States. These comparisons are popular since a revealed preference type of argument suggests that the benefits of monetary union outweigh the costs for the United States. There are essentially three components to comparisons of the consequences of monetary unification for the United States to those expected for Europe. The first consists of pointing out that labor is less mobile in Europe than in the United States, even within countries. The second compares the process of adjustment to aggregate supply and demand shocks in the European Union to that in the United States. The third involves estimating and comparing the relative importance of symmetric and asymmetric, and temporary and permanent, regional shocks.

The natural presumption is that labor is much less mobile in Europe than within either the United States or Canada for reasons of national identity, culture, and language. But the relative immobility of labor also holds within national borders. For example, 3.3 percent of the U.S. population moved between states in 1980, while 1.3 percent of the German population moved between *Länder* the same year.[12] But the difference between rates of interregional migration for the United States and the European Union may not have any significant relevance for monetary union. To play the role of nominal exchange rate movements in the adjustment process, labor migration would have to respond to temporary shocks and be transitory. That is, monetary policies are important for short-run adjustment, so that if migration is a replacement for them labor must move across regions in response to temporary regional employment shocks. Because independent monetary policies also allow governments to ease the adjustment to permanent asymmetric regional shocks, labor movements that respond to permanent real shocks could partially offset the loss of exchange rate flexibility with monetary union as long as the response lag is similar to the time frame for nominal exchange rate adjustments.[13]

Blanchard and Katz (1992) and Eberts and Stone (1992) study the adjustment of labor markets in the United States. Blanchard and Katz examine labor market adjustment at the state level, while Eberts and Stone study major metropolitan labor markets. Both studies find that relative unemployment rates adjust more rapidly than relative wages across regions of the United States. The adjustment process takes up to a decade or more in the data used by Eberts and Stone but between five and 10 years in Blanchard and Katz's analysis of state-level data. Both articles argue that unemployment rates eventually converge more through migration than other means. Eberts and Stone find that migration plays a smaller role in local labor market adjustment than does labor force participation and provide evidence that interregional migration responds slowly to local labor demand shocks. The empirical literature on regional labor market adjustment in the United States that investigates the role played by migration does not provide much support for the hypothesis that labor mobility makes an important contribution to the advantages of a common currency for the United States.

Short-run adjustment to both temporary and permanent disturbances displays significant differences between the United States and the European Union. Bayoumi and Thomas (1995), among others, show that relative price movements play a primary role in short-run adjustment to temporary and permanent aggregate shocks in Europe, while in the United States prices and wages are unresponsive to asymmetric regional shocks. On the other hand, output and employment respond quickly to asymmetric shocks in the United States. Bayoumi and Thomas, in particular, demonstrate that aggregate demand shocks affect relative prices and wages far more and relative outputs much less in the European Union than in the United States. For aggregate supply shocks, the adjustment processes are qualitatively similar. As expected, fluctuations in relative prices are generally correlated with nominal exchange rate movements.

These results suggest that independent monetary policies and flexible exchange rates are important for easing the adjustment to asymmetric disturbances in the European Union. These estimates are obtained using a structural vector autoregression model that incorporates a priori restrictions to identify supply and demand shocks, but none of the restrictions can identify real and nominal demand shocks. The estimation of the supply and demand disturbances that is used to compare the responses of relative prices and outputs between the European Union and the United States relies on the assumption that relative price movements for Europe are due to real shocks.

This implies that if there are nominal shocks in the original data, similar shocks are not being compared between the United States and the European Union.

There are three reasons to suspect that nominal shocks may be included and be important for the estimation results, so that the conclusions are problematic. The first is that the differences reported by Bayoumi and Thomas (1995) appear in the responses to aggregate disturbances that are identified as demand shocks and so are likely to include nominal shocks to aggregate demand.[14] The second is that independent monetary policies are a potential source of nominal shocks, so that monetary autonomy itself may be responsible for some of the demand shocks for Europe. Indeed, a strong argument can be made that inadequate coordination of monetary policies has been responsible for many significant exchange rate movements in Europe in recent years, including the abandonment of the narrow band ERM following the speculative attacks that began in September 1992. The third is that a significant share of relative price fluctuations for the European Union is due to nominal exchange rate movements. If prices are rigid in terms of domestic currency, then exchange rate fluctuations affect employment and output to the extent that export sales are a fraction of national output and firms do not hedge against the relative price risk caused by exchange risk in the forward market. The price fluctuations used to estimate supply and demand shocks may have significant components due to nominal shocks in the case of Europe that cannot be in the data for interregional variation for the United States, so that what is estimated is not an adjustment process but, rather, the relationship between nominal exchange rate fluctuations and real economic variables.

The third step in comparisons between the United States as a currency area and the European Union as a prospective one is the estimation of the relative magnitude of idiosyncratic regional shocks. Bayoumi and Eichengreen (1993) decompose shocks to output growth and inflation rates for individual member states of the European Union and for eight regions of the United States into asymmetric and symmetric components. They also break down these shocks into permanent and temporary parts.[15] The average correlation coefficients for permanent output growth shocks are found to be 0.33 for the European Union relative to Germany and 0.46 for the United States relative to the middle Atlantic region. The average correlation coefficients of temporary disturbances are found to be 0.18 and 0.37 for the European Union and the United States, respectively. These results suggest that asymmetric shocks are relatively more important for the European Union than the United States.[16] Bayoumi and

Eichengreen also find that the standard deviation of permanent shocks (as a fraction of output) averages 2.1 percent for the European Union compared with 1.5 percent for the United States, while the standard deviation of temporary shocks averages 1.7 percent for the European Union and 2.1 percent for regions of the United States. These authors suggest that the larger relative magnitude of temporary shocks for the United States is due to the greater regional specialization in production brought about by the absence of real exchange rate fluctuations under monetary union. If this is the case, then the magnitude of temporary shocks might be expected to increase in Europe after monetary unification.

The estimates of Bayoumi and Eichengreen (1993) are obtained using a structural vector autoregression model that cannot distinguish nominal from real disturbances to outputs and relative price levels.[17] This implies that it is difficult to use these estimates to reach conclusions about the effects of monetary unification. Since nominal shocks cause transitory fluctuations in real variables that are unrelated to changes in economic fundamentals, the magnitude of asymmetric shocks and the volatility of employment, output, and other real measures of economic performance could be reduced by the establishment of a permanently fixed exchange rate regime. It is possible that some of the idiosyncratic shocks measured by these studies are due to exchange rate flexibility itself through the impact of nominal shocks or extrinsic noise on financial markets, so that monetary unification could lead to a reduction in the size of transitory idiosyncratic shocks.

In sum, recent empirical investigations motivated by the prospect of monetary unification in Europe demonstate the importance of asymmetric regional shocks for both the European Union and the United States. The implications of similar shocks for the performance of a monetary union could differ if the economies display different capacities to adjust to real disturbances. Although the evidence indicates that real wages and labor supplies adjust more rapidly in the United States than within member states of the European Union, the response of the labor market in the United States may be too sluggish to serve as a significant replacement for nominal exchange rate adjustment. The argument that monetary unification should be more costly for the European Union than for the United States because relative prices are more important for stabilizing regional economies in the face of asymmetric disturbances in Europe is vulnerable to the critique that the shocks identified by the econometric procedure for the European Union are not necessarily comparable with those identified for the United States. If nominal shocks are the predominant source of temporary demand disturbances, then this evidence would tend to favor monetary unification, while if real shocks dominate then the implication that monetary unification will be costly would tend to be supported.

4. Fiscal Insurance as an Alternative to Monetary Independence

The importance of asymmetric shocks to output growth and the limited degree of interregional labor mobility in the European Union imply that fiscal policies will need to bear more of the burden of adjustment to asymmetric shocks with a common currency. Ingram (1959) suggests that transfers between the federal government and states of the United States serve as a replacement for exchange rate flexibility under monetary union. His argument is that fiscal federalism at least partly replaces independent regional monetary policies in large political and monetary unions. In the U.S. case, automatic stabilizers acting through proportional income taxation and means-tested transfer payments, such as unemployment compensation, activate resource transfers in response to idiosyncratic regional supply and demand shocks. Further, federal taxation and federal government spending programs redistribute incomes across regions.

Sachs and Sala-i-Martin (1992) argue that fiscal transfers within the United States are important policy tools for stabilizing regional purchasing power. They find that net reductions in federal tax liabilities and increases in transfers from the federal government offset about 35 percent of a state's income loss during recession. Von Hagen (1990) criticizes their conclusion that the absence of a mechanism for effecting fiscal transfers within the European Union will have serious consequences for stabilization of regional incomes by noting that Sachs and Sala-i-Martin fail to distinguish permanent from transitory transfers. He argues that a large share of interstate transfers serve to compensate for divergent long-term income trends across states. The estimation procedure used by Bayoumi and Masson (1994) separates permanent components of interstate transfers in the United States from temporary components. They estimate that permanent income differentials are offset by approximately 20 percent through interstate redistribution and that about 28 percent of temporary asymmetric income fluctuations are offset by net interjurisdictional transfers.

The argument that the European Union will need to replace nominal exchange rate flexibility with a system of fiscal insurance has become a popular topic in the debate over monetary unification.[18] Because the entire budget of the European Union equals approximately 1 percent of GDP, a move to a system of fiscal insurance would appear to imply significant political changes. Surprisingly, neither the public debate nor the analytical literature has investigated the logic of Ingram's original argument that fiscal insurance plays the role in macroeconomic stabilization vacated by monetary autonomy. The purpose of this section is to discuss the benefits of international or interregional fiscal insurance in order to identify the possible roles of fiscal transfer schemes for macroeconomic stabilization. The approach is to focus on how the addition of fiscal transfer schemes to national fiscal policies contributes to the capacity of fiscal authorities to influence resource allocation.

In general, governments can realize mutual social welfare gains through international fiscal insurance when there is no role for monetary policy, that is, in a nonmonetary economy in which all prices and wages are perfectly flexible. This will be the case if markets for international insurance are incomplete and there are asymmetric national disturbances to incomes. Fiscal transfers between governments can facilitate desirable international risk sharing that markets are unable to provide directly. For example, idiosyncratic productivity shocks mean that young workers face lifetime income risk upon entering the labor market that is typically not insurable. Taxes, transfers, and public sector borrowing can provide for the sharing of risks over time and across households within the country, but cross-border insurance is needed to share asymmetric aggregate national income risks.

Two related reasons why a fiscal insurance scheme might be desirable for the European Union are raised by Eichengreen (1992a). These involve the idea that monetary union may reduce the range of fiscal policies available to national governments. One is that the fiscal convergence criteria may restrict the extent to which national governments can use deficit financing in economic stabilization programs. The second is the standard argument that economic integration tends to reduce the capacity of individual states to pursue divergent fiscal policies because increasing factor mobility causes the elasticity of the tax base with respect to tax rates to rise so that the ability of member governments to service public debt is restricted and deficit financing is hampered. Eichengreen points out that fiscal insurance may play the role of replacing the fiscal instruments that governments lose. However, neither of these arguments is directly related to the permanent fixing of the exchange rate. The first is associated with monetary unification only because of the Maastricht Treaty's prescription of fiscal restraints. The second concerns economic integration, and it is not clear that monetary union itself will further increase factor mobility in the already highly integrated post-1992 European economy.

The literature proposing that interregional fiscal transfers compensate for exchange rate flexibility is not particularly systematic about how such transfers contribute to the set of fiscal instruments governments have available for macroeconomic stabilization. It is useful to distinguish two comparisons. The first compares monetary union with and without a system of international fiscal transfers. In this case, the issue is whether fiscal transfers add to the capacity of national fiscal policies to replace monetary policy independence in macroeconomic stabilization. The other considers whether the permanent fixing of exchange rates reduces the set of fiscal instruments available to each government and thereby creates a need for international fiscal transfers to replace a lost fiscal instrument. It compares the role of fiscal policy with and without monetary unification.

The next two subsections discuss these two aspects of international fiscal transfer schemes in economies in which monetary policies have short-run effects on economic performance.

4.1. Fiscal Policies as Stabilizers under Monetary Union

Under monetary union, fiscal policy can be used to stimulate output and employment in a member state suffering an adverse real supply or demand disturbance by shifting purchasing power across households and raising demand for the output of that country. Fiscal transfers can perform this function by shifting permanent income from some member states to others. Understanding how fiscal transfer schemes add to the capacity of national fiscal policies to influence private resource allocation requires study of how fiscal policies affect the lifetime budget constraints of households and the returns to the activities of producers.

Consider the case in which each country has a single representative household that is infinitely lived. The home government receives a transfer at some date t from another government, relaxing the home country's intertemporal public sector budget constraint. The single-period budget identities for the home and foreign governments are

$$B_{t+1} = (1 + i_t)B_t + G_t - T_t + X_t \tag{4}$$

and

$$B_{t+1}^* = (1 + i_t^*)B_t^* + G_t^* - T_t^* - X_t, \tag{5}$$

respectively, where X_t is the fiscal transfer made at date t. Because there is a single currency, $i_t = i_t^*$ for nominally indexed debt unless there is differential public sector default risk. This transfer is equivalent to the assumption of a portion of the home country's public debt by the foreign country. It allows the home fiscal authority to increase the net transfer to (equivalently, reduce net taxes paid by) the home country household in present value terms and requires a reduction in transfers, a fall in public goods spending, or an increase in taxes in present value terms in the foreign country. If public spending on goods and services is held constant in each country, then consumption will rise in the home country and decline in the foreign country. It does not matter when each government actually changes its fiscal policies as long as the transfer is not simply a loan to be repaid on the same terms as other public debt. In the representative agent model, international fiscal transfers increase the ability of national authorities to influence relative prices and the regional pattern of employment and investment at time t.

A richer description of the private sector is provided by an overlapping generations model. In an overlapping generations economy, each consumer has a finite lifetime, new generations are born each year, and some members of each generation do not wish to make bequests to future generations. In this case, fiscal transfers between members of a monetary union do not increase the capacity of the national fiscal authorities to influence the distribution of purchasing power across countries. Transfers do add to the ability of fiscal authorities to influence the growth path of the economy, but they do not augment the set of fiscal tools for managing aggregate demands in the short run outside exceptional circumstances.

This is shown in stages. The first part of the argument is that a given fiscal transfer can be made later in equal present value terms without changing the equilibrium of the private economy. The second part explains when the fiscal transfer can be eliminated without changing the short-run equilibrium path of real and nominal variables. This implies that as long as money is neutral in the long run transfers do not enhance the usefulness of fiscal policies for replacing independent monetary policies. The caveats to this claim are spelled out at the end of this subsection.

I divide the lifetime of each consumer into two periods, young and old, as in the Diamond-Samuelson overlapping generations model. In the first period, the household makes its first-period consumption, saving, and labor supply decisions and determines its financial portfolio. Since there can be uncertainty about aggregate demands and supplies or policies in the second period, financial assets are risky. In the second period, the household receives the gross returns to its savings. For a household without a bequest motive, second-period savings is always zero. The first-period budget constraint for the typical household of the generation born at date t is given by

$$w_t l_t \geq P_t c_t + \tau_t + s_t + M_t, \tag{6}$$

where w_t is the (nominal) wage rate, l_t is labor supply, c_t is household consumption, τ_t represents taxes paid net of transfers received, s_t is nonmonetary savings, and M_t equals money holdings, all at date t. The budget constraint is given by

$$R_{t+1} s_t + w_{t+1} l_{t+1} + M_t \geq P_{t+1} c_{t+1} + \tau_{t+1}, \tag{7}$$

where $R_{t+1} s_t$ represents the second-period equilibrium gross (nominal) return to the portfolio held by the household. For example, savings may be held in the form of public debt issued either by government or as equity claims on the earnings of capital located in either country. In this case, the gross return to household savings (unearned income) in the second period is the sum of the gross interest on holdings of public debt and gross earnings on equities held by the household as given by

$$R_{t+1} s_t = [(1 + i_{t+1})b_t + (1 + i^*_{t+1})b^*_t]$$
$$+ [P_{t+1}(1 + \rho_{t+1})k_t + P^*_{t+1}(1 + \rho^*_{t+1})k^*_t]. \tag{8}$$

The household's demands for home (foreign) public debt and equities are denoted b_t and k_t (b^*_t and k^*_t), respectively. $P_{t+1}(1 + \rho_{t+1})$ is the gross value marginal product of home country capital (ρ_{t+1} is the net real rate of return to investment and is subject to real shocks) and similarly for foreign capital. Equilibrium in capital markets requires that total savings by the young in both countries equal the total outstanding stock of public debt plus the gross capital stock carried into the next period:

$$N_t s_t + N_t^* s_t^* = (B_t + B_t^*) + (P_t K_t + P_t^* K_t^*).$$ (9)

The total number of households of the young generation at time t for the home and foreign country are denoted by N_t and N_t^*, respectively. K_t and K_t^* denote (gross) physical investment at time t in the home and foreign country, respectively.

Household behavior depends on prices and wages prevailing at time t, those expected for time $t + 1$, and net taxes owed in each period. Consumption and labor supply at any age depend on the lifetime budget constraint for the household, which depends on the present value of lifetime resources, but an individual's savings decision also depends on how income net of taxes and transfers is distributed over the life cycle. The distribution of returns to various assets influences savings and the financial portfolio chosen by each household. Fiscal policies affect output, employment, and capital accumulation by changing the budget constraints for households, the returns to production and investment decisions by firms, and the stock of public debt.

Suppose that the fiscal transfer, X_t, is made from the foreign country to the home country at date t as part of a given pair of fiscal policies. These policies imply a particular path for the tax obligations and transfer entitlements of every household currently alive or yet to be born and determine the stock of public debt issued by each government that, in asset market equilibrium, must be held by all households. Now consider a different pair of fiscal policies. Under these alternative policies, the taxes and transfers made to any generation alive at date t or later are the same as under the original policy pair. Public spending on goods and services by each government and any taxes or subsidies imposed on firms are also held constant. The only difference is that the fiscal transfer is not made at date t, but an equal present value transfer is made T periods later, at date $t + T$.

Using the budget identities, this implies that the value of the public debt for the home country is larger by the amount X_t at date $t + 1$, and the debt of the foreign government is smaller by the same amount, under the substitute policies than under the original policies. By not changing any other aspects of either country's fiscal policy path, the home government is essentially borrowing X_t and paying off the additional accumulated debt at date $t + T$. The foreign country makes a loan of matching value. The home country repays this addition to its outstanding public debt with certainty. Therefore, the transfer made at date $t + T$ by the foreign country to the home country under the substitute policies equals X_t plus the accumulated interest at the implicit risk-free rate.

If the substitute policies are to support exactly the same equilibrium for all real economic variables, the outstanding stock of public debt that must be held by households in asset market equilibrium must be the same as under the initial fiscal policies. If it is, then fiscal policies will have exactly the same effect on private sector behavior in the two cases. Because the transfer is made with certainty, the value of the additional debt for the home country exactly equals the value of the debt reduction for the foreign country at every date between t and $t + T$. This holds even if there is a risk of default by either government or if the maturity, indexation, or other contractual characteristics of the public debt issued by each are different. The change of timing of the transfer has no effect on the intertemporal budget constraints of either government at any date, so that the distribution of returns to the total portfolio of outstanding public liabilities issued by both countries is identical at every date under the two policies. This implies that, given the original equilibrium path of prices, wages, and interest rates, households demand the same portfolios of privately issued financial claims and firms undertake the same investments under the two policies. No assumptions were made about the nature of the tax or transfer instruments used by the governments; taxes can be distortionary, and tax collection and transfer administration can be costly.

The next step is to consider a final pair of fiscal policies that support identical paths for all transfers, taxes, subsidies, and public expenditures between time t and $t + T$ but do not include the intergovernmental transfer at $t + T$. After $t + T$, the public debt for each country is different under this third policy pair than it was under the two policy paths with a fiscal transfer.

Begin with the case in which the two countries' public debts are perfect substitutes. Only the total quantity of outstanding public debt issued by the two governments, and not its national composition, matters for asset market equilibrium. This should be the case if there is no risk of default, the legal rights and obligations of debt holders do not vary with nationality, and each government minimizes its expected present value cost of borrowing.[19] It is not feasible for either government to change its fiscal policy at any time from date t onward in this case (including after date $t + T$). This is because only the sum of the national public debts of the two members of the monetary union affects the allocation of resources. When the public debts are perfect substitutes, the aggregate public sector budget identity for the two countries,

$$B_{t+1} + B^*_{t+1} = (1 + i_t)(B_t + B^*_t) + (G_t + G^*_t - T_t - T^*_t) \tag{10}$$

is unchanged. With the same fiscal policies for all dates and contingencies, household savings and the decisions of firms are the same functions of prices, wages, and rates of return under all three financing policies. If the fiscal policies are feasible for each country under either plan incorporating an international fiscal transfer, then they must also be feasible without the transfer. Note that allowing two government debts to be imperfect substitutes does not matter; the quantities B_t and B^*_t would need to be interpreted as market equilibrium values.

This implies, however, that if each government remained solvent under the original plan with an international transfer, then the home government is now running a Ponzi debt scheme exactly matched by the foreign government's Ponzi credit scheme. In place of an explicit fiscal transfer at date $t + T$, the foreign government makes a loan of equal value, intermediated by the world financial market, to the home country that is never repaid. To eliminate the international fiscal transfer, public sector solvency constraints will have to be imposed on the fiscal-financial plans for each government separately, ruling out the extension of credit by one government to the other that is never repaid.

Consider a last change in the policies pursued. At date $t + T$, the fiscal policies of each government adjust to maintain solvency without an international fiscal transfer (between t and $t + T$, the fiscal policies are identical to the original, transfer-inclusive, policies). Using the simple overlapping generations economy, let T exceed the lifetime of those alive at date t. The budget constraints for households alive at date t, equations 6 and 7, imply that household consumption and savings at date t will be unchanged as long as the real wage and real interest rate are the same. The value of the stock of public debt for the integrated economy (as in eq. 10) is also unchanged under the proposed policy pair. The real interest rate for period $t + 1$ is a function of investment at time t. This is just the excess of savings over public debt. The budget constraints imply that the real interest rate depends only on the actions of households alive at date t. Therefore, equilibrium employment, investment, consumption, and the real interest rate are the same at date t with and without a fiscal transfer. The effects of eliminating the transfer are passed to households entering the economy after date t through larger taxes net of transfers in the home country and lower taxes net of transfers in the foreign country. At date $t + T$ and beyond, the equilibrium path for the economy is different under the two policy pairs.

This implies that it is feasible to replicate the short-run effects of feasible fiscal policies with a fiscal transfer using feasible fiscal policies, subject to each government's intertemporal budget constraint, that do not involve the transfer. The capacity to make fiscal transfers between members of a monetary union may affect the growth path of each country, but it does not add to the ability of national fiscal authorities to influence short-run employment and output. That is, a system of fiscal insurance does not contribute an additional instrument to make up for the loss of exchange rate flexibility when money is neutral in the long run.

There is one caveat to this argument. The model expressed by equations 6 and 7 has a single relative price, the real interest rate. Adding a second commodity, the budget constraints become

$$w_t l_t \geq P_t^1 c_t^1 + P_t^2 c_t^2 + \tau_t + s_t + M_t \tag{11}$$

and

$$R_{t+1} s_t + w_{t+1} l_{t+1} + M_t \geq P_{t+1}^1 c_{t+1}^1 + P_{t+1}^2 c_{t+1}^2 + \tau_{t+1}, \tag{12}$$

where c^1 and P^1 denote consumption and nominal price of the first good, respectively. In this more general economy, relative spot prices at a future date will be affected by the taxes and transfers imposed on future generations of consumers. When households alive at date t expect to consume in future years simultaneously with future generations, short-term consumption and savings can differ between the two policies to the extent that future spot commodity relative prices affect them. But such effects are almost certain to be of minimal importance for realistically sized temporary fiscal transfers.

In the comparison of monetary union with and without a system of fiscal insurance, fiscal transfers increase the set of tools for short-run stabilization only to the extent that future reductions in national public debt matched by increases in foreign public debt affect current relative prices. This does not imply that fiscal transfers between states or provinces are not useful for short-run stabilization in the presence of asymmetric real supply and demand shocks for countries with systems of fiscal federalism such as the United States and

Canada. But such transfers may add little to the capacity of fiscal tools to replace independent regional monetary policies as short-run stabilizers when regional fiscal authorities do not give up their ability to issue public debt as well as money. Within a nation, interregional transfers may substitute for deficit financing of public expenditures at the state or provincial level for historical and political reasons. In the case of the United States, a wide variety of restrictions, some stronger than others, has been placed on the issue of public debt by all but one of the states. Such restrictions reduce the set of fiscal instruments available to state authorities in comparison with the set of instruments available to the sovereign member states of the European Union. The argument made earlier indicates that the role of fiscal federalism for doing some of the work of monetary autonomy arises as a replacement for the active use of public debt. In their historical study of restrictions on deficit financing at the subnational level, Eichengreen and von Hagen (1995) find an association between the federal government assuming a significant share of the responsibility for taxation and restraints on subnational public debt.

4.2.   The Loss of Fiscal Instruments with Monetary Unification

With separate national currencies and flexible exchange rates, each government can issue public debt indexed to the domestic currency. To the extent that foreign residents hold home country nominally indexed debt, the home country govenment can arrange an incoming international real resource transfer through the *unanticipated* inflation tax. This instrument of fiscal policy is largely lost with the adoption of a common currency.

Nominal indexation with national currencies implies that international fiscal transfers occur in response to both nominal and real shocks. In particular, they may occur in response to financial market noise that is unrelated to the asymmetric disturbances to real economic variables motivating arguments for a system of fiscal federalism under monetary unification and may even exacerbate the impact of such noise on economic activity. This implies that while an instrument of fiscal policy is lost with monetary unification, some of its effects may be undesirable due to financial market incompleteness. Because some degree of fiscal insurance is possible for member states of the European Union, an argument for fiscal transfers based on monetary unification, rather than economic integration, exists. Unfortunately, international systems of accounting do not allow us to estimate the size of these transfers or estimate the share that is noise generated.[20]

5. Fiscal Insurance with and without Political Union

The preceding argument concludes that the primary role of systems of fiscal federalism in monetary unions is not to increase the set of fiscal instruments in a manner that compensates for the loss of independent monetary policies. Fiscal insurance schemes in political-monetary unions may replace deficit financing by individual regions of a union. In actual practice, the deficit and debt limits proposed by the Treaty of Maastricht will be critical for deciding the importance of fiscal transfers. As already noted, fiscal insurance schemes can be used to promote economic welfare without reference to monetary unification as long as existing insurance markets are incomplete. That is, the presence of asymmetric supply and demand shocks implies that there are gains to be had by adopting an international fiscal insurance scheme even if fiscal restrictions are not imposed.

The primary reason for systems of fiscal transfers in countries with economically diverse regions could be due to the ability of a political union to enforce social welfare–improving insurance schemes and impose and administer taxes more efficiently under economic union. The relevance of arguments for a system of fiscal federalism for the European Union is frequently questioned on the grounds that the entire budget of the union is only 1 percent of total GDP at present and political unification would need to precede any significant expansion. This section considers how a scheme of fiscal insurance might be possible without requiring more than coordination by the union. First, the possibility that international fiscal transfers may be feasible for smoothing national purchasing power with each member state retaining sovereignty over its fiscal policies is discussed using a simple game-theoretic model. Second, the additional gains from fiscal insurance if some of the fiscal sovereignty of member states is subordinate to the union as a whole are discussed.

A two-country case is used to illustrate the possibilities of cooperative fiscal insurance that does not rely on the power of a supranational government. For simplicity, assume that each government seeks to smooth deviations of national income from the full-employment level. This objective is written in an intertemporally additively separable form, and each government discounts future deviations at the same constant social discount rate. Let the natural level of output be constant and ignore nominal shocks. Focusing only on temporary shocks, the objective functions to be maximized by each government are

$$W_t = u(\epsilon_t + x_t) + E_t \sum_{-i=t+1}^{\infty} \beta^{i-t}u(\epsilon_i + x_i)$$

(13)

$$W_t^* = u^*(\epsilon_t^* - x_t) + E_t \sum_{-i=t+1}^{\infty} \beta^{i-t}u^*(\epsilon_i^* - x_i),$$

where $\epsilon_t = y_t - \bar{y}$ is the transitory shock to output in the home country at date t, x_t is the net real resource transfer received from the foreign country, and β, such that $0 < \beta < 1$, is the discount factor. The shocks are assumed to be imperfectly correlated and drawn from stationary stochastic processes. The net resource transfer, x_t, from the foreign country can be either positive or negative. (A negative value would be a positive fiscal transfer from the home country to the foreign.)

The optimum can be achieved by an insurance contract under which the two governments pool asymmetric risks. Borrowing and lending using standard debt contracts and imposing solvency cannot lead to the same allocation of resources across the two countries. This is because an insurance contract allows for a payment by one party at date t in exchange for a promise of a state-contingent indemnity payment in the future. Future payments (in net present value) vary with realized shocks. In a standard debtor-creditor relationship without default, a creditor country receives the same net present value repayment in the future for every realization of shocks. A role for international transfers arises because deficit financing and public debt cannot yield the optimal degree of pooling of asymmetric output shocks for the two countries. Any additional insurance that can be achieved using international fiscal transfers necessarily involves temporary transfers that result in permanent transfers of wealth. (Recall that in a competitive insurance market the insured pays the expected present value of future indemnity payments ex ante but in an adverse event receives a positive net present value payment.)

If commitment is possible, then the two governments should negotiate a contract that would maximize a weighted sum of W_t and W_t^*. However, such a contract would commit either country to make payments to others that would leave it worse off than if it refused to participate further, suffering the consequences of shocks as best as it can using domestic resources and policy instruments. This would seem to be the relevant case if sovereignty is respected.

Define the minimum level of reduced-form social welfare that each government can be forced to accept as

$$\overline{W}_t = u(\epsilon_t) + E_t \sum_{-i=t+1}^{\infty} \beta^{i-t} u(\epsilon_i)$$

$$\tag{14}$$

$$\overline{W}_t^* = u^*(\epsilon_t^*) + E_t \sum_{-i=t+1}^{\infty} \beta^{i-t} u^*(\epsilon_i^*),$$

where other opportunities for minimizing output fluctuations are incorporated in the (residual) shocks ϵ_t and ϵ_t^*. The restrictions that either country can renege on any long-term agreement to make wealth transfers to the other are given by

$$W_t \geq \overline{W}_t$$

$$\tag{15}$$

$$W_t^* \geq \overline{W}_t^*$$

for every date t.

This model is analogous to the repeated game model of sovereign borrowing and lending of Kletzer and Wright (1995).[21] With infinite repetition, cooperative outcomes are possible, where cooperation means any path of policies such that at least one of the governments realizes social welfare higher than the noncooperative (barred) level. Partial pooling of asymmetric shocks is feasible without any exogenous or external enforcement of agreements in this model as long as the common rate of discount, β, is not too small. This is an application of the folk theorem for perfect equilibria of repeated games.

The idea is that the foreign country makes a positive transfer to the home country when $\epsilon_t^* > \epsilon_t$ because the future transfers that the foreign country will receive from the home country in a cooperative equilibrium make up for the reduction in current foreign absorption. That is, the foreign government makes a transfer because this increases its social welfare looking forward. To be successful, such paths require punishments for support. Adequate punishments give a government that fails to make a transfer expected in the cooperative equilibrium the same social welfare it would achieve if the two countries simply abandoned the mutual output-smoothing scheme. This means that a transfer, x_t, from the foreign country is possible as part of long-term fiscal cooperation if the following inequality is satisfied by the infinite horizon path of contingent fiscal transfers:

$$W_t^* = u^*(\epsilon_t^* - x_t) + E_t \sum_{-i=t+1}^{\infty} \beta^{i-t} u^*(\epsilon_i^* - x_i) \geq \overline{W}_t^* \qquad (16)$$

For $x_t > 0$, this implies that future x_t will be negative, that is, the foreign country will receive positive inflows from the home country.

Kletzer and Wright (1995) prove that reversion to noncooperative behavior is not necessary to sustain cooperative behavior without commitment in this type of economy. They also show that cooperation can be supported when there are any number of participating sovereigns.[22] (The full game-theoretic analysis is beyond the scope or purposes of this chapter, and interested or concerned readers are referred to that article.)

A formal analysis shows that international insurance schemes for stabilizing national outputs in the presence of asymmetric transitory shocks can be supported without a central fiscal or political authority. As long as the participating governments act in the long-term interest of their nations, mutually beneficial cooperation using intertemporal fiscal transfers is possible that allows the countries to realize some gains from international social insurance beyond what they could achieve using cooperative fiscal policies restricted by national solvency constraints.[23] The constraints on cooperation in a international mutual insurance scheme assume that either country can refuse to make a net real resource transfer to the other at any date without requiring any disruption of other economic or political relationships between the countries. If threats of market disruption or political reprisal are credible, then more cooperation in a fiscal insurance scheme could be supported as punishments become costlier. In the context of the European Union, it seems reasonable to ignore such possibilities. One role for a unionwide political body may be to facilitate such cooperation.

Cooperative outcomes are also possible in alternate game-theoretic models, with policymakers possessing uncertain horizons or overlapping ones with feasible short-run commitments. However, if national governments only care about deviations from potential output over finite horizons, then cooperation in a system of mutual social insurance is not possible without third-party enforcement.

The simple model also implies a role for fiscal federalism under political union. When the two constraints

$$W_t \geq \overline{W}_t$$

$$W_t^* \geq \overline{W}_t^*$$

can be relaxed, more mutual smoothing of national real output is possible, allowing higher levels of social welfare for both countries. Relaxation of these constraints requires that the union be able to force net transfers of resources between states; it must be able to impose taxes on member countries or activities within their domains. The additional insurance that is possible for a nation with economically diverse regions gives one incentive for the states to yield fiscal authority to the federal government by adopting a system of fiscal federalism. (Note that this discussion disregards any external benefits that paying regions might realize by making transfers to other regions.)

The European policy discussion has also motivated the theory of fiscal federalism presented in papers by Persson and Tabellini (1992, 1993) and Alesina and Perotti (1995). Both models demonstrate that centralized fiscal distribution can create adverse incentives for subfederal levels of governments. In the Persson and Tabellini model, the federal government makes transfers to member states as block grants or as transfer payments to households for the purpose of pooling consumption risk in the presence of asymmetric output fluctuations. Subfederal authorities can take actions that increase the riskiness of domestic production, so that block grants may not raise social welfare as a consequence of moral hazard. They also show that direct transfers to individuals may or may not dominate block grants. In the model of Alesina and Perotti, the taxes imposed by subfederal governments are endogenous with respect to the fiscal transfers made by the federal authority. These authors show that centralized fiscal redistribution may reduce the social welfare of the federation.[24]

6. Conclusion

This chapter has analyzed the implications of monetary unification for the ability of fiscal authorities to stabilize economic performance in the presence of asymmetric disturbances to aggregate supplies and demands. Among the issues discussed was the role of exchange rate flexibility in the adjustment to asymmetric shocks and the consequences of its loss for macroeconomic stabilization. A number of points were made against the existing literature. One concerned the largely neglected importance of financial market and other nominal shocks for explaining certain asymmetric disturbances to activity and the significance of exchange rate flexibility in the adjustment process in the European Union. The volatility of foreign exchange markets, episodes of speculative attack, and the possibility that noise unrelated to fundamentals can generate exchange rate movements that affect real variables all suggest that the presence of nominal shocks should not be neglected in estimating the relative importance of symmetric and asymmetric aggregate supply and demand disturbances.

A focus of the chapter was the logic behind the widely held presumption that fiscal federalism can replace regional monetary autonomy. This notion has led to suggestions that monetary unification will succeed only if Europe also adopts an international fiscal insurance scheme. It was argued that, while fiscal transfers increase the capacity of fiscal policies to influence resource allocation, they do not do so in a way that augments the ability of fiscal authorities to replace the role of monetary policy independence under flexible exchange rates. Restrictions on the ability of member states to use public sector budget deficits and public debt as temporary policy instruments eliminate fiscal tools that were available to national authorities before monetary integration, creating a need for fiscal transfers to replace them. Such restrictions, mandated by the Treaty of Maastricht and proposed recently in stricter form, may be unnecessary when member states retain overwhelming control over taxation and undesirable for political reasons since they imply a need for supranational enforcement. To the extent that political unification is necessary to sustain a system of fiscal insurance, the arguments of this chapter suggest that monetary union does not necessitate political union.

Finally, the idea that a system of fiscal insurance can only be sustained under political union was reviewed. A game-theoretic model was sketched to explain how cooperation in a sequence of reciprocal temporary international transfers was possible without violating the sovereignty of individual member states. This implies that political union is not necessarily the only way to obtain fiscal insurance in a union of similar countries experiencing idiosyncratic temporary disturbances to supplies and demands. Political unification does, however, allow more extensive fiscal insurance schemes that provide larger social welfare benefits in the general case.

NOTES

1. In particular, Buiter and Kletzer (1991a), Buiter, Corsetti, and Roubini (1993), Eichengreen and von Hagen (1995), Hutchison and Kletzer (1995), and Eichengreen (1996) cover a broad range of arguments against imposing fiscal restrictions as a requirement of monetary unification. Canzoneri and Diba (1991) argue from the perspective of optimal taxation that fiscal restrictions can be efficiency enhancing. Buiter and Kletzer (1991b) analyze the welfare economics of fiscal policies in interdependent economies.

2. h_t will remain constant over time if the velocity of base money is constant and expected inflation equals actual inflation.

3. The data are taken from the International Monetary Fund, International Financial Statistics, June 1995. Seignorage is calculated as the average annual rate of change in reserve money divided by nominal GDP. Inflation is measured by the annual change in the GDP deflator.

4. Buiter and Kletzer (1991a), Buiter, Corsetti, and Roubini (1993), Eichengreen (1992a), and Froot and Rogoff (1991), among others, question the desirability of restrictions on deficits and debt. Hutchison and Kletzer (1995) discuss the redundancy of deficit and debt limits and problems of credibility for the no-financing and no-bailout clauses.

5. One solution to the problem that the optimal policy for an independent central bank is not time consistent is to appoint a central banker committed to low inflation, as suggested by Rogoff (1985), following the general idea of appointing agents who have different preferences than the principals (Schelling 1960). Cukierman (1992) discusses central bank independence and the proposed constitution and governance of the European Central Bank.

6. Forty-nine of the 50 states impose restrictions, which vary in legal terms and impact. Vermont is the exception.

7. Buiter and Kletzer (1991a) stress the distinction between technological externalities and spillovers that redistribute income or wealth across agents. If markets are incomplete or subject to preexisting distortions, then redistributive spillovers affect allocative efficiency and provide an efficiency-based argument for intervention.

8. See, for example, Ingram 1973, Bayoumi and Eichengreen 1993, Bayoumi and Masson 1994, Bayoumi and Thomas 1995, de Grauwe and Vanhaverbeke 1991, Dehesa and Krugman 1993, Eichengreen and Wyplosz 1993, Kenen 1992, Krugman 1993, Melitz 1991, and von Hagen and Hammond 1995, among others.

9. The theory of optimum currency areas is further elaborated in McKinnon 1963, Kenen 1969, and Ishiyama 1975.

10. Krugman (1993), for example, suggests that regional monetary autonomy and exchange rate flexibility could affect long-run real output growth differentials between

regions of the United States and that the permanent fixing of exchange rates within the European Union might have real long-term consequences because of hysteresis in the natural rate. Long-run neutrality of money may also fail if the long-run Phillips curve is not vertical, implying that an increase in core inflation does not lead to an equal increase in actual inflation. The long-run growth rate of the monetary base can affect output even in the absence of nominal rigidities. The primary example is the Mundell-Tobin effect under which a higher money growth rate leading to higher anticipated inflation causes savers to substitute claims on capital for money in their portfolios, resulting in a higher steady state capital stock. As noted in the text, the choice of exchange rate regime does not matter in this case.

11. Indeed, the elimination of one trading opportunity in an economy with incomplete financial markets can be welfare improving. This implies that permanently fixing exchange rates could improve resource allocation in the presence of nominal rigidities by eliminating trade in financial assets denominated in different currencies.

12. These figures are reported in Eichengreen 1992a.

13. One natural hypothesis is that temporary shocks have permanent effects at the level of the household, so that migration may respond to temporary aggregate shocks and be reversible, with different households making permanent moves. For example, cyclical downturns lead to permanent firm exit and permanently displaced workers, and such workers should be prime candidates for migratory job searches. As summarized by Eberts and Stone (1992), only about 2 percent of these workers report moving between metropolitan areas to find work, and they are relatively underrepresented among those who do move in the United States, for these workers tend to be young and college educated.

14. If the estimated demand shocks for the European Union are combinations of real and nominal demand disturbances, then the supply shocks are not estimated in a comparable fashion between the United States and the European Union. The similar relative magnitudes of the responses of relative prices and outputs to supply shocks for the United States and the European Union may be meaningful, however, because of the identification procedure, even though a comparison of the magnitudes of the output and price responses may not be informative.

15. Bayoumi and Eichengreen (1993) use vector autoregressions with identifying restrictions (structural VARs) to decompose shocks into permanent and temporary components using the technique of Blanchard and Quah (1989). Temporary shocks apply to both output and inflation and are interpreted in this literature as demand shocks, while permanent shocks to output are identified as supply shocks.

16. Bayoumi and Eichengreen (1993) also find that the average correlation coefficient for permanent disturbances is lower for the EU core than for the periphery.

17. Several authors, including Bayoumi and Eichengreen (1993), Cohen and Wyplosz (1989), and Weber (1991), estimate the impact of shocks on nominal variables (inflation rates). This is not the same as estimating the impact of financial market or other nominal shocks.

18. Examples in the economics literature include van Rompuy, Abraham, and Heremans 1991, Eichengreen 1992a, Courchene 1993, and Bayoumi and Masson 1994.

19. More precisely, differential default risk must be ruled out. That is, debts can be perfect substitutes even if both governments potentially default, but they must default in response to the same events (which is unrealistic with asymmetric shocks to national aggregate supplies and demands). Equal legal treatment implies, for example, that German citizens cannot avoid taxes on interest earned by holding French public debt, so that the composition of the total debt stock matters. The third condition implies that the marginal bond will carry the same terms (for example, maturity and indexation) without regard to which government issues it.

20. Neumeyer (1995) presents an interesting formal analysis of the welfare economics of eliminating nominally indexed public debt instruments in general equilibrium with incomplete markets.

21. Here both sides of the relationship are risk averse, while in the model used by Kletzer and Wright (1995) to study intertemporal barter one side is risk averse and the other risk neutral. What matters is that there are gains from intertemporal exchange and cooperation.

22. Kletzer and Wright (1995) demonstrate that renegotiation-proof punishments exist that support the efficient perfect equilibrium path in the two-country case and find coalition-proof strategies when there are more than two countries.

23. Properly, policymakers need to have infinite horizons and be sufficiently patient in the model with perfect information adapted from Kletzer and Wright 1995.

24. Endogenous government policy responses and moral hazard could be added to the voluntary mutual international insurance scheme outlined here by applying the theory of repeated games under imperfect monitoring. That literature implies that gains from cooperation are still possible. The introduction of centralized redistribution for the purpose of extending risk sharing (by relaxing the sovereignty constraints) leads to the problems raised by Persson and Tabellini.

REFERENCES

Alesina, Alberto, and Roberto Perotti. 1995. "Economic Risk and Political Risk in Fiscal Unions." National Bureau of Economic Research Working Paper, no. 4992. January.

Bayoumi, Tamim, and Barry Eichengreen. 1993. "Shocking Aspects of European Monetary Unification." In *The Transition to Economic and Monetary Union in Europe*, edited by Francesco Giavazzi and Francisco Torres. New York: Cambridge University Press.

Bayoumi, Tamim, and Paul Masson. 1994. "Fiscal Flows in the United States and Canada: Lessons for Monetary Union in Europe." Centre for Economic Policy Research, London. Discussion Papers, no. 1057. Typescript.

Bayoumi, Tamim, and Alun Thomas. 1995. "Relative Prices and Economic Adjustment in the United States and the European Union: A Real Story about EMU." *IMF Staff Papers* 42:108–33.

Blanchard, Olivier, and Lawrence Katz. 1992. "Regional Evolutions." *Brookings Papers on Economic Activity*, no. 1: 1–61.

Blanchard, Olivier, and Danny Quah. 1989. "The Dynamic Effects of Aggregate Demand and Supply Disturbances." *American Economic Review* 79 (September): 655–73.

Buiter, Willem. 1995. "Macroeconomic Policy during a Transition to Monetary Union." University of Cambridge, Department of Economics. Mimeo.

Buiter, Willem, Giancarlo Corsetti, and Nouriel Roubini. 1993. "Excessive Deficits: Sense and Nonsense in the Treaty of Maastricht." *Economic Policy* 16 (April): 57–100.

Buiter, Willem, and Kenneth Kletzer. 1991a. "Fiscal Implications of a Common Currency." In *European Financial Integration*, edited by Alberto Giovannini and Colin Mayer. New York: Cambridge University Press.

———. 1991b. "The Welfare Economics of Cooperative and Noncooperative Fiscal Policy." *Journal of Economic Dynamics and Control* 15:215–44.

Canzoneri, Matthew, and Behzad Diba. 1991. "Fiscal Deficits, Financial Integration, and a Central Bank for Europe." *Journal of the Japanese and International Economies* 5:381–403.

Cohen, Daniel, and Charles Wyplosz. 1989. "The European Monetary Union: An Agnostic Evaluation." Centre for Economic Policy Research, London. Discussion Paper, no. 306. Typescript.

Courchene, Thomas. 1993. "Reflections on Canadian Federalism: Are There Implications for the European Economic and Monetary Union?" In "The Economics of Community Public Finance," *European Economy*, special issue, no. 4: 23–166.

Cukierman, Alex. 1992. *Central Bank Strategy, Credibility, and Independence: Theory and Evidence.* Cambridge: MIT Press.

de Grauwe, Paul, and Wim Vanhaverbeke. 1991. "Is Europe an Optimum Currency Area? Evidence from Regional Data." Centre for Economic Policy Research, London. Discussion Papers, no. 555. Typescript.

Dehesa, Guillermo de la, and Paul Krugman. 1993. "Monetary Union, Regional Cohesion and Regional Shocks." In *The Monetary Future of Europe*, edited by Guillermo de la Dehesa, Alberto Giovannini, Manuel Guitian, and Richard Portes. Cambridge: Cambridge University Press.

Eberts, Randall, and Joe Stone. 1992. *Wage and Employment Adjustment in Local Labor Markets.* Kalamazoo, Mich.: W. E. Upjohn Institute for Employment Research.

Eichengreen, Barry. 1992a. *Should the Maastricht Treaty Be Saved?* Princeton Studies in International Finance, no. 74. International Finance Section, Department of Economics, Princeton University.

———. 1992b. "Is Europe an Optimum Currency Area?" In *The European Community after 1992: The View from the Outside,* edited by S. Borner and H. Gruble. London: Macmillan.

———. 1993. "Labor Markets and European Monetary Unification." In *Labor and an Integrated Europe,* edited by Lloyd Ulman, Barry Eichengreen, and William Dickens. Washington, D.C.: Brookings Institution.

———. 1996. *A More Perfect Union? The Logic of Economic Integration.* Princeton Essays in International Finance, no. 198. International Finance Section, Department of Economics, Princeton University.

Eichengreen, Barry, and Jürgen von Hagen. 1995. "Fiscal Policy and Monetary Union: Federalism, Fiscal Restrictions, and the No-Bailout Rule." Conference Paper, Kiel Institute of World Economics, Kiel, Germany, June 21–22.

Eichengreen, Barry, and Charles Wyplosz. 1993. "The Unstable EMS." *Brookings Papers on Economic Activity,* no. 1: 51–124.

Froot, Kenneth, and Kenneth Rogoff. 1991. "The EMS, the EMU, and the Transition to a Common Currency." In *NBER Macroeconomics Annual, 1991,* edited by Olivier Blanchard and Stanley Fischer. Cambridge: MIT Press.

Hutchison, Michael, and Kenneth Kletzer. 1995. "Fiscal Convergence Criteria, Factor Mobility, and Credibility in Transition to Monetary Union in Europe." In *Monetary and Fiscal Policy in an Integrated Europe,* edited by Barry Eichengreen, Jeffry Frieden, and Jürgen von Hagen. Berlin: Springer.

Ingram, James. 1959. "State and Regional Payments Mechanisms." *Quarterly Journal of Economics* 73:619–32.

———. 1973. "The Case for European Monetary Integration." Princeton Essays in International Finance, no. 98. International Finance Section, Department of Economics, Princeton University.

Ishiyama, Yoshihide. 1975. "The Theory of Optimum Currency Areas: A Survey." *IMF Staff Papers* 22:344–83.

Kenen, Peter B. 1969. "The Theory of Optimum Currency Areas: An Eclectic View." In *Monetary Problems in the International Economy,* edited by Robert A. Mundell and A. K. Swoboda. Chicago: University of Chicago Press.

———. 1992. *After Maastricht.* Washington, D.C.: Group of Thirty.

Kletzer, Kenneth, and Brian Wright. 1995. "Sovereign Debt as Intertemporal Barter." University of California. Manuscript.

Krugman, Paul. 1993. "Lessons of Massachusetts for EMU." In *Adjustment and Growth in the European Monetary Union,* edited by Francesco Torres and F. Giavazzi. New York: Cambridge University Press.

Mankiw, N. Gregory. 1987. "The Optimal Collection of Seignorage: Theory and Evidence." *Journal of Monetary Economics* 20:327–41.

McKinnon, Ronald. 1963. "Optimum Currency Areas." *American Economic Review* 53:717–25.

Melitz, Jacques. 1991. "A Suggested Reformulation of the Theory of Optimal Currency Areas." Centre for Economic Policy Research, London. Discussion Papers, no. 590. Typescript.

Mundell, Robert A. 1961. "A Theory of Optimum Currency Areas." *American Economic Review* 51:657–75.

Neumeyer, Pablo A. 1995. "Currencies and the Allocation of Risk: The Welfare Economics of a Monetary Union. Working paper, Department of Economics, University of Southern California.

Persson, Torsten, and Guido Tabellini. 1992. "Federal Fiscal Constitutions: Risk Sharing and Moral Hazard." Working paper, Institute for International Economic Studies, Stockholm. March (revised September 1994).

———. 1993. "Federal Fiscal Constitutions II: Risk Sharing and Redistribution." Working paper, Institute for International Economic Studies, Stockholm.

Rogoff, Kenneth. 1985. "The Optimal Degree of Commitment to an Intermediate Monetary Target." *Quarterly Journal of Economics* 100 (November): 1168–89.

Sachs, Jeffrey, and Xavier Sala-i-Martin. 1992. "Fiscal Federalism and Optimum Currency Areas: Evidence for Europe from the United States." Centre for Economic Policy Research, London. Discussion Papers, no. 632. Typescript.

Sargent, Thomas. 1986. *Rational Expectations and Inflation.* New York: Harper and Row.

Schelling, Thomas. 1960. *The Strategy of Conflict.* Cambridge, Mass.: Harvard University Press.

van Rompuy, Paul, Filip Abraham, and Dirk Heremans. 1991. "Economic Federalism and the EMU." *European Economy,* special issue, no. 1: 109–35.

von Hagen, Jürgen. 1992. "Fiscal Arrangements in a Monetary Union: Evidence from the U.S." In *Fiscal Policy, Taxes and the Financial System in an Increasingly Integrated Europe,* edited by Donald Fair and Christian de Boissieu. Boston: Kluwer Academic.

von Hagen, Jürgen, and George Hammond. 1995. "Regional Insurance against Asymmetric Shocks: An Empirical Study for the European Community." Centre for Economic Policy Research, London. Discussion Papers, no. 1170. Typescript.

Weber, Axel. 1991. "EMU and Asymmetries and Adjustment Problems in the EMS: Some Empirical Evidence." *European Economy,* special issue, no. 1: 187–207.

Part 2
Political Institutions

CHAPTER 5

Economic and Political Integration: Institutional Challenge and Response

Lisa L. Martin

After the Treaty on European Union (TEU, also known as the Maastricht Treaty) was negotiated in 1991, it confronted unprecedented and unexpected problems with the necessary ratification processes in the member states. A Danish popular majority initially voted against the treaty. In France, one of the two countries seen as the center of the European Union, it was barely approved by a majority.[1] Even Germany, the other central member state, ran into legal and political difficulties during ratification.

These ratification crises were eventually overcome, but they have led to extensive reevaluation of the processes of European integration and reconsideration by governments of the constraints of popular and organized political opinion. Many of the ratification difficulties can be traced to an underlying sense that the decision-making processes of the EU are too undemocratic. Indeed, many believe that the "democratic deficit" in the EU was, if anything, growing prior to the Maastricht Intergovernmental Conference (IGC). Until the mid-1980s, the EU made policy in areas that were seen largely as technical or in which a widespread consensus existed about the basic outlines of policy, such as trade liberalization. But, by the late 1980s, the EU was deeply involved in areas much closer to the everyday lives of its citizens and that were more highly politicized. In this context, a perception that EU policy making was beyond the control, or indeed the intelligibility, of normal democratic processes led to a sense of crisis and demands for fundamental institutional reform.

This chapter examines the institutional challenges posed by concern for democratic control of the EU. First, it considers the definition of the "democratic deficit," lending some precision to this loose concept and asking in which institutions, if any, such a deficit lies. This analysis suggests that there is indeed legitimate concern that the EU has, at a number of levels, developed policy-making processes that give decision makers considerably more autonomy than is commonly accepted in democratic political systems. The deficit cannot be corrected merely by improving the procedures used by an individual institution, such as the Council of Ministers or the European Commission. Instead, it results from these procedures, from the ways in which the EU institutions interact with one another, and from frequent failure by national political structures to develop adequate oversight and control mechanisms.

The demands for representation and accountability in the EU thus present a complex agenda for institutional reform, one that governments and EU bureaucrats must confront if economic and political integration are to continue. Potential responses to these challenges range from marginal tinkering with existing mechanisms to wholesale creation of new institutions and the destruction of old ones. I organize the gamut of potential responses, and focus on the most salient ones, by concentrating on responses at two levels: the level of the EU institutions themselves and the domestic level.

At the EU level, each of the three major bodies—the Council, the Commission, and the European Parliament (EP)—has taken steps to redress problems of representation and/or accountability and is debating further steps.[2] While reforms in the Council and Commission may improve the accountability problem at the margins, an increased role for the EP is seen by most of those concerned about the democratic deficit as the only real solution to problems of both representation and accountability. The second section of this essay will concentrate primarily on the EP, considering its development, current organization, and the debate about its influence on policy in the EU.

While some still predict a federal future for the EU, for the time being and the foreseeable future it is an international institution comprised of states. Inevitably, this suggests that at least some processes of accountability will occur at the domestic level. The third section turns to the national and subnational levels to examine how institutional reforms here are related to the goal of bringing EU policy making under control. National parliaments, long seen as lacking the necessary capabilities and interests to influence the course of integration, are increasingly organizing themselves and reasserting their rights in the European arena. In addition, movements to devolve significant powers to subnational structures, such as regional governments, are gaining ground in many member states. The logic of economic integration suggests that such devolution is not coincidental but is likely to continue and spread. Devolution and fragmentation raise a new set of problems, and potential solutions, centering around the relations among regions, states, and supranational institutions.

This chapter concludes by considering the implications of institutional challenges for the new circumstances confronting the EU. In particular, problems of enlargement and development of a "flexible architecture" for integration will further challenge those who hope to implement institutional reforms. I conclude that, while the EP is a more powerful institution than many analysts have realized, attempts to improve processes of representation and accountability in the EU are misguided if they focus on the EP alone. In the foreseeable future, national institutions will continue to play a major role in providing democratic control of European integration, and these processes will proceed most efficiently if they respond to the demands of domestic institutions rather than searching for mechanisms to circumvent them.

The Challenge: The Democratic Deficit

Complaints about a "democratic deficit" in the EU have become frequent and loud over the last few years (Williams 1991). Yet such worries are not new. In the 1970s, the dominant approach to studying the activities of the then EC was neofunctionalism, with its emphasis on technical rather than political solutions to problems (Haas 1958). In this vision, the process of European integration was elite driven, compelled by functional necessity, and inexorable. This view provoked some resistance by those who worried that such an elitist, bureaucratic process would create dynamics of integration outside the control of any democratic structures. Fears of lack of democratic control led to calls for increasing the representative nature of EC institutions, particularly the EP. Only the EP, observers claimed, could effectively control the Commission and the Council (Herman and Lodge 1978, 21). Such concerns led to the introduction of direct elections to the EP in 1979.

What exactly is the purported democratic deficit that so concerns observers of the EU, both historically and in the present? Developing a precise definition would require an extensive analysis of the meaning of democracy and potential tradeoffs between democracy and other goals, and as such is well beyond the scope of this chapter.[3] However, in looking at analyses of the purported democratic deficit, we see a common core of concerns about lack of *representation* and *accountability* in EU decision-making processes. These concerns are common to different theoretical approaches to democracy, reflecting the tension between majority rule and constraints such as division of powers or the rule of law (Dahl 1956). Williams, in one of the best contemporary arguments, defines the democratic deficit as "the gap between the powers transferred to the Community and the efficacy of European Parliamentary oversight and control" (1991, 155). While Williams's focus on loss of national powers and problems of oversight and control is accurate, her emphasis on the EP to the exclusion of other institutions assumes a particular kind of solution to such problems and so unnecessarily restricts the scope of studies of representation and accountability.

Boyce (1993) summarizes contemporary concerns about the democratic deficit and proposed solutions, offering a more general analysis if no precise definition. She discusses the major failings of EU structures from the viewpoint of assuring democratic control. To begin, extensive decision-making powers have been transferred from national parliaments to the EU level but have not been located in the democratically elected EP. This transfer of authority is large and growing. For example, Jacques Delors predicted in 1988 that within 10 years 80 percent of economic legislation would be of EU rather than national origin (Bogdanor and Woodcock 1991, 487), an assessment that does not seem wildly off the mark. Concern about the decline of national parliaments is related to the role of the Council. The Council of Ministers is the dominant legislative and executive body in the EU. Although it is made up of democratically selected national ministers, there is a near consensus that the chains of accountability between the Council and national parliaments are weak (Herman and van Schendelen 1979; Marquand 1981).

Another frequently expressed concern relates to the role of the Commission, which is entirely unelected but plays a major role in EU decision making, including having the sole right to initiate legislation and extensive power to modify EP amendments to legislation. The EP, while at least an elected body, suffers from low visibility, low turnout in elections, and, most fundamentally, a restricted role in the legislative process. Concerns also arise about the clouded separation of powers within the EU. The executive and legislative powers, in particular, are not clearly delegated to separate institutions, as in most democratic systems. All these problems are exacerbated by a general lack of transparency in EU proceedings, particularly in the Council and Commission, and the increasing complexity of legislative and regulatory procedures.

Other specific failures of the EU to meet generally accepted norms of democratic practice could be listed, but I will summarize the concerns by arguing that representation and accountability of policy-making structures within the EU fall short of the level that would be required to lead citizens to view the EU as a responsive and responsible institution. This is not to argue that national systems of representation and accountability are without their faults. Indeed, some political activists, especially those on the left in some domestic political arenas, have hoped that the EU would correct national-level democratic deficits. But over the last decade such hopes have gone unfulfilled, as the EU greatly expanded the scope of its legislative activities without much improving procedures designed to make such activities accountable to any system of political control.

Let me first focus on the Commission. The Commission is chosen by the consensus of the governments, and this is the body for which worries about representation are most acute. Recently the EP has gained the power to reject the proposed president of the Commission, or the rest of the Commission as a whole, but this process remains one in which the decision is many steps removed from popular control and a very blunt tool. The EP's right of veto, as will be discussed, provides it with significantly less leverage than would a more integrated role in the selection process.

Concerns about representation on the Commission would carry less force if the Commission were constrained to a typical bureaucratic role of carrying out legislation. But the Commission plays a much deeper role in the legislative process of the EU (Ludlow 1991). It has legislative functions as well and is the repository of most policy expertise in the EU. As the intense conflict about finding a successor to Jacques Delors, the former president of the Commission, suggests, member states recognize the Commission as a powerful actor. On the other hand, the most representative body in the EU, the EP, has a restricted role in policy making. The recently established cooperation and codecision procedures mark a significant increase in the EP's ability to influence legislation. But the impact of these procedures is limited by the narrow range of legislative activities to which they apply, the need to form coalitions with the Commission and some Council members to exercise conditional influence, and internal organizational problems of the EP, including the fact that its proceedings take place in three different geographical locations.

Turning to the Council, the primary concern is that it is accountable to neither national parliaments nor the EP. Its actions traditionally have taken place behind closed doors, with the results of votes not even recorded, making the exercise of any kind of scrutiny extremely difficult. Responding to concerns about this lack of transparency, the Council agreed at Maastricht to publicize its proceedings by making public the results of voting. However, the quality of information disclosed thus far has been disappointing. With the exception of Denmark (and perhaps the partial exception of the United Kingdom), national parliaments have been slow to develop mechanisms that provide them with information about what their ministers are doing in the Council and with leverage to put constraints on the positions ministers take in Council negotiations. This is not to argue that national parliaments have been without influence in European integration or to suggest that they cannot develop more effective oversight mechanisms. But until now the mechanisms available to national parliaments often have been post hoc, through their ability to obstruct implementation of EU legislation (Martin 1994). This has put parliaments in an obstructionist rather than a constructive position and has left a gap in the chain of accountability.

The development of the Council and Commission as bodies not subject to tight democratic controls is no accident. The visions of key figures in the founding of the EU, such as Jean Monnet, and of national governments converged on one point. Both saw the EU as appropriately an arena to be dominated by elites and took steps to create structures that would give them a relatively free hand in making policy. In other words, the creation of the democratic deficit was largely intentional. Featherstone (1994) shows how Monnet's vision of European integration was technocratic and elitist. The Commission was not supposed to be representative or accountable, since its role was to solve technical problems and exercise leadership (163). Likewise, the Council has proven a fertile ground for national governments' attempts to evade the constraints of domestic politics. Moravcsik (1994) argues that the closed processes, legislative power, and cooperative nature of the Council have led to an increase in executive strength vis-à-vis parliaments.[4] This shift in powers, he argues, goes far to explain executive support for the EU. Contrary to Williams's (1991, 162) argument, the weakening of national parliaments as a result of integration was not "unforeseen" but planned (Lodge 1996, 188).

But the ability of governments to use the Council in this manner is likely reaching its limits. Forums for international cooperation do not provide unlimited capacity to break the bonds of accountability in a democracy. As Emil Kirchner has argued, "the view that the EC was elite inspired and is elite driven still has a certain validity, though the time of the 'permissive consensus' of the masses is clearly over" (1994, 264). The strategy of creating a democratic deficit may have been a shortsighted one, as it has led to the current backlash against the EU seen in popular opinion and on the part of domestic political actors. At a minimum, this strategy has endowed the EU with a set of problems of democratic legitimacy that it must now confront if processes of integration are to continue. Integration is not inherently an elite-driven process, and it could only remain so as long as supranational decision making was limited to matters not of much interest to the average citizen. Most elites and analysts misread lack of public involvement in EU debates and easy ratification of EU deals up until the TEU as a sign that governments had found a successful way to free themselves from democratic constraints. Instead, it appears that such constraints have always existed, and the EU is bumping up against them now.

Proponents of integration have often been quite explicitly opposed to the introduction of more democratic procedures in the EU policy-making process. However, the belief that appropriate institutional design can allow governments to pursue policies of deep and immediate interest to many citizens without worrying about representation and accountability generally is misplaced in democratic systems. As will be discussed, past practices of attempting to circumvent national parliaments have had the unintended effect of creating inefficiencies in the implementation of policies. This pattern of implementation delays, along with problems such as the initial Danish rejection of the Maastricht Treaty, provides evidence that important national interests continue to have influence in spite of attempts to close them out. As the scope of integration deepens, the current structure of informal, post hoc representation of interests is creating a great deal of resentment and inefficiency and a resulting legitimacy crisis. In view of these results, institutional reformers would be well advised to move beyond an elitist fear of democracy to consider solutions that would allow for both some resolution of concerns about democratic deficiencies and continued pursuit of welfare-enhancing integration. As I will argue, these goals are not as deeply in conflict as is widely assumed.

Some of the current outcry about the democratic deficit is surely overblown, as analysts hold the EU up to standards of ideal rather than practicing democracy. But this occasional exaggeration of the problem does not mean that no problem exists. Public opinion sees the EU as too distant, with its most representative body having limited policy influence and unrepresentative bodies being largely unaccountable but endowed with strong policy-making powers. This perception is backed up by analysis of EU institutions, which finds grounds in the legislative procedures and formal powers of the various institutions to argue that they do not live up to usual standards of representation and accountability. As David Martin, a member of the EP, has argued: "If the European Community was a state . . . and applied to join the Community, it would be turned down on the grounds that it was not a democracy" (quoted in Bogdanor and Woodcock 1991, 482).

Responses: European Union Level

A problem of democratic legitimacy is facing the EU. Part of this problem is public perception, but the perception is based on facts about the unique policy-making procedures used by the EU. With the crises of ratifying the TEU, EU elites have realized that major reforms are necessary if they are to gain the necessary popular and domestic support to push ahead with integration efforts. Such support is not a luxury but a necessary condition for effective policy making. This recognition has led to innumerable proposals for institutional reform. I will concentrate here on the reforms that have been implemented or seem most feasible, assessing the degree to which they might make a difference in the exercise of influence within the EU.

The Council and the Commission

One of the intriguing aspects of the debate about the democratic deficit has been the degree to which different observers locate the key problem in different institutions. Some have focused primarily on the lack of transparency and accountability in the Council, others on the lack of representation and accountability in the Commission. The previous analysis suggests that both institutions are subject to criticism, and both have undertaken some reforms in response.

Lodge (1994) argues that the original concerns about the democratic deficit focused on the Council of Ministers. Certainly, if one looks at analyses published in the 1970s and 1980s, it is true that the difficulties of national parliaments in controlling the Council and its lack of accountability to the EP are common complaints. These concerns were exacerbated by the acceptance of qualified majority voting in the Council with the Single European Act (SEA) in 1985. Previously, member states could invoke the Luxembourg Compromise to veto any proposals they deemed to be of "vital national interest." This veto power provided at least a minimal degree of transparency, as national parliaments knew when ministers had failed to exercise their veto. The veto power also provided a mechanism for domestic accountability, although a blunt one. When qualified majority voting was introduced without concomitant changes in publicizing the proceedings of the Council, even these minimal forms of oversight were compromised.

Thus, calls to improve the accountability of the Council focused on removing the secrecy of its proceedings and introducing clearer accountability mechanisms. Attempts to increase accountability, in particular, threatened the dominant role of the Council in EU policy making. If accountability were increased on the national level, it would increase parliamentary influence at the expense of executives. Other proposals called for increased accountability to the EP, for example, by moving toward a bicameral European legislature, with the Council reduced to the role of an upper house and significant powers moving to the EP.

The Council responded to these threats in three ways. First, it agreed to an apparent increase in the role of the EP, although the magnitude of this increase is subject to question, as will be discussed. Second, it took steps to increase the transparency of its proceedings. Lodge (1994, 346) argues that the decision to focus on transparency was a strategic move on the part of member governments, as it constituted only a minimal change in the way the Council did business but allowed them to follow a third strategy: shifting blame for any democratic deficit to the Commission. She finds that the emphasis on transparency was intended to apply only to the Commission but came back to haunt the Council, as national parliaments demanded that the transparency of Council actions be increased (348–49). The Maastricht agreement responded to these demands with a "declaration on transparency," which called for greater openness in all EU institutions without specifying how such openness was to be achieved.

Other observers, such as Featherstone (1994), trace the source of the democratic deficit to the Commission rather than the Council. Certainly the public's perception that too many decisions are being made in Brussels rather than closer to home reflects a dissatisfaction with the Commission more than the Council. To some extent, the Council's tactics may account for this perception, but it remains true that the Commission is not chosen through directly representative mechanisms and that its workings remain opaque, although it may be quite open to the influence of organized lobbying groups. Ambitious reformers call for direct elections to the Commission, giving it a clearer and more legitimate role as the Union's executive.

In the meantime, the Commission has taken more moderate steps toward reform. The declaration on transparency applies to the Commission, although it is unclear what it will mean in practice. Responsibility for informing national bodies about draft legislation, ongoing negotiations, and other EU business remains primarily with member state governments. The major reform to which the Commission has committed itself goes under the vague heading of "subsidiarity." The Commission presented a declaration on subsidiarity at the Edinburgh summit in December 1992 (Commission of the European Communities 1992). While subsidiarity may mean different things to different people (see Scott, Peterson, and Millar 1994), the fundamental idea is that political decisions should be made at the lowest possible level. In practice, this seems to mean that the EU should not take upon itself responsibility for making policies that could as efficiently be made at the national level. While implementing such a principle remains difficult—who is to decide which policies "require" supranational intervention?—the idea clearly was for the Commission to put substantive and procedural limits on its stated rights to make policy.

In spite of its ambiguities, a consensus has grown that subsidiarity is an admirable principle and one that will address the democratic deficit by bringing decisions closer to the people. The ambiguity of subsidiarity may be one of the factors behind its success. Antifederalist governments, such as those of the United Kingdom and Denmark, can applaud subsidiarity as it promises to return policy-making authority to the national level. More prointegrationist states can also support subsidiarity for its promise to make decision making more accountable, thus increasing the democratic legitimacy of European institutions. However, as will be discussed, support of subsidiarity has had an effect probably unanticipated and certainly unintended by the United Kingdom. If decisions are to be made at the lowest feasible level, it may imply a significant devolution of power away from the national level to *subnational* levels, particularly regions. As devolution was anathema to the Major government and deeply controversial in the British political system, the Tories argued that the principle of subsidiarity applied only at the EU, not at the national, level. At the other end of the spectrum, some see the principle of subsidiarity as opening the door to a "Europe of the regions," fully representative and accountable to popular will, where the nation-state plays only a minimal role.

The principle of subsidiarity is a difficult one with which to quarrel, as it appears to combine the virtues of efficiency and democracy. Efficiency gains are, according to the principle, the only legitimate reason for making policy at higher levels, further removed from direct popular control. But subsidiarity is a concept in which the devil is in the details. Efficiency gains are difficult to measure ex ante, as would be required for effective implementation. Controversies are sure to arise about the "most efficient" level for decision making, even with a presumption in favor of lower levels. Implementation of subsidiarity would require creation of a dispute settlement body or other mechanism to determine the appropriate decision-making level. And such a body would thereby wield tremendous power. A strong case exists for making sure that any such body is composed of policy experts, who presumably be in the best position to make efficiency calculations. But a body of experts might itself violate principles of democratic representation unless it were elected, and election of a body of experts is generally understood to be a contradiction in terms. Thus, subsidiarity itself is not a solution to the problem of the democratic deficit. Instead, it opens up a large new set of institutional challenges.

The European Parliament

Most analysts of the democratic problems of the EU have concluded that empowerment of the EP is an essential part of any solution. National parliaments, the argument goes, simply do not have the capacity effectively to control governments' actions in the Council; were they to develop such capacity, it would paralyze the decision-making processes of the Union. (I consider the validity of this argument subsequently.) For integration to have democratic legitimacy, its decision-making bodies must be accountable to a representative, supranational body; the Parliament is the only such body in the EU.

Proposals for reforming the powers of the Parliament have attended to its relations with both the Commission and the Council. With respect to the Commission, the emphasis has been on mechanisms that would increase the EP's role in approving the appointment of commissioners. Until Maastricht, the EP had only the right to dismiss the Commission as a whole, including the president (Westlake 1994, 114–15). Since this was obviously an extremely blunt instrument, and one whose exercise would bring the activities of the EU to a screeching halt, it provided the EP with little influence over either appointments to the Commission or its activities. The TEU increased the EP's say in the appointment process by giving it a consultative role in the selection of the president and commissioners. With respect to commissioners, the EP's power is primarily consultative; it can only reject the Commission as a whole, not individually. But the EP gained the right to veto the Council's nominee for president and made threats of this nature during the tortuous 1994 selection process. Whether such threats were credible, and what impact they might have had on the eventual result, must await further research. But at least one authoritative study of the EP concludes that these reforms "fundamentally changed the nature of the relationship between the Commission and the Parliament" (Westlake 1994, 116).

With respect to relations with the Council, the major concern of reformers has been to increase the legislative powers of the EP. The SEA took a large step forward by creating the cooperation procedure, which for the first time gave the Parliament a recognizable legislative role with an ability to make amendments to legislation to veto it (Nugent 1991). Demands for greater parliamentary powers during the Maastricht negotiations focused on giving the EP a genuinely "colegislative" role with the Council, a proposal vigorously contested by antifederalist states, especially the United Kingdom. A new procedure was implemented in Article 189b of the TEU, widely known as the codecision procedure, in spite of British objections (Nicoll 1994, 408–9).

These new procedures increase the legislative powers of the EP, although the extent to which they do so remains a contentious issue. Most observers still see the Parliament as a weak organization. Even if its formal powers have been increased, the degree to which the EP is able to exercise these powers effectively remains questionable. One problem is chronic absenteeism. EP decisions generally require approval of an absolute majority of its members. But low attendance means that mustering an absolute majority, even for important proposals, is difficult. Questions are also raised about the quality of members of the EP (MEPs). Some political parties see the EP as a sort of dumping ground for party members nearing retirement or as a reward for various political favors. These activities do not contribute to the development of policy expertise or sensitivity to constituent concerns within the EP. Internal organizational problems also persist, aggravated by the fact that EP holds its proceedings in three different locations: Strasbourg, Luxembourg, and Brussels. The process of party formation in the EP is not yet stabilized, with shifting coalitions that are unable to enforce much party discipline (Duff 1994).

In spite of these difficulties, recent research is building a growing body of evidence that the EP is increasing its capacity to influence decisions and is exercising this influence. Many of the amendments proposed by the Parliament are eventually integrated into EC legislation. The committee system of the EP is well developed, and most of the work of the EP takes place in committees, as in any influential legislature (Tsebelis 1995b; Jacobs, Corbett, and Shackleton 1992). A body of empirical work that provides evidence of EP influence on specific policies is growing (e.g., see Judge and Earnshaw 1994). To a large extent, treating the EP's organizational or personnel problems as an impediment to exercising influence seems misguided. Instead, such problems are largely endogenous. As long as the EP had no legislative authority, why not use it as a place to send inconvenient party members? Why should a legislature with no role beyond consultation in the legislative process behave as anything other than a talking shop? But, as the external constraints and opportunities for the EP have changed, for example, with the introduction of direct elections and the SEA, its internal organization has changed accordingly. Only when the body can hope to have some impact on decisions does it organize itself in such a way that it can make decisions. We can expect this internal reorganization to continue as the EP acquires more powers, suggesting that current internal weaknesses of the EP are not a good justification for refusing to grant it more authority.

What do we know about the powers of the EP and the conditions under which they can be exercised? Tsebelis (1994, 1995a, 1995b) has presented the most rigorous and theoretically informed analysis of the powers of the EP under the cooperation and codecision procedures. Using spatial models, he characterizes the EP under the cooperation procedure as a "conditional agenda-setter" (Tsebelis 1994). Under specified conditions concerning the policy preferences of the governments, Commission, and EP, the cooperation procedure gives the EP the ability to present the Council with legislation that it finds easier to accept than to override. Later work (Tsebelis 1995b) shows that these results are not dependent on the simplifying assumption that the EP is a unitary actor and that the predicted ability of the EP to influence legislation has empirical support in a number of recent cases. Rather than observing the lowest common denominator results that we would expect if the EP was an unimportant actor, we instead sometimes see legislation that exceeds the lowest common denominator by a great deal. In fact, legislation at times exceeds the standards set by *any* member state, let alone the least stringent member-state standards.

Under the Maastricht Treaty, the cooperation procedure was largely replaced by the codecision procedure. The codecision procedure will also be used in a number of new areas of EU authority such as education and consumer protection. Most analysts, and apparently members of the EP, have seen the codecision procedure as leading to a major increase in their ability to influence legislation (Westlake 1994, 146). For example, one 30-year member of the EP concludes that Maastricht represents a "tremendous step forward" for the EP (Scott-Hopkins 1994, 24). Tsebelis (1995a), extending his formal analysis of the cooperation procedure, questions this assessment. While he acknowledges that in some areas the EP's powers increase under the TEU, his primary finding is that under the codecision procedure the EP has sacrificed its power as a conditional agenda setter to accept veto power it previously did not have. Since agenda setting generally provides for more policy influence than does veto power, he concludes that the EP actually has lost influence over legislation through the codecision procedure as compared with the cooperation procedure. Garrett (1995) agrees with this assessment, using modified spatial models for his analysis of institutional changes moving from the Luxembourg Compromise through the introduction of the codecision procedure.

Tsebelis cites the difference between presidential and parliamentary systems to illustrate the claim that agenda-setting power is more valuable than veto power is (1995a, 7–8). In a presidential system such as that of the United States, the legislature is understood to be more powerful than in parliamentary systems. This is because Congress has agenda-setting power, while the president can only veto legislation. In parliamentary systems, the situation is reversed. The executive has the right of initiative, leading to parliaments less able to influence the course of legislation than is the U.S. Congress.

While Tsebelis relies on two-dimensional models that can be generalized to N dimensions, the general point about the advantages of agenda-setting versus veto power can be made simply in a one-dimensional example. Figure 5.1 shows a generic decision problem in a one-dimensional policy space. Consider points to the right to represent more "integrationist" policies. Point SQ is the status quo policy, while C is the policy the Council would most prefer to see adopted. Point P is the policy the EP would most like to implement.[5]

Consider two decision-making processes. In the first, the Council is able to make a policy proposal and the Parliament has the choice of accepting or vetoing it (no amendments are allowed, as in the last stage of the cooperation or codecision procedures). In the second, the roles are reversed. The first process, with the Parliament having veto power, will result in a policy outcome of C. The Council can propose its most preferred policy, and, since this is better from the EP's perspective than the status quo, it will accept it. But when the Parliament has agenda-setting power it can do better. In this case, it can propose a policy at point x, which is the same distance from the Council's ideal point as is the status quo. Assuming symmetrically shaped utility functions, this will leave the Council indifferent between the status quo and x, allowing the EP to get a policy outcome significantly closer to its ideal point than it could with veto power.

While this result must be modified and qualified when extended to more than one dimension, the essential insight remains: agenda-setting power provides more ability to influence policies than does veto power. Thus, Tsebelis concludes (1995a), the EP was better off under cooperation than under codecision. The Maastricht Treaty will not reduce the democratic deficit.

This finding is sure to be controversial. While Tsebelis has done a great service by subjecting the EP's procedures to the same level of analysis as is typically applied to other legislative mechanisms and showing that not all aspects of the TEU unambiguously increase the EP's powers, the overall effect remains ambiguous. First, as Tsebelis acknowledges, the TEU made changes in the EP's powers outside the creation of the codecision procedure. It increased the accountability of the Council and Commission to the EP by giving the EP

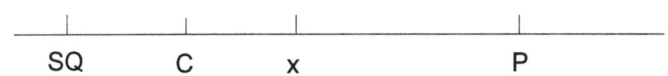

SQ: The status quo policy
C: The Council's preferred policy; also the outcome when the
    Council has agenda-setting and the Parliament veto power
P: The Parliament's preferred position
x: The outcome when the parliament has agenda-setting and
    the Council veto power

Fig. 5.1. Agenda setting and veto power

power to reject the Council's recommendation for president of the Commission. The EP has also acquired the formal right to request that the Commission introduce legislation, and the issues subject to the cooperation procedure have increased, as mentioned previously. While this outcome falls short of the EP's demands to be given the power of initiative, it does represent an increase in EP powers.

But, as Tsebelis argues (1995a), the codecision procedure is really the key to any new role for the EP. Analysis of the effects of this new procedure therefore will determine the extent to which the EP has gained influence. At least two considerations suggest that Tsebelis's results must be qualified. First, the EP's powers as an agenda-setter vis-à-vis the Council under the cooperation procedure were *conditional,* not unconditional. The EP did not have the right, at the second reading, to present the Council with a take it or leave it position. Instead, the Council had the right to take it, leave it, or *amend* it if the Council could muster a unanimous vote. The results of the cooperation procedure through 1993 show that the Council could indeed round up all its members to amend EP proposals at the second reading, as it accepted only 23.6 percent (253 out of 1,074) amendments proposed at this stage by the EP (Westlake 1994, 265).

Second, the EP's agenda-setting power under the cooperation procedure was conditional on its ability to reach agreement with the Commission. After the Parliament proposed amendments at both the first and second readings, they were forwarded to the Commission. They reached the Council only if the Commission approved them. This allowed the Commission to modify substantially the Parliament's proposal in accord with its own preferences.[6] The Commission frequently has exercised its power to accept or reject EP amendments, having accepted only 54.7 percent (2,499 out of 4,572) at the first reading and 44.2 percent (475 out of 1,074) at the second reading. The codecision procedure decisively changes the balance of power between the Commission and the EP through its provisions for representation on conciliation committees at the final stage of the legislative process. Conciliation committees are made up of equal numbers of parliamentary and Council representatives; the Commission is represented only as an observer (Laursen 1996, 131). Any agreement reached by the Conciliation Committee can be accepted by an absolute majority in the EP and a qualified majority in the Council. Thus, in situations in which there is significant disagreement between the Commission and the EP, the codecision procedure provides the EP with a mechanism by which to override the Commission that was not present under the cooperation procedure. To this extent, it does increase democratic accountability by taking power out of the hands of an unrepresentative body, the Commission, and putting it in the hands of an elected body, the Parliament. Not surprisingly, the Commission has expressed its displeasure with losing its "traditional proprietorial rights over draft legislation" at the final stage of the codecision procedure (Westlake 1994, 145) in spite of the fact that it had initially proposed the idea of codecision (Wester 1992, 209).

The debate over the formal and realized powers of the EP will doubtless continue for many years. Tsebelis's analysis is valuable in preventing complacence about ever increasing EP powers, suggesting that changes that apparently meet demands for increased powers may have more ambiguous effects. One proper conclusion at this point is that the TEU reduced the powers of the Commission. The degree to which it enhanced or decreased the power of the EP, and under what conditions, remains in question. It appears that under some conditions, given the configuration of Council, Commission, and EP preferences, the EP's powers are increased. Under others, they are limited by the surrender of agenda-setting power. Analysis of EP influence, including precise specification of these conditions, should prove to be one of the most fruitful areas in the study of EU institutions over the next few years.

Responses: Domestic Level

Although reform of EU institutions has occupied center stage in attempts to provide more democratic accountability, we also observe movements on the domestic level that could have major impacts on the future of European integration. For one, national parliaments are rediscovering and reasserting their supposedly lost powers to constrain government representatives in the Council. While many see the resurgence of national parliaments as a threat to integration, such fears may be overblown. Another domestic development, hinted at in the earlier discussion of subsidiarity, is the increasing role of regions and potentially other subnational actors in EU business. While a "Europe of the regions" is far from being realized, in many states we see increasing responsibility for implementing legislation devolving to regional actors, which is leading to an increase in their influence at the policy-making stage.

National Parliaments

Analyses of European integration uniformly agree that national parliaments have not been influential actors in this process, nor in foreign policy more generally (Milward 1992; Wallace 1973, 13; Niblock 1971, 16). While opponents of deeper integration call for greater parliamentary engagement, those who favor federalism or deeper integration generally find the possibility of greater parliamentary influence threatening. Both perspectives rely on a common assumption: that there is a fundamental tradeoff between efficiency and national parliamentary democracy (Moravcsik 1993, 515; *Economist,* July 7, 1990, 34; Wessels 1996, 59). I argue that this assumption is not justified. National parliaments do have the ability to influence integration, and it is where they have been most active that we find the *best* records for implementation of EU-level legislation.

Models of national parliaments that find them fundamentally unable to bring governments under control are *abdication models.* Such a perspective dominates the study of parliaments in the EU and argues that the intergovernmental and/or supranational processes of integration have inexorably weakened national legislatures. The abdication approach is consistent with the emphasis on the elitist, technocratic nature of integration discussed earlier. In contrast to abdication models, *delegation models* see governments' room for maneuver as contingent on parliamentary organization and preferences (Martin 1994). Governments that appear to be free of parliamentary constraints actually may be working within the boundaries set by parliaments; lack of legislative activity does not imply lack of legislative influence. It may instead imply legislative consent to executive activities.

If the delegation perspective is correct, it has a number of observable implications. First, it implies that if governments misunderstand their role and attempt to operate outside the bounds set by parliaments we should see parliamentary activity to rein governments back in. Second, it suggests that patterns in implementation of EU legislation should be dependent on parliamentary involvement in EU negotiations. National parliaments retain explicit, formal authority to translate much EU legislation into national law. This power at the implementation stage provides parliaments with indirect leverage in the integration process. If they are involved in a transparent, regularized manner that allows them to influence the actions of their representatives in the Council, we should see smooth implementation of EU agreements. If they are excluded from negotiations and then asked to implement agreements on which they have not been consulted, we should see difficulties during implementation. While this argument contradicts traditional ways of thinking about European parliaments, it deserves to be treated as a testable hypothesis.

Patterns of implementation are thus important because they reveal something about the role of national parliaments. They are also important for purely substantive reasons, as failures of implementation are becoming one of the key concerns of those who study integration. Analysts have pointed to an "integration deficit" that may be as troubling as the democratic deficit (Bronckers 1989; Colchester and Buchan 1990, 131–38); here I argue that the two are directly related. Concerns about rates of implementation have arisen especially in the context of the 300 White Paper directives that were intended to complete the Single Market by the end of 1992. Responding to these concerns, the Commission has undertaken regular studies that measure the percentage of directives that have been implemented by the legislated deadline in each member state. Figure 5.2 shows some of these data for the period December 1989 to August 1992, when the bulk of the implementation work was undertaken.

Looking at these figures, a number of interesting patterns emerge. First, we might note that the United Kingdom, which prides itself on having an excellent implementation record and frequently complains about those of other member states, is not clearly ahead of the other major members of the Union. Its record is comparable with those of France and Germany, above average but not at the top. This spot goes consistently to Denmark, which always has implementation records better than those of other member states, hovering around 90 percent.[7] This observation is surprising, because Denmark is not known to be a promoter of integration. On the contrary, it has a reputation of being a foot dragger and tough negotiator, leery of moves toward federalism (Toonen 1992, 11–12). Its "no" vote on the Maastricht Treaty merely reinforced this reputation. So why does it implement EU legislation efficiently?

It appears that Denmark's record is accounted for by the fact that its parliament, the Folketing, has a uniquely formalized role in EU negotiations. Williams (1991, 159) argues that Denmark is the only member state in which

Percent of directives implemented

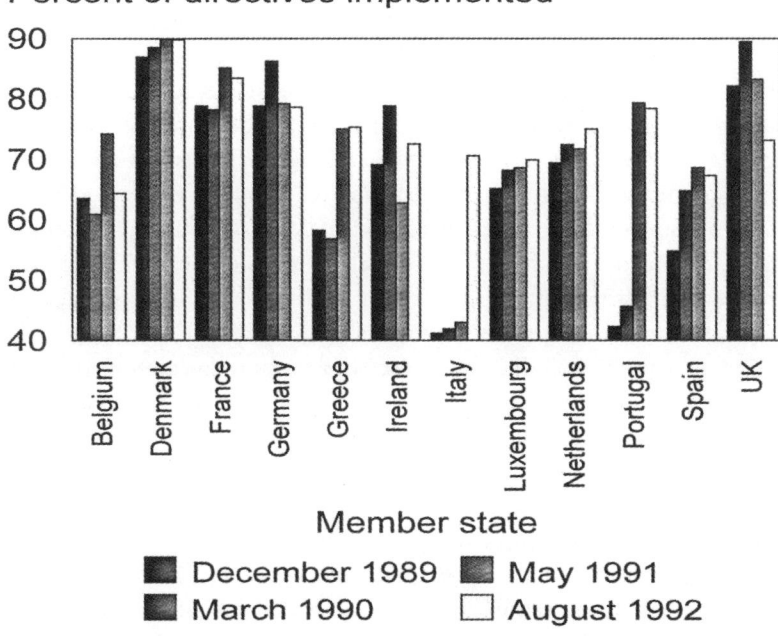

Member state

■ December 1989   ■ May 1991
■ March 1990   □ August 1992

Fig. 5.2. Implementation rates. (Data from Commission reports.)

the parliament effectively constrains its negotiators in Council proceedings. Even prior to its entry to the EC in 1973, the Danish Parliament organized a committee, the Market Relations Committee (MRC), that would exercise tight control over government actions in the Council (Fitzmaurice 1976). The MRC has been successful, through frequent meetings with the executive branch and occasional implementation of threats, in gaining timely information about EU negotiations and handing down a negotiating mandate to the government (Rasmussen 1988; Møller 1983). While EU committees have now been established in all national parliaments, others do not have the institutionalized, early involvement in EU activities that we see in Denmark. Instead, other legislatures exercise their influence post hoc by dragging their feet when it comes time to implement legislation, sometimes forcing renegotiation or extension of deadlines.

The finding that parliaments that are excluded from negotiations can stymie efficient implementation suggests that we need to reconsider the conventional wisdom that involving national parliaments more regularly in the integration process will introduce debilitating inefficiencies. Instead, it appears that attempts to circumvent parliaments create inefficiencies, although they arise at the implementation rather than the negotiation stage. More formal parliamentary involvement would undeniably have an effect on the integration process. We would expect government negotiators to be more constrained and tougher, as the Danish negotiators are.[8] But this would be offset to at least some extent by more reliable, efficient implementation. Member states could be sure that any agreement they reached would in fact be carried out, as the commitments of negotiators who have received parliamentary authorization would be more credible. Parliamentary involvement thus appears to be a much less significant threat to integration than many have argued.

This is a positive finding for those who support integration since the movement of national parliaments to exert their often latent powers is gaining momentum (Lequesne 1996, 77). As noted, all member states now have some version of the MRC. Some of these committees have been sending delegations to Denmark to gain an understanding of how the MRC operates so they can adapt their procedures to their own political systems. The three newest members of the EU, Sweden, Finland, and Austria, have studied Denmark's system intensively in their preparations for entry (Rösiö 1995). An Interparliamentary Conference of these bodies has begun meeting twice annually (Govaere and Hélin 1990), although it remains unclear whether much coordination has arisen from this particular forum. The Council's reluctant agreement to provide more information about votes and other details of its proceedings has resulted largely from parliamentary demands. While many other states may not reach the level of parliamentary influence seen in Denmark—this is hard to imagine, for example, in the disorganized Italian Parliament—the trend toward increasing formal involvement of parliaments is unmistakable. While this will have a substantial impact on negotiating processes, the evidence suggests that it will not introduce the level of inefficiency many fear and will bring measurable benefits. In addition, as elaborated subsequently, a system that relied on national parliamentary accountability would provide for the flexibility that will be necessary as some form of variable geometry emerges in the EU.

The Paradox of Subsidiarity: Regional Powers

National parliaments are not the only domestic actors with formal responsibility for implementation. Increasingly, subnational actors, such as regional governments, are gaining such responsibility. This trend is most marked in federal systems, such as Germany's, and in states that have relied on regional autonomy to deal with ethnic and linguistic conflicts, such as Spain and Belgium. Increased devolution to regions is one suggested remedy to the democratic deficit. Additionally, it raises questions similar to those raised by an increased role for parliaments: will devolution create severe inefficiencies? The answer I propose here is similar to my argument about national parliaments. An increased role for regions is likely, and not necessarily threatening to the process of integration, if it is confronted openly.

Looking at implementation records again provides a starting point to analyze the role of regions. We might expect that devolving responsibility to regions for implementation would lead to delays, as it would create yet another layer of responsibility and set of political concerns (From and Stava 1993). Evidence for this view comes in looking at the implementation records of Spain and, especially, Belgium (see fig. 5.2). In spite of being home to many EU institutions and apparently an enthusiastic supporter of integration, as of August 1992 Belgium had the worst implementation record in the Union. Analysts attribute this to the fact that, while responsibility for implementation lies with the regions, they are not consulted by ministers during EU negotiations (Defalque 1985, 19). Spain also has significant regional autonomy and has continued to have an implementation record that lags behind those of Portugal and Greece, which confronted similar problems of democratic consolidation and entered the Union at about the same time as Spain.

But Germany's record calls this generalization into question. Its federal system means that the German *Länder* are deeply involved in implementation of EU directives. Yet Germany has a very good implementation record. As in my analysis of parliamentary involvement, I would argue that this pattern is explained by the different ways that regional governments are integrated into the EU negotiating process. In Belgium and Spain, they are largely excluded and so are asked to implement legislation on which they have had no input. Not surprisingly, this creates problems. But in Germany the *Länder* are involved in the negotiating process early on (Hrbek 1992). They have long had a seat at the negotiating table, and their role in the negotiation process was increased as a condition for ratification of the Maastricht Treaty (Kirchner 1994, 259). This organized, early, and transparent method of bringing regions into the integration process means that their objections and potential difficulties of implementation can be anticipated, allowing for a smoother implementation process.

The role of regions is likely to grow for at least two reasons. The first, referred to earlier, is the acceptance of subsidiarity as the principle that should govern decisions about the appropriate level for policy making. The paradox of subsidiarity is that it was promoted, by the United Kingdom in particular, as a mechanism to shift power away from the Commission and back to the state level. But the logic of subsidiarity suggests that the appropriate level of decision making may not be the state but the subnational level. Proponents of subsidiarity and strong states may have thus backed themselves into a corner by having promoted a principle that has proven a powerful weapon in the hands of those who favor increased regional autonomy.

The second reason to expect increased regional influence has to do with the logic of economic integration itself. As Alesina and Spolaore (1994) demonstrate, economic integration removes one of the fundamental reasons for large states to hold together. Their model is specifically about the number of states we would expect to see under different conditions of economic integration. They find that economic integration across national boundaries decreases the economic advantages of large states and so predict an increase in the number of states as integration proceeds. Even if we do not see a formal increase in the number of states in an economically integrated Europe, the model suggests that we should see increased pressures for regional autonomy and smaller-scale policy making on many issues. When economic well-being is no longer dependent on the welfare of the state as a whole, as results when economic integration deepens, the argument for state-level policy making is weakened significantly. Instead, individuals can increase their well-being by forming small-scale groupings that make policy as a unit. This devolution allows more variety and flexibility in the nature of political arrangements without sacrificing the economic advantages of state-level policy making that existed prior to economic integration.

Both the underlying logic of integration and the political decision to adopt subsidiarity are creating pressures for increased regional autonomy and influence on EU policy making. A "Europe of the regions" will be a long time coming, as states will continue to safeguard their powers to make policy and actual economic integration, as opposed to formal integration, will take time to realize. However, short of this idealized outcome, we can expect increased regional activity and influence. EU and national institutions can best adapt to this process not by denying it but by developing structures through which regions have a greater say in EU negotiations, perhaps through the development of national-level mechanisms of representation. Failure to develop such mechanisms is sure to lead to delays and inefficiencies as regions acquire the right to implement EU legislation.

Implications

EU institutions suffer from weak patterns of representation and accountability. However, accepting that a problem exists does not lead logically to any particular solution. The number of potential reforms is infinite; a debate about the advantages and disadvantages of particular reforms dominated the 1996 IGC and will continue for many years afterward. I conclude this analysis of the challenges to EU institutions by arguing that current related developments in the structure of the EU imply that strengthening the EP will not, on its own, be an adequate solution to problems of the democratic deficit. While a powerful EP is consistent with the vision of an eventual "United States of Europe," the current movement of the EU is in a very different direction.

The two major changes in the EU's structure I would highlight here are its enlargement and the movement toward some form of different obligations for different member states. The ways in which patterns of obligation and cooperation may vary across member states are the source of rapidly proliferating "Eurojargon": Europe à la carte, variable geometry, flexible architecture, hard core, concentric circles, multispeed Europe, and so on.[9] Each of these terms denotes a different vision of the exact development of the EU. But common to them is the idea that not all members of the EU will have the same obligations in all issue areas. Those states with common interests in monetary union, for example, may be able to push ahead in this area while others stay behind, opt out, or accept some other form of monetary cooperation. The same applies to defense cooperation, common immigration rules, and countless other areas of EU policy making.

This development represents a fundamental shift in the nature of the EU. Initially, and until quite recently, all members were assumed to have accepted the same obligations. New members sometimes were given more time to adopt EU standards, but the assumption was that all states had the same obligations and duties, with only inconsequential delays in their acceptance by new members. As the EU has grown, both in the number of states it encompasses and the range of issues on which it makes policy, such an ideal seems increasingly unrealistic. While accepting a multispeed Europe is sure to have some negative consequences, particularly in the decline of transfers to poorer states, it seems inevitable. The entry of Sweden, Austria, and Finland is not likely to have major consequences for this process, as they are relatively rich states, well integrated into the Western European economy. But further enlargement to the East will accelerate the fragmentation of EU obligations, as the EU will be forced to deal with the difficulties of accommodating a group of poor, newly democratized states with foreign policy interests that may diverge significantly from those of the older members.

What does this imply for the development of institutions to improve representation and accountability? It suggests that putting sole emphasis on the EP as the appropriate arena in which to address such concerns would be a mistake. The Parliament is a federalist institution, making common policy for all member states and encouraging the development of political groupings that are not differentiated by state. How is such a body to make policy in areas where not all member states would be subject to its decisions? The logical, ethical, and institutional complexities of such a procedure would be mind-boggling. Instead, what would likely happen would be the development of a powerful EP whose jurisdiction will be limited to those few areas in which policy applies equally to all member states. Indeed, we see this process already, as the EP is excluded from participation in IGCs and ratification of amendments to the Rome Treaties and at Maastricht was excluded from two of the three "pillars" of European integration. Such a restricted EP role would leave unresolved the problems of democratic accountability in most issue areas.

The incongruity between a powerful EP and a multispeed Europe, whatever form it eventually takes, leads to the conclusion that many problems of representation and accountability must be addressed on the domestic level.[10] The analysis in this chapter suggests that movements in this direction will not necessarily pose the major threat to integration that many suppose. Coordination among national parliaments can enhance the effectiveness of both domestic oversight and international bargaining processes and deserves more serious study. To have any impact, such coordination depends on organization within national parliaments. National-level organization is occurring rapidly, suggesting that this necessary condition may be met. If so, coordination among parliaments could improve the quality of information available to them, allow them to learn from one another about institutional strategies for exercising oversight, and help mitigate the inefficiencies that many fear will result from greater parliamentary involvement. Developing workable systems that reach out to national parliaments and regions is likely the only solution that will allow states to trust that one another will actually implement EU agreements, a necessary condition for further economic and political integration.

Conclusion

Popular and scholarly concern about a democratic deficit in the EU rests on genuine problems of representation and accountability in EU institutions.

While concerns have been exaggerated by tactical mistakes on the part of the Council and Commission, particularly the rush to integration by elites at Maastricht, they cannot and should not be dismissed. Integration can best proceed not by sticking to the narrowly technocratic, elitist view of integration that has dominated analysis of the EU thus far but by developing well-organized and transparent mechanisms of representation and accountability. While it was possible for EU institutions to avoid developing such mechanisms previously, now that EU policy making reaches deeply into the traditional prerogatives of national parliaments and the daily lives of citizens, continued evasion of the problem will only hamstring prointegration forces.

The findings of this analysis of problems of representation and account-ability highlight some reasons for optimism, even as European integration reaches a particularly difficult phase. Some of the farthest reaching schemes for solving the democratic deficit are surely unworkable. But analyses that con-clude that even more modest steps in this direction will bring the process of integration to a screeching halt are misguided, as they rely on the mistaken assumption of a deep conflict between democracy and efficiency. The process of economic and political integration in Europe is highly institutionalized, but institutionalization has in the past often removed policy making from demo-cratic control. Those who favor continued integration should be as committed to increasing democratic representation and accountability as those who worry about democratic deficiencies per se.

NOTES

I would like to thank Jim Alt, Jeff Frieden, Geoff Garrett, Bob Keohane, Yves Meny, Andy Moravcsik, Ron Rogowski, and George Tsebelis for comments on earlier versions of this chapter.

1. Many references cited in this chapter refer to the EU as the European Com-munity, using its older name.

2. A fourth major EU institution, the European Court of Justice (ECJ), will not receive extensive analysis in this chapter. While the ECJ surely plays a major role in making policy in the EU (see Shapiro 1992 and Burley and Mattli 1993), most analyses of the democratic deficit have not focused on it. (For exceptions, see Boyce 1993, 458; and Caldeira and Gibson 1995.) If the ECJ were to step outside its current practice of acting in a politically unbiased manner, concerns about accountability would likely arise.

3. For an excellent introduction to such an analysis in the context of Europe, see Weiler 1993.

4. This argument follows a tradition that finds international organization conducive to the formation of executive cartels at the expense of the public interest (Vaubel 1986; Kaiser 1971).

5. For ease of illustration, the Commission is not included in this grossly simplified example. It could be included most simply by assuming it has preferences very close to those of the EP.

6. My thanks to Andy Moravcsik for clarifying this point.

7. The patterns of transposition examined here are very similar to those found in data on enforcement records. See Martin 1994, 18.

8. See Putnam 1988.

9. Von Hagen and Fratianni (this volume) provide a cogent discussion of the issues involved in moving toward a more fragmented pattern of policy making.

10. See Wallerstein (this volume) for a discussion of the ability of member states to carry out national policies under conditions of deep integration.

REFERENCES

Alesina, Alberto, and Enrico Spolaore. 1994. On the Number and Size of Nations. Harvard University. Manuscript.

Andersen, Svein S., and Kjell A. Elissen, eds. 1996. *The European Union: How Democratic Is It?* London: Sage.

Bogdanor, Vernon, and Geoffrey Woodcock. 1991. The European Community and Sovereignty. *Parliamentary Affairs* 44:481–92.

Boyce, Brigitte. 1993. The Democratic Deficit of the European Community. *Parliamentary Affairs* 46:458–77.

Bronckers, Marco C. E. J. 1989. Private Enforcement of 1992: Do Trade and Industry Stand a Chance against the Member States? *Common Market Law Review* 26:513–33.

Burley, Anne-Marie, and Walter Mattli. 1993. Europe before the Court: A Political Theory of Legal Integration. *International Organization* 47:41–76.

Caldeira, Gregory A., and James L. Gibson. 1995. The Legitimacy of the Court of Justice in the European Union: Models of Institutional Support. *American Political Science Review* 89:356–76.

Colchester, Nicholas, and David Buchan. 1990. *Europe Relaunched: Truths and Illusions on the Way to 1992.* London: Economist Books.

Commission of the European Communities. 1992. *The Principle of Subsidiarity.* Brussels: Commission of the European Communities. Communication of the Commission to the Council and the European Parliament.

Dahl, Robert A. 1956. *A Preface to Democratic Theory.* Chicago: University of Chicago Press.

Defalque, Lucette. 1985. Belgique: Synthése Nationale. In *The Implementation of EC Law by the Member States*, edited by Giuseppe Ciavarini Azzi. Maastricht: European Institute of Public Administration.

Duff, Andrew. 1994. Building a Parliamentary Europe. *Government and Opposition* 29:147–65.

Featherstone, Kevin. 1994. Jean Monnet and the "Democratic Deficit" in the European Union. *Journal of Common Market Studies* 32:149–70.

From, Johan, and Per Stava. 1993. Implementation of Community Law: The Last Stronghold of National Control? In *Making Policy in Europe: The Europeification of National Policy-Making*, edited by Svein S. Andersen and Kjell A. Eliassen. London: Sage.

Garrett, Geoffrey. 1995. From the Luxembourg Compromise to Codecision: Decision Making in the European Union. Stanford University. Manuscript.

Govaere, Inge, and Frédérique Hélin. 1990. Implementing the Internal Market: Problems and Perspectives. In *The 1992 Challenge at National Level*, edited by Jürgen Schwarze, Inge Govaere, Frédérique Hélin, and Peter Van den Bossche. Baden-Baden: Nomos Verlagsgesellschaft.

Haas, Ernst B. 1958. *The Uniting of Europe: Political, Economic, and Social Forces, 1950–1957*. Stanford: Stanford University Press.

Herman, Valentine, and Juliet Lodge. 1978. *The European Parliament and the European Community*. New York: St. Martin's.

Herman, Valentine, and Rinus van Schendelen, eds. 1979. *The European Parliament and the National Parliaments*. Westmead, Eng.: Saxon House.

Hrbek, Rudolf. 1992. The German Länder and EC Integration. *Journal of European Integration* 15:173–93.

Jacobs, Francis, Richard Corbett, and Michael Shackleton. 1992. *The European Parliament*. 2d ed. Essex: Longman.

Judge, David, and David Earnshaw. 1994. Weak European Parliament Influence? A Study of the Environment Committee of the European Parliament. *Government and Opposition* 29:262–76.

Kaiser, K. 1971. Transnational Relations as a Threat to the Democratic Process. *International Organization* 25:706–20.

Keohane, Robert O., and Stanley Hoffmann, eds. 1991. *The New European Community: Decisionmaking and Institutional Change*. Boulder: Westview.

Kirchner, Emil J. 1994. The European Community: A Transnational Democracy? In *Developing Democracy*, edited by Ian Budge and David McKay. London: Sage.

Laursen, Finn. 1996. The Role of the Commission. In Andersen and Eliassen 1996.

Lequesne, Christian. 1996. The French EU Decision-Making: Between Destabilization and Adaptation. In Andersen and Eliassen 1996.

Lodge, Juliet. 1996. The European Parliament. In Andersen and Eliassen 1996.

———. 1994. Transparency and Democratic Legitimacy. *Journal of Common Market Studies* 32:343–68.

Ludlow, Peter. 1991. The European Commission. In Keohane and Hoffmann 1991.

Marquand, David. 1981. Parliamentary Accountability and the European Community. *Journal of Common Market Studies* 19:221–36.

Martin, Lisa L. 1994. The Influence of National Parliaments on European Integration. Working Paper, 94–10. Center for International Affairs, Harvard University.

Milward, Alan S. 1992. *The European Rescue of the Nation-State.* Berkeley: University of California Press.

Møller, J. Ørstrøm. 1983. Danish EC Decision-Making: An Insider's View. *Journal of Common Market Studies* 21:245–60.

Moravcsik, Andrew. 1994. Why the European Community Strengthens the State. Paper presented at the American Political Science Association annual meeting, New York.

———. 1993. Preferences and Power in the European Community: A Liberal Inter-governmentalist Approach. *Journal of Common Market Studies* 31:473–523.

Morgan, Robert, ed. 1994. *Guide to the European Parliament, 1994.* London: Times Books.

Niblock, Michael. 1971. *The EEC: National Parliaments in Community Decision-Making.* London: Chatham House.

Nicoll, William. 1994. The European Parliament's Post-Maastricht Rules of Procedure. *Journal of Common Market Studies* 32:403–10.

Nugent, Neill. 1991. *The Government and Politics of the European Community,* 2d ed. Durham: Duke University Press.

Putnam, Robert D. 1988. Diplomacy and Domestic Politics: The Logic of Two-Level Games. *International Organization* 42 (Summer): 427–60.

Rasmussen, Hjalte. 1988. Denmark. In *Making European Policies Work: The Implementation of Community Legislation in the Member States,* edited by Heinrich Siedentopf and Jacques Ziller. Vol. 2. London: Sage.

Rösiö, Ninna. 1995. Bridging the Democratic Gap and Strengthening the Public Support for the EU. Center for International Affairs, Harvard University. Manuscript.

Scott, Andrew, John Peterson, and David Millar. 1994. Subsidiarity: A "Europe of the Regions" v. the British Constitution? *Journal of Common Market Studies* 32:47–67.

Scott-Hopkins, James. 1994. Radical Changes Have Made the Parliament Unrecognisable. In Morgan 1994.

Shapiro, Martin. 1992. The European Court of Justice. In *Euro-Politics: Institutions and Policymaking in the "New" European Community,* edited by Alberta M. Sbragia. Washington, D.C.: Brookings Institution.

Toonen, Theo A. J. 1992. Europe of the Administrations: The Challenges of '92 (and Beyond). *Public Administration Review* 52:108–15.

Tsebelis, George. 1994. The Power of the European Parliament as a Conditional Agenda Setter. *American Political Science Review* 88:128–42.

———. 1995a. Will Maastricht Reduce the "Democratic Deficit?" Paper presented at the American Political Science Association annual meeting, Chicago.

———. 1995b. Conditional Agenda Setting and Decision Making inside the European Parliament. *Journal of Legislative Studies* 1:65–93.

Vaubel, Roland. 1986. A Public Choice Approach to International Organization. *Public Choice* 51:39–57.

Wallace, Helen. 1973. *National Governments and the European Communities.* London: Chatham House.

Weiler, Joseph H. H. 1993. After Maastricht: Community Legitimacy in Post-1992 Europe. In *Singular Europe: Economy and Polity of the European Community after 1992,* edited by William James Adams. Ann Arbor: University of Michigan Press.

Wessels, Wolfgang. 1996. The Modern West European State and the European Union: Democratic Erosion or a New Kind of Polity? In Andersen and Eliassen 1996.

Wester, Robert. 1992. The European Commission. In *The Intergovernmental Conference on Political Union,* edited by Finn Laursen and Sophie Vanhoonacker. Dordrecht, Netherlands: Martinus Nijhoff.

Westlake, Martin. 1994. *A Modern Guide to the European Parliament.* London: Pinter.

Williams, Shirley. 1991. Sovereignty and Accountability in the European Community. In Keohane and Hoffmann 1991.

CHAPTER 6

Banking Regulation with Variable Geometry

Jürgen von Hagen and Michele Fratianni

I. Introduction

Toward the end of the current century and well into the next, European integration will face two conflicting forces, enlargement and deepening of the European Union (EU). The impulse to enlarge comes from the restructuring of the political map following the end of the Cold War. Since the breakup of the socialist bloc, countries of Eastern and Central Europe have expressed a strong desire to join the EU to speed up the transformation and modernization of their economies. The EU has signed Europe Agreements with the four Visegrad countries (Poland, the Czech Republic, the Slovak Republic, and Hungary), the three Baltic republics (Estonia, Latvia, and Lithuania), Bulgaria, Romania, and Slovenia. These agreements are "an important step toward economic integration in Europe" (Baldwin 1996, 4).[1] Of current EU members, Germany is the keenest for eastern enlargement. Chancellor Helmut Kohl worked hard at "his" Essen summit in the fall of 1994 to obtain a firm promise for an eastern enlargement in the foreseeable future from the EU. German politicians fear that otherwise they will be left alone in dealing with political instabilities in Eastern and Central Europe and that involvement in Eastern and Central European politics might draw Germany out of the EU.[2] Opposition to enlargement stems from its likely impact on redistributive policies. Since the new members will contribute little to the Community's resources in relation to their requests for transfers, those members—Greece, Portugal, and Spain—and those sectors—mainly agriculture—that are now the main beneficiaries are also the main opponents of an eastern enlargement (Baldwin 1994, chap. 7). To keep the

159

EU from becoming too oriented toward the east, the Mediterranean countries have begun to pursue a southern enlargement, lining up Malta and Cyprus as the next candidates for membership and giving Turkey a closer association.

The impetus to deepen European integration comes mainly from the older EU members who wish to strengthen European political integration and solidarity. Deepening European integration includes the realization of European monetary union (EMU) but also closer cooperation in areas of social policy (e.g., the Social Charter), foreign policy, and home affairs, and, ultimately, the vision of a European political union. As deepening has proceeded, conflicts have arisen also among the existing members. The United Kingdom, for example, has objected to the drive for EMU and has asked for and obtained an option, formalized in the Treaty on European Union (TEU, also known as the Maastricht Treaty), not to participate in monetary integration. Denmark has obtained a similar option. Other member states, like Italy, while sharing the objective of monetary unification, may find they cannot meet the criteria for joining EMU by the prescribed deadline.

Enlargement will add additional tensions because it will slow down the process of deepening. First, deepening raises the entry hurdle for the newcomers (Baldwin 1994). Second, the prospect of having to include less developed and politically less stable countries in deeper forms of European integration reduces the value of integration for old EU members striving for further deepening (von Hagen 1995). Third, enlargement will raise the number of members that does not share the founders' vision of a European political union. This will make it harder to obtain the necessary consensus for deepening the community.

The growing dissatisfaction of those members who wish to go forward with deepening and feel that they are being held back by the others has led to the concept of *variable geometry* (VG). First mentioned by the late President François Mitterrand in a message to the French people on December 31, 1990, the idea was developed by Karl Lamers of the German Christian Democrats (CDU 1994) and by Eduard Balladur (1994) in a response to that essay.[3] At the heart of VG lies the distinction between a core and a periphery of the EU. The core includes what all members have in common. The periphery contains those policies that are shared by some but not all EU members. Thus, the principle of VG is that it does not require all members to participate in all areas of integration (Fratianni 1995b). This stands in contrast to the traditional doctrine that all EU members strive to participate fully in all areas of common or Community policies. VG would allow different members to achieve different degrees of integration not only temporarily—allowing new members time to achieve the common level of integration has been a principle of European integration since the first enlargement in the 1970s—but permanently.

The TEU incorporates some elements of variability but not to the extent of VG. One such element is manifested in the derogations the United Kingdom, Denmark, and Sweden obtained from EMU. Another is the exemption the United Kingdom obtained from the social union. In the most recent enlargement, Sweden even obtained an exemption from the Single Market, though only in a negligible area.[4] However, these exemptions and derogations are exceptional and, being the product of international treaty negotiations, hard to repeat. Recent proposals go beyond that and intend to introduce variability as a normal characteristic in European integration.[5]

This chapter explores the political economy of VG in the EU using banking regulation as an example. Banking regulation is an interesting case for two reasons. First, given the role of banking in financial intermediation, money creation, and the payment mechanism, this industry fits into two distinct EU activities. As part of the financial industry, banking fits into the Single Market Program, a core and common area of the EU; for the rest, banking fits into the EMU category. While EMU is conventionally regarded as a common area of integration like the Single Market Program, tensions among the old members and between the old and new members are likely to make it more limited in scope. Second, integration of banking regulation creates both positive and negative externalities for EU countries, depending on their different stages of financial development. Negative as well as positive externalities are of particular interest to us because they influence the nature of VG. Generally speaking, the core will be defined in terms of activities that generate gains for all member countries, whereas peripheries include activities that may generate negative externalities.

Our central message is that the German version of VG promotes compromises among countries pursuing different goals for integration in the same area but that it also has a built-in risk that may lower the likelihood of an agreement and may in fact lead to no integration. The French version of VG promotes the formation of different coalitions among countries and a larger degree of variation in European integration. It turns out—in a historical oddity—that German interests would be better served by the French proposal than the German, whereas a country like Italy—and also France—ought to prefer the German proposal to the French.

The plan of this chapter is as follows. Section 2 reviews banking regulation in the EU. Section 3 defines the concept of VG. Section 4 analyzes the relevant themes of political economy using banking regulation as an example: the choice of a particular form of VG and the treatment of banking regulation within it. Section 5 presents the main conclusions.

2.   Principles of Banking Regulation in the EC

2.1.   Reasons for Financial Regulation

Two basic motives explain financial regulation. One reason for regulating the financial industry is the same as for regulating any other industry, namely, to protect producers from the effects of competition. The other motive for financial regulation—one that is usually emphasized in the literature—finds its raison d'être in market failures. Along this second dimension, it is useful to distinguish three reasons, each leading to different modes and instruments of regulation.[6] The first is the protection of small depositors against the risk of bank failure. It is motivated by the observation that small depositors find it excessively costly to monitor the lending activities of their banks and are therefore unable to prevent banks from pursuing risky lending strategies. Small depositors, therefore, are exposed to excessive risk and supply suboptimal amounts of savings to the banking sector.

Banks can insure their deposits to avoid this problem. But deposit insurance is difficult to organize on a market basis because information asymmetries between the insurer and the bank make it impossible to price deposit risk in an actuarially fair way, and mispricing induces moral hazard on the part of the insured (Chan, Greenbaum, and Thakor 1992). As a result, bank deposits are commonly insured by government agencies or through cooperative industry arrangements promoted and enforced by the government. Banks are typically charged flat fees for the insurance—as was the case with the prereform Federal Deposit Insurance Corporation (FDIC) in the United States. The resulting incentive for depositors to reduce their monitoring activities can be mitigated by setting upper limits on the insurable amounts. To address the moral hazard problems for the banks, the providers of deposit insurance typically introduce other elements of banking regulation such as capital and publication requirements.[7]

The second reason for financial regulation is to prevent financial contagion, that is, the effects that large withdrawals of deposits at one bank may have on the industry. Financing illiquid assets with liquid liabilities is a central activity of banks. The mismatch in maturity between bank assets and liabilities creates the risk that depositors will withdraw their funds from a bank when even a slight suspicion arises that the bank is unable to repay its liabilities (see, e.g., Diamond and Dybvig 1983). Since the bank's reserves are limited, each depositor wants to be first in line to obtain his deposit before the bank shuts down; hence the self-propelling nature of the bank run. If depositors at other banks read the closure of one bank as a signal that their banks are also in financial trouble, the run can spread (Tirole 1992).

Bank panics can be prevented by strengthening the credibility of the banks' promise to honor their liabilities. Regulatory strategies to prevent bank runs involve measures to convince depositors of the financial soundness of the banking sector, such as limiting the risk exposure of the banks with prudential rules and forcing banks to hold sufficient reserves to meet sudden increases in the demand for cash. Furthermore, bank panics can be prevented by a credible lender of last resort (LLR) that guarantees the liquidity of the banking system. If depositors are assured that banks can always obtain the necessary reserves to pay out their deposits, then the value of being first in line disappears and bank panics do not arise. Note that this bank-runs-related LLR (R-LLR) function addresses a different type of problem than deposit insurance. Deposit insurance comes into play when the bank's liabilities exceed the value of its assets—that is, the bank is insolvent—whereas R-LLR aims at correcting an externality that results from maturity transformation by solvent banks.

The third reason for financial regulation is to preserve the integrity of payment mechanisms (Goodhart and Schoenmaker 1993; Hartman 1995). Payment systems help to economize on the reserve medium (mostly central bank money) and avoid long delays in payment. They create credit relations among the participants during the time interval between the initiation and the final settlement of payments. This is particularly true in *net* settlement systems, in which funds are transferred only on the basis of the net interbank positions at the end of a settlement period but also in *gross* settlement systems, in which funds are transferred for every transaction (if such systems contain overdraft facilities.) Thus, payment systems create their own credit risk. If a participant proves unable to meet its obligations, other participants may be affected, given the interdependence of credit relations. The system would then grind to a halt and all payments would have to unwind to isolate the failing institution from other participants, a procedure that would be lengthy, costly, and at times impossible.

To avoid such a breakdown, the clearing agent, often the central bank operating the system, must stand ready to provide the system with the necessary reserves if one or more participants is unable to honor its liabilities. Thus, the smooth operation of payment systems demands another, payment-related (P-LLR) lender of last resort. To reduce the credit risk shifted on the P-LLR provider, mechanisms like overdraft, float pricing, and collateral can be used. However, credit risk is not completely eliminated unless transactions are settled in real time, on a gross basis, and without recourse to overdraft facilities, a costly procedure.

The P-LLR function is quite different from the R-LLR function. The latter focuses on liquidity in the context of credits and debits that banks create voluntarily after assessing their counterparts. In contrast, a payment system makes banks extend credit to other banks without choice or assessment of their counterparts, as these credits result from the activities of other banks (Angelini and Passacantando 1993; Goodhart and Schoenmaker 1993). For this reason, regulatory provisions surrounding the P-LLR and R-LLR functions are different. R-LLR regulation focuses on the quality of the bank's assets, reserves, and capital. In contrast, P-LLR regulation requires information about the quality of risk controls, computing, backup facilities, and network technologies over and above information about the solvency of the bank.

Banking regulation in these three areas can and does involve different institutions. Deposit insurance, LLR functions, and prudential rules (inclusive of capital adequacy ratios) can be delivered cooperatively by the banking industry, the central bank, another government agency specializing in these activities, or a mixture of all three.[8] In Germany, for example, deposit insurance is provided by an industry fund operating under the auspices of the Bundesbank;[9] prudential rules and their enforcement are the authority of the independent Federal Regulatory Authority for Financial Institutions, while payment-systems-related regulation falls under the jurisdiction of the Bundesbank. The ability of a central bank to provide, in principle, unlimited liquidity by creating claims against itself makes this institution the most credible LLR provider.

These three types of banking regulation involve the reallocation of risk and therefore a wealth transfer. But those who benefit are not the same in the three cases. Deposit insurance (particularly when the size of insurable deposits is limited) primarily benefits small savers. Prevention of bank panics primarily benefits equity owners of banks that are financially sound but would suffer from panics otherwise, as well as those on the other side of the maturity transformation provided by the banking sector, namely, individuals and firms that borrow from the banks. Securing the smooth functioning of the payment system generates a benefit for the banks and the users of the medium of exchange.[10]

In an international setting, the identification of the primary beneficiaries of banking regulation raises interesting and more complex issues. First, governments have a greater incentive to protect domestic depositors against the risk of bank failure than do foreign depositors. If deposit insurance is administered by a government agency or a central bank, it involves taxation of the public for the benefit of bank depositors. Since a transfer of tax revenues to foreigners is not politically attractive, governments tend to be reluctant to rescue foreign bank depositors and delay payments or refrain from honoring their obligations altogether if deposit losses are large.[11] The failure of Banco Ambrosiano in 1983 illustrates this point. The Italian Banco Ambrosiano Spa controlled a Luxembourg holding company, BAH, which became involved in unauthorized and dubious transactions not properly scrutinized by either the Italian or the Luxembourg regulators. When the failure of the holding company brought down the Italian bank:

> All the creditors of Banco Ambrosiano Spa were repaid promptly, creditors of BAH received only partial repayment after considerable delay. Disregarding the question of whether official supervision prevents bank failures, sophisticated market participants inferred that in the event of trouble, *governments are unlikely to assist entities for which they do not have primary supervisory responsibility.* (Herring and Litan 1995, 102; emphasis ours)

Second, governments do have an incentive to extend the LLR coverage to foreign banks operating in their countries, since a run on or the illiquidity of a foreign bank operating in the domestic market may spill over to the domestic banking sector. Goodhart and Schoenmaker's survey of bank failures (1993) supports that point by illustrating governments' interest in rescuing foreign-owned banks operating in domestic markets.[12] In contrast, governments are unlikely to care much about the ripples financially troubled, domestic banks may cause in foreign markets. This is nicely illustrated in the Herstatt case (von Hagen 1992) in which the German authorities closed down the operations of the bank after the German market ended but while the New York market was still in operation, not worrying about the financial distress this caused for Herstatt's New York creditors in unsettled daily transactions. By implication, governments will be reluctant to stand by as providers of LLR functions to domestic banks operating mainly in foreign economies. This, in turn, means that the incentive to enforce domestic regulation on banks operating abroad to reduce the risk exposure of foreign LLR providers is weak, since the benefits of enforcement accrue to the foreign government.[13]

2.2. Regulation and Competition

Regulation, even where socially desirable, raises the cost of doing business. Regulated financial institutions offer lower yields on their deposits and charge higher interest rates on their assets than unregulated institutions. Countries with tighter regulatory regimes offer more protection to depositors but lose business to countries with looser regulatory regimes. The birth and expansion of the Eurocurrency markets were driven largely by the fact that the host countries (where offshore banks are located) compete with home countries through lower regulatory burden.[14]

A second link between competition and regulation revolves around the institutional design of banking regulation and, in particular, deposit insurance (Goodhart and Schoenmaker 1993). In many European countries, regulation and protection of depositors were traditionally organized on the basis of close cooperation between industry organizations and the central bank or a government agency. Such cooperative arrangements become more difficult to maintain in an environment of international competition for two reasons: competition tends to destroy the traditional, insider-club nature of industry relations, and banks acquire additional activities, such as insurance, resulting in a fuzzier industry structure than the traditional one. The increasing intensity of competition has, therefore, induced a tendency to develop more formal structures of regulation and deposit insurance, turning away from the traditional approach.

2.3. The European Approach to Regulation

EU banking regulations distinguish prudential supervision, deposit insurance, and maintenance of payments systems. This distinction mixes elements of all three basic functions of regulation, which, as argued in section 2.2, all involve elements of prudential supervision. According to the Second Banking Directive of 1989, prudential supervision falls under the home-country principle. Banks are regulated by the relevant authorities of their home countries irrespective of where they do business in the EU, and regulatory authorities have the right and the obligation to regulate and supervise the activities of all banks chartered in their countries regardless of where these activities are performed. Since all member states accept this principle, national regulatory standards are mutually recognized.

Mutual recognition works if the participants trust one another and agree that the lowest national standard in the group is an acceptable minimum standard of regulation for all or if the group has negotiated a common minimum standard. To facilitate trust and agreement, mutual recognition requires sufficient homogeneity of preferences. Through a variety of directives, such as the Own Fund Directive, the Solvency Directive, and the Large Exposure Directive, the EU has supplemented home-country rule by minimum standards. This strategy was deemed superior to the alternative of ex ante coordination that might provide a first-best solution but is more difficult to implement (Fratianni 1995a).

With the Directive on Deposit Guarantee Schemes, passed in May 1994, home-country rule has been extended to the area of deposit insurance. All financial institutions must participate in deposit insurance schemes. Beginning on July 1, 1995, deposit insurance schemes must provide insurance for all deposits with maximum coverage no less than 20,000 ECUs.[15] Introducing home-country rule in this area implies that depositors in each country face different deposit risks at domestic and foreign banks. A bank operating in a foreign country can join the host country's deposit scheme voluntarily if that scheme provides higher coverage than does the scheme of its home country.

The home-country principle does not apply with regard to regulation aimed at the maintenance of payment systems. All European central banks are involved in this area of regulation, even those, like the Bundesbank and the Danish Nationalbank, which are not involved in matters of prudential supervision. This is a consequence of the fact that all European central banks are engaged in the operation of national payment systems.[16] As each central bank remains responsible for the functioning of the payment system in its home country, subsidiaries of foreign banks are subject to the regulations of the national payment system such as solvency requirements, minimum transaction volumes, participation fees, technical requirements, and certification by the central bank. This principle has been maintained recently by the Working Group on EC Payment Systems, a committee of EC central banks (Hartmann 1995). It is partially inconsistent with the principle of mutual recognition because the national authorities charged with the maintenance of the payment system need information and hence must rely on the monitoring activities of the regulatory agencies involved in ordinary banking regulation as regards foreign banks.

TABLE 6.1.   The TEU on Banking Regulation, Supervision, and Payment Mechanism

The European System of Central Banks (ESCB) is assigned the role of promoting "the smooth operation of payment systems" (Council of European Communities, 1992, protocol 3, Art. 3.1, 149).

"The ESCB shall contribute to the smooth conduct of policies pursued by the competent authorities relating to the prudential supervision of credit institutions and the stability of the financial sytem" (protocol 3, Art. 3.3, 149).

"The ECB [European Central Bank] and national central banks may provide facilities, and the ECB may make regulations, to ensure efficient and sound clearing and payment systems within the Community and with other countries" (protocol 3, Art. 22, 158).

"The ECB may offer advice to and be consulted by the Council, the Commission and the competent authorities of the Member States on the scope and implementation of Community legislation relating to the prudential supervision of credit institutions and to the stability of the financial system" (protocol 3, Art. 25.1, 159).

"The ECB may perform specific tasks concerning policies relating to the prudential supervision of credit institutions with the exception of insurance undertakings" (protocol 3, Art. 25.2, 159).

"The EMI [European Monetary Institute] shall . . . facilitate the use of the ECU and oversee its development, including the smooth functioning of the ECU clearing system" (protocol 4, Art. 4.1, 173).

"The EMI shall in particular . . . promote the efficiency of cross-border payments" (protocol 4, Art. 4.2, 174).

A division exists among the member countries concerning the degree of involvement of the central bank in prudential supervision.[17] Strong and weak central bank involvement coexist: among the 14 current central banks in the EU, six—the Austrian, Belgian, Danish, German, Finnish, and Swedish central banks—are not involved in supervision at all or have only a small administrative role. In these countries, banking supervision falls under the jurisdiction of separate government agencies. The remaining central banks have substantial responsibilities in this area. This division is reflected in the text of the TEU, which, in contrast with EMU, is vague about banking regulation and supervision beyond the regulation and supervision of ECU clearing systems and cross-border payments (see table 6.1).

In sum, prudential supervision, deposit insurance, and, though not mentioned explicitly, R-LLR are likely to remain under national authority and, furthermore, will not necessarily be an area of competence of central banks, since they currently fall under the competence of other government agencies or industry arrangements in some countries. Even in the domain of payment systems, the current interpretation is that the treaty places the responsibility with the national central banks rather than the ECB (Hartmann 1995).

2.4. The Irrelevance of Home-Country Rule in the EU

The assignment of regulatory competencies in the EU reveals a peculiar pattern. Rather than distinguishing between the different types of regulation, the EU puts all prudential rules legislation and its enforcement under the home-country principle. Presumably, this assignment was designed to facilitate competition in banking and among national regulatory approaches. In contrast, regulatory activities involving resource transfers generally remain under the jurisdictions of the host countries. Deposit insurance, which in principle falls under the home-country rule, leaves banks the option to apply the host-country principle.

The assignment of home- and host-country rules according to instruments rather than functions of banking regulation will make the home-country rule practically irrelevant for the EU. We base this prediction on the fact that the current system creates an overwhelming incentive for banks to charter in the national markets where they operate and adopt the different national regulatory regimes through subsidiaries rather than operating from a single base, across borders, through branches. This incentive results from the competitive disadvantages foreign branches face in domestic markets. To begin with, deposit insurance of a foreign branch lacks credibility due to the home government's reluctance to effect transfers to citizens of other countries. This implies that depositors will turn away from foreign branches unless they are compensated by an appropriate risk premium. In order to avoid such premiums, banks will find it more attractive to set up subsidiaries, under national licenses, and will accept the host country's regulatory requirements in order to participate in the national deposit insurance scheme. Furthermore, the inability to participate in the national payment system restricts foreign branches in competing with domestic banks. This, again, creates an incentive to accept the regulatory requirements of the host country in order to enjoy the benefits of the national payment system. Last but not least, R-LLR is bound to remain a national function if for no other reason than that it has been ignored by current EU regulations.

In sum, notwithstanding the prevalence of the home-country rule, banks have strong incentives to conform to national regulation. As a result, member states will continue to use diversity in regulation as barriers to entry. On this basis, we will proceed on the assumption that countries can unilaterally set regulatory standards for their own markets.

3.   Concepts of Variable Geometry

The incentives national governments will retain in operating different regulatory systems make it unlikely that governments will readily agree on a common EU-wide standard. This raises the possibility of VG in the financial sphere. With VG, members of the EU have choices regarding the policy areas in which they wish to participate with other countries in common, integrated policies and arrangements. The important constitutional question is to what extent these choices must be structured and limited.

The most radical form of variability is Europe à la carte. *À la carte* means literally that each member country would be free to "pick and choose" the areas of integration in which it wants to participate. There would be no restrictions on how policy spheres could be combined, meaning that each of them would be treated independently. The attractiveness of this model lies in the fact that no member is constrained to accept any policy that it dislikes.

VG is more restrictive than Europe à la carte. Critical to VG is the distinction between a common *core* of integration, to which all EU members must adhere, and a set of *peripheries* or optional integration areas. Also critical to VG is the question of what goes in the core and what goes in the peripheries.[18] There are two aspects to this question: (1) which policy domains must be in the core? and, (2) by which principles can members choose among peripheries? Three principles apply to the first aspect. First, the core establishes basic values that all EU members share. The free movement of goods, services, capital, and individuals—that is, the Single Market—is surely part of the core. In contrast, neither monetary integration (MU) nor social policy belongs to the core in light of the fact that the EU has already granted "derogations" in these policy domains to some member countries.[19]

Second, the core can be regarded as an instrument for constructing package deals. Take the Single Market as an example. In the past, member countries were unwilling to accept particular elements of the Single Market unless they were compensated for adjustment costs. The EU has been able to push forward the integration process by offering attractive side deals to those members. The existence and growth of regional, structural, and social funds must be interpreted as part of these package deals to expand the size and depth of the core.

Third, the core must include all policies that regulate the creation of peripheral spheres of integration, that is, it must include the constitution of the EU. As an implication of these three criteria, coordination of policies in peripheral areas can take place only if it does not endanger the integrity of the core.

4. Banking Regulation and Variable Geometry

In this section, we explore how VG might work for the EU using banking regulation as a specific example. We proceed in three steps. In the next section, we consider where banking regulation should be placed in the framework of VG. Following that, we discuss the organization of the periphery in the context of banking regulation and EMU. Finally, we bring enlargement into the picture to show how it affects VG.

4.1. Banking Regulation: Core or Periphery?

We have seen that the motivation for banking regulation can differ. Deposit insurance aims at protecting the wealth of small savers and falls primarily under the jurisdiction of the country where the protected individuals live. LLR functions aim at correcting negative externalities and also fall under the jurisdication of the host market, where the benefits from a well-functioning payment mechanism and a stable financial system accrue.

The incentive to coordinate or integrate LLR functions derives from the benefit to create larger, integrated markets for banking services and payment systems. Both offer economies of scale and scope. In addition, an integrated banking market offers a more efficient allocation of capital, and an integrated payment system generates lower transaction costs in international trade. The impetus for creating integrated banking markets and an integrated payment system will thus come primarily from countries with highly developed and competitive banking industries that wish to expand and from countries with export-oriented industries that wish to rid themselves of barriers to trade created by separation of banking markets and payment systems. In contrast, countries with weak and noncompetitive banking industries will resist such efforts. As noted in section 2, one motivation for regulating the financial sector is to protect producers from competition. Weak incumbents put pressure on regulators, who tend to identify with the interests of the industry.[20]

Suppose that all EU members have the choice to participate in free integrated trade in goods and services, integrated markets for banking services, an integrated payment system, and integrated LLR functions. There are three possible configurations: countries with a competitive banking industry and a competitive goods industry would wish to participate in free trade and integrated banking markets and payment systems. Countries with competitive industries and noncompetitive banking sectors would prefer free trade in goods and services and a common payment system, but they would use domestic banking regulation as a barrier to entry into the domestic banking market. Countries with noncompetitive goods industries and competitive banking industries would wish to participate in an integrated banking market but would use trade restrictions to protect their domestic industries. Countries with noncompetitive goods and banking industries would opt to keep trade barriers in both areas.

The problem with Europe à la carte is that it does not encourage deals among the second and third groups in which each accepts open markets where it is weak in exchange for open markets where it is strong. Europe à la carte would mean, therefore, free trade in goods and banking services only among the countries belonging to the first group. Disaggregating "goods" and "banking industries" further, one can see that Europe à la carte would lead to a patchwork of sectoral free trade agreements rather than an integrated European market, as each country has some strong and some weak industries. Thus, by offering unstructured variability, Europe à la carte destroys the Single Market in goods, services, and financial assets.

Let us now assume that the EU will adopt VG as an organizing principle and that free trade in goods and banking will be in the core because of positive externalities. If banking regulation is excluded from the core, countries with weak banking industries can use regulation to erect barriers to entry around their home markets. In this sense, uncoordinated banking regulation will threaten the proper working of the core. This line of reasoning presumably led the EU to introduce the home-country rule. However, as has been argued, the home-country rule is unfit to achieve the desired results. The proper functioning of the core instead demands a minimal degree of coordination of banking regulation.

Since the host-country principle effectively applies, minimum standards are not relevant here. What matters, rather, is to limit the misuse of regulatory provisions as barriers to entry, that is, to limit variation in regulatory provisions and assure equal treatment for domestic and foreign banks. Such monitoring of national regulatory activities could become an activity of the European Commission, whose task would be to enforce the proper working of the core. Beyond that, national regulatory functions could operate independently.

With an integrated market for financial services as part of the core, bank crises arising in one country may spill over to another. If, for example, branches of Dutch banks become very active in northern Germany, a run on banks in Rotterdam could easily spread to Dutch banks in Bremen and Hamburg and from there to other banks in the German market. Thus, integration of banking markets creates a joint responsibility for maintaining the stability of the banking industry. This shared responsibility implies that there is a need to coordinate R-LLR across countries, too. Otherwise, national R-LLR providers would have an incentive to free ride on other countries' providers. There would be underprovision of R-LLR in the integrated banking market, generating too much market instability in equilibrium. But the independent provision of R-LLR by different governments in an integrated banking market is inefficient, since prudential rules set by one provider affect the risk exposure of other providers of R-LLR. Finally, R-LLR requires rapid action concerning banks located in various places in the integrated market. Independent providers find it hard to move fast.

In conclusion, R-LLR belongs to the core either under a common, European provider or through cooperation by national providers operating under identical prudential and regulatory standards.

Things are different with regard to deposit insurance. Again, some coordination is necessary to prevent countries from misusing deposit-insurance-related regulation as barriers to entry. An incentive to integrate deposit insurance schemes comes from the incentive to pool risks. This incentive is independent of the existence of a common market in banking services; it may even be stronger where such a market does not exist, since market segmentation would reduce the correlation of default risk across banks. Since each government is interested in protecting its own citizens, the host-country principle creates no free riding among independent, national providers. Thus, apart from the risk-pooling incentive, there is no compelling reason to coordinate deposit insurance.

Just like other forms of insurance, the interest in pooling risks is different among countries whose banking systems have achieved different degrees of financial stability. Countries with weak systems want to pool with countries with strong systems, but not vice versa. This implies that forcing countries to pool deposit insurance will induce those countries whose banks are low risks to opt for a low, suboptimal level of insurance. Consequently, given the potential for a negative externality, deposit insurance should be placed in the EU periphery countries with similar banking industries so that they can pool risk if they wish.

However, there is a link between R-LLR functions and deposit insurance that arises from the sequence of events. It is plausible that the LLR provider will be called first to rescue a bank; that provider is uncertain about the nature of the problem but injects reserves to keep the payment system running and prevent the bank failure at the same time. Deposit insurance becomes relevant only when the LLR provider subsequently realizes that the bank is insolvent and not simply illiquid. Thus, an incentive may arise for the LLR provider to judge in favor of closing down too often in order to preserve its own financial integrity. In this way, the LLR provider can shift risk to the deposit insurance provider.

This externality would suggest that LLR and deposit insurance be integrated and made part of the core if LLR is part of the core to begin with. However, the externality can be eliminated by setting up a system of arbitration to which the deposit insurance provider can appeal if it feels that the LLR provider has misbehaved. The arbitrator could then force the LLR provider to repay the insurance provider. Anticipating arbitration would eliminate the incentive to shift risk.

Finally, the P-LLR function does not belong to the core, as it is intimately linked to the payments system, which is not itself part of the core.

4.2.   Organizing the Periphery

Two approaches have been proposed regarding the organization of peripheral areas under VG: the German *concentric circles* approach (CDU 1994) and the French *excentric circles* (Balladur 1994). Figures 6.1 and 6.2 give a visual interpretation of the two alternatives. In both proposals all member countries participate in the integration core of the EU. Under excentric circles, different members may participate in different peripheral policy areas; the sets need not be fully overlapping but can partially overlap or not overlap at all. Under concentric circles, the structure of peripheries is more restrictive. Starting from the core, a member can enter a particular sphere of integration only if it participates in all the preceding ones. Thus, a subset of members may participate, say, in a common social policy, a smaller subset in MU, and an even smaller subset in a joint defense policy.

The figures reveal two important differences between the two models. One is that only the concentric circles define a sequence of steps countries must take to go from the core to the highest sphere of integration. In contrast, with excentric circles, each country can join the peripheral arrangement which it prefers.

The second difference is that, with concentric circles, there is at most one peripheral arrangement for each sphere of integration. A country that wishes

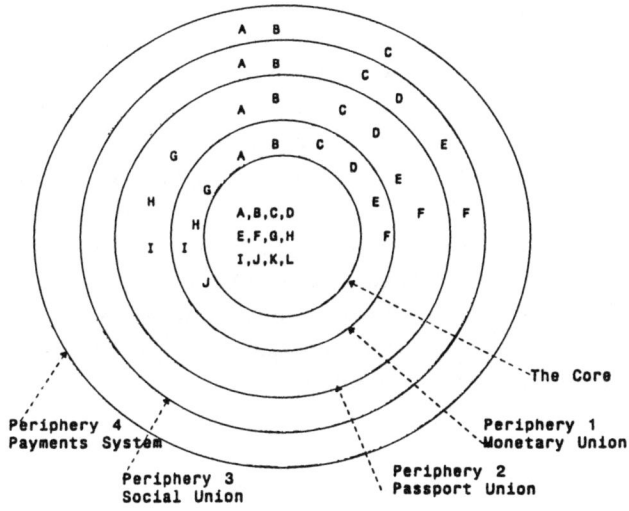

Fig. 6.1. Variable geometry: concentric circles

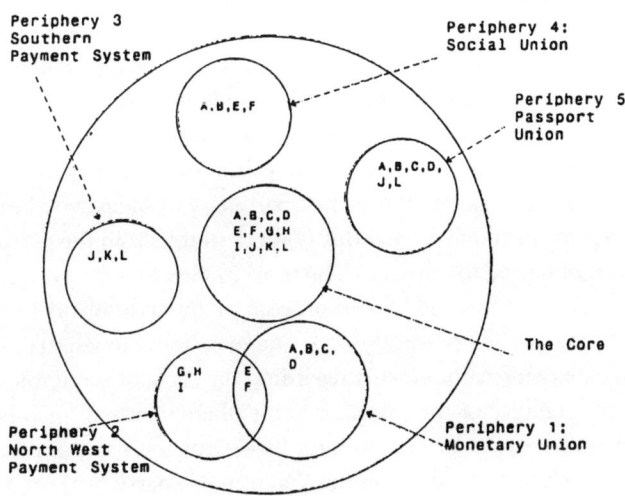

Fig. 6.2. Variable geometry: excentric circles

to participate in a particular sphere can only join the existing group or join no group. In contrast, excentric circles include the possibility of multiple cooperative arrangements among EU countries for the same field of policy, such as multiple, separate payment systems among different member countries. Similarly, excentric circles allow countries to overcome the problem of increasing heterogeneity of EU members as enlargement proceeds: countries with similar preferences or economic structures can form subgroups to set up cooperative arrangements and thus enjoy larger benefits from integration.

These differences have implications for the governance of a union with VG. Given a set of existing circles, the formation of a new one and the definition of its contents will result from the initiative of a subgroup of EU members. The question then is: who can make the relevant decision to set up a new periphery and determine its members? Consider the concentric circles approach first. The decision to set up a new periphery affects not only the participants (the insiders) but also other EU members (the outsiders) simultaneously, since it determines how the entire EU proceeds with integration. Thus, the decision to set up a new periphery exerts a large externality on the outsiders. This suggests that all members should be given a voice in the development of the new periphery. Otherwise, conflicts would arise between insiders and outsiders, who would feel uncertain about the sequence of further integration. Note that the negotiations over EMU proceeded according to this principle.

Giving a voice to the outsiders in the decision-making process would have three implications. One is that all EU members would participate in the design of the new periphery, including its institutions. The resulting design would thus reflect the preferences of both insiders and outsiders. This implies that countries may refrain from forming new peripheries because outsiders' interference may force them to adopt an inferior solution. The second implication is that all members belonging to the farthest periphery would have to be given the option to join the next one, even if this is not desirable from the perspective of the countries initiating the process. The third implication is that future entry into the new periphery would have to proceed on the basis of rules adopted at the time the new periphery was formed. The easiest way to handle this would be to formulate entry requirements regarding the stage of economic development and the stability of the prospective members. Since all members must agree in the first case, entry clauses for a higher sphere of integration cannot permanently exclude a member country that wants to participate. At best, entry requirements can delay entry of countries deemed undesirable by other participants.

The same externality does not exist under excentric circles. If a group of countries were to initiate a new periphery, outsiders would not be compelled to follow suit before entering other arrangements. This suggests that the design and the membership of the periphery under excentric circles can be left entirely to the initiators of a new arrangement; membership enlargement can be decided by insiders. Thus, new spheres of integration reflect the preferences of the initiators more closely under this approach. As compensation for the possibility of permanent exclusion from a given periphery, outsiders are free to pursue alternative arrangements. All that excentric circles require is an agreement by all members that a new periphery neither interferes with the proper working of the core nor creates negative externalities for other peripheries. Following current practices, such a decision could be made by the European Council and/or the European Parliament upon recommendation by the European Commission. It would prevent countries from forming peripheries that would reintroduce barriers to trade and mobility.[21]

4.3. VG Applied to Banking Regulation and EMU

Consider first the EU of 15 that is trying to tackle the issue of EMU. To facilitate discussion, we distinguish three groups of countries, A, B, and, C. Group A consists of countries with similar low-inflation preferences and highly developed banking industries willing to form a monetary union in order to lower transaction costs. In this group we would include Germany, Austria, Belgium, Luxembourg, the Netherlands, Denmark, Ireland, and France.[22] Group B consists of countries that, having a lesser commitment to price stability and less developed banking industries, wish to join the monetary union of group A to gain the credibility of low-inflation policies.[23] In this group we would include Italy, Spain, Portugal, Greece, Sweden, and Finland. Countries in group C have well-developed banking industries but are not keen on EMU. The United Kingdom clearly fits into Group C.

The desired outcome for group A is to limit membership in the EMU and to equip it with a highly integrated regulatory system for banks. This group would set up a common central bank to manage a common payment system and act as a lender of last resort providing both the P and R functions. Either the central bank or a common insurance fund would manage the provision of deposit insurance.

The desired outcome for group B is to join EMU both to gain credibility and to have some influence over European monetary policy. In contrast, these countries would be less interested in integrated regulatory functions. Group A would have an incentive to exclude B from EMU because of the higher implied inflation rate (von Hagen and Süppel 1994) and the risk exposure of the common deposit insurance and payment system. Group C's preferred outcome would be not to have both EMU and harmonized banking regulation, since the latter would reduce the international competitiveness of C's banking industry. On the other hand, in EMU C would have an incentive to join with A to establish an integrated LLR and a deposit insurance system in order to remain competitive.

There would be different expected outcomes depending on the form of VG. Consider first the French excentric approach. Under this scenario, group A could form EMU and exclude B, which would be free to create alternative arrangements. If A and C had sufficiently similar banking structures and regulatory preferences, they could agree to integrate LLR, deposit insurance, and payment systems. The expected outcome would be the creation of at least two peripheries, a monetary union limited to A on the one hand and an integrated LLR, deposit insurance, and payment system involving both A and C on the other. The existence of two peripheries would dictate that the LLR function and deposit insurance could not be placed under the jurisdiction of the central bank of the monetary union.[24]

Group B, while excluded from both peripheries, would not lose relative to the initial situation of no monetary union and unintegrated banking regulation. This is true as long as the rules for setting up peripheries do not interfere with the core. Furthermore, B would be free to create peripheries of its own, for example, a monetary union with a higher average inflation rate than the German-led monetary union.

The logic of VG changes under the German concentric approach which does not permit the formation of competing functional areas. Thus, all member states would have to agree ex ante on the sequence of integration—for example, should EMU occur before or after integrated regulatory functions?—and on a set of entry rules. The latter necessitates objective measures of performance to determine whether a country is fit to enter the next level of integration (witness the entry requirements formulated for EMU in the TEU). The ability to measure performance in a precise and independent way is critical for eliminating the potential for discrimination against outsiders. The noted lack of precision of the TEU on banking regulation and supervision reflects the importance each member state assigns to this area and the deep divisions among member states in reaching a common policy (Fratianni 1995a). This suggests that group A would prefer to create EMU before integrated banking regulation, a strategy that would allow A to set up tough standards and delay the entry of B. Group C would support A's position on the grounds that monetary union would be delayed.

To obtain additional predictions, we need to know more about how group A would react to B's membership. Two scenarios are of interest: the first assumes that an enlarged membership would reduce A's payoff without making it negative, and the second assumes instead that A's payoff would become negative, a likely possibility if B's banks had sufficient financial troubles to add significant risk in running the common LLR and deposit insurance systems. Under the first scenario, A would form a monetary union combined with an integrated regulatory arrangement and try to harden as much as possible the entry requirements for monetary union, being fully aware that B's entry could be postponed but not denied. This is the situation that best describes the game in the EU now. The Franco-German bloc, which is the core of group A, has accepted the principle that the southern countries, typified by Italy, cannot be excluded from EMU. Tough entry standards serve the purpose of aligning the southern countries to the policies pursued by the Franco-German bloc. Under the second scenario, A would instead refuse to set up an integrated regulatory arrangement. The result would then be only one periphery, namely, monetary union. Furthermore, if monetary union and integrated regulatory functions were deemed strongly complementary by A, it would not join in a monetary union with B. In this case, concentric circles would inhibit the formation of any periphery.[25]

In sum, group A favors the excentric circles version of VG because that scheme permits it to exclude B. In contrast, B prefers the concentric circles version of VG because it guarantees entry into higher spheres of integration, even against the opposition of A, unless A is willing to deny itself entry. Group C's preference is ambiguous. It prefers excentric circles if monetary union happens anyway but concentric circles if A's marginal benefit from including B is sufficiently negative to preempt monetary union.

4.4.   The Consequences of Enlargement

Enlargement to the east and south of the existing EU will have the consequence of adding countries characterized by weak banking sectors and low commitment to price stability. Consequently, enlargement increases the number of countries belonging to group B. New entrants may even be keen on joint regulatory functions, seeing an opportunity to shift some risk of bank failure to the common regulatory institutions.

Enlargement affects the outcome with excentric circles only to the extent that the old and new members of group B find it mutually beneficial to pool regulatory functions among themselves. Thus, enlargement increases the scope for additional peripheries.

Under concentric circles, in contrast, enlargement raises group A's concern that it will have to accept members in the monetary union and the regulatory arrangement that are sources of negative externalities. In view of that, enlargement would induce A to raise the entry requirements for monetary union. Group C would also support this move. As a result, enlargement would slow down entry into monetary union of the original members of B. Furthermore, it would raise the likelihood of ending with either one periphery (monetary union) or none.

From this perspective, neither group A nor group B has an incentive to favor enlargement. However, as we have argued, at least one member of A, Germany, favors enlargement for other reasons. Suppose that Germany can persuade the other members of A to support enlargement. One way to resolve the conflict between A and B would be for B to accept the model of excentric circles on the condition that a monetary union including B be formed immediately. This would allow the original members of B to exclude the new members from the benefits of monetary union. In this sense, enlargement could speed the formation of monetary union in Europe. Group A could then form an additional, regulatory arrangement excluding B in order to enjoy the benefits of a common payment system. Group C would favor both enlargement and concentric circles as a strategy to prevent both monetary union and common regulatory functions.

5.   Conclusions

VG has been proposed as a solution to the problem of making enlargement consistent with the desire for deepening the EU. The distinguishing feature of VG is the combination of a common core of integration and a set of peripheries or arrangements for integrated policies in which not all member countries participate. Two forms of VG are under consideration, one called concentric circles, relying on a hierarchical structure of peripheries, and the other called excentric circles, placing all peripheries on the same level. Using banking regulation as an example, we have explored the consequences of these two approaches.

An important feature of European integration today is that different countries have different motivations for pursuing cooperation in a given field of economic policy. Another important feature is that the benefits from further integration shrink with the increasing heterogeneity of the participants; integration among a small group of countries pursuing the same interest often seems more beneficial than integration among a large group of countries pursuing different interests.

The concentric circles approach promotes compromises among countries pursuing different goals, but in doing so it runs the risk that "bundling" issues may lower the likelihood of an agreement; the status quo of no integration may in the end prevail. The excentric circles approach promotes the formation of different groups among countries pursuing different goals; consequently, it leaves room for a larger degree of variation in European integration.

Our arguments suggest that the two approaches would set the EU on very different integration paths. The hierarchical model would lead to a union in which all countries would ultimately share the same, relatively low level of integration. The alternative model would lead to a union in which different members "play the integration game" with different intensities; inevitably, some members would achieve a high degree of integration while others would opt for a lower degree. A practical corollary of these propositions is that countries like Italy would prefer the hierarchical structure of concentric circles because it would ensure a common end result, whereas countries like Germany would prefer the nonhierachical approach because it would ensure deeper forms of integration and would effectively discriminate among members with different degrees of commitment to integration.

Ultimately, the choice between these two models depends on the vision the members have for the EU of the twenty-first century. If that vision stresses commonality, the hierarchical model will prevail. If the vision stresses opportunity for change, benefits from cooperation, and learning through new forms of integration, the alternative model will be chosen. The ongoing Intergovernmental Conference will have to address these issues and make a choice.

NOTES

We thank Jim Alt, Jerry Cohen, Barry Eichengreen, Jeffry Frieden, Miles Kahler, and Lisa Martin for comments and suggestions.
    1. The Europe Agreements do not promise accession or set a date or a timetable.
    2. Lamers (CDU 1994) makes this point very clearly.
    3. For a review of the debate on variable geometry, see Dewatripont et al. 1995.

4. The accession treaty allows Sweden to produce and consume snuff, which is prohibited in the rest of the EU.

5. See CDU 1994, Balladur 1994, and Bocquet 1994.

6. We ignore some secondary reasons related to the smoothness of the money supply process and credit allocation schemes driven by social policy goals.

7. Most industrial countries and all EU countries have subscribed to the capital standards defined in the Basle Accord under the auspices of the Bank for International Settlements.

8. Folkerts-Landau and Garber (1992) argue that different jurisdictional responsibilities lead to different financial structures. A "broad" central bank, one that is responsible not only for monetary policy but also for lending in the last resort, regulation, and supervision, enhances the development of liquid and securitized financial markets with an efficient payment system.

9. The central bank is the leader of the banking industry and organizes rescue operations, as in the case of the failure of Bankhaus Herstatt of Cologne in 1974.

10. In the last two cases, larger additional externalities to the entire economy exist. This is emphasized in Diamond and Dybvig's analysis of R-LLR (1983).

11. In practice, governments have ways to limit the potential transfer of tax revenues to foreigners, for example, charging banks a fee for supplying deposit insurance and the use of coinsurance. However, fair pricing of deposit insurance is extremely difficult, and international competition in financial services limits the scope for making banks pay for deposit insurance. Thus, we assume that the potential tax transfers are sizable.

12. Goodhart and Schoenmaker (1993, app.). For example, Banque Andes, with a large proportion of foreign shareholders, faced a run and received a line of credit from the Belgian Rediscount and Guarantee Institute. Also, the foreign-owned Banque Internationale pour l'Afrique Occidentale, BAII UBAf and Kuwaiti French Bank, and Al Saudi Bank were helped by the French regulator.

13. One may criticize our view of governments pursuing national economic interests by pointing to European economic integration as an example of fruitful economic cooperation. While we do not deny that there is a tradition of cooperation in Europe, we cannot help observing that day-to-day politics is often driven by economic self-interest.

14. This does not suggest that the tradeoff between the two is linear or continuous.

15. In the transition period from July 1, 1995, to December 31, 1999, member states can limit the guarantee to 15,000 ECUs (Fratianni 1995a, 160).

16. In most EC countries, central banks are involved only in payment systems handling large-scale payments. Most banks leave technical operations to private clearinghouses but execute the final settlement of payments on the central bank accounts of the participating banks. Central bank involvement in this activity is regarded as a necessary condition for effective use of monetary policy instruments (Hartmann 1995).

17. For a discussion of the pros and cons of a "broad" central bank, see Folkerts-

Landau and Garber 1992, Goodhart and Schoenmaker 1993, Baltensperger 1993, Angelini and Passacantando 1993, Fratianni 1995a, and Masciandaro 1996.

18. Here we will ignore the fact that the current members of the EU have already agreed on a set of common policies that might define a core.

19. The TEU grants derogations to Denmark and the United Kingdom on monetary union and to the United Kingdom on social policy.

20. There is a significant body of literature stressing regulation as a rent-seeking activity (Mueller 1989, 235–38).

21. Further designs of the periphery are, of course, conceivable. Here we limit our attention to those that have been proposed in the political debate.

22. Group A corresponds to the first three groupings in Garrett (this volume, table 2.7). Note that our criterion is much simpler than Garrett's four-variable proxy for the expected economic consequences of being part of EMU.

23. For a discussion of such a constellation of preferences, see Alesina and Grilli 1993 and von Hagen 1995.

24. A plausible alternative would be that C limits its participation to the integrated deposit insurance fund and the R-LLR facility, counting on the incentive of A to extend P-LLR coverage to C-banks operating in A. Group A would then have an incentive to limit participation in its joint payments mechanism to banks complying with its regulatory standards.

25. Note that in our case "bundling" issues raises the likelihood of no agreement, as in Alt and Eichengreen 1989. In contrast, much of the literature seems to suggest that "bundling" raises the likelihood of an agreement (see Eichengreen and Frieden, this volume).

REFERENCES

Alesina, A., and V. Grilli. 1993. On the feasibility of a one-speed or multi-speed European Monetary Union. *Economics and Politics* 5:145–66.

Alt, J., and B. Eichengreen. 1989. Parallel and overlapping games. *Economics and Politics* 1:119–44.

Angelini, P., and F. Passacantando. 1993. Central banks' role in the payments system and its relationship with monetary policy and supervision. In *Prudential Regulation, Supervision, and Monetary Policy,* edited by F. Bruni, 453–92. Giornale Degli Economisti e Annali di Economia, no. 60. Milan: Bocconi University.

Baldwin, R. E. 1994. *Towards an Integrated Europe.* London: CEPR.

———. 1996. Concepts and speed of an eastern enlargement. Geneva, Graduate Institute of International Studies. Mimeo.

Balladur, E. 1994. Pour un nouveau traité de l'Elysée. *Le Monde,* November 30.

Baltensperger, E. 1993. Central bank policy and lending of last resort. In *Prudential Regulation, Supervision, and Monetary Policy,* edited by F. Bruni, 441–52.

Giornale Degli Economisti e Annali di Economia, no. 60, Milan: Bocconi University.

Bocquet, D. 1994. *Ce que la France doit repondre à l'Allemagne.* Paris: Mouvement Européen France.

Chan, Y., S. I. Greenbaum, and A. V. Thakor. 1992. Is fairly priced deposit insurance possible? *Journal of Finance* 47:227–45.

CDU/CSU Fraktion des Deutschen Bundestages. 1994. Überlegungen zur europäischen politik. Bonn. Mimeo.

Council of European Communities. 1992. *Treaty on European Union.* Luxembourg: Office of the Official Publications of the European Communities.

Dewatripont, M., F. Giavazzi, J. von Hagen, I. Harden, T. Persson, H. Rosenthal, G. Roland, A. Sapir, and G. Tabellini. 1995. *Flexible Integration.* Monitoring European Integration, no. 6. London: CEPR.

Diamond, D. W., and P. H. Dybvig. 1983. Bank runs, deposit insurance, and liquidity. *Journal of Political Economy* 91:401–19.

Folkerts-Landau, D., and P. M. Garber. 1992. *The European Central Bank: A Bank or a Monetary Policy Rule?* NBER Working Papers, no. 4016. Cambridge: National Bureau of Economic Research.

Fratianni, M. 1995a. Bank deposit insurance in the EU. In *Monetary and Fiscal Policy in an Integrated Europe,* edited by B. Eichengreen, J. Frieden, and J. von Hagen. European and Transatlantic Studies, no. 1. Heidelberg: Springer.

———. 1995b. Variable integration in the European Union. Paper presented at Forum CEIS Q8, Porto Cervo, September 22–23.

Goodhart, C., and D. Schoenmaker. 1993. Institutional separation between supervisory and monetary agencies. In *Prudential Regulation, Supervision, and Monetary Policy,* edited by F. Bruni, 353–440. Giornale Degli Economisti e Annali di Economia, no. 60. Milan: Bocconi University.

Hartmann, W. 1995. Die rolle der zentralbanken im europäischen zahlungsverkehr. *Auszüge aus Presseartikeln,* March 1, 1–6.

Herring, R. J., and R. E. Litan. 1995. *Financial Regulation in the Global Economy.* Washington, D.C.: Brookings Institution.

Masciandaro, D. 1995. Designing a central bank: Social player, monetary agent, or banking agent? *Open Economies Review* 6:399–410.

Mueller, D. C. 1989. *Public Choice II: A Revisited Edition of Public Choice.* Cambridge: Cambridge University Press.

von Hagen, J. 1992. Herstatt crisis. In *The New Palgrave Dictionary of Money and Finance,* edited by J. Eatwell, M. Milgate, and P. Newman. New York: Stockton Press.

———. 1995. Credible ways to EMU. In *The Financial System under Stress,* edited by M. Uzan. London: Routledge.

von Hagen, J., and R. Süppel. 1994. Central bank constitutions for federal monetary unions. *European Economic Review* 38:774–82.

CHAPTER 7

The Impact of Economic Integration on European Wage-Setting Institutions

Michael Wallerstein

I. Introduction

What is the impact of European economic integration on the structure of industrial relations and wage setting in the countries of Western Europe? Does the distinctive pattern of industrial relations in North and Central Europe—a pattern characterized by strong unions, high levels of union coverage, and multitier bargaining with the base wage increase set at the industry or national level—have a future within the Single Market of the European Union? Will economic integration compel European unions to accept the decentralization of wage setting and the loss of influence already experienced by unions in the United States?

For those who view the centralized wage-setting institutions of Western Europe as largely beneficial, recent events have been dispiriting to say the least. In Britain, unions have lost a third of their membership since 1979, the year that union membership peaked. The number of British workers covered by industry-level agreements has also fallen by a third, as multiemployer bargaining has been increasingly replaced with single-employer bargaining (Howell 1995).[1] In Sweden, the pattern of centralized negotiations covering the entire private sector that began in 1956 came to an end in 1983. Since 1983, the predominant locus of bargaining in Sweden has increasingly shifted to the industry level. Although central agreements were still signed in the majority of bargaining rounds in the 1980s, the central agreement no longer imposed an industrial peace obligation on the subsequent industry-level talks. In 1993, the Swedish national employers' association began to advocate decentralizing wage negotiations further, to the level of the firm, while retaining industry-level bargaining for nonwage issues such as working time (Pontusson and Swenson 1996).

The pattern of change is not so simple, however. In Denmark, the role of the national union confederation in wage setting was largely eliminated in the 1980s, but control over wage setting at the industry level has increased. Labor agreements in the 1980s and early 1990s have increased restrictions on locally negotiated supplements to industry-level contracts (Scheuer 1992). In addition, industry-level bargaining has become increasingly concentrated. The amalgam of industry, craft, and general unions in Denmark are in the process of forming five large bargaining cartels that together cover the entire labor market, both public and private (Due et al. 1993). In other countries in North and Central Europe, little change in wage-setting institutions can be observed, at least so far (Wallerstein, Golden, and Lange 1997).

In spite of the divergence of national trends, it is common today to argue that strong unions and centralized bargaining institutions at the national level are being undermined by the creation of a Single European Market. After all, the starting date for the Single European Market—January 1, 1993—was not long ago. Sweden, Finland, and Austria voted to enter the EU in the summer and fall of 1994. The fact that dramatic change in wage-setting institutions has not occurred in the majority of countries in North and Central Europe to date may only indicate that the full impact of economic integration on European industrial relations and collective bargaining has yet to be observed.

Changes in the centralization of bargaining have potentially large consequences for the distribution of income, particularly the distribution of income among wage earners. Centralized bargaining systems generate, on average, a more equal distribution of wages than either decentralized bargaining systems or nonunion labor markets (Moene and Wallerstein 1997). The egalitarian impact of centralized bargaining has been most evident in Scandinavia, where the unions adopted an explicit policy of compressing wage differentials (Hibbs and Locking 1995a, 1995b; Edin and Topel 1995). Even in countries where unions have not openly pushed for a more egalitarian wage structure, the correlation between centralized bargaining and wage equality is strong (Freeman 1988).

Politically, the debate over the effect of economic integration on wage-setting institutions is a piece of a larger debate over the future of social democracy in an integrated European market. Unlike their rivals on the left, social democrats have long accepted the view that union moderation is essential for adequate aggregate economic performance. Where social democrats differed from their rivals on the right was on how union moderation was best obtained. While conservatives argued for measures to weaken the power of unions, social democrats sought to simultaneously protect union power and encourage moderation in the exercise of that power. One of the main institutional arrangements for achieving wage restraint and strengthening the union organizations at the same time was centralized bargaining. If centralized wage negotiations are now being undermined by economic integration, an important component of the social democratic program will have been abandoned.

Two arguments regarding the impact of economic integration on union strength and centralized bargaining are particularly prominent. What could be called the "union monopoly" argument starts from the proposition that the ultimate source of union strength is monopoly power in the labor market (Reder and Ulman 1993). Unions achieve gains for their members by reducing competition among workers for jobs. Organizing a firm's potential supply of labor, however, may not be sufficient if the firm lacks monopoly power in the market for goods. Unless there are firm-specific rents to be shared, an increase in wages that does not result in a price increase will drive the firm out of business. The only way to raise the price in a competitive industry is to raise the wage for all producers. In this view, unions succeed by either obtaining a share of the firm's rents or creating monopoly rents where none existed through an industrywide wage increase. As Ulman (1955) first argued with regard to the development of national unions in the United States in the nineteenth century, unions must organize on the same scale as the market for goods to be effective.

By this reasoning, economic integration poses a stark challenge to unions. As Mancur Olson put it in *The Rise and Decline of Nations:* "A monopoly over a small part of an integrated market is, of course, no monopoly at all" (1982, 125). Either the unions grow as large as the market for goods or unions lose their ability to raise wages and attract members. As Reder and Ulman (1993) pose the alternatives, European unions must follow the pattern of American unions in the late nineteenth century and centralize control over bargaining on a Europeanwide basis or the European unions will follow the more recent pattern of American unions and decline into insignificance. Since the prospects for pan-European unions are bleak, the conclusion that economic integration in Europe will result in union shrinkage and decentralization of wage setting, as has already happened in Britain, seems inescapable.

The most prominent argument in the political science literature is different, but the conclusion is the same. What could be called the "corporatist" argument starts from the premise that there is an intimate link between centralized wage bargaining at the national level and government attempts to control inflation without unemployment through formal or informal income policies. Successful macroeconomic policy, the argument goes, requires the cooperation of unions where unions are too strong to be ignored in order to restrain wages and ensure that an increase in demand results in an increase of employment rather than an increase in inflation. In a decentralized bargaining system, obtaining the cooperation of wage setters is difficult, if not impossible. Hence, according to the analysis of Philippe Schmitter and Wolfgang Streeck (Schmitter 1989; Streeck and Schmitter 1991; Streeck 1993), governments strengthened national union confederations and encouraged central bargaining in order to have actors in the labor market with whom those governments could negotiate.

Schmitter and Streeck proceed to argue that corporatism, the label given to the interweaving of public and private decisions in which governments extend fiscal and welfare policy concessions in return for moderation in private-sector wage and price setting, depended on political conditions that are vanishing at the national level and are unlikely to emerge at the level of the EU.[2] The essence of corporatism, according to the logic of Schmitter and Streeck, was an exchange between the central organizations of unions and the government. In return for union cooperation in restraining wage increases and maintaining industrial peace, governments provided a variety of subsidies, organizational support, and, above all, a macroeconomic policy commitment to full employment.

With increased economic integration, the argument goes, governments have lost much of their policy autonomy. Governments can no longer offer influence over macroeconomic policy in exchange for influence over wage growth, since governments no longer have enough policy autonomy to give away. Without the possibility of Keynesian policies at the national level, corporatism at the national level loses its purpose. One might expect the development of corporatism on a European scale if the EU develops into a government with macroeconomic policies of its own and if unions are strong enough at the EU level to make their cooperation indispensable. But the possibility of bilateral or trilateral wage bargaining in coordination with macroeconomic policy choices at the EU level is too remote to take seriously. Thus, Schmitter and Streeck predict that interest representation and collective bargaining in the EU will look more like those of United States than those of Germany, let alone pre-1983 Sweden.

We have two different arguments from two different fields that yield the same conclusion: Economic integration has undermined the traditional wage-setting institutions of Western Europe. Unions may or may not maintain their membership. The examples of Belgium, Denmark, Sweden, and Finland, where the unions provide unemployment insurance and membership has continued to grow throughout the 1980s, indicate the potential importance of nonwage services to members. What unions are losing everywhere, it is argued, is the ability to set wages in a centralized fashion at the sectoral or industrial level or, even, to influence wages at all.

Yet, on closer examination, the two arguments do not strengthen each other. In fact, the two rest on contradictory assumptions about how unions influence wages in centralized systems. The union monopoly argument starts from the premise that unions set wages centrally in order to raise wages. The corporatist argument starts from the contrary premise that the purpose of centralized wage setting was to prevent wages from rising. Clearly, both can't be right, at least not at the same time and place.

In this chapter, I argue that both arguments are at least partly wrong. The next section addresses the union monopoly argument and the relationship between centralized bargaining and international trade. The third section reviews the relationship between centralized bargaining and macroeconomic policy. In the fourth section, I suggest another explanation for the link between economic integration and the potential or—in the case of Sweden and Great Britain—actual decline of centralized bargaining. The fifth section concludes.

Before proceeding, however, it is worth noting two ways in which the scope of the chapter is limited. I do not offer a comprehensive review of explanations for the decentralization of bargaining in Sweden or Britain. Explanations of decentralization that bear little necessary relationship to trade or factor mobility are discussed only briefly. Nor does this essay present an empirical overview of the extent to which decentralization has actually occurred in Western Europe as a whole. That is partly done in Wallerstein, Golden, and Lange 1997.

2. Union Monopoly and Economic Openness

In a competitive industry, unions' ability to raise wages is limited unless they raise wages for all producers. If the competitive industry is in the traded goods sector, raising wages for all requires either international unions or trade protection. More generally, an increase in the degree of competition in product markets caused by economic integration raises the cost of wage increases in terms of employment (or increases the elasticity of the demand for labor).

Thus, it is natural for to think that strong unions and trade protection go hand in hand.

Yet, most work on corporatism in political science has noted that the empirical association between economic openness and many measures of union strength, including union density and centralized wage setting, is positive, not negative. Cameron 1978 was probably the most important article in establishing the surprising impact of economic openness as an independent variable in cross-national comparisons. Cameron found that economic openness (measured by the sum of exports plus imports as a share of GDP) was the single best predictor of welfare effort (measured by government revenues as a share of GDP) in a simple cross-sectional analysis of OECD countries. Welfare spending is not the same as centralized wage setting, but it is no surprise that the countries with high levels of welfare spending are also, by and large, countries with more centralized systems of wage determination.

Cameron did not challenge the conventional wisdom because he did not conclude that trade openness was a cause of either high welfare spending or centralized bargaining. Instead, he suggested that the correlation was spurious. In his view, the cause of all three is a particular historical pattern of economic development followed by the small countries on the northern fringe of Europe that began late, proceeded exceptionally rapidly, and was oriented toward export markets. Drawing on the thesis proposed by Geoffrey Ingham (1974), Cameron argued that late, rapid development led to an industrial and occupational structure conducive to the formation of strong industrial unions whose electoral support of social democratic parties led to the rapid growth of welfare expenditures.[3]

Some of the scholars who followed Cameron, however, did challenge the conventional economic wisdom by attributing a causal role to economic openness in explaining both welfare effort and centralized bargaining. Wallerstein (1985) and, much more prominently, Peter Katzenstein (1983, 1984, 1985) argued that an export orientation engendered a political commitment to free trade policies, which, in turn, affected the organization of interests and policies in other arenas. Katzenstein's (1983) argument centered on the vulnerability of small, export-dependent countries (including Germany, which Kastzenstein claimed acted like a small country despite its size) subject to continual economic shocks from abroad. Vulnerability, suggested Katzenstein, spurred efforts to attain domestic compromise between contending interests, especially between employers and unions. The centralization of bargaining was the concrete expression of class compromise, according to Katzenstein, in which employers accepted the unions' right to negotiate over wages at the industry level or higher and the unions accepted managerial authority at the plant level. The growth of welfare spending, in Katzenstein's argument, was explained by the absence of other means of protecting citizens from international economic shocks in countries that were too dependent on trade to consider protectionist policies. Katzenstein (1985) added a historical argument that centered on the weakness of landed nobility in the small European states, which resulted in a divided Right, a moderate Left, and a willingness to share political power through proportional representation.

The most historically informed and convincing accounts of the link between trade dependence and centralized bargaining, however, are Peter Swenson's (1989, 1991a) studies of the origins of centralization in Sweden and Denmark. The Norwegian story, which is strikingly similar to the Swedish story, can only be found in Norwegian in Jorunn Bjørgum 1985. In both Norway and Sweden, the initial step toward centralization took the form of a conflict between the national organization of employers and the national confederation of unions, on the one side, and construction workers on the other. In Norway, the union confederation, the Landsorganisasjonen, or LO, intervened to end an illegal strike of construction workers in 1928, a strike that threatened the unity of the national employers' association. In Sweden, the first step toward centralization occurred with the intervention of the LO in a strike of construction workers in 1933. In both countries, there were political considerations in the background. The Norwegian LO was afraid that the strike would provoke the bourgeois majority in Parliament to pass antiunion legislation. The Swedish LO feared that the new social democratic government would intervene to end the strike if it didn't do so itself. In Sweden, the LO was also fearful that employers would respond with a general lockout.

In addition to the political considerations, however, there was a powerful economic rationale for intervention by the LO. The initial steps toward multi-industry wage bargaining in Sweden and Norway (and, much earlier, in Denmark) represented, according to Swenson, an attempt by employers and workers in the metalworking sector to control wages throughout the economy in line with prices in the traded goods sector (Swenson 1991). Construction workers were the target in both Sweden and Norway because they were highly paid, militant, and sheltered from foreign competition. Since construction workers were employed in the export sector as well as in home construction, higher construction wages raised costs in the export sector. The more construction workers were paid, the more metalworkers had to reduce their wages in order to maintain employment with declining export markets and the more metalworkers resented the wage reductions they were asked to accept. In Scandinavia, centralized bargaining was created as a mechanism for allowing those workers who were directly subject to international competition to set the pace of wage increases for the rest of the economy.[4] The German system, in which the 16 industrial unions that comprise the Deutscher Gewerkschaftsbund, or DGB, allow the metalworkers union to act as the wage leader, is not so different in this respect (Markovitz 1986; Thelen 1991). Far from being the product of a closed economy, centralized bargaining institutions were adopted in countries with high levels of trade dependence.

The recent decentralization of wage setting in Sweden does not contradict the empirical association of trade openness and centralized wage setting as much as is commonly believed. Exports plus imports as a share of GDP have risen in all European countries during the postwar period. Employment in the traded goods sector, however, has fallen as a share of employment, especially in Sweden. With higher than average productivity growth, the traded goods sector contributes more to output with relatively fewer workers. In the past two decades, almost all employment growth in Scandinavia has been in the public sector.

As employment has shifted to the public sector in Sweden, so has union membership. The share of public sector workers in the Swedish LO grew from 17 percent in 1950 to 37 percent in 1987 (Martin 1991, 26). By the 1980s, the metalworkers, traditionally the dominant union in the LO, had been surpassed in size by the union of district and municipal employees. Of the five largest unions in the Swedish LO in 1989 (which together contained two-thirds of the LO's membership), only one represented workers in the traded goods sector of the economy. Moreover, the blue-collar union confederation had declined relative to the white-collar and professional union confederations in which public sector workers constituted an even larger share of membership. In sum, the relative share of union members employed in industries exposed to international competition declined significantly between the first centralized bargaining rounds in the 1950s and the end of centralized bargaining in 1983.[5]

The relationship between the growth of sheltered sector unions and the decline of centralized bargaining is subtle. As Iversen (1996) points out, the sheltered sector unions are the strongest advocates of centralized bargaining in Scandinavia today, since the egalitarian wage policy pursued through centralized bargaining has been particularly beneficial for the relatively low-wage workers in the public and retail sectors. The growing weight of public sector and white-collar workers in collective bargaining, however, altered the character of centralized bargaining in ways that employers in the traded goods sector found objectionable. Swedish employers in the traded goods sector played a central role in the establishment of centralized bargaining in the 1950s and, as I discuss in section 4, an equally central role in the disestablishment of centralized bargaining in the 1980s.

If the argument about the association of centralized bargaining with trade dependence is correct, one might ask why free trade among the American states didn't lead to the development of multi-industry bargaining at the state level rather than the growth of craft and industrial unions that attempted to coordinate wage setting at the national level. One answer is that the United States constitutes a single market for labor as well as goods. The mobility of labor across state lines was a powerful force for the establishment of American unions on a national scale, as Ulman (1955) documents. In principle, there is free movement of labor as well as goods inside the European Union. In practice, the mobility of labor across countries in the European Union remains far less than that across states in the United States in spite of the absence of legal restrictions.

A second answer to the question of why American unions attempted to organize on a national or binational scale is that, to the extent that they were successful, their ability to raise wages increased substantially. The inability of unions to "take wages out of the competition" in the traded goods sector of small open economies implies that such unions' impact on the average wage received by their members is small. Unions in North and Central Europe have never been able to obtain the wage premiums enjoyed by union members in the United States. According to the estimates of David Blanchflower and Richard Freeman (1992), in 1985–87 the union-nonunion wage differential was 18 to 22 percent in the United States, 10 percent in Britain, and only 5 to 8 percent in Austria and Germany. Moreover, the wage differential in Austria and Germany is mostly due to local wage increases above the terms of the union contract since the industry-level agreements cover all employers who belong to the employers' association (which is almost all employers in practice) whether their workers are union members or not. In Norway and Sweden, union contracts cover the entire labor force and unemployment rarely reached 3 percent until the recession of 1990–93. Under such conditions, average wages could not have been lower even if the Nordic labor markets had been completely unorganized. Indeed, the widespread evidence of labor shortages in Norway and Sweden in much of the postwar period suggests that union wages were lower than the wages that would have prevailed in the absence of unions.

In conclusion, the empirical association between centralized wage setting institutions and trade openness has the wrong sign for the monopoly union argument. In Scandinavia, the need to maintain control over labor costs in industries exposed to international competition helps explain the origins of centralized bargaining institutions. While the premise that economic integration sharpens the tradeoff between wage increases and unemployment is correct, the premise that control over labor costs is more difficult to achieve with centralized wage setting is doubtful.[6]

3. Corporatism and Macroeconomic Policy

That centralized systems of bargaining were established to keep wages low rather than push wages up is the fundamental claim of the literature on corporatism. The argument was first made by Bruce Headey (1970), who suggested that centralized bargaining and social democratic participation in government were, in the European experience, necessary conditions for the successful implementation of voluntary incomes policies. Most of the subsequent research on corporatism and economic performance that followed was based on the proposition that the benefits of wage moderation are, to a significant degree, received by actors other than those bearing the sacrifice. In the words of an influential OECD report from the 1970s: "Unless wage bargaining is highly centralized, individual unions can rationally hope that an improvement in their real wages can be achieved at the expense of profits and hence employment elsewhere in the economy" (1977, 159).

Many different externalities in the wage-setting process have been suggested. In the model of Lars Calmfors and John Driffill (1988), the source of the externality is the impact of wage increases in one industry on consumer prices and therefore real consumer wages received by workers outside the industry. In the model of Wallerstein (1990), the source of the externality is the impact of wage increases for one category of worker on the demand for the labor of other types of workers who are complements in production. Richard Jackman (1990) emphasizes the externality that comes from the need to finance unemployment benefits out of taxes, including taxes on wages. Peter Lange and Geoffrey Garrett (1985) and Garrett and Lange (1986) think of the continual survival of a social democratic government as a kind of externality that leads centralized unions to moderate wages when the Left is in power. Andrew Oswald (1979) included the idea that union members care about their relative wage (the own wage relative to the wages of others) as well as their real wage (their own wage relative to the consumer price level). All of these articles point in the same direction. A union confederation or a single union that covers a large share of the labor market would internalize much of the externality and accept lower wages than less centralized wage setters, at least over some range of centralization.[7] The claim that centralization results in wage moderation with beneficial consequences for the economy has long been a staple of comparative studies of macroeconomic performance among OECD countries in both political science and economics.[8]

If the corporatist literature is correct in its fundamental premise that centralized wage-setting institutions were supported by governments, employers, and union leaders in order to hold wages down and improve macroeconomic performance, what is wrong with attributing the decline of centralization to the loss of macroeconomic policy autonomy at the national level? One can question the extent to which macroeconomic policy autonomy of West European countries has been reduced in comparison with the 1950s or 1960s. Richard Cooper (1987), for example, argues that a world in which countries have ready access to an international financial market provides policymakers with more freedom than when international capital mobility was low and government debt had to be financed domestically. Of course, policy autonomy will be lost if the EU acquires a common currency and imposes controls on the fiscal policy of members as well, but these are political choices rather than matters of economic necessity.

For our topic, the question of whether or not policy autonomy has declined is a side issue. What is more important is that none of the mechanisms that have been suggested connecting the centralization of wage setting with lower wage demands have anything to do with the business cycle or macroeconomic policy. All of the mechanisms discussed in the literature imply that centralized bargaining lowers wages and raises employment over the entire business cycle, whatever the mix of fiscal and monetary policy. This could be a failing of the literature rather than a true statement about the world. Nevertheless, nothing in the existing literature provides a reason why the incentive for unions to solve their collective action problem and accept lower wages in exchange for higher employment or growth is only present when the government is committed to maintaining full employment with discretionary macroeconomic policies.[9] One might think that the willingness to sacrifice wage increases for employment growth would increase as unemployment rises.

One might continue to defend the corporatist explanation by arguing that high unemployment is a substitute for centralized bargaining from the point of view of employers and governments. If the government is committed to full employment, the argument goes, self-restraint on the part of unions is essential if labor costs are to be controlled. But if union militancy declines for other reasons, such as high unemployment, centralized bargaining may become superfluous. When unemployment is high, unions are in no position to raise wages whether they are self-restrained or not.

This is the most convincing argument but, like other arguments in the corporatist literature, it assumes that the critical actors are unions. It is the unions whose wage demands have to be restrained, either by centralized bargaining or by high unemployment. The impact of centralized bargaining on employers' wage offers, however, may be more important than the effects of centralization on the unions' wage demands. If employers' ability to attract, retain, and motivate workers is affected by the wage they offer—a plausible assumption—then centralized wage setting reduces wage levels and increases employment even if wages are unilaterally set by employers. Since this point is not well known, it is worth illustrating with a simple model.[10]

The basic premise of a wide class of efficiency wage models is that workers' efficiency, denoted e, is a positive function of their wage relative to wages and employment possibilities elsewhere. If, for any reason, the efficiency of labor is affected by the wage, then employers may find it optimal to pay wages higher than the market-clearing level. Let the firm choose both the number of employees, L, and the wage rate, w. Then the firm's decision can be written as

$$\max_{w,L} R[e(w)L] - wL, \tag{1}$$

where $R(\cdot)$ is the firm's revenues and $e(w)$ indicates the way that workers' efficiency depends on the wage. The functions $R(\cdot)$ and $e(w)$ are both assumed to be strictly concave. In particular, it is assumed that efficiency increases as the wage rises but at a declining rate. In the case of an interior solution, the first-order conditions can be written as

$$R'(eL) - (w/e) = 0 \tag{2}$$

$$R'(eL)(de/dw) - 1 = 0. \tag{3}$$

Let $\lambda(w) \equiv (de/dw)(w/e)$ be the elasticity of workers' efficiency with respect to the wage. Then equations 2 and 3 can be combined to yield

$$\lambda(w) - 1 = 0 \tag{4}$$

as the basic optimality condition in the efficiency wage model. The assumption that $e(w)$ is strictly concave implies that the second-order condition of $\lambda'(w) < 0$ when $\lambda(w) = 1$ is satisfied.

There are many possible reasons why the wage might affect workers' efficiency. For example, a higher relative wage might lower turnover and thus reduce the costs associated with finding and training new workers (Calvo 1979). Or a higher relative wage increases the loss associated with being fired and thus may reduce shirking on the job (Calvo and Wellisz 1978; Shapiro and Stiglitz 1984; Bowles 1985). In either case, what matters is the difference or, more conveniently, the ratio between a worker's current wage, w, and what a worker would obtain if he or she quit or were fired. We assume for convenience that the probability of finding another job after a separation is equal to one minus the aggregate rate of unemployment. Workers' expected income after a separation can then be written as $\mu w^* + (1 - \mu)bw^*$ where w^* is the wage level elsewhere, b is the replacement ratio (the percentage of wage income that is replaced by unemployment benefits), and μ is the employment rate (one minus the rate of unemployment). Thus, we have

$$e = e\left(\frac{w}{w^*[\mu + (1 - \mu)b]}\right),\qquad(5)$$

with $e'(\cdot) > 0$, as the equation representing the dependence of efficiency on wages.

Workers' outside opportunity, the denominator in equation 5, is exogenous from the point of view of each employer. Therefore, the elasticity of efficiency with respect to the wage in the case of decentralized wage setting is

$$\lambda^D = \left[\frac{w/w^*}{(1 - b)\mu + b}\right]\frac{e'(\cdot)}{e(\cdot)},\qquad(6)$$

which firms set equal to one by equation 4. As each employer tries to raise wages relative to others, none succeed, but the aggregate wage level and rate of unemployment increase until equation 4 is satisfied at $w = w^*$.

With centralized wage setting, all wages are raised together. When $w = w^*$, both terms drop out of the expression for e in equation 5. At the same time, centralized employers would take into consideration the effect of higher wages on unemployment: $\mu = \mu(w)$ with $\mu'(w) < 0$. As Michal Kalecki (1943) argued, employers benefit from higher unemployment to the extent that it increases the "threat of the sack." Calculating the elasticity of workers' efficiency with respect to centrally set wages, one obtains

$$\lambda^C = -\left[\frac{w\mu'(w)}{\mu(w)}\right]\left[\frac{(1 - b)\mu(w)}{((1 - b)\mu(w) + b)^2}\right]\frac{e'(\cdot)}{e(\cdot)}$$

$$= -\left[\frac{w\mu'(w)}{\mu(w)}\right]\left[\frac{(1-b)\mu(w)}{(1-b)\mu(w)+b}\right]\lambda^D. \tag{7}$$

This last equation can be simplified further, assuming a fixed number of identical firms. The first term, $w\mu'(w)/\mu(w)$, is the elasticity of the demand for labor. Equations 2 and 4 imply that this elasticity must equal negative one. To see this, differentiate equation 2 with respect to w to obtain

$$R''(\cdot)\left(L\frac{de}{dw} + e\frac{dL}{dw}\right) = \frac{1}{e^2}\left(e - w\frac{de}{dw}\right),$$

which can be rewritten as

$$R''(\cdot)\left[\lambda + \frac{w\mu'(w)}{\mu(w)}\right] = \frac{w}{e^2 L}(1-\lambda).$$

Since $\lambda = 1$ from equation 4, we conclude that $w\mu'(w)/\mu(w) = -1$. Therefore, equation 7 simplifies to

$$\lambda^C = \left[\frac{(1-b)\mu}{(1-b)\mu + b}\right]\lambda^D < \lambda^D, \tag{8}$$

provided that $b > 0$. Thus $\lambda^C(w) - 1 < 0$ when evaluated at the equilibrium wage with decentralized wage setting. To achieve the optimum of $\lambda^C(w) = 1$, the wage must be reduced, since $\lambda'(w) < 0$ by the second-order condition. Thus, a centralized confederation of employers would set lower wages through a national agreement than would be chosen in equilibrium by each employer acting independently. Through centralized wage setting, firms are able to curtail self-defeating attempts by each to raise its wage offers above what other employers are paying.

The model highlights two externalities in decentralized wage setting that remain in a labor market even when workers' bargaining power vanishes. The first is the negative externality that one firm's wage increase imposes on other employers' ability to attract and motivate workers without also paying higher wages. Swenson (1992) describes internal debates within the Swedish employers' association during the early postwar boom in which leading employers complain repeatedly of the "unsolidaristic wage policies" of employers who try to steal their workers by paying higher wages. The second externality is the positive effect of wage increases elsewhere in the economy of reducing the aggregate demand for labor, thereby raising unemployment and increasing employers' ability to find and retain workers without a wage increase. In the absence of unemployment insurance, that is, when $b = 0$, these two externalities exactly cancel each other such that centralized wage setters would choose the same wage as would decentralized wage setters. With unemployment insurance, however, the wage-restraining effect of unemployment is lessened. If $b >$ 0, the direct gain to employers of avoiding the attempt by each to raise wages above wages elsewhere outweighs the indirect loss of decreased discipline due to lower unemployment.

The efficiency wage argument differs from the more common argument that coordinated wage setting allows employers to exercise monopsony power in the labor market, that is, to raise profits by holding wages below the market-clearing level. The key difference concerns the relationship between centralized wage setting and employment. According to the monopsony wage model, all workers who want employment at the current wage are employed. A wage decrease can only lower employment by reducing the number of people willing to work. According to the efficiency wage model, in contrast, a share of the work force remains unemployed in the decentralized equilibrium. If employers are able to reduce wages through centralized bargaining, employment expands.

In conclusion, employers can increase their profits by limiting self-defeating attempts by each employer to pay more than others in order to increase employees' loyalty and willingness to work. Of course, in such a situation, employers have a constant incentive to free ride and try to pay their workers more than the central agreement allows. The central employers' association may receive valuable help from the unions in preventing "unsolidaristic" wage increases if unions are strong enough to impose some discipline on their members and support a policy of wage restraint for reasons of their own. In Scandinavia, union leaders cooperated with employers in restraining wages for two reasons. The first was their willingness to work with social democratic governments to preserve low unemployment without high inflation. The second was the union desire to use centralized bargaining to impose a more egalitarian distribution of wages among workers.

4. An Alternative View of Centralized Bargaining and Economic Integration

An alternative view is that European economic integration per se may have little impact on centralization of collective bargaining, at least as long as labor mobility across countries within the EU remains low. Yet changes in collective bargaining and the drive to create a single European market may be related in the sense that both represent responses to the same underlying problem: years of slow growth and, in most of Western Europe, high unemployment. The most important change in the political economy of Western Europe and the United States since the mid 1970s is the decline in the demand for labor. While the decline in the demand for labor was initially viewed as a cyclical phenomenon, expected to vanish as the economies recovered from the sharp recessions of 1974–75 and 1980–81, private sector employment in Europe remained stagnant even during the long expansion of the 1980s.

Two decades of high unemployment and/or low wage growth has rearranged the political landscape of Western Europe, both weakening unions and empowering employers.[11] When unemployment is high, employers' power as "employment givers," to use the German phrase, becomes painfully apparent. Increasing public employment can protect workers from a decline in the private demand for labor for awhile, and public employment growth contributed significantly to the maintenance of full employment in Austria and the Nordic countries during the 1980s. The combination of public sector employment growth and private sector employment stagnation is a recipe for an increasing tax burden, however, and there is a limit to the growth of taxes as a share of national income, even in Sweden. Moreover, Swedish workers paid a price for the maintenance of full employment in the 1970s and 1980s. Real wages in Sweden were sharply reduced in the late 1970s and early 1980s. The willingness of European unions to support, or at least not fight, the creation of a Single Market within the EU may be explained by the unions' hope that integration would spur economic growth and provide a means of escaping the dismal choice between high unemployment and falling wages.

Yet the fact that employers are in the driver's seat doesn't mean that dramatic decentralization is around the corner. One reason is that, in much of Western Europe, the unions retain sufficient strength to defeat unilateral attempts by employers to restructure bargaining institutions. The attempt by German employers in the metalworking industry to weaken industry-level bargaining in 1993 was defeated by a surprisingly successful strike waged by workers in eastern Germany (Turner 1994).

A second reason why centralized bargaining institutions survive is that the beneficiaries of the current system include many employers as well as workers. Employers in Europe are far from united over whether bargaining should be decentralized. The battle lines among employers seem to vary from country to country. In Germany, employers in western Germany, especially large employers, defend centralized bargaining. Even in eastern Germany, most large and medium-sized employers have joined the employers' association (Turner

1994). In Sweden, large, multinational employers have been the primary advocates for the decentralization of bargaining (Martin 1991; Pontusson and Swenson 1996).[12]

So far, large changes in the level of bargaining have only occurred in Britain and Sweden. Both countries are special cases for different reasons. British employers faced unions that were the most similar to unions in the United States. Centralized pay setting was always limited to a minority of industries. The union-nonunion wage differential was higher than anywhere else in Europe. With political encouragement from the Thatcher government, British employers have followed the example of American employers and acted to either replace the traditional unions with enterprise unions or eliminate unions altogether in new plants (Howell 1995).

In Sweden, employers' complaints centered less on the unions' impact on average wages than on relative wages. As much as Swedish employers benefited from centralized wage restraints, employers had to pay a price in terms of the compression of wage differentials. Swedish unions needed some quid pro quo for their cooperation in imposing wage restraints, and a central benefit that the Swedish unions obtained was a reduction in wage inequality. The union commitment to wage equality was not very expensive in the 1950s and 1960s, when the relative demand for unskilled and semiskilled workers was rising throughout Europe and North America. The reduction in wage inequality was universal among advanced industrial societies in the early postwar period. Thus, the policy of solidaristic bargaining adopted in all four Nordic countries accelerated a change in the structure of pay that would have occurred anyway in the 1950s and 1960s, albeit to a lesser extent (Edin and Topel 1995). Moreover, theoretical work by Moene and Wallerstein (1997) and the empirical work by Hibbs and Locking (1995a, 1995b) conclude that the initial effects of solidaristic bargaining, the equalization of wages between firms within industries and between industries, was beneficial for Swedish industry. In the 1970s, however, Swedish unions increasingly began to demand wage compression between different occupations and, according to Hibbs and Locking (1995a, 1995b), productivity growth suffered.

Wage compression, however, does not distinguish Sweden from the other Scandinavian countries. Wages were equally compressed in Norway, where decentralization has not occurred at all, and in Denmark, where decentralized has occurred to a much lesser extent. What does distinguish Sweden from its neighbors is the hostile relations that existed between employers and unions, stemming from political battles during the 1970s, particularly the fight over the union proposal to establish wage-earner funds that would have resulted in eventual union ownership of all large Swedish firms if the original proposal been adopted. According to this interpretation, Swedish employers were willing to forego the advantages of centralized pay setting in order to gain the ability to increase wage differentials and reduce the influence of the unions in Swedish politics.[13]

5. Conclusion

In this essay I have argued that the two leading arguments regarding the impact of economic integration on collective bargaining institutions are flawed. The union monopoly argument mistakenly views the purpose of centralization as increasing the unions' ability to obtain rents. In fact, the opposite was the case. Centralization was a means by which employers limited the rents unions received. The corporatism argument asserts that centralization was tied to Keynesian policies of demand management and has declined as the room for discretionary macroeconomic policy has shrunk. I argue that there are many benefits of centralization that do not depend on full employment or demand management. High unemployment, or the threat of high unemployment in the near future, may make the prospect of negotiating wage restraints at the central level more appealing, not less.

Nevertheless, both arguments contain an element that is worth retaining. While centralized wage setting, at its inception, was a means of subjecting the entire labor market to the ability to pay of the traded goods sector, over time workers in the traded goods sector have lost their pay-setting role in countries where public sector employment, and hence public sector union membership, has grown dramatically. In both the 1950s and the 1980s, Nordic employers in the traded goods sector wanted to restrain wage increases in the sheltered sector and were unhappy about the unwillingness of sheltered sector employers to "stand up to" the unions. In the 1950s, wage restraint in the sheltered sector was imposed via centralization. In the 1980s and 1990s, many employers have advocated decentralization to achieve the same end.

There may be also be an important link between the macroeconomic environment and the survival of centralized bargaining at low levels of inflation. Unions find it very difficult to acquiesce to nominal wage reductions, no matter what the bargaining system. With a moderate amount of inflation, real wage reductions can be accomplished with a small increase in the nominal wage. When inflation is close to zero, the room to lower real wages without cutting nominal wages is limited. In such an environment, employers may only be able to reduce their labor costs by withdrawing from collective bargaining altogether, which is incompatible with the continuation of centralized bargaining.

The most compelling relationship between the decentralization of bargaining and economic integration may be that both are responses to a common problem, poor economic performance since the mid-1970s. A long-term decline in the demand for labor has significantly strengthened employers relative to unions. This does not mean that centralized bargaining is being dismantled everywhere, for many of the benefits of centralization were received by employers. Only in a few countries, notably Britain and Sweden, have employers united in opposition to centralized bargaining. It is an indication of the change that has occurred in the past two decades, however, that the future of centralized bargaining is being largely decided in internal debates among employers, with the unions relegated to the sidelines.

NOTES

An earlier version of this essay was presented at the conference "The Political Economy of European Integration: The Challenges Ahead," hosted by the Center for German and European Studies, University of California, Berkeley, April 20–22, 1995. I thank Lloyd Ulman, Peter Swenson, Kathy Thelen, Miriam Golden, Jeff Frieden, and participants of the conference for helpful comments.

1. This sentence overstates the decline of centralization in Britain, as wage setting, in most industries, had already devolved to the shop floor by the 1960s in spite of being covered by an industry-level agreement. Unlike in the Germanic and Nordic countries, local bargaining in Britain was not restricted by an industrial peace clause. Moreover, the growth of single-employer agreements in Britain constitutes a centralization of wage setting insofar as multiple craft unions are being replaced with a single union that represents all workers in the firm.

2. In fairness to Schmitter and Streeck, it should be noted that the argument summarized here is one of several that they offer for the decline of corporatism. They also point to changes in occupational structure, values, and technology that they think have contributed to the decline of corporatism independent of economic integration.

3. For a recent exchange on the plausibility of Ingham's thesis as an explanation of cross-national difference of union density, see Stephens 1991, Wallerstein 1991, and Western and Jackman 1994. Swenson 1991a also contains a criticism of Ingham's thesis.

4. That workers in the traded goods sector act as the pattern setters for the determination of wages throughout the economy is the central assumption of the Aukrust, or Scandinavian, model of inflation (see Aukrust 1977).

5. See Garrett and Way 1994 for a study of corporatism and economic performance that emphasizes the importance of the relative size of public sector and private sector unions.

6. One should be careful not to confuse the outcomes in a labor market which is largely unorganized, as in the US, with the likely results of decentralizing wage-setting in a labor market where almost all workers are union members, as in the Nordic countries.

7. As Calmfors and Driffill (1988) pointed out, at some point continual decentralization results in one union per worker which is equivalent to a competitive labor market. Therefore, the impact of centralization must be hump-shaped rather than monotonic over the entire range of possible centralization.

8. See, for example, Bruno and Sachs 1985 or Layard, Nickell, and Jackman 1991.

9. Garrett and Lange (1991) find that macroeconomic policy in countries with social democratic government and centralized bargaining institutions was no more expansionary than in other countries in the postwar period.

10. The argument that centralized wage setting would reduce wages in an efficiency wage model was first made by Asbjørn Rødseth (1990). The model presented here is taken from Moene, Wallerstein, and Hoel 1993.

11. In this respect, I agree with the argument of Streeck and Schmitter (1991).

12. One reason for the difference is that union membership is much more widespread in Sweden than in Germany. Employees in small firms in Germany are unlikely to belong to the union. Thus, small employers in Germany can escape the provisions of the collective agreement by not joining the employers' association. In Sweden, where virtually the entire labor force is organized, only large employers welcome negotiating with the unions without the support of a strong employers' association.

13. It should be noted that there is no consensus in the literature on the causes of decentralization in Sweden. My conclusion is derived from a study of continuity and change in collective bargaining institutions in the Nordic countries since 1950, reported in Wallerstein and Golden 1997. For other views on the causes of the decline of the Swedish model of wage bargaining, see Lash 1985, Swenson 1991b, Hernes 1991, Moene and Wallerstein 1993, Martin 1991, Iversen 1996 and Pontusson and Swenson 1996.

REFERENCES

Aukrust, Odd. 1977. Inflation in an Open Economy: A Norwegian Model. In *Worldwide Inflation: Theory and Recent Experience*, edited by Lawrence B. Krause and Walter S. Salant. Washington, D.C.: Brookings Institution.

Bjørgum, Jorunn. 1985. LO og NAF, 1899–1940. *Tidsskrift for Arbeiderbevegelsens Historie* 1985, no. 2: 85–114.

Blanchflower, David G., and Richard B. Freeman. 1992. Unionism in the United States and Other Advanced OECD Countries. *Industrial Relations* 31:56–79.

Bowles, Samuel. 1985. The Production Process in a Competitive Economy: Walrasian, Neo-Hobbesian, and Marxian Models. *American Economic Review* 75:16–36.

Bruno, Michael, and Jeffrey Sachs. 1985. *The Economics of Worldwide Stagflation*. Cambridge: Harvard University Press.

Calmfors, Lars, and John Driffill. 1988. Bargaining Structure, Corporatism, and Macroeconomic Performance. *Economic Policy* 3:13–61.

Calvo, G. A. 1979. Quasi-Walrasian Theory of Unemployment. *American Economic Review* 69:102–7.

Calvo, G. A., and S. Wellisz. 1978. Supervision, Loss of Control, and the Optimum Size of the Firm. *Journal of Political Economy* 86:943–52.

Cameron, David R. 1978. The Expansion of the Public Economy: A Comparative Analysis. *American Political Science Review* 72:1243–61.

Cooper, Richard N. 1987. External Constraints on European Growth. In *Barriers to European Growth: A Transatlantic View,* edited by Robert Z. Lawrence and Charles L. Schultze. Washington, D.C.: Brookings Institution.

Due, Jesper, Jorgen Steen Madsen, Carsten Stroby Jensen, and Lars Kjerulff Petersen. 1993. *The Survival of the Danish Model.* Copenhagen: DJOF Publishers.

Edin, Per-Aners, and Robert Topel. 1995. Wage Policy and Restructuring: The Swedish Labor Market since 1960. In *Reforming the Welfare State,* edited by Richard B. Freeman and Robert Topel. Chicago: University of Chicago Press.

Garrett, Geoffrey, and Peter Lange. 1986. Economic Growth in Capitalist Democracies, 1974–1982. *World Politics* 38:517–45.

———. 1991. Political Responses to Interdependence: What's "Left" for the Left? *International Organization* 45:539–64.

Garrett, Geoffrey, and Christopher Way. 1995. The Sectoral Composition of Trade Unions, Corporatism, and Economic Performance. In *Monetary and Fiscal Policy in an Integrated Europe,* edited by Barry Eichengreen, Jeffry Frieden, and Jürgen von Hagen. Berlin: Springer.

Headey, Bruce W. 1970. Trade Unions and National Wages Policies. *Journal of Politics* 32:407–39.

Hernes, Gudmund. 1991. The Dilemmas of Social Democracies: The Case of Norway and Sweden. *Acta Sociologica* 34:239–60.

Hibbs, Douglas A., Jr., and Håkan Locking. 1995a. Wage Dispersion and Productive Efficiency: Evidence from Sweden. Stockholm, Trade Union Institute for Economic Research. Manuscript.

———. 1995b. Solidarity Wage Policies and Industrial Productivity in Sweden. *Nordic Journal of Political Economy* 22:95–108.

Howell, Chris. 1995. Trade Unions and the State: A Critique of British Industrial Relations. *Politics and Society* 23:149–83.

Ingham, Geoffrey. 1974. *Strikes and Industrial Conflict: Britain and Scandinavia.* London: Macmillan.

Iversen, Torben. 1996. Power, Flexibility, and the Breakdown of Centralized Wage Bargaining: The Cases of Denmark and Sweden in Comparative Perspective. *Comparative Politics* 28:399–436.

Jackman, Richard. 1990. Wage Formation in the Nordic Countries Viewed from an International Perspective. In *Wage Formation and Macroeconomic Policy*

206 Forging an Integrated Europe

in the Nordic Countries, edited by Lars Calmfors. Oxford: Oxford University Press.

Kalecki, Michal. 1943. Political Aspects of Full Employment. *Political Quarterly* (October-December): 322–31.

Katzenstein, Peter. 1983. The Small European States in the International Economy: Economic Dependence and Corporatist Politics. In *The Antinomies of Interdependence,* edited by J. R. Ruggie. New York: Columbia University Press.

———. 1984. *Corporatism and Change: Austria, Switzerland, and the Politics of Industry.* Ithaca: Cornell University Press.

———. 1985. *Small States in World Markets: Industrial Policy in Europe.* Ithaca: Cornell University Press.

Lange, Peter, and Geoffrey Garrett. 1985. The Politics of Growth. *Journal of Politics* 47:792–827.

Lash, Scott. 1985. The End of Neo-corporatism? The Breakdown of Centralized Bargaining in Sweden. *British Journal of Industrial Relations* 23:215–39.

Layard, Richard, Stephen Nickell, and Richard Jackman. 1991. *Unemployment, Macroeconomic Performance, and the Labour Market.* Oxford: Oxford University Press.

Markovits, Andrei S. 1986. *The Politics of the West German Trade Unions.* Cambridge: Cambridge University Press.

Martin, Andrew. 1991. Wage Bargaining and Swedish Politics: The Political Implications of the End of Central Negotiations. Working Papers, no. 6. Cambridge, Center for European Studies, Harvard University.

Moene, Karl Ove, and Michael Wallerstein. 1993. What's Wrong with Social Democracy? In *Market Socialism: The Current Debate,* edited by Pranab Bardhan and John Roemer. Oxford: Oxford University Press.

———. 1997. Pay Inequality and Job Creation. *Journal of Labor Economics,* forthcoming.

Moene, Karl Ove, Michael Wallerstein, and Michael Hoel. 1993. Bargaining Structure and Economic Performance. In *Trade Union Behavior, Pay Bargaining, and Economic Performance,* Robert Flanagan, Karl Ove Moene, and Michael Wallerstein. Oxford: Oxford University Press.

Olson, Mancur. 1982. *The Rise and Decline of Nations.* New Haven: Yale University Press.

Organization for Economic Cooperation and Development. 1977. *Towards Full Employment and Price Stability.* Paris: OECD.

Oswald, Andrew J. 1979. Wage Determination in an Economy with Many Trade Unions. *Oxford Economic Papers* 31:369–85.

Pontusson, Jonas, and Peter Swenson. 1996. Labor Markets, Production Strategies, and Wage Bargaining Institutions: The Swedish Employer Offensive in Comparative Perspective. *Comparative Political Studies* 29:223–50.

Reder, Melvin, and Lloyd Ulman. 1993. Unionism and Unification. In *Labor and an*

Integrated Europe, edited by Lloyd Ulman, Barry Eichengreen, and William T. Dickens. Washington, D.C.: Brookings Institution.

Rødseth, Asbjørn. 1990. Efficiency Wages and Local versus Central Bargaining. Working paper, University of Oslo, Department of Economics.

Scheuer, Steen. 1992. Denmark: Return to Decentralization. In *Industrial Relations in the New Europe,* edited by Anthony Ferner and Richard Hyman. Oxford: Blackwell.

Schmitter, Philippe C. 1989. Corporatism is Dead! Long Live Corporatism. *Government and Opposition* 24:54–73.

Shapiro, Carl, and Joseph Stiglitz. 1984. Equilibrium Unemployment as a Worker Discipline Device. *American Economic Review* 74:433–44.

Stephens, John D. 1991. Industrial Concentration, Country Size, and Union Membership. *American Political Science Review,* 85:941–49.

Streeck, Wolfgang. 1993. The Rise and Decline of Neocorporatism. In *Labor and an Integrated Europe,* edited by Lloyd Ulman, Barry Eichengreen, and William T. Dickens. Washington, D.C.: Brookings Institution.

Streeck, Wolfgang, and Philippe C. Schmitter. 1991. From National Corporatism to Transnational Pluralism: Organized Interests in the Single European Market. *Politics and Society* 19:133–64.

Swenson, Peter. 1989. *Fair Shares: Unions, Pay, and Politics in Sweden and West Germany.* Ithaca: Cornell University Press.

———. 1991a. Bringing Capital Back in, or Social Democracy Reconsidered. *World Politics* 43, no. 4:513–44.

———. 1991b. Labor and the Limits of the Welfare State: The Politics of Intraclass Conflict and Cross-Class Alliances in Sweden and West Germany. *Comparative Politics* 23:379–99.

———. 1992. Managing the Managers: The Swedish Employers' Confederation, Labor Scarcity, and the Suppression of Labor Market Segmentation. *Scandinavian Journal of History* 16:335–56.

Thelen, Kathleen A. 1991. *Union of Parts: Labor Politics in Postwar Germany.* Ithaca: Cornell University Press.

Ulman, Lloyd. 1955. *The Rise of the National Trade Union.* Cambridge: Harvard University Press.

Wallerstein, Michael. 1985. Working Class Solidarity and Rational Behavior. Ph.D. diss., University of Chicago.

———. 1990. Centralized Bargaining and Wage Restraint. *American Journal of Political Science* 34:982–1004.

———. 1991. Industrial Concentration, Country Size, and Union Membership: Response to Stephens. *American Political Science Review* 85:949–53.

Wallerstein, Michael, and Miriam Golden. 1997. The Fragmentation of the Bargaining Society: Wage-Setting in the Nordic Countries, 1950–1992. *Comparative Political Studies,* forthcoming.

Wallerstein, Michael, Miriam Golden, and Peter Lange. 1997. Unions, Employers Associations, and Wage-Setting Institutions in North and Central Europe, *Industrial and Labor Relations Review* 50:379–401.

Western, Bruce, and Simon Jackman. 1994. Bayesian Inference for Comparative Research. *American Political Science Review* 88:412–23.

Part 3
Enlargement

CHAPTER 8

Nordic Accession: An Analysis of the EU Referendums

Jonathon W. Moses and Anders Todal Jenssen

The intent was clear: in domino fashion the Nordic countries would fall into the ranks of the European Union. The timing of the Nordic referendums was designed in such a fashion as to ensure that the most enthusiastic potential member, Finland, would set the stage and generate the momentum to help convince Swedish and Norwegian voters of the need to follow suit. The outcome was not as planned. While Sweden followed the Finnish example, the Norwegian electorate proved obstinately opposed. This chapter argues that timing was not the most relevant determinate of outcomes in the three Nordic countries. Rather, we ask whether the nature of each country's economic integration (or lack thereof) with the European Union might provide better guidance for interpreting the variation in referendum outcomes.

On October 16, 56.9 percent of voting Finns declared their support for Finnish membership in the European Union in an advisory referendum. While the aggregate numbers showed support for membership, their geographic distribution suggests that the country was severely split on the issue. Indeed, 70 percent, or 326, of the 445 municipalities (*kommuner*) were opposed to membership. Of the supportive counties (*län*), all of them lay in the urban-dominated southern part of the country (see fig. 8.1). The county surrounding the capital city, Helsinki, voted 73.6 percent in favor of membership. The northern counties were all opposed to membership, with the strongest opposition found in Uleåborg (56.1 percent opposed) and Vasa (55.6 percent opposed) counties.

A similar story unfolded in Sweden just a month later; on November 13, Swedes supported EU membership by 52.3 percent. Whereas the number of counties opposed to membership was equal to the number that supported it

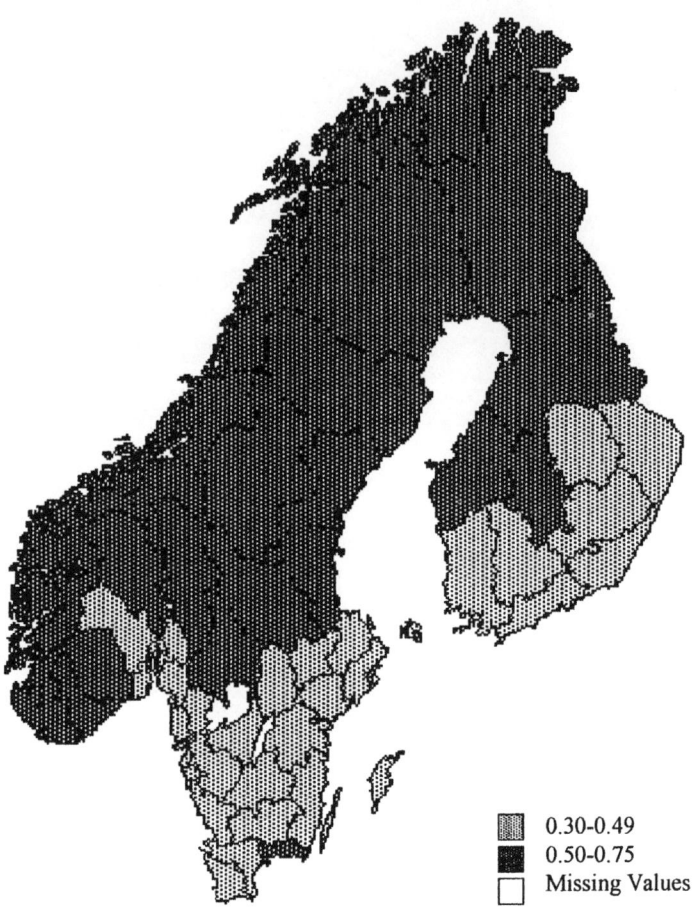

Fig. 8.1. Nordic referendum outcomes, percentage of no votes

(12), there was large variation among counties: from the 66 percent of the electorate in Malmöhus Län, which supported membership, to the 72 percent in Jämtlan, which opposed it. As in Finland, opposition to the referendum was more concentrated in the northern, more rural part of the country (see fig. 8.1). The pattern was similar in Norway but with a different result. On November 28, the Norwegian electorate narrowly (52.2 percent) opposed membership. As in the other two Nordic countries, the yes votes were heavily concentrated in the urban centers, with the northern and western counties providing strong opposition. Of Norway's 19 counties, 14 contained majorities that opposed membership, with Finnmark Fylke—in northern Norway—opposing membership by 75 percent.

There are a myriad of potential explanations for the variance in outcomes.[1] Opinions about membership in the European Union have been influenced by a number of elements, several of which were not even conceivable just a handful of years ago. Worse, membership itself crosses many issue areas and crosses several of the traditional cleavages in the Nordic body politic. Because of the complex nature of the decisions, explanations of the referendums threaten to be ideographic and ad hoc.

How do we begin to understand these variations at both the national and regional levels? We propose a parsimonious political economy explanation. Our working hypothesis is that variations among and within the Nordic countries can be explained by their unique economic relationship with the European Union. In particular, the more economically integrated a nation, region, or individual is with the European Union, the more likely it will support Union membership in the respective referendums. In order to test this hypothesis, we examine economic structures and attitudes at three different levels of analysis: national, county, and individual.[2]

This chapter is divided into four sections, wherein each level of analysis is prioritized. After a brief introduction on integration, the second section compares the economic structure and export dependence of each of the Nordic countries vis-à-vis the European Union. Each economy relies on different export structures, which are more or less dependent on markets within the European Union. While the Norwegian economy is shown to be the most integrated with European export markets, the nature of its export (oil) and its relative wealth make it insensitive to membership pressures.

In the third section, the same questions are analyzed at the regional level by employing a series of simple regressions on county-level data. County-level aggregate data are used to establish that the arguments supported at the national level can be sustained at the regional level. We hypothesize that those counties that are more dependent on sheltered sector incomes would be less likely to support membership, and the regression evidence in this section suggests that the economic integration argument is supported at the county level as well. Indeed, the political economy hypothesis finds its strongest support at the county level.

In the fourth section, we attempt to provide microfoundations for the premises worked out in the previous two sections. It is, after all, individuals who vote. The individual-level data only grudgingly support the conclusions of the previous two sections. While economic factors were frequently used to support membership attitudes, they were not the only factors mentioned, nor were they always the most significant.

We conclude by arguing that an economic integration argument goes some distance in explaining Nordic EU membership aspirations but that the effect of that integration is not always or forcefully apparent in the individual responses of voters. There appears to be a strong political economy argument in effect at the county level, moderate support at the national level, and more nuanced and varied support at the individual level. The results of the individual-level analysis should not be surprising: individual attitudes are affected by a variety of factors. Even in the individual responses that name ideological or political variables as significant in determining their position with respect to EU membership, it is likely that political economy factors nevertheless lie beneath these responses.

I. Integration

Our story begins by assuming that each of the Nordic countries would rather *not* join the European Union. Our justifications for doing this are threefold. First, membership entails too many political constraints on national sovereignty to be attractive in its own right. Second, small neighboring states under the European Economic Agreement (EEA) umbrella have the potential for free riding on European solutions. Finally, as members, the potential influence of each of the Nordic states (individually) is relatively small. Instead, we assume that small neighboring nations might be willing to bear the costs of membership—given a greater degree of national economic integration with the European Union. Economic integration, from this perspective, functions as a justification for membership. But what is the relationship between economic and political integration?

Unfortunately, most of the political integration literature is of little utility when trying to explain the incentives for *entering* (as opposed to building) a relatively integrated market.[3] Nor can we expect assistance from the ranks of trade theorists. Although much of contemporary trade theory recognizes a relationship between economic dependence and political affiliation, it positions the causal arrow in a direction pointing *from* political affiliation *to* economic integration. Trade, in these models, follows the flag.[4] Nevertheless, literature from both the integration and trade theory traditions can be modified to account for enlargement incentives. In particular, we intend to explain membership expansion in terms borrowed from industrial organization theory, cognitive theory, and neofunctionalism.

It is our proposition that the flag follows trade, at least in the case of small open economies on the margins of Europe. This is so for at least three reasons. First, an integrated market is developing and has developed in Europe, and Nordic firms—to varying degrees—are participants.[5] Second, economic integration functions as a sort of communicative interactionism[6] in which exchange interactions form communities. Whereas Karl Deutsch (1953, 1968) originally posited that security communities formed as the result of increased communication (mail flows, telephone calls, tourism, etc.), the same sense of community may be formed by economic exchanges. Finally, and concomitantly, economic integration may have its own spillover effects. Generally, as economic integration accelerates and spreads it can potentially encroach further and further into the political realm, so that political integration might be built on the cognitive foundations of the interactive community. From these generalizations we can form a specific hypothesis: the more economically integrated an entity is with the EU, the greater the likelihood that the entity will desire membership in the Union.

2. National Level

The next stage of the puzzle is operationalization. Whereas support for EU membership is easy to gauge from the recent referendums, indicators for economic integration are more amorphous. At the national level, we propose to measure levels of economic dependence along three fronts: general economic well-being (i.e., autonomy or the lack of dependence), foreign direct investment flows, and trade exposure. As we only need to establish relative levels of integration among the three countries, this measure should be sufficient.

Along the first front, economic autonomy, we assume that wealth encourages autonomy. In other words, the poorer a country, the greater the likelihood that it will prefer membership. There are at least two justifications for this assumption. First, and most simply, membership in the European Union is costly for the richer countries.[7] Richer countries can expect to pay more into Union coffers than they receive in return (via such things as larger VAT and GNP resource contributions). Although we are not talking about very much in terms of overall European GDP (under 1.7 percent), these are not insignificant transfers for individual nation-states. Second, membership in the EU and its accompanying designs for economic and monetary union entails significant constraints on national economic policy. In particular, countries that have serious inflation and budget, debt, or exchange rate problems can use membership in the European Monetary System as a means of providing an ambitious external source of legitimacy for national policies. Economic policies suffering a legitimation deficit are more likely to benefit from membership.[8]

In the second area, we are interested in investment flows. We expect that countries that are experiencing a large outflow of foreign direct investment into Europe would be more likely to join the European Union.[9] High levels of outward FDI could be important for EU membership, even if the investments are going outside of Europe. Continual exit by investment capital weakens the resolve of nation-states, weary from growing unemployment levels. In these cases, outward-oriented multinational corporations are seen to pull their respective countries into the European Union. The more national capital flight into Europe, the stronger the pull on the nation-state to follow.[10]

The final area of economic integration is the most straightforward. We expect to find that the more trade dependent a country is on the EU for its export market the more likely it is to support membership. Increased trade integration is expected to facilitate community building and undermine the initial resistance to membership. In other words, given the referendum outcomes, we would expect that the Norwegian economy was less export dependent on the EU than either the Swedish or Finnish economy.

If these hypotheses are accurate, we should expect to find that these three elements of economic integration are correlated with the outcomes in Finland, Sweden, and Norway. The Norwegian economy should be the least integrated in the European market, the Swedish and Finnish economies more.

2.1. General Economic Conditions

The first measures of integration to consider are those that depict the general economic health of each of the three Nordic countries. As we argue that membership in itself is not attractive for nations with stronger economies, measuring the relative strength of each economy should provide a rough indicator of membership attitudes. The difficulty comes in trying to operationalize strength. As credibility concerns play a role in this decision, we think it most useful to measure each Nordic country's record in terms of the EU's so-called convergence criteria. If a country intends to use EU membership as a means of introducing economic frugality, we would expect the most enthusiastic members to have the worst record in terms of these criteria. In addition to the four traditional criteria, we have listed a fifth—percent unemployed—to give a better all-around picture of the economic health of each of the economies (see table 8.1).

TABLE 8.1.   Convergence criteria plus unemployment, 1993

	Inflation	Deficit	Interest Rate	Debt	Unemployment
EU criteria	<2.9%	<3.0%	<9.46%	<60.0%	—
Finland	2.2[a]	10.8	8.9[a]	37.0[a]	18.0
Norway	3.7	3.4	7.2[a]	43.3[a]	6.0
Sweden	4.5	13.0	8.8[a]	53.0[a]	8.2

Sources: European Commission 1996; Nordisk Råd 1995.

Note: Annual change in consumer prices should not exceed by more than 1.5 percent above the three lowest EU inflation rates. The general government budget deficit as a percentage of GDP should not exceed 3 percent. The yields of long-term government bonds should not exceed the yields on the three lowest inflation countries by more than two points. The general government debt as a proportion of GDP should not exceed 60 percent.

[a]Convergence criteria have been met.

Although these figures only offer a slice of time (1993), the picture that develops is as follows. Despite the fact that Finland satisfied the greatest number of convergence criteria in 1993, it had a phenomenally large unemployment problem. The Swedish economy was also experiencing great difficulties, though these were of a different nature. Swedish debt figures were growing at such a rate that they would soon be outside the criteria's margins, and the deficit, at 13 percent, was frighteningly large. Generally speaking, then, the Norwegian economy seems to be the strongest. Not only was Norway's unemployment level lower than the other two, but it was fairly close to meeting both the deficit and inflation criteria.

2.2.   Foreign Direct Investment

Immediately after the Swedish EU referendum, a large Swedish firm, Ericsson Ltd., took out full-page ads in several pan-European newspapers to declare that Sweden had finally followed Ericsson's lead in joining the European Union. This advertisement is indicative of the attitude that several internationally oriented Nordic firms took toward the European Union. In the run-up to the referendums, Nordic firms exercised explicit threats of exit (to the European Union) if the national referendums should result in opposition to membership. Several internationally oriented firms had already taken up residence in Europe to defend against that possibility.

Figures 8.2–8.4 show the degree to which capital was already flowing from each of the Nordic economies in the run-up to the referendums.[11] As is evident in all three figures, the EU share of FDI from each of the countries is significant, though it is less so in Finland than in the other two countries. In both

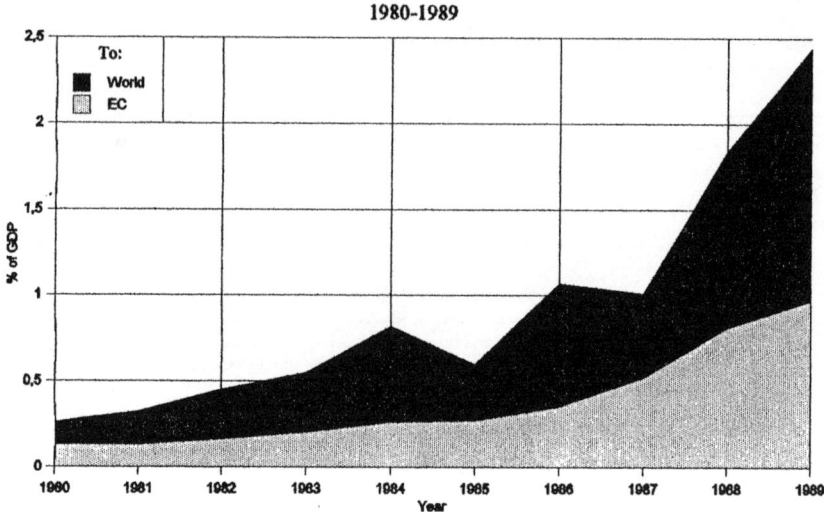

Fig. 8.2. FDI from Finland. (Data from Karlsen 1990 and IMF 1994.)

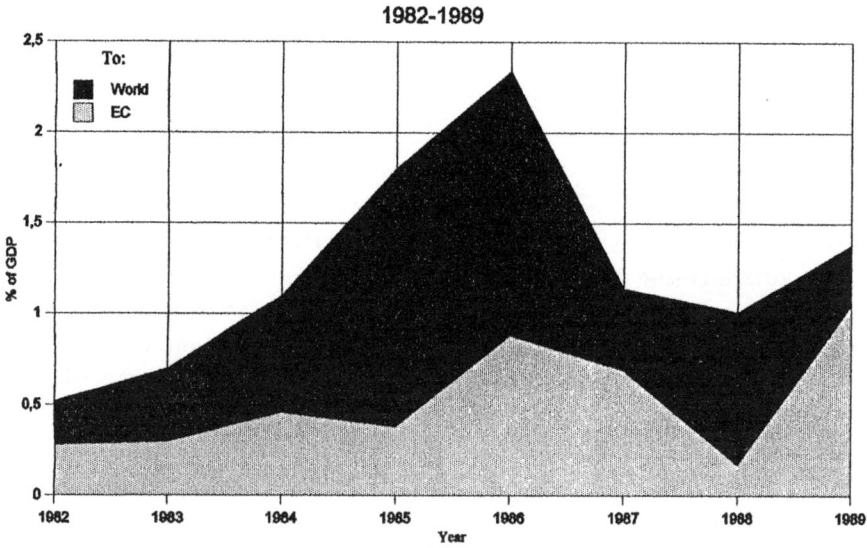

Fig. 8.3. FDI from Norway. (Data from Karlsen 1990 and IMF 1994.)

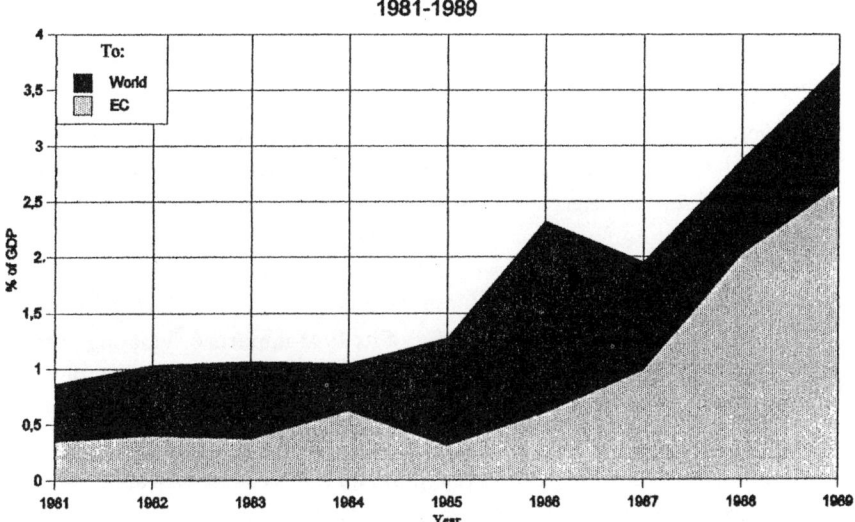

Fig. 8.4. FDI from Sweden. (Data from Karlsen 1990 and IMF 1994.)

Finland (fig. 8.2) and Sweden (fig. 8.4) the EC share of their world FDI is actually decreasing over time, while in Norway (fig. 8.3) the EU share of its world FDI has grown enormously since 1988. These figures reveal two patterns. First of all, outbound FDI is increasing rapidly in all three countries—to both world and EU markets. Second, the rate of growth (for the EU/world share) varies between Norway, on the one hand, and Sweden and Finland on the other. Either Swedish and Finnish capital has reached its saturation limit in terms of European FDI shares (unlikely) or there is some other explanation for the growth rates of European-directed FDI.

The Norwegian figures halfheartedly challenge our working hypothesis. As a larger (relative) share of Norwegian outward FDI is landing in Europe (larger than is the case in either Sweden or Finland), and because the relative growth of the Norwegian EU/world share of direct investment is higher than in either of the other two countries, we might expect that Norway would be more likely than the other two to entertain membership ambitions. On the other hand, outward FDI is of a larger magnitude (in terms of percentage of GDP) for both Finland and Sweden than is the case in Norway. Thus, it would appear that Sweden and Finland are more susceptible to the threat of capital flight.

2.3. Trade Dependence

By international standards, all of the Nordic countries are fairly reliant on trade. In 1993, export incomes were above 23 percent of GDP in all three countries, with Norway exporting at about the 31 percent level. In terms of imports, all three countries are relatively equally dependent. However, when we begin to look at the degree to which each economy relies on the European Union as a receptor of its export products, we find more variation in the degree of dependence. On the import side, all three countries receive about half of their imports from the European Union. Finland appears to be the least dependent in this regard, with only 47 percent of its 1993 imports originating in the EU. On the export side, however, Norway appears to be more dependent on the European market than any of the other countries, with 67 percent of its 1993 world exports heading toward European markets.

By disaggregating the figures even more, we can get some idea about which specific countries are the primary target markets for Finnish, Swedish, and Norwegian export goods. Table 8.2 lists the top five export markets for the Nordic countries in 1993. All three countries focused their exports in EU markets, with the United States and Norway being the only non-EU markets to make it among the top five. Curiously, Norway was the only country to have all of its top five export markets in the EU. Both Sweden and Finland are relatively dependent on the American market—Sweden, in particular, with 10 percent of its total export share going to the U.S. market. Table 8.2's overall figures suggest that the Norwegian export market is most concentrated in the EU (63 percent), while the markets for Finnish and Swedish exports are less densely concentrated (either in Europe or generally).

Generally, the trade picture presented in table 8.2 is not encouraging for our working hypothesis. More than either Finland or Sweden, the Norwegian economy is dependent on the European market as a receptor for its exports. In both the aggregate figures and its export concentration, Norway would seem to be most integrated into the European goods market. There are two potential explanations for this. First, it may be that Norwegians opposed membership despite the consequences in terms of market integration. Alternatively, the specific nature of Norway's trade relationship with the European Union might not have been affected by membership. The first possibility has been accounted for in the preceding section. Norway's relative economic strength allows it a cushion of autonomy. The latter possibility can be entertained by examining the sorts of products on which each country depends for the majority of its

TABLE 8.2.   The Top Five Export Countries, 1993 (percentage of world exports, ranking)

To	From Finland	From Norway	From Sweden
Denmark			7 (5)
France	5 (5)	8 (5)	
Germany	13 (1)	13 (2)	14 (1)
Netherlands		8 (4)	
Norway			8 (4)
Sweden	11 (2)	9 (3)	
United States	8 (4)		10 (2)
United Kingdom	10 (3)	25 (1)	8 (3)
Total	47	63	47

Source: Nordisk Råd 1995.

export income. Quite possibly, the nature of Norway's export income makes membership less enticing.

Table 8.3 lists the five most important export items, at the two-digit Standard International Trade Classification (SITC) level, for each of the three countries. This table introduces two important types of information. First, it is interesting to note that the Finnish and Swedish export economies rely heavily on paper and paper products, whereas the Norwegian export economy relies primarily on petroleum. In other words, all three export economies are heavily reliant on natural resource extraction. Second, there are important differences in the degree of concentration for each export economy. The Norwegian export economy is by far the most concentrated in that 70 percent (!) of its total export earnings are concentrated in the top five sectors, with petroleum taking the lion's share.

Thus, while the Norwegian economy is most dependent on European markets as receptors for its exports, the specific nature of its export economy make it less susceptible to economic blackmail. The importance of oil and petroleum imports to the European economies makes it highly unlikely that they will close off their markets to Norwegian exports. Because of this, Norwegian voters may have decided against membership despite their export dependence on Europe.

Obviously, these oil incomes are largely responsible for Norway's relative economic strength mentioned in the first section. It would appear, then, that oil incomes have become a determinate factor in influencing Norwegian atti-

TABLE 8.3.   The Five Most Important Export Items at the Two-Digit SITC Level (percentage of total exports, ranking)

Product Group	Finland	Norway	Sweden
03 Seafood and seafood preparation		7 (3)	
24 Cork and wood	5 (5)		
33 Petroleum and its products		44[a] (1)	
34 Gas, natural and manufactured		7 (2)	
64 Paper and paper products	25 (1)		10 (2)
67 Iron and steel	6 (2)		6 (5)
68 Nonferrous metals		7 (4)	
72 Specialized industrial machinery	6 (3)		
74 General industrial machinery			7 (3)
76 Telecommunications equipment	5 (4)		6 (4)
78 Road vehicles			12 (1)
79 Other transportation equipment		5 (4)	
Total	47	70	41

Sources: Nordisk Råd 1995; SSB 1995.

[a]The Norwegian petroleum export figures in the Nordisk Råd 1995 are obviously incorrect. The yearbook would have that sector representing only 4 percent of Norway's export earnings! The figures in the table have been replaced with those from SSB 1995.

tudes on membership. *Despite* Norway's export dependence, and the rate at which Norwegian capital is leaving for the continent, it would seem that the Norwegian economy—in the eyes of the Norwegian electorate—floats unaffected on its oil revenues. Norwegians apparently feel that they can afford to remain outside the Union.

Generally, the political economy hypothesis finds only moderate support at the national level. To understand Norway's hesitant attitude toward EU membership, we have to go beyond simple integration arguments and look at the specific nature and structure of its economy. In short, the hypothesis only holds with ad hoc modification.

3.   County Level

3.1.   Integration

An extension of the economic integration argument formulated in the first section might be generated to explain variations within each of the Nordic countries. If economic integration can explain membership attitudes at the national level, we would expect that these pressures would be just as effective at the county level. In short, our hypothesis at this level of analysis can be formulated as follows: counties that harbor more sheltered economic sectors are more likely to oppose membership in the EU. Or, in other words, sectors and/or counties that are heavily involved in European trade and investment should be more pro-EU than not.

It is our intent in this section to trace the relationship between some of the economic conclusions in the previous section against data collected at the county (*fylke* or *län*) level in all three countries.[12] Unfortunately, the cross-national data at this level are scant and patchy. Whereas it possible to obtain low-level data (municipal) in the Norwegian case,[13] many of the polling and political economy variables are not available in a comparative format for the remaining two countries. It is because of these difficulties that we have pursued our hypothesis at a variety of levels. Still, despite the limited nature of the data, some relationships can be tested.

This section is divided in two. The first part takes all of the county-level data from the three Nordic countries and runs a series of regressions on the most interesting employment variables. The aggregate data set includes 55 observations: for 12 Finnish, 19 Norwegian, and 24 Swedish counties. The remaining part runs two dummied regressions, which allow us to control for specific sectoral effects within each of the three countries. Together, these regressions should help us to evaluate the degree to which there was some linear relationship between the dependence of a given county on a specific sector (in terms of percentage of the population employed in that sector) and that county's referendum outcome.

As a sector's importance in income terms is different than what it is in employment terms, and as these county-level variables look at the *employment* strength of various sectors, table 8.4 shows Nordic employment strength and distributions by sector. In all three countries, the social services, sales, and manufacturing sectors are the strongest employers. The primary sector, despite its strong showing in the export incomes of Norway and Finland, is a small employer in all three countries. From the economic integration hypothesis, we would expect that those employed in either the sales or manufacturing (i.e., exposed) sectors would support membership, whereas those employed in the more sheltered sectors (such as social services) would be opposed. There are two justifications for this expectation. First, the sheltered sectors—by definition—are less affected by foreign influences and can be expected to prioritize domestic policy autonomy at the expense of integration. Second, we can assume that EU membership will help both import-export traders directly and the commercial sectors more generally.

With the data available, we have been able to operationalize five sectoral

TABLE 8.4.   Employment, by Sector 1993, Single-Digit SITC (percentage of total employment, ranking)

Industrial Branch	Finland		Norway		Sweden	
1 Agriculture, hunting, forestry, and fishing	9		6		3	
2 Mining and quarrying	0.2		1		0.3	
3 Manufacturing	19	(2)	15	(3)	18	(2)
4 Electricity, gas, and water	1		1		0.9	
5 Construction	6		6		6	
6 Wholesale and retail trade	15	(3)	17	(2)	14	(3)
7 Transport, storage, and communications	8		8		7	
8 Financing, insurance, and business services	9		8		9	
9 Community, social, and personal services	33	(1)	39	(1)	40	(1)

Source: Nordisk Råd 1995.

variables (at the single-digit SITC level). They represent the percentage of the population employed in the: (1) primary sector (PRIMSEC),[14] (2) public sector (PUBSEC), (3) manufacturing sector (MANUF), (4) oil extraction, mining, and quarrying industries (OIL), and (5) wholesale and retail trade (TRADE). Each variable has been run in a series of bivariate and multivariate equations in both the aggregate and national batches.

3.2.   Aggregate Data

Whereas the mean vote was fairly similar in all three countries, the spread varied significantly across counties in all three countries. Table 8.5 lists the significant descriptive statistics for the batches. Not surprisingly, the county with the strongest opposition to EU membership was in Norway; the weakest opposition was found in Finland. On this data, four different multivariate batches were run, in addition to several bivariate regressions. The bivariate regressions were used to check the robustness of specific relationships and appear only in parenthetical references.

In the multivariate regressions we found a strong negative correlation between the PRIMSEC and TRADE variables, such that inclusion of them both as independent variables was problematic. This was especially true for the Finnish and Norwegian data. To control for this, we had to decide which of the two to include. This was no simple matter, as they both had their advantages in all of the models. Eventually, we decided to run two models (A and B) for each set, but in our analysis we rely most heavily on the TRADE variable model (A), as

TABLE 8.5.   No Vote in Referendums (percentages)

	Mean	Standard Deviation	Minimum	Maximum	N
Finland	47	8	30	56	12
Sweden	50	9	34	72	24
Norway	56	12	33	75	19
Aggregate	52	10	30	75	55

TABLE 8.6.   Aggregate Regression Coefficients (t-statistics, percentage of no votes)

Variable	Model A		Model B	
PUBSEC (β)	.250	(.98)	1.30	(5.59)[a]
MANUF (δ)	−.577	(−2.18)[a]	.291	(1.48)
OIL (δ)	3.91	(3.05)	3.89	(3.68)[a]
TRADE (ϵ)	−1.67	(−3.53)[a]		
PRIMSEC (ϵ)			1.63	(6.27)[a]
Constant (α)	.764	(4.6)	−1.28	(−1.13)
R^2	.37		.57	

Note:
Model A
$$Y_{NO} = \alpha + \beta(\text{PUBSEC}) + \gamma(\text{MANUF}) + \delta(\text{OIL}) + \epsilon(\text{TRADE}) + u$$
Model B
$$Y_{NO} = \alpha + \beta(\text{PUBSEC}) + \gamma(\text{MANUF}) + \delta(\text{OIL}) + \epsilon(\text{PRIMSEC}) + u$$
[a]Significant at the 95 percent confidence level. PUBSEC, MANUF, OIL, TRADE, and PRIMSEC represent the percentage of the population employed in the public sector; manufacturing; the oil extraction, mining and quarrying industries; the wholesale and retail sales sectors; and the primary sector, respectively.

this sector is more important, in employment terms, in all three countries. It is important to note that the two models produce somewhat different outcomes.

Table 8.6 presents the findings of our multivariate aggregate batch regressions. In these regressions, national disturbances were overlooked in order to focus on the common political economy determinants of EU opposition among the Nordic countries. In model A, we found statistically significant relationships for three of the four explanatory variables, MANUF, OIL, and TRADE. For the MANUF and TRADE variables we find a fairly strong and statistically significant relationship between the relative strength of employment in those sectors for a given county and its support in the EU referendum. As the MANUF and TRADE sectors are the most outward-oriented sectors of the economy, these findings are consistent with our hypothesis. The same can be said, in reverse, for the findings with respect to the OIL variable.[15] Indeed, all of the coefficient signs in this model are consistent with our theoretical expectations.

In model B, the TRADE variable was replaced with one representing employment strength in the primary sector, PRIMSEC. This model is statistically more robust, with very strong t-scores and an R^2 of .57. Together models A and B support our general hypothesis. Counties that are heavily reliant on sheltered sector employment tended to oppose membership, while those employing more integrated sectors tended to support membership.

3.3. National Data

The next set of regressions employed a series of dummy variables to capture the relationships *within* each country, the results of which can be found in table 8.7. In general, what is most noteworthy is the apparent relationship between TRADE and/or PRIMSEC strength and support for Union membership across all three countries. The regression results in this section are generally consistent with our hypothesis.

The Finnish data show a significant relationship between a county's dependence (in employment terms) on the primary sector and its tendency to oppose the referendum. The same can be said, in reverse, of the TRADE variable's relationship to EU support. In the bivariate regressions run on these two variables (TRADE and PRIMSEC), both regressions explained over half of the proportion of the referendum variance.[16] Among the Finnish variables, there were few surprises. In model A, the only significant variable remained TRADE, though its significance declined relative to the bivariate regressions. In model B, both the PUBSEC and PRIMSEC variables were significant.

The same story could be told for Norway. Here the coastal and northern counties, which rely heavily on fishing, farming, and hunting for their livelihoods, were strongly opposed to membership. In the model B variant, the PRIMSEC, PUBSEC, and OIL variables are all statistically significant, the first two being quite robust. In model A, the TRADE and PUBSEC variables remain statistically significant.

Finally, the Swedish case was—quite possibly—the most interesting.[17] Sweden was the only country that did not show a significant PRIMSEC coefficient in either the bivariate or the multivariate regressions (i.e., model B). This suggests that the primary sector counties in Sweden were less engaged in opposing EU membership than in the other two countries. For example, Gotlands Län, a county where 12 percent of the population is employed in the

TABLE 8.7. National Regression Coefficients (t-statistics, percentage of no votes)

Variable			Finland		Sweden		Norway	
Model A								
PUBSEC (β)			.632	(.728)	.125	(.287)	1.33	(2.58)[a]
MANUF (γ)			−.359	(−.982)	−.347	(−1.21)	.094	(.215)
OIL (δ)			−1.62	(−.107)	4.21	(2.06)[a]	1.16	(1.06)
TRADE (ϵ)			−3.58	(−3.19)[a]	−2.87	(−3.69)[a]	−4.73	(−7.72)[a]
Constant (α)	.885	(3.65)[a]						
R^2		.75						
Model B								
PUBSEC (β)			2.40	(3.34)[a]	1.98	(3.94)[a]	2.00	(4.15)[a]
MANUF (γ)			.702	(1.84)	.803	(2.67)[a]	.817	(1.87)
OIL (δ)			−14.89	(−1.06)	4.65	(2.02)	3.01	(2.46)[a]
PRIMSEC (ϵ)			1.59	(3.39)[a]	.689	(1.15)	2.21	(5.92)[a]
Constant (α)	−.466	(−2.10)						
R^2		.68						
N		55	12		24		19	

Note:

Model A

$$Y_{NO} = \alpha + \beta_N(\text{PUBSEC}^*D_N) + \beta_S(\text{PUBSEC}^*D_S) + \beta_F(\text{PUBSEC}^*D_F)$$
$$+ \gamma_N(\text{MANUF}^*D_N) + \gamma_S(\text{MANUF}^*D_S) + \gamma_F(\text{MANUF}^*D_F)$$
$$+ \delta_N(\text{OIL}^*D_N) + \delta_S(\text{OIL}^*D_S) + \delta_F(\text{OIL}^*D_F)$$
$$+ \epsilon_N(\text{TRADE}^*D_N) + \epsilon_S(\text{TRADE}^*D_S) + \epsilon_F(\text{TRADE}^*D_F) + u$$

Model B

$$Y_{NO} = \alpha + \beta_N(\text{PUBSEC}^*D_N) + \beta_S(\text{PUBSEC}^*D_S) + \beta_F(\text{PUBSEC}^*D_F)$$
$$+ \gamma_N(\text{MANUF}^*D_N) + \gamma_S(\text{MANUF}^*D_S) + \gamma_F(\text{MANUF}^*D_F)$$
$$+ \delta_N(\text{OIL}^*D_N) + \delta_S(\text{OIL}^*D_S) + \delta_F(\text{OIL}^*D_F)$$
$$+ \epsilon_N(\text{PRIMSEC}^*D_N) + \epsilon_S(\text{PRIMSEC}^*D_S) + \epsilon_F(\text{PRIMSEC}^*D_F) + u$$

[a]Significant at the 95 percent confidence level. PUBSEC, MANUF, OIL, TRADE, and PRIMSEC represent the percentage of the population employed in the public sector; manufacturing; the oil extraction, mining, and quarrying industries; the wholesale and retail sales sectors; and the primary sectors, respectively. D_N, D_S, and D_F are dummy variables for Norway, Sweden, and Finland, respectively.

primary sector (the most in Sweden), narrowly opposed EU membership in aggregate. Indeed, among the rest of the 55 cases, the only other county to support membership with a strong primary sector was St. Michels Län in Finland.

In concluding this county-level study, our findings provide some support for the political economy hypothesis. Employment in the sheltered sectors was highly and significantly correlated with opposition to EU membership in all three countries. In all of the countries, both the TRADE variable (in model A) and the PUBSEC variable (in model B) were significantly correlated with the referendum outcomes. In model B's results, the PRIMSEC variables were significant in both the Finnish and Norwegian cases.

4. Individual Level

Moving from aggregate-level analyses to the individual level implies a change of perspective in more than one sense. First, the reflections of the average voter are rather vague, obscure, and particularistic compared with the hypotheses we have discussed so far. Second, we must take into account that some voters may experience cross-pressures: for instance, some may think of membership as an asset to the country but as a setback to their personal economy. Third, the economic effects of membership may have only a marginal impact on the EU vote compared with other considerations, especially if the economic aspects of membership are too complicated to be grasped. In aggregate-level analyses, these types of phenomena tend to disappear as "noise" in the data. A few well-informed "ideologues" are sufficient to produce substantial aggregate-level correlations if attitudes in the general public are randomly distributed. In microlevel analyses, we have to take all voters into consideration.

This part of the chapter is divided into three subsections. So far, we have taken for granted that the voters in the three countries were familiar with their countries' economic situations as well as their personal economic conditions. In the first section, we simply ask: is this a viable assumption? Do voters hold opinions on these questions? Are Norwegians more content with their economic conditions than are Swedes and Finns? Our purpose here is to evaluate further some of our earlier findings and interpretations.

In the second subsection we explore the links between: (1) an individual's position in the economic structure, (2) his or her perceived personal and national economic interests, and (3) his or her EU vote. As far as possible, we will investigate the same key variables as in our county-level analysis. Unfortunately, we will have to rely exclusively on data from Norway for most of this inquiry.

In the final subsection, we seek to asses the relative importance of economic considerations on the EU vote compared with other aspects of the issue (national sovereignty, international cooperation, cultural integration, etc.). We do so by exploring the voters' answers to an open-ended question on the reasons behind their positions on the issue.

4.1. Perceptions of the Personal and National Economy

In the first part of the chapter we argued that Norwegians were more likely than Finns and Swedes to feel economically independent of EU membership due to a stronger national economy and the petroleum industry. If this is the

TABLE 8.8. Subjective Retrospective Change over the Previous Two or Three Years (percentages)

	In National Economy			In Personal Economic Condition		
	Norway	Sweden	Finland	Norway	Sweden	Finland
Improved	49	5	5	33	24	12
The same	28	7	10	50	41	38
Worse	17	86	84	17	34	49
Don't know	6	3	1	1	1	1
Total	100	101	100	101	100	100
N	(2,947)	(1,807)	(1,559)	(2,947)	(1,807)	(1,559)

Note: The questions asked were: (1) "According to your judgment, how has the economy changed in the last two or three years? Has it *improved,* stayed *the same,* or has it *worsened?*"; and (2) "If you compare your personal economic condition with the situation two or three years ago, has it *improved,* stayed *the same,* or has it *declined?*"

case, we might expect Norwegians to be relatively more satisfied than Swedes and Finns are with their country's economic development. We expect the perceptions of change in personal economic conditions to display the same pattern, though to a lesser extent, as a substantial portion of the population in the three countries are protected from the ups and downs of the national economies.

In table 8.8, we have displayed the one-way distributions of responses to identical questions asked in the three countries.[18] As we expected, there are significant differences. More than 80 percent of the adult population in Finland and Sweden judge the national economy to have worsened in the past two or three years. Only 5 percent in both countries had the impression that the economy had improved. The contrast to the Norwegian situation is striking. Fifty-one percent of the Norwegians believe their nation's economy has improved. In Finland and Sweden, few respondents report no knowledge on the issue. The results so far strongly support our interpretation: economic recovery was a far more important concern to Finns and Swedes compared with Norwegians in the fall of 1994. However, we must also take one's personal economic condition into consideration.

The "personal economic conditions" results are similar to those for the "national economy," but the differences are less remarkable, and the Swedish case seems to fall somewhere between the two (Norwegian and Finnish) extremes. Nearly half of the Finns consider themselves to be less well off than two or three years ago. In comparison, only 17 percent of the Norwegian sample falls into the same category. The Finnish result may well reflect the high unemployment rate in Finland (18 percent in 1993; see table 8.1). When it

TABLE 8.9. Subjective Prospective Change (percentages)

	In National Economy			In Personal Economic Condition		
	Norway	Sweden	Finland	Norway	Sweden	Finland
Improved	28	50	44	26	27	23
No change	44	28	30	58	47	49
Worse	13	16	23	12	22	24
Don't know	14	6	4	4	4	4
Total	100	100	101	100	100	100
N	(2,947)	(1,803)	(1,599)	(2,947)	(1,807)	(1,559)

comes to their personal economy, only 1 percent in each country was unable to make a judgment. Although the results in table 8.8 are in line with our expectations, they cannot be considered a critical test of our assumptions. Comparing distributions from different countries tells relatively little about the accuracy of individual impressions.

The answers to our retrospective questions yield important insights, but they tell only half the story. Just as important are expected economic changes in the near future. These evaluations are hardly based on hard evidence, but they reveal important information on the psychological state of the electorate. If, for instance, Finns and Swedes have—in addition to past hardship—given up hope of economic recovery, they might start looking for radical solutions. In other words, they may have jumped on the EU bandwagon in hopes of a rapid economic recovery. The results reported in table 8.9 suggest that this was not the case for the majority in either country.

The electorates in all three countries seem to be rather optimistic, Swedes in particular. Every second Swede expected an improvement in the national economy within the coming two or three years. The number was almost as high in Finland: 44 percent. The expectations seem to have been more modest in Norway, as was to be expected from the recent past (many Norwegians were well aware of the situation in the neighboring countries), but 27 percent hoped for an improvement, while 13 percent feared economic decline.

Voters in Sweden and Finland seemed to be less optimistic when it came to the question of future changes in personal economic conditions. The personal-level distribution for Norway comes close to the results for perceived future national economy. On average, the Swedes and Finns are slightly less optimistic than are the Norwegians with regard to their future personal economy. More striking, however, is the gap between expected change in national and personal economy. Both Swedes and Finns harbor higher hopes for the national economy than for their future personal prosperity. This finding mirrors the perceptions of past economic developments reported in table 8.8. There seems to be a general tendency among voters to envision the changes in the national economy as more dramatic than changes in personal economic condition.[19]

One of the main concerns of the EU is to promote economic growth and wealth in its member nations. The reports in the mass media in the Nordic countries have given a rather mixed impression of the EU's achievements in this field. When asked to rate future economic development within the EU, voters in Norway and Finland gave slightly different answers (reported in table 8.10). In both countries, however, the median answer is "no change." Evaluations in the Finnish electorate seem to be more polarized partly due to frequent "don't know" answering in Norway. In other words, the EU is not considered an economic miracle in the eyes of the average voter. However, to people distressed by economic hardship, "no change" within the EU may stand out as a favorable option.

So far, we have not looked into the key question: did EU membership really matter to personal and national economies in the eyes of the voters? The results to this question, reported in table 8.11, are rather mixed. In all three countries, a majority of the voters believe EU membership will make a difference to the national economy. In Finland and Sweden majorities believe that membership will improve the economies of their respective countries. In Norway, 31 percent believe membership will lead to economic decline on the national level, whereas 28 percent consider membership an advantage to Norway's economy. These results are in line with the outcome of the referendums and our findings at the other two levels. Voters in Norway and Sweden are less likely to believe membership to have consequences for their *personal* economic conditions. Again, the results indicate that the economic well-being of the nation may have been of greater concern to many voters than their personal pocketbooks.

Relatively few respondents gave "don't know" answers to these two questions. This may come as a surprise. In Norway, for instance, leading economists were ambivalent and divided over the issue. When many experts failed to give straight answers to these two questions, how did the common voter come up with an answer? Many, but not all, voters belong to groups with well-defined economic interests, for instance, through employment in the primary sector or industries heavily dependent on the European market. We will discuss this in the next subsection. Others, and especially the more extreme on both sides of the debate, may well have formed an opinion on the basis of their general attitude toward EU membership, the "logic" being that since EU membership

TABLE 8.10. Subjective Prospective Economic Change in EU
Countries (percentages)

	Norway	Sweden	Finland
Improved	15	Question not asked	24
No change	41		42
Worse	21		29
Don't know	23		13
Total	100		99
N	(2,947)		(1,559)

TABLE 8.11. Subjective Prospective Change in Personal and National Economies
under EU Membership (percentages)

	Norway		Sweden		Finland
	Personal	National	Personal	National	National
Improved	5	27	17	52	63
No change	71	35	58	23	18
Worse	17	32	15	20	14
Don't know	8	7	10	5	5
Total	101	101	100	100	100
N	(2,947)	(2,947)	(1,804)	(1,799)	(1,559)

Note: The wording of the personal question was: "If we become an EU member, do you believe your personal economic condition will improve notably or decline notably compared with our standing outside the EU, or do you believe your economic condition will not be influenced whether we get into the EU or not?" The national question was: "How do you suppose membership in the EU would influence the development of the country in the following fields? . . . the economy."

is good or bad for everything else, it must be good or bad for the economy as well. The multivariate analysis in the next subsection will throw further light on this question.

4.2. Economic Interests, Considerations, and the EU Vote

So far, our individual findings are in line with the arguments in the first part of this chapter. The inhabitants of the three countries are aware of the economic situations of their respective countries, and the differences between the electorates are in accordance with key indicators like unemployment, inflation, and the trade deficit. The distributions are more similar when it comes to prospective economic change with some important exceptions: the Finns and Swedes have on average greater expectations about future national economic develop-

TABLE 8.12. Percentage Voting "Yes" by Perception of Personal and National Economic Conditions

		Norway	Sweden	Finland
Retrospective: personal economy	Improved	55	63	64
	The same	48	56	60
	Declined	41 (14)	48 (15)	60 (4)
Retrospective: national economy	Improved	56	62	66
	The same	46	55	63
	Declined	37 (19)	55 (7)[a]	60 (6)[a]
Prospective: personal economy	Improve	57	59	69
	No change	50	54	62
	Decline	37 (20)	50 (9)	50 (19)
Prospective: national economy	Improve	63	62	69
	No change	48	48	57
	Decline	34 (28)	45 (17)	47 (22)
Prospective: development in EU countries	Improve	80	Question not asked	88
	No change	54		61
	Decline	20 (60)		25 (62)
Prospective: personal economy if EU member	Improve	75	81	Question not asked
	No change	58	57	
	Decline	9 (66)	27 (54)	
Prospective: national economy if EU member	Improve	84	78	78
	No change	53	33	31
	Decline	14 (70)	14 (64)	16 (62)

Note: Differences between yes votes in "improve" and "decline" groups are in parentheses.
[a]Not statistically significant at the 5 percent level.

ments, and they have far more positive evaluations of the possible effects of EU membership than do the Norwegians.

Our next step is to investigate the associations between the different perceptions and EU vote. In table 8.12, we report the proportion voting "yes" in each subcategory in tables 8.8 to 8.11. Some voters may have thought of EU membership as a solution to national and personal economic problems, but they appear to be exceptions. Voters reporting past improvements and optimism for the near future are more likely to favor EU membership in all three countries. This pattern becomes more pronounced when we move from the retrospective to the prospective questions.

The statistical associations are impressive when we come to the questions on future economic development within the EU and possible economic effects of EU membership on personal and national economies. In Norway, for instance, those who believed membership would lead to economic progress were seven or eight times more likely to favor membership than those who feared economic decline. Indeed, these questions—when they address the likelihood of personal economic benefit from EU membership—come the closest to a test of our working hypothesis. If we can assume that people who feel most economically dependent on EU membership are those who expect their personal economic conditions to improve with membership, then we find very high support in the two countries where the questions were posed (Norway and Sweden). The problem, as we shall see, is that individual respondents may be letting their predisposed attitudes about EU membership color their expectations about national and personal economic benefit. Thus, though it may appear that the question of EU membership was first and foremost an economic issue, we are not yet ready to accept that conclusion. First, we have to establish the links between positions in the economic structure, perceived economic interests, and EU vote.[20]

One important aspect of the EU debate in Norway was the mobilization of interest groups. Both sides tried to define the economic interests associated with EU membership for different categories of voters and mobilize them. When the "no" side argued that cuts in public spending were one consequence of EU membership, the Labor government countered by guaranteeing the incomes of state pensioners. The leadership of the peak labor organization (the LO), dominated by members of the Labor Party, supported the "yes" alternative, but the extraordinary LO congress in the fall of 1994 opposed membership by a close margin. Public sector unions also overwhelmingly supported the no alternative. While spokesmen for the oil industry and the minister of energy, Stoltenberg, advocated membership, the union of oil workers was opposed.

TABLE 8.13. Multiple OLS regressions (N = 1,666)

	Model 1		Model 2		Model 3	
	B	t-value	B	t-value	B	t-value
Constant	.60	24.0	1.07	17.0	.49	5.7
PRIMSEC	.36	.65	.35	6.5	.14	3.1
MANUF	−.06	−1.8	−.04	−1.2	−.04	−1.3
TRADE	−.10	−2.9	−.08	−2.4	−.06	−2.0
WORKCL[a]	.02	1.1	.03	1.3	.01	.6
PUBSEC	.09	2.8	.10	3.2	.06	2.5
INCOME[b]	$-7.8^{.0000001}$	−7.6	$-6.4^{.0000001}$	−6.3	$-4.2^{.00000001}$	−4.8
RETROSP. NAT.[c]			−.02	−1.0	.01	.5
RETROSP. PRIV.			−.06	−3.4	−.03	−2.0
PROSPECT. NAT.			−.12	−6.7	−.00	−.1
PROSPECT. PRIV.			−.02	−1.3	−.03	−1.6
PROSPECT. EU					−.11	−6.6
PROSPECT. NAT. IF					−.26	−17.4
PROSPECT. PRIV. IF					−.13	−5.1
R^2		.09		.13		.39

[a]The coding of this variable is based on Goldthorpe's class index (see Erikson and Goldthorpe 1992). Our variable WORKCL includes classes 6 and 7 in his typology.
[b]INCOME in Norwegian crowns.
[c]Favorable perceptions are coded high.

Thus, declaring one group's "true economic interests" to be either compatible or inconsistent with membership was a highly controversial matter.

To try and map the relationship between an individual's economic condition, interests/perceptions, and EU vote, we have regressed individual votes against professional, work skills, and income-related variables. Our dependent variable, vote in the EU referendum, has an almost perfect 50/50 distribution so we decided to apply standard ordinary least squares (OLS) regression in our multivariate analysis. The advantage is that the B-coefficients for the independent dummy variables can be interpreted as the percentage of change in the "no" vote directly. The regression was also performed as a logistic regression to make sure the t-values in the OLS regression were not misleading (see Aldrich and Nelson 1984).

The interpretation of the results in table 8.13 is relatively straightforward. Position in the economic structure explains relatively little of the EU vote (9 percent of the total variance). Two variables stand out as important: employment in the primary sector and income. Public employees are somewhat more likely to vote "no" and those working in trade, finance, and private services are significantly more likely to vote "yes," but in both cases the differences are modest: 8 and 10 percent, respectively. These are all consistent with our county-level findings.

Adding perceptions of national and personal economic development (model 2) improves the explanatory power only marginally. It is important to note that only perceptions of national economic development have a significant impact on the EU vote. This result is in line with the "sociotropic" voting theory of Kinder and Kiewiet (1981, 1979). People who judge the national economy to have improved in the past, and believe in future progress, are more likely to favor EU membership. The effects of the variables from the first bloc hardly changes from model 1 to model 2, with a possible exception for INCOME. In other words, perception of changes in the personal and national economy are not very different among the various interest groups. A closer look at the bivariate correlations confirms this interpretation.

The variables included in the third bloc improve the amount of variance accounted for by the independent variables significantly, but the effects may be disregarded as tautological. The effects of attachment to the primary sector and income are profoundly reduced in model 3, compared with models 1 and 2. Hence, people in the primary sector and people with low incomes are likely to believe the consequences of EU membership to be negative for themselves and the nation.[21] However, the three new variables in model 3 do much more than funnel the modest effects of position in the economic structure. The amount of variance explained has tripled from model 2 to model 3. How are we to account for this? We have already argued that some of the respondents may have answered these questions on the basis of their general attitude toward EU membership. In other words, model 3 is tautological. However, this is not the only possible explanation. The answers given to our questions may also reflect ideological predispositions and exposure to the campaign messages from the "yes" and "no" organizations and parties. Unfortunately, it is beyond the scope of this chapter to investigate these possibilities in detail.

4.3. Relative Importance: Issue Salience

The results obtained in models 1 and 2 (presented in table 8.13) are far from impressive. Position in the economic structure and assessment of changes in national and personal economic conditions have only moderate effects on the EU vote. We suspect that the reason for this is simple. The question of EU membership is complicated, and voters had to take a large number of arguments into consideration. During the campaign, the economic aspects of membership were not the main argument on either side. The experiences of the EU debate in 1972 restrained both camps.[22] To assess the relative importance of the economic arguments, we have categorized the answers to an open-ended question, which asked respondents to give personal reasons for their stands on the issue. Each respondent was allowed to give three reasons. The results for the "yes" and "no" voters are given in figures 8.5 and 8.6, respectively.

Economic arguments are the most frequently given reason for voting "yes." However, this category of arguments is rather heterogeneous. Most of the arguments are clearly of an ideological nature and are not linked to specific interests, sectors, or industries. Most of these respondents favor the four freedoms of the EU, less state intervention, and so on. A substantial portion of the "yes" voters argue in favor of free access to the EU market. However, the economic arguments taken together (economic policy, employment, food, agriculture, and fisheries) add up to about one-third of the arguments mentioned for voting "yes."

National sovereignty and democracy are by far the largest category of "no" arguments. Arguments related to economic questions rank second.[23] As with the "yes" arguments, the category includes both ideological and more specific, interest-oriented arguments. The more ideological arguments are typically left-wing arguments favoring state intervention and market control and in some cases anticapitalist opinions. Others argue more practically and in defense of specific interests like the food-processing industry. Some also argue in favor of the EEA agreement; in other words, they regard close economic relations with the EU to be in Norway's best interest, but they oppose political integration. The Christian People's Party and the "no" faction within the Labor Party advocated this position. Summing up, the economic arguments on the "no" side (economic policy, agriculture, employment, and fisheries) constitute close to one-third of the "no" arguments.

The individual-level data show a more nuanced picture of support for EU membership. In terms of our specific hypothesis, there was a very strong relationship between support for EU and the likelihood that one's personal economy would be strengthened by EU membership (table 8.12). If this can be interpreted as a surrogate for "economic dependence," we feel confident that our hypothesis was supported. But, by looking at the more open-ended questions about why individual voters supported EU membership (figs. 8.5 and

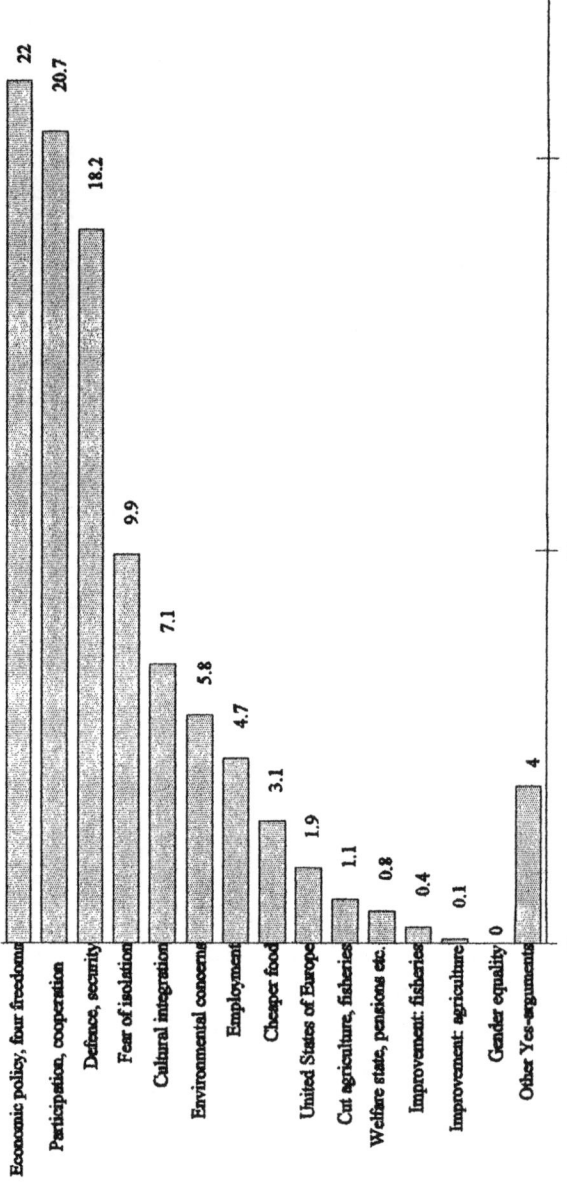

Fig. 8.5. Arguments given for voting "yes" to Norwegian membership in the European Union, percentages of all arguments

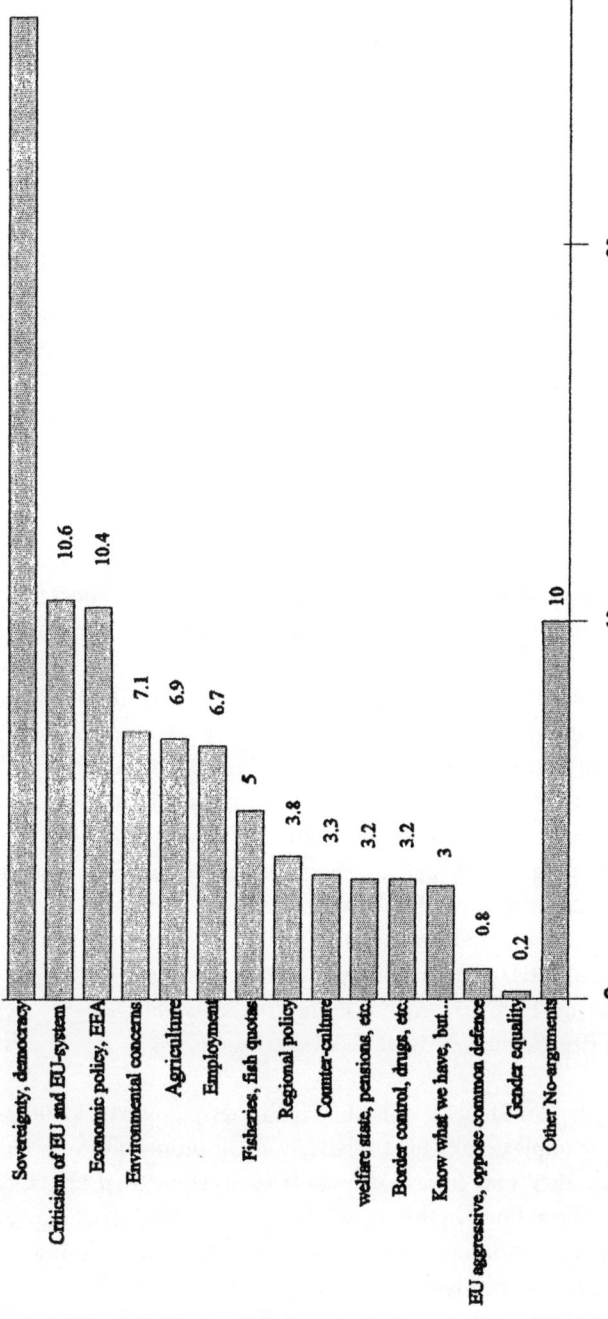

Fig. 8.6. Arguments given for voting "no" to Norwegian membership in the European Union, percentages of all arguments

8.6), it appears that several ideological, political, and social factors are also influencing voter attitudes.[24] This is not at all surprising in that EU membership entails choices across several issue areas.

5. Conclusion

In conclusion, we argue that a political economy hypothesis, based on a theory of economic integration, goes some distance in explaining the variation across the Nordic countries and among their respective counties. Support was strongest at the county level, while the national-level analysis required some modification. Economic integration alone was not sufficient to explain variations in the national referendum outcomes. At the individual level, several of our national- and county-level arguments were supported, but other explanations were also voiced in support of or opposition to membership.

At the national level, Norway's opposition to membership is best explained by its relative wealth and the nature of its export relationship to the EU. Despite the fact that Norway was more export dependent than either Finland or Sweden on European export markets, its relative wealth and export structure made it less susceptible to dependency pressures. Finland and Sweden are both heavily dependent on European markets (both goods and capital) and are economies in search of recovery. Arguably, membership in the European Union offered them this hope.

At the county level, a similar picture develops. Counties that harbored high employment levels in sheltered sectors (in particular, the primary and public sectors) were highly and significantly correlated with those counties' opposition to EU membership in the respective referendums. The opposite was the case for counties that employed heavily in the retail and wholesale trades. To the extent that trade and manufacturing sectors (though manufacturing was less statistically relevant in our county-level findings) can be assumed to be dependent on European markets, and to the extent that the sheltered sectors are less dependent, our hypothesis was supported in the county-level data.

The county-level findings can also be explained by contextual effects. Even if farmers (for example) make up a relatively small proportion of a county's total population, they may have a strong effect, in contextual terms, on the opinions of their neighbors. In this regard, living in a farm district may project more relevant information on a given voter's attitudes than knowing the specific occupation of that resident.

At the individual level, as expected, the findings were more varied. Although many of our economic findings (from the national level) in terms of perceptions of economic strength and dependence were supported in the polling data, we are more cautious in interpreting this as support for our hypothesis. In particular, it is difficult to interpret the degree to which individuals felt economically dependent on EU membership. When asked the reasons for voting as they did, economic arguments played a significant role for those Norwegians who voiced support of membership, but they played a much smaller role in the ranks of the opposition.

Generally, it appears as though voters may have been most concerned about the effects of EU membership on their national (as opposed to individual) economies. The results in table 8.11 suggest that EU membership would bring to Finland and Sweden the promise of an improved national economy. Such a promise was lacking and less relevant for richer Norwegian voters. These findings bring us full circle and support the evidence presented in the two earlier sections.

No simple hypothesis can explain a phenomenon as multidimensional as support for EU membership. Still, we must begin somewhere. This chapter has proposed a simple political economy hypothesis as a first attempt at understanding the variation in Nordic referendum outcomes. This hypothesis found its strongest support in the county-level analysis, but it was consistent with many of the data in the other two levels of analyses. Considering the multifaceted nature of the issue, it is surprising to us both that a simple economic integration argument can explain so much of the variation at all three levels of analysis.

NOTES

The original essay was presented to the conference "The Political Economy of European Integration: The Challenges Ahead," held at the University of California, Berkeley, April 20–22, 1995. The interview data were collected by the survey division of Statistics Norway. In addition, we would like to thank Hernik Oskarson at the University of Götenborg, and Pertti Pesonen at the University of Tampere for the data that they provided. The cross-national county-level data were generously provided by Norwegian Social Science Data Services. The authors would like to thank Jeff Frieden, Doug Rivers, Ron Rogowski, and Michael Wallerstein for their useful remarks and comments. Obviously, all responsibility remains with the authors.

1. See Arndt's contribution to this volume for a thorough description of relevant explanators for EU membership.

2. This three-level test imposes certain methodological constraints, as the as-

sumptions common to macrolevel analyses differ significantly from those common in microlevel studies. In particular, the assumption of rationality is often relaxed (or challenged) in individual-level analyses. We are aware of this potential conflict but feel that it is important to try and cross the analytical divide that separates behavioralists from macrocomparativists.

3. The integration literature is voluminous and largely ideological. Originally, federalists, functionalists, and neofunctionalists spent most of their energy arguing over *how* to integrate rather than *why* one might wish to integrate (see, e.g., Mitrany 1946 and Haas 1958). Realists and their intergovernmentalist brethren, on the other hand, recognized the potential costs of integration. However, these schools tended to focus on security or sovereignty costs, assuming that economic integration was largely beneficial—unless it encroached on economic policy autonomy (see e.g., Taylor 1983 and Keohane 1984, 1986).

4. Gowa (1989) and Hirschman (1945) offer two variants. See Busch and Milner (1994) for an overview.

5. The expansion of foreign direct investment (FDI) into Europe can be explained by industrial organization and transaction cost theories. For influential examples, see Hymer 1976, Caves 1982, and Teece 1986.

6. This term comes from Mutimer's (1994) characterization of Deutsch's work.

7. This proposition should be made delicately. There are several things that contribute to a nation's cost of membership. Britain's infamous 1979 row over the size of its budget contribution, for example, was the result of its taste for tariff-burdened imports (from beyond the EU) and its efficient farm sector (Dinan 1994, 109–15). Nevertheless, patterns do develop, and current national contributions to the EU budget are as follows: the United Kingdom, Germany, and France are net contributors; Italy and Netherlands are roughly in balance; and all other countries are net recipients. Each of the Nordic countries would have been net contributors (Nugent 1994, 343).

8. This sort of argument is prevalent among economists looking at the disciplinary incentives of the EMS. See, for example, de Grauwe 1989, Giavazzi and Pagano 1988, Giavazzi and Giovannini 1989, and Mélitz 1988.

9. To the (lesser) extent that FDI flows are coming *into* the respective economies, despite being outside the EU, we argue that these flows, ceteris paribus, will be unaffected by membership and therefore lay outside the focus of this analysis.

10. As Arndt's contribution to this volume argues, FDI can also be used as a surrogate for membership: Swiss firms needed membership less because they already had productive facilities in Europe. Instead, our argument is based on employment considerations. Norwegian firms investing in Brussels are not investing in Norwegian jobs. To the extent that these flows are a response to fear of a potential "Fortress Europe," they can be stopped with membership.

11. Unfortunately, more current figures are not available, as the EC-share figures are the result of a Herculean effort by Karl Karlsen—who accumulated the data firsthand from the respective central banks.

12. The cross-national county-level data used in this section were generously provided by Norwegian Social Science Data Services.

13. For a current analysis employing these data, see Pettersen et al. 1995.

14. In particular, this includes those employed in agriculture, fishing, forestry, and hunting.

15. Among the bivariate regressions, the strongest relationship was between OIL and the referendum outcomes, but the scatter plot on these regressions suggests that the relationship is heavily influenced by the pull of three outlier counties: Norrbottens Län in Sweden and Rogaland and Finnmark Fylker in Norway. On this variable there simply is not enough variation. Red flags are also tagged on the interpretive estimates in this model. The large beta-coefficient for the OIL variable suggests that the model is misspecified. Thus, great care should be taken when interpreting the significance of the OIL variable in these regressions.

16. The Finnish primary sector variable should be read with great care, as it includes the cleavage currently dividing the Finnish Center Party: both farming interests (which are opposed to membership) and timber interests (which generally support membership) are included therein.

17. What is perhaps most interesting about the Swedish case is not its uniqueness when compared with the other two countries but the contrasting story offered by the two different models. Here two particular differences present themselves. First, it is peculiar that the PUBSEC and OIL variables are significant in only one of the two models' results. The OIL findings can be explained by closer inspection of the Swedish bivariate scatter plots. It appears that the (apparently significant) relationship is being drawn by Norrbottens Län—which was both strongly opposed to membership and holds Sweden's highest proportion of workers in those sectors. When the Norrbotten case is removed, the rest of Sweden's counties are tightly packed around zero. There are not many oil, mining, or quarry workers remaining in Sweden.

Second, given our theoretical priors, it is surprising that the Swedish MANUF variable was not significant in the model A variant and was significant (but with the wrong sign!) in the model B results. Because of Sweden's heavy reliance on the export of manufactured goods, we might expect that counties with strong manufacturing sectors would be more likely to support membership. Closer inspection of the Swedish bivariate regression data reveals them to be heavily spread at the low end of the manufacturing scale. In other words, those counties with relatively small manufacturing bases are strongly opposed and strongly supportive of EU membership. Alternatively, at the other end of the scale, those counties that depend most heavily on manufacturing jobs seemed to split (at very close margins) over supporting EU membership. In other words, no clear linear relationship presents itself in the data.

18. The individual-level data used in this section were collected in a cross-national survey involving the Universities of Trondheim and Oslo in Norway, the University of Göteborg in Sweden and the University of Tampere in Finland. Anders Todal Jenssen was the project coordinator.

19. One may object to these interpretations in that some of the respondents may have counted on EU membership when they answered our questions on prospective economic development. This may have been the case in Finland, where the opinion polls indicated a comfortable victory, but the outcomes of the referendums in Sweden and Norway were far from obvious at the time of interviewing.

20. For a more detailed description and analysis of this linkage, see Jenssen 1997.

21. A look at the bivariate correlations supports this interpretation.

22. In the Norwegian EU debate prior to the 1972 referendum, the "yes" side focused on the economic aspects of membership. Both the employers' organization (NAF), important industrialists, and the leading figures in the LO painted a rather gloomy picture of Norway's future economic situation if membership was rejected in the referendum. The "no" side countered by describing this as an effort to scare people into voting for EU membership. As it turned out, the 1972–78 period turned out to be prosperous. Whether this came as a result of the "no" victory or of growing oil incomes did not really matter. The "yes" side lost credibility in the eyes of many voters. Hence, the spokesmen of the employers' organization chose a different rhetorical style in the 1994 campaign.

23. The reader is advised to employ some caution in interpreting these figures, as there are aggregation fallacies involved. Several of the economic, ideological, and social factors could be combined in various ways to skew the distribution.

24. Interpreting the open-ended questionnaires is complicated by a debate within the discipline about the processes informing voter behavior. Our interpretation here is consistent with an "on-line," as opposed to a "memory-based," process. See Rahn et al. 1994 for a discussion.

REFERENCES

Aldrich, John H., and Forrest D. Nelson. 1984. *Linear Probability, Logit, and Probit Models.* Beverly Hills: Sage.

Busch, Marc L., and Helen V. Milner. 1994. "The Future of the International Trading System: International Firms, Regionalism, and Domestic Politics." In *Political Economy and the Changing Global Order,* edited by Richard Stubbs and Geoffrey R. D. Underhill, 259–76. London: Macmillan.

Caves, Richard. 1982. *Multinational Enterprise and Economic Analysis.* Cambridge: Cambridge University Press.

de Grauwe, Paul. 1989. "The Cost of Disinflation and the European Monetary System." CEPS Working Documents, no. 40. Manuscript.

Deutsch, Karl W. 1953. "The Growth of Nations: Some Recurrent Patterns of Political and Social Integration." *World Politics* 5:168–95.

Deutsch, Karl W., et al. 1968. *Political Community and the North Atlantic Area: International Organization in the Light of Historical Experience.* Princeton: Princeton University Press.

Dinan, Desmond. 1994. *Ever Closer Union?* London: Macmillan.

Erikson, Robert, and John H. Goldthorpe. 1992. *The Constant Flux: A Study of Class Mobility in Industrial Societies.* Oxford: Clarendon Press.

European Commission. 1996. AMECO Database (September).

Giavazzi, Francesco, and Alberto Giovannini. 1989. *Limiting Exchange Rate Flexibility: The European Monetary System.* Cambridge: MIT Press.

Giavazzi, Francesco, and Marco Pagano. 1988. "The Advantage of Tying One's Hands: EMS Discipline and Central Bank Credibility." *European Economic Review* (June): 1055–74.

Gowa, Joanne. 1989. "Bipolarity, Multipolarity, and Free Trade." *American Political Science Review* 83, no. 4: 1245–56.

Haas, Ernst B. 1958. *The Uniting of Europe: Political, Economic, and Social Forces, 1950–1957.* Stanford: Stanford University Press.

Hirschman, Albert O. [1945] 1980. *National Power and the Structure of Foreign Trade.* Berkeley: University of California Press.

Hymer, Stephen. 1976. *The International Operations of National Firms: A Study of Direct Foreign Investment.* Cambridge: MIT Press.

IMF. 1994. *International Financial Statistics Yearbook, 1994.* Geneva: International Monetary Fund.

Jenssen, Anders Todal. 1997. "Personal Economies and Economic Expectations." In *To Join or Not to Join: Three Nordic Referenda on Membership in the European Union,* edited by Pertti Pesonen, Anders Todal Jenssen, and Mikael Gilljam. Oslo, forthcoming.

Karlsen, Jan Karl. 1990. "Business Strategy and National Policy concerning Integration: Nordic Direct Foreign Investments in the European Community." Paper presented at the Danish Summer Research Institute, Gilleleje, August 20–31.

Keohane, Robert. 1984. *After Hegemony: Cooperation and Discord in the World Political Economy.* Princeton: Princeton University Press.

———, ed. 1986. *Neo-Realism and Its Critics.* New York: Columbia University Press.

Kiewiet, D. Roderick, and Donald R. Kinder. 1979. "Economic Discontent and Political Behaviour: The Role of Personal Grievances and Collective Economic Judgements in Congressional Voting." *American Journal of Political Science* 23:495–527.

Kinder, Donald R., and D. Roderick Kiewiet. 1981. "Sociotropic Politics: The American Case." *British Journal of Political Science* 11:129–61.

Mélitz, Jacques. 1988. "Monetary Discipline and Cooperation in the EMS: A Synthesis." CEPR Discussion Papers, no. 219. Manuscript.

Mitrany, David. 1946. *A Working Peace System.* London: Royal Institute of International Affairs.

Mutimer, David. 1994. "Theories of Political Integration." In *European Integration: Theories and Approaches,* edited by Hans J. Michelmann and Panayotis Soldatos, 13–42. Lanham, Md., and London: University Press of America.

Nordisk Råd. 1995. *Yearbook of Nordic Statistics, 1995.* Copenhagen: Nordisk Råd.

Nugent, Neill. 1994. *The Government and Politics of the European Union*. 3d ed. London: Macmillan.

Pettersen, Per Arnt, Anders Todal Jenssen, and Ola Listhaug. 1995. "The 1994 EU Referendum in Norway: Continuity and Change." Paper presented at the annual meeting of the Midwest Political Science Association, Chicago, April 6–8.

Rahn, Wendy M., Jon A. Krosnick, and Marijke Breuning. 1994. "Rationalization and Derivation Processes in Survey Studies of Political Candidate Evaluation." *American Journal of Political Science* 38, no. 3 (August): 582–600.

SSB. 1995. *Statistisk Årbok 1994*. Oslo: Statistisk Sentralbyrå.

Taylor, Paul. 1983. *The Limits of European Integration*. Beckenham, Eng: Croom Helm.

Teece, David J. 1986. "Transaction Cost Economics and the Multinational Enterprise: An Assessment." *Journal of Economic Behavior and Organization* 7:21–45.

CHAPTER 9

Alpine Contrasts: Swiss and Austrian Responses to the EU

Sven W. Arndt

Introduction

The European Community's[1] Single-Market project—popularly known as Europe 1992—was launched at a time of sluggish economic performance throughout Europe and of uncertainty about the future of the Community itself. Europeans spoke anxiously about "Euro-sclerosis" and fretted endlessly about competition from the United States and Japan. A major initiative seemed to be needed in order to reinvigorate the integration progress and generate the political will required to push it forward.

In introducing the project, the EC Commission released a series of studies showing that the customs union had failed to create a Single Market: Europe's goods and services markets, not to mention its factor markets, remained heavily segmented.[2] The proposed policy initiative would "complete" the internal market by eliminating costly border formalities and ridding the Community of policies and practices that stood in the way of fuller integration.

While the global objective of Europe 1992 was to enable European firms to compete more effectively with their Japanese and American rivals, its announcement rekindled anxieties among members of the European Free Trade Area (EFTA) about their own economic viability. These concerns were intensified as a succession of studies warned that Europe 1992 would create problems for the EFTA nations.[3]

These studies, as well as the Commission's own work, placed a great deal of emphasis on "nontraditional" sources of the gains from trade. Imperfect competition, economies of scale, and investment-led economic growth not only

247

were prominently featured but made the predicted welfare gains from further integration significantly larger than would otherwise have been the case. Although the models used were largely empirically untested, the forecasts appear to have been widely accepted by policymakers and the public.

Those forecasts and predictions were important in the Austrian policy debate and to a lesser extent in Switzerland. Although various "dynamic" considerations were used to puff up the predicted welfare gains from the Single Market for EU members and from membership for outsiders, the quantifiable effects were nevertheless relatively small. There was no escaping the fact that Europe was already significantly integrated and that the major gains from trade and specialization had already been captured. This meant that noneconomic and nonquantifiable considerations of various kinds could play an important role in the membership decisions of EFTA countries. In the end, Sweden, Finland, and Austria joined the European Union, while Switzerland and Norway did not. This chapter examines Austrian and Swiss reactions and seeks to understand why the two Alpine nations, which are similar in so many ways, chose such diametrically opposite solutions to the challenge of the Single Market. The next section briefly reviews the predicted effects of Europe 1992; it is followed by an evaluation of the options available to outsiders like Austria and Switzerland. Next, the experts' forecasts and the means by which they were generated are assessed, after which the specifics of the Austrian and Swiss cases, respectively, are examined. A concluding section completes the discussion.

Predicting the Effects of the Single Market Program

Europe 1992 was expected to manifest itself in two major ways: first, in lower trade costs as border formalities, customs procedures, and various nontrade barriers were eliminated;[4] and, second, in reduced inefficiencies due to imperfect competition and market segmentation. Although market segmentation is often the result of factors beyond the control of policymakers, the Community was determined to eliminate government's contribution by improving technical standards and regulatory procedures and by liberalizing public procurement practices.

The European Commission estimated the total gain from the project to run between 4.5 and 6.5 percent of GDP. This estimate was based on a series of studies, using a variety of modeling approaches and specifications.[5] The studies played a major role not only in shaping public acceptance of Europe 1992 in the Community but in shifting public opinion in favor of membership in a number of EFTA countries. In Austria and other countries, the Commission's

TABLE 9.1. EU and EFTA and the Single Market (changes in percentages)

	EU without EFTA		EFTA in EU	
	EU	EFTA	EU	EFTA
Real income	.64 (.40)	−.68 (−.15)	.68 (.45)	1.13 (.78)
Real factor prices				
Skilled labor	.77 (.51)	−.45 (−.40)	.77 (.51)	1.69 (1.11)
Unskilled labor	.59 (.38)	−.18 (−.14)	.65 (.43)	1.00 (.58)
Capital	.66 (.35)	−.08 (+.15)	.67 (.39)	1.74 (1.05)

Source: Haaland 1993.

Note: Figures in parentheses give the effects of reduced trade costs only; others cover the full effects of EU integration.

forecasts quickly became the basis for estimating the spillover effects of Europe 1992.[6]

All along, the word from outside experts was that Europe 1992 was bad news for any EFTA country that chose to remain a nonmember. The intellectual establishment weighed in early and heavily on the side of membership as the only solution for the EFTA countries.[7] The predominant view among expert observers was that Europe 1992 would impair the competitive standing of EFTA producers and hence make EFTA countries less attractive to home and foreign investors. EFTA producers would take an immediate competitive hit and then would suffer the long-run erosion of what is known in Austria and Switzerland as the "Industriestandort" position. Representative estimates of the effects of Europe 1992 on EFTA are given in table 9.1.

The Options

EFTA countries had three options. They could stay with their strategy of nonmembership while continuing bilateral and group efforts to integrate their economies further with the European Union. This approach had produced significant reductions in trade barriers and market segmentation between the two blocs in the past and could be expected to achieve further integration and cooperation in the future.

Each EFTA country had a bilateral free trade agreement with the EU and a variety of arrangements covering specific aspects of services trade and capital flows. For Austria and Switzerland, the chances of reducing border formalities still further were excellent, not least because the two countries sit astride major trading routes linking the EU's northern and southern members.

Austria had successfully maintained a fixed exchange rate regime vis-à-vis Germany, proving that exchange rates can be fixed unilaterally as well as through multicountry coordination mechanisms like the European Monetary System. Switzerland, too, had maintained exchange rate stability by tying Swiss monetary policy to German monetary conditions.

The second option was full membership. It would fully and completely integrate the EFTA economies into the European Union, enabling them to reap all the benefits available under existing policies and giving them a full voice in future policy making, but it would obligate them to share the burden of financing the EU's programs.

An intermediate position between nonmembership and full membership was available in the European Economic Area. The EEA was a compromise solution, advanced by the EU after earlier attempts to form a customs union between the two blocs had failed. The EEA would give EFTA countries access to the EU market without requiring them to adopt the common external tariff. It would exempt them from the Common Agricultural Policy and a variety of fiscal burdens. It would, however, require new members to accept existing EU rules and procedures covering a wide range of policy areas—the so-called *aquis communautaire.*

This degree of independence, however, would come at a price. For one thing, EU imports from EFTA countries would be subject to costly border formalities and cumbersome rules of origin tests. These had proven especially bothersome in connection with foreign sourcing and processing. For another, the EU would not allow EEA countries a formal role in the design of EU policies; nor would it guarantee that its future policies would not discriminate against them.

The Arguments

In Austria and Switzerland, nonmembership was seen as a viable option, the net welfare effects of which were widely expected to be positive. Early Austrian studies showed that the Single Market's dominant effect would be a spillover boost to Austrian growth. This growth dividend was expected to be large enough to dominate the negative effects of changes in competitiveness. Swiss researchers reached similar conclusions.[8]

Estimates of the costs of nonmembership were probably biased upward because they assumed the status quo and thus did not allow for future improvements in economic cooperation between the Alpine countries and the EU. There can be little doubt that such improvements would have been forthcoming. Austria, for example, gave every indication prior to joining the EEA that it intended to seek to expand cooperation with the European Union. Switzerland still has that option today and is capable of achieving many of the benefits of EU membership by means of unilateral policy reforms.

Opinion makers in Austria and Switzerland expected the major costs of nonmembership to flow from classical trade diversion and from deterioration in the competitiveness of domestic producers in home and EU markets.

Trade Diversion

Removal of border controls and harmonization of regulatory policies reduces the cost of doing business among members and thereby changes trade patterns. Trade among members replaces trade with nonmembers. The effect is strongest for homogeneous products, weaker when products are differentiated, and weaker still when nonmembers supply niche markets. Overall, however, the effect of trade diversion on Swiss and Austrian shares of the EU market was expected by most observers to be relatively small.[9]

The Single Market would bestow some benefits on EFTA exporters to the extent that elimination of intra-EU border controls reduces the cost of trans-shipping products among member countries because, once inside the EU, EFTA products would move more freely among countries. Intra-EU harmonization of standards and regulatory policies would also reduce the cost of selling in the EU if it required EFTA exporters to comply with one uniform standard rather than one for each national market. EFTA firms with production facilities in the EU, such as Swiss chemicals and financial services producers, would not only be in a position to capture the benefits of the Single Market, but they might be able to use their position as established multinationals to obtain first-mover advantages vis-à-vis indigenous firms.

Of course, any decline in EU demand for EFTA products brought about by trade diversion would benefit EFTA consumers to the extent that it would reduce the home prices of exportables. Consumers in EFTA countries would benefit in addition if lower trade costs reduced the prices of imports from the European Union. Inasmuch as prices in Switzerland and Austria were higher in terms of purchasing power than those in the EU, stronger pressures forcing Austrian and Swiss prices toward EU levels would benefit consumers.[10]

Imperfect Competition and Market Segmentation

As noted, the Commission saw in governmental policies and practices a major cause of market segmentation, and this sentiment was echoed by expert observers. Whether of partial or general equilibrium in conception, most studies endeavored to model at least some aspects of imperfect competition. Imperfect competition was believed to be important because much of intra-EU trade was observed to be intraindustry trade. The belief that market inefficiencies were widespread was further supported by price differentials across European markets that were greater than those found across the United States and could not be explained by transportation costs.

A weakness of many of the models used in these computational exercises is that they were not adequately tested empirically before being applied to Europe 1992. This is surprising in view of the availability of information on prior episodes of trade liberalization and market integration against which models could have been tested. Assumptions and selection of parameter values were often optimistic regarding the welfare implications of membership, while estimates of nonmembership tended to be biased in the opposite direction, often simply because further trade liberalization and market integration between outsiders and the EU was not taken into account.

The choice of sample period created problems, especially since accession dates were unknown. Breuss and Schebeck (1989), for example, apply their model to the period 1982–87, calculating what would have been the result in 1987 if Austria had (1) joined the European Economic Area (EEA) in 1982 or (2) joined the European Community in 1982. The results estimated for 1987 are then compared with actual developments during 1982–87. A less biased comparison, but one more difficult to carry out, would have been against a scenario of nonmembership combined with further bilateral trade-liberalizing and policy-harmonizing initiatives between Austria and the EU.

Imperfect-competition models of the kind employed in many of these studies are sensitive to parameter calibration and behavior assumptions.[11] Since the models have in general not been empirically tested, it would have been useful to experiment with alternative specifications, especially of producer behavior with respect to scale economies, of consumer choice with respect to variety, and, perhaps most important of all, of adjustment speeds in labor markets.

In general, modelers assumed the effects of the Single Market to manifest themselves in terms of one or more of the following: scale economies, product variety, and endogenous growth. The Commission (Emerson 1988) and others placed major emphasis on the role of scale economies and the effect of the Single Market on growth. The growth effect, moreover, was not just a one-time boost but a "permanent" change brought about by the expected effect of competition on investment in research and development and on innovation. Baldwin (1989, 1992, 1993) formalized this growth effect in a model using insights from the modern theory of economic growth. Breuss (1992) adopted the Baldwin model and found that its growth assumptions generated significant additional benefits for Austria, with or without membership.[12]

The Commission focused on the role of scale economies at industry levels, while Baldwin's focus is on the aggregate economy. Applied to Europe, where labor force growth is virtually nonexistent, the economics of scale are really the economics of capital accumulation. According to Baldwin, the Single Market will raise the return on investment in the EU, raising the equilibrium capital stock and initiating a period of faster growth fueled by capital accumulation. Consequently, he obtains an overall effect of Europe 1992 on EU GDP that is several times as large as the Commission's original estimates.

It is somewhat surprising to see how quickly the Baldwin approach made its way into "practical" policy modeling. As noted, when Breuss (1992) applied the approach to Austria, the total benefit from membership was almost double the "static" effects.

The importance of "dynamic" or growth effects was further enhanced when the Baldwin approach was extended from physical to human capital. Now Europe 1992 could be expected to raise the return on human capital in the EU while reducing it in EFTA countries.[13] These losses in EFTA welfare, added to the negative effects on physical capital, implied "that the EFTA countries would experience a brain drain if they did not join the EEA."[14]

These and other predictions were highly sensitive to calibration. Real world developments would have to follow model prescriptions extremely closely in order to prevent significant departures from predicted results.

One way in which real world developments might deviate from model specifications is in the area of labor market responses. The structural adjustments needed to enable European industry to realize the dynamic benefits predicted by modelers would necessitate nontrivial reallocations of labor. The modeled effects will not materialize and the benefits of the single market will be *significantly* smaller if labor is immobile and the requisite labor market adjustments are not forthcoming. Indeed, if labor is immobile enough, the net effect may well be negative, because labor shed in contracting industries will not be easily reemployed, making it more likely that rationalization of resource deployment will cause initial reductions in output growth rather than the growth spurt postulated by modelers.

By contrast, the Commission, most of the outside experts, and policymakers generally expected the gains from the single market to materialize relatively quickly. The Austrian forecasts, for example, expect half the GDP gains to be realized within the first two years.

There is very little discussion, by the Commission or the experts, of the degree of labor mobility required to deliver the projected results within the projected time. Given the speed with which the results of the Single Market or full membership materialize in these exercises, labor markets will have to be quite responsive. Keuschnigg and Kohler (1996), for example, simply assume perfectly competitive labor markets for Austria. The well-known and well-documented inflexibility of European labor makes many of these specifications appear to be rather heroic.[15]

The European public was sold extraordinarily optimistic economic forecasts, the predictions of which are unlikely to be realized. If the "dynamic" effects fail to be realized, then members' gains from the Single Market will be much smaller, especially if the costs of implementing the program are taken into account. For nonmembers, reductions in benefits will make the costs of membership loom larger, particularly the fiscal burden for rich countries.

Product Variety

In their recent study, Keuschnigg and Kohler (1996) make product variety the centerpiece of a model with imperfect competition in which returns to scale are constant at the level of the firm but increasing at the level of the economy. Scale economies manifest themselves through variations in product variety. The authors expect variety to increase in Austria and Switzerland as a result of full membership and thereby to boost the gains from membership relative to traditional trade creation-diversion calculations and relative to the benefits of lower trade costs. Table 9.2 reproduces the main results of the study, in which the net effect of membership is given in terms of permanent income streams in percentage of initial GDP. The effect of variety is obviously important.

Although the model is specified to generate an increase in variety and hence to raise welfare, the alternatives should have been explored. It is not that the chosen outcome cannot occur but that less attractive alternatives are no less likely to occur. Product variety need not rise; it may actually fall, as Gasiorek et al. (1992) have found.[16] This model, like the others, could and should have been tested against evidence from earlier liberalization episodes.

As before, there are reasons to take the numbers with a grain of salt. If adjustment turns out to be less efficient and less extensive than predicted, there will be disappointments. Weaker, less smooth, and more protracted structural

TABLE 9.2. Membership in the EU (Effects in percentage of GDP)

	Austria	Switzerland
Reduction of real trade costs	1.318	1.453
Adoption of common tariff	.041	− .004
Agriculture	.622	.598
Subtotal	1.981	2.047
Membership contributions	− 1.222	− 1.222
Subtotal	.759	.825
Variety	.425	.469
Total	1.184	1.294

Source: Keuschnigg and Kohler 1996.

Note: Figures indicate permanent income streams in percentages of GDP.

transformation would affect nonmembers in at least two important ways. If improvements in the competitive standing of EU firms come more slowly, the challenges to be met by Austria and Switzerland will be sharply reduced. Slower responses in the EU will give EFTA producers more time to respond. Slower or incomplete responses will make Europe 1992 less compelling as an economic argument for EU membership.

The reactions of Swiss and Austrian producers to the Single Market may also have been misjudged by many modelers. It has been axiomatic that, once inside the EU, Austrian and Swiss firms would hold their own against their EU rivals, exploiting scale economies, augmenting product variety, and gaining the efficiencies and cost reductions that would be needed to maintain (if not increase) market share and capture the gains from membership. While such an outcome is possible, it may not be the most likely outcome.

Swiss firms are, of course, already operating in the EU. The OECD (1991) estimates Swiss firms to be responsible for around one million jobs in the European Union. But those producers do not need Swiss EU membership to take advantage of the Single Market Program.

Factor Market Integration

One of the four freedoms promised by EU membership is the movement of persons. In both Austria and Switzerland, labor market considerations played an important part in the debate over membership. Close to a quarter of the Swiss labor force consists of foreign workers. The inflow of foreign labor is controlled by policies whose aim is to ensure a supply of low-skilled workers to certain industries, including tourism, agriculture, and construction.

This bias in Switzerland's immigration policy toward admitting unskilled workers has been blamed for contributing to relative shortages of skilled workers, high manufacturing wages, and upward pressures on costs of production.[17] Proponents of joining the EU hoped that membership would change not the number of foreign workers in Switzerland but their skill composition, shifting the weight from unskilled to skilled workers. That change was expected to have beneficial effects on productivity and the international competitiveness of Swiss producers.

This problem, however, like many others, is something that can be solved without EU membership. Switzerland has the freedom to alter its immigration policies at any time. If the political will is lacking, of course, then membership may be necessary in order to bring about changes in policies. This view of EU membership as a catalyst for action and change appears throughout the EU debate in both Switzerland and Austria.

Austria's foreign labor problem is different from its neighbor's and pertains to inflows—often uncontrolled or difficult to control—of workers from Central and Eastern Europe. Many Austrians saw EU membership as an opportunity to shift the problem of the westward migration of workers to the EU and to seek solutions at that level, but such considerations were probably not a major preoccupation for most voters.

The implications of membership for factor returns also played a role in the policy debate in both countries. As noted earlier, some studies—including Haaland and Norman 1992, Baldwin et al. 1992, and Haaland 1993—suggested that failure to join would have adverse impacts on skilled workers. Haaland, for example, concludes that completion of the Single Market will cause skill-intensive sectors in EFTA countries to decline, as competition from the EU forces EFTA resources to be shifted to capital-intensive sectors. If skilled workers accepted this forecast, their vote would favor membership, as the data suggest.

Agriculture

Agriculture represented one of the major challenges of membership. The inefficiency of European agriculture is well known, but Austria and Switzerland have agricultural sectors that are less efficient than even the EU. Since the EEA exempts agriculture, it was possible for Austria to join the EEA without having to deal with the knotty problem of agriculture. The contemplated move to EU membership changed all that.

Simply put, EU membership would be bad for farmers and food processors, two important components of a vocal political constituency. It would be bad because it would force prices down. For that reason, membership would be good for consumers. As table 9.2 shows, agriculture is a major source of the projected benefits of membership. The gains come in part from reduced prices for agricultural products and processed foods and in part, though more in the long run than the short, from reduced budget outlays for support of the agricultural sector.[18]

Recognizing the importance of the potential opposition among farmers and their allies, Austria's policymakers moved early and deftly to neutralize the opposition—essentially by arranging for an extended phase-in period and for significant compensation payments. The latter would come partly out of the national budget, but they would be supplemented by transfers from the EU. The arrangement effectively silenced a significant element of the opposition.

Switzerland's problem with agriculture was, in a sense, not a problem because the Swiss were merely voting to join the EEA. It is unclear to what extent the heavy negative vote of rural Switzerland was influenced by expectations of future challenges to Swiss agriculture. Exit polls suggest that a large majority of Swiss voters believed that EEA membership did not necessarily imply EU membership.

Austria in the EEA

The European Economic Area was proposed by Jacques Delors in 1989, and negotiations continued through 1990 and 1991. The agreement was signed in early 1992. It was rejected by Swiss voters in late 1992, whereupon the agreement was revised and signed anew in 1993, with implementation set for the beginning of 1994. Austria, which had applied for membership in 1989, entered the EEA at that time.

From the beginning, many Austrians saw the EEA as a mere transitional arrangement. Moreover, as Kramer (1994) points out, agriculture notwithstanding, some of the toughest adjustments occur upon entry into the EEA not the EU. Still, the question of EU membership received intense and sustained discussion.

With or without the EEA, the degree of economic integration between Austria and the EU is very high. Moses and Jenssen suggest in this volume that countries with already high degrees of integration with the EU should find it easier to take additional integrative steps than will countries with less integration.

Although there is some evidence in support of this thesis for Europe generally,[19] and although Moses and Jenssen find Nordic behavior to be largely consistent with it, the evidence is ambiguous for the Alpine nations, at least as far as trade integration is concerned. The proportions of Swiss exports and imports with the EU in 1989 were 57 and 71 percent, respectively, and for Austria 64 and 68 percent. Indeed, Switzerland led all OECD countries in terms of the share of imports that came from the EU (Hauser and Bradke 1991). Yet the Swiss rejected further integration when they voted against the EEA.

It is not clear why the relationship between willingness to integrate further and degree of integration already achieved must necessarily be positive. The relevant comparison, surely, is not the degree of integration still to come relative to what has already been accomplished but the costs of further integration relative to the benefits. Although the prospects were widely believed to be positive for both countries, the net benefits were expected to be small and contingent on "dynamic" elements that were somewhat speculative. Uncertainties about the measurable effects of membership thus left room for nonquantifiable considerations to assert themselves.

In Austria, the government coalition supported membership and, in spite of some internal squabbles, conducted a campaign in favor of it.[20] The major political parties and broad segments of the academic and media establishments also favored membership. And, although the outcome of the referendum was uncertain until the end in view of large numbers of undecided voters, 66.6 percent of voters ultimately chose membership.

During the debate, the public was fed a rich diet of data and forecasts. Beginning with the early study by Breuss (1989), the Austrian Institute of Economic Research issued a succession of studies, analyses, and evaluations showing that the quantifiable elements favored membership.

As noted earlier, however, uncertainty about when membership would commence forced researchers to choose arbitrary starting dates and test periods for their simulation exercises. The official starting date would, in any event, not necessarily be the obvious point at which to start simulating the effects because markets would act in anticipation of the start date. Modelers at WIFO solved the problem by simulating the effects of EEA and EU, respectively, as if membership had started in 1982, and allowing for an adjustment period of six years, namely, the length of time the Commission had set aside for realization of the main effects of Europe 1992. Table 9.3 compares the estimated effects for Austria with those predicted by the Commission for the EU.

Unlike foreign experts, many Austrians believed that there would be positive spillover effects from Europe 1992 regardless of whether Austria joined or not. Table 9.4 compares the effects of nonmembership (scenario A) with two

TABLE 9.3. Early Estimates of Single Market Effects

	EU[a]	Austria[b]
Removal of border controls	.36	.00
Government procurement	.55	−.10
Liberalization of financial services	1.46	.60
Supply-side effects[c]	2.14	1.10
Budgetary effects	—	.30
Other	—	1.60
Total	4.51	3.50

Source: Breuss and Schebeck 1989.
[a]Selected by Breuss and Schebeck (1989) from Emerson et al. 1988.
[b]Additional GDP in the sixth year relative to 1982–87 actual GDP.
[c]Including scale economies and greater competition.

TABLE 9.4. Austria's Three Options Compared

	Year					
	1	2	3	4	5	6
A. Nonmembership						
Real GDP	.3	.7	1.0	1.2	1.2	1.6
Consumption deflator	−.2	−.5	−1.0	−1.3	−1.5	−1.6
Unemployment rate	−.1	−.2	−.2	−.3	−.3	−.4
Labor productivity	.2	.5	.6	.7	.8	.8
Net lending by government (% of GDP)	.2	.3	.3	.3	.4	.4
B. EU membership without budgetary correction[a]						
Real GDP	.7	1.6	2.2	2.7	3.1	3.5
Consumption deflator	−1.8	−3.4	−4.3	−4.8	−5.0	−5.2
Unemployment rate	.3	.1	−.2	−.5	−.7	−.9
Labor productivity	.9	1.5	1.8	1.8	1.9	1.9
Net lending by government (% of GDP)	−1.2	−1.4	−1.4	−1.3	−1.2	−1.1
C. EU membership with budgetary correction[a]						
Real GDP	.2	.9	1.5	1.8	2.2	2.5
Consumption deflator	−1.7	−3.2	−4.1	−4.7	−5.0	−5.2
Unemployment rate	.4	.3	.1	−.1	−.4	−.6
Labor productivity	.6	1.1	1.4	1.5	1.5	1.5
Net lending by government (% of GDP)	−.1	−.3	−.3	−.2	−.1	0

Source: Breuss and Schebeck 1989.
Note: Deviations are from the base scenario, and realized results are for 1982–87.
[a]Corrections via fiscal measures to keep budget balanced.

TABLE 9.5.   Static and Dynamic Effects of EU Membership (point estimates in percentage of GDP)

	EU	Austria
Static effects[a]	4.5	3.5
Dynamic effects[b]	4.75	2.5
Total	9.25	6.0

Source: Breuss 1992.

[a]For the EU, static effects are drawn by Breuss (1992) from Emerson et al. 1988. For Austria, see Breuss and Schebeck 1989. See also table 9.4.

[b]Dynamic effects are due to exploitation of scale economies and stimulation of investment (endogenous growth). For the EU, effects are drawn by Breuss from Emerson et al. 1988, Baldwin 1989, 1992. For Austria, adoption is by Breuss from the Baldwin approach, with multiplier values drawn from Baldwin 1992.

versions of membership (scenarios B and C). The difference between the latter two reflects alternative assumptions about the budget implications of membership.

In the third of the scenarios (C), government revenues and outlays are adjusted in order to prevent the fiscal costs of membership from worsening the budget; in the second scenario (B), the budget deficit is allowed to increase by 1.1% over the base scenario.[21] According to WIFO calculations, at the end of the sixth year GDP would have been 1.6 percent higher than the base case if Austria chose not to join the EU and either 2.5 percent or 3.5 percent higher if it did join.

The numbers show the positive effect of the Single Market on inflation and unemployment in Austria, which decline in all three cases; meanwhile, labor productivity rises in all three cases. The relatively small differences between nonmembership and membership under budget discipline are particularly striking.

As noted, WIFO researchers accepted the emphasis placed by the Commission on the role of imperfect competition and market segmentation. They also found the growth model advanced by Baldwin (1989, 1992) compelling. Table 9.5 summarizes WIFO's estimates of the static and dynamic effects for Austria. The Baldwin "multiplier," referenced in the notes to the table, is a function of scale economies and capital-output elasticities. The dynamic effect of Europe 1992 is obtained by multiplying the static effects by the appropriate Baldwin multiplier.

When the date of accession to the EU became known, WIFO used that date in its simulations. Table 9.6 gives the effects, in the first year and the remaining five years, in terms of cumulative deviations from membership in

TABLE 9.6. Austria: EEA and EU Compared

	1995	1996	1997	1998	1999	2000
Real GDP	.8	1.4	1.8	2.2	2.5	2.8
Consumption deflator	−1.8	−2.3	−2.7	−2.9	−3.1	−3.3
Real disposable personal income	2.1	2.1	2.5	2.8	3.1	3.4
Unemployment rate	−.2	−.3	−.2	−.3	−.3	−.3
Labor productivity	.7	.8	1.1	1.2	1.4	1.4
Net lending by government (% of GDP)	−1.5	−1.1	−1.0	−1.0	−.9	−.9

Source: Breuss, Kratena, and Schebeck 1994.
Note: EU effects are cumulative deviations from EEA.

the EEA. It shows that by the year 2000 Austrian GDP will be 2.8 percent higher than it would have been under the EEA and that the consumption deflator will be 3.3 percent lower. Table 9.7 provides a disaggregated view of the estimated effects. The importance rationalization of agriculture plays in these calculations is readily apparent.

Overall, the benefits of EU membership are thus considerable by WIFO's calculations. Keuschnigg and Kohler (1996) obtain similar magnitudes (2.6 percent compared with WIFO's 2.8 percent for GDP). Flam (1995), on the other hand, obtains net gains for Austria of a mere .08 percent, albeit on the basis of back-of-the-envelope calculations, in which gains from rationalization of agriculture are roughly offset by the costs of fiscal transfers.

Although the economic effects, especially the quantifiable ones, received much attention, Austrians also fretted about matters that are not easily expressed in terms of numbers.[22] Ability to influence EU policy and fear of isolation were two of these. Another was Austria's future as a gateway to the East. Vienna, in particular, likes to see itself as a gateway to the emerging economies of Central and Eastern Europe. Although Austria had already profited from the opening of the Eastern economies and the reunification of Germany, opinion makers believed that the gateway role could be better realized within the EU. That would be particularly true in the case of an eastern enlargement of the EU.

In the end, broad segments of Austria's voters found the package of arguments favoring membership compelling. The overall yes vote of 66.6 percent was matched or nearly matched across a wide range of voter types and categories. The two government parties and the Liberal Forum supported membership. The fringe parties, including the Greens, opposed membership. The major newspapers were promembership.

TABLE 9.7.   Disaggregated Effects of EU Membership for Austria (deviations from EEA in percentages)

	Real GDP		Consumption Deflator	
	1995	2000	1995	2000
Integration effects	.2	2.0	−.3	−1.8
Customs union	.0	.1	−.1	−.2
Trade costs	.1	.9	.0	−.2
Location[a]	.0	.6	.0	.0
Competition[b]	.1	.4	−.2	−1.4
Agriculture	.4	.3	−1.4	−1.4
Budgetary effects	.2	.5	−.1	−.1
Total	.8	2.8	1.8	3.3

Source: Breuss 1995.

[a]Represents Austria's improved status for investment.

[b]"Dynamic" supply-side effects, including scale economies and greater competition.

Not only was the positive vote stronger than had been anticipated but the disaggregated results largely followed the overall pattern.[23] The vote in all nine provinces (*Laender*) was strongly positive, ranging from a high yes vote of 74.7 percent in economically disadvantaged Burgenland to a low of 56.7 percent in Tirol. Burgenland would have been expected by many analysts to oppose membership in order to preserve an element of protection for its relatively weak economy. The strong positive vote is explained by the fact that Burgenland voters reacted to the promised inflow into the region of structural and other transfers from the EU. The "low" yes vote in Tirol was influenced by that region's unhappiness with Austrian and EU policies regarding road transit through the Brenner Pass.

Further disaggregation of the regions into voter districts leaves the voting pattern largely unchanged: strong majorities in favor of union. If there was an urban-rural split, it was reflected mainly in smaller yes votes rather than rejection of membership. Rural agricultural areas, rural areas with blue-collar communities, and rural areas in which services played a major role provided yes votes of 61.5, 67.1, and 64.9 percent, respectively, while urban industrial areas and urban areas in which services were economically significant voted yes, with 68.5 and 67.2 percent, respectively. Population centers came in with yes votes of 66.6 percent.

In general, economically weaker regions tended to have the largest proportion of no votes, but they still chose membership (Plasser, Sommer, and Ulram 1995, 338). In that limited sense, the results are consistent with expectations that weakly competitive regions and areas with sheltered economic activities would feel threatened by the opening to Europe. In many of these poor regions, however, negative sentiments were swamped by expectations of resource transfers from Brussels.

In cities with traditional blue-collar communities, the yes vote was 65.3 percent, and in urban centers with significant concentrations of skilled service workers it was 67.6 percent (Plasser, Sommer, and Ulram 1995, 340). Many voters appeared to follow their parties' positions when casting their vote. Strong positive votes in blue-collar communities, for example, may reflect workers' membership in the Socialist Party (SPO), which supported EU membership.

Gender, age, and education played a role but mainly in determining the size of the yes vote. Men (70 percent) favored membership more than did women (62 percent), older voters more than younger voters,[24] and highly educated voters more than less skilled ones.[25] Women, young voters, and less educated voters also tended to wait longer before making up their minds. They were heavily represented among undecided voters. Mistrust of government and institutions played a role, with 83 percent of those who trusted government voting in favor of EU membership, while 62 percent of those who did not trust government voted no.

Among arguments and considerations that seemed to affect large numbers of voters, the expectation of personal benefit contributed to a positive vote and appeared to be more important among educated voters. Many voters felt that membership would contribute to national security. Among general economic considerations, expectations of lower consumer prices were important, as were hopes that membership would contribute to economic growth and the creation of new jobs. On the negative side, there were fears about job security, the environment, erosion in the quality of social services, transit and transportation problems, Austria's neutrality, and, above all, agriculture. It is clear that whatever their concerns and misgivings two-thirds of Austria's voters found the expected benefits more compelling.

Switzerland Opts Out

Issues of neutrality and questions about the effect of the EEA or the EU on Swiss traditions of direct democracy arose very early in the debate on membership. These issues were officially addressed (Schweizerischer Bundesrat 1988) and initially judged to be insuperable. The government eventually changed its mind, but the issue remained relevant in the opinion of many.

TABLE 9.8.   Integration in Switzerland (deviations in percentages from base scenario)

A.   General equilibrium model

	Scenarios			
	1	2	3	4
GDP	.25%	.26%	2.0%	.26%

Scenarios

1.   Removal of nontariff barriers on Swiss manufacturing imports.
2.   Scenario 1 plus removal of nontariff barriers on Swiss exports to the EU.
3.   Scenario 2 plus free cross-border movement of labor.
4.   Removal of cartel structures in certain Swiss sectors.

B.   Partial equilibrium studies of selected Swiss industries (deviations in percentages from base scenario in the year 2000)

	EEA	EU
GDP	3.5	4.3

C.   Summary conclusions based on various studies

	Additional GDP
Structural reform in Swiss industry	1.5 to 2.5%
Removal of trade costs; supply-side effects;[a] free movement of labor	2.5 to 3.5%

Source: Hauser and Bradke 1991.

Note: The base scenario represents realized outcomes for 1985; deviations are calculated for 1985.

A total effect of 4 to 6 percent translates into an annual growth rate of GDP of .4 to .6 percent for an adjustment period of 10 years.

[a]Includes scale economies and stronger competition.

The bulk of the empirical work on EU membership was done by a group of researchers coordinated by Professor H. Hauser of St. Gallen. The findings of several component studies are summarized in Hauser and Bradke 1991, and the main results are captured in table 9.8. The net effects of membership, in the EEA or the EU, were judged to be positive but relatively small.

Swiss researchers, moreover, emphasized the extent to which those benefits were due to structural change and policy reforms in Switzerland rather than integration per se. This is evident in the summary statistics of table 9.8, especially those of part B, where liberalization of Swiss labor immigration policies and removal of Swiss restraints on imports provide the dominant effects.

Hauser and Bradke (1991) point out repeatedly that Switzerland is capable of achieving most of the benefits of EU membership unilaterally simply by changing relevant domestic policies. Since neutrality, sovereignty, and other noneconomic issues loom so large in considerations of membership, the latter would be needed only if the political will to make those unilateral policy changes were lacking.

The Swiss vote on EEA membership took place in December 1992. It ran 50.3 to 49.7 percent against the EEA. The election produced one of the largest voter turnouts in postwar history. The closeness of the popular vote, however, was not reflected in the vote of the cantons, which rejected the EEA by a majority of 26 to 17 (see fig. 9.1).

The bulk of the opposition came from the German-speaking cantons, reflecting the division of opinion between the two main language groups along what is known as the "*Roestigraben*" or roast potato trench. Even in the dual-language cantons of Freiburg (Fribourg) and Wallis (Valais), the vote was split along language lines.

In addition to language, there appeared to be an urban-rural split. Sixty percent of the large-city vote favored membership, as against 45 percent of the rest (Kriesi et al. 1993). Even in German-speaking regions, all major cities except St. Gallen voted for membership. When they voted for the EEA, German-speaking cities did so with bare majorities of 53 percent, compared with majorities of 86 percent in French-speaking cities.

The yes vote in the French-speaking countryside was 53 percent, while the German-speaking rural areas delivered yes votes of 39 percent. This urban-rural split is not atypical in Switzerland, especially when national identity is involved. In her study of earlier Swiss referenda on major economic issues, Weck-Hannemann (1990) finds similar urban-rural divisions.

In comparison with language and location, other factors played smaller and often more ambiguous roles. Education, gender, and age, for example, seemed to matter but less so. Similarly, differences in atttitudes between Left and Right were less important. The Left voted for membership and the Right against, but the strongest opposition came from the ideological middle ground (Kriesi et al. 1993, 35).

Indeed, the third most important element would appear to have been distrust of the "political class" and official organs and institutions. Leaders of the opposition effectively exploited populist antipathy toward centralized government and institutions. Exit polls showed that 70 percent of voters who expressed confidence in central government voted for membership against 27 percent of voters who did not.

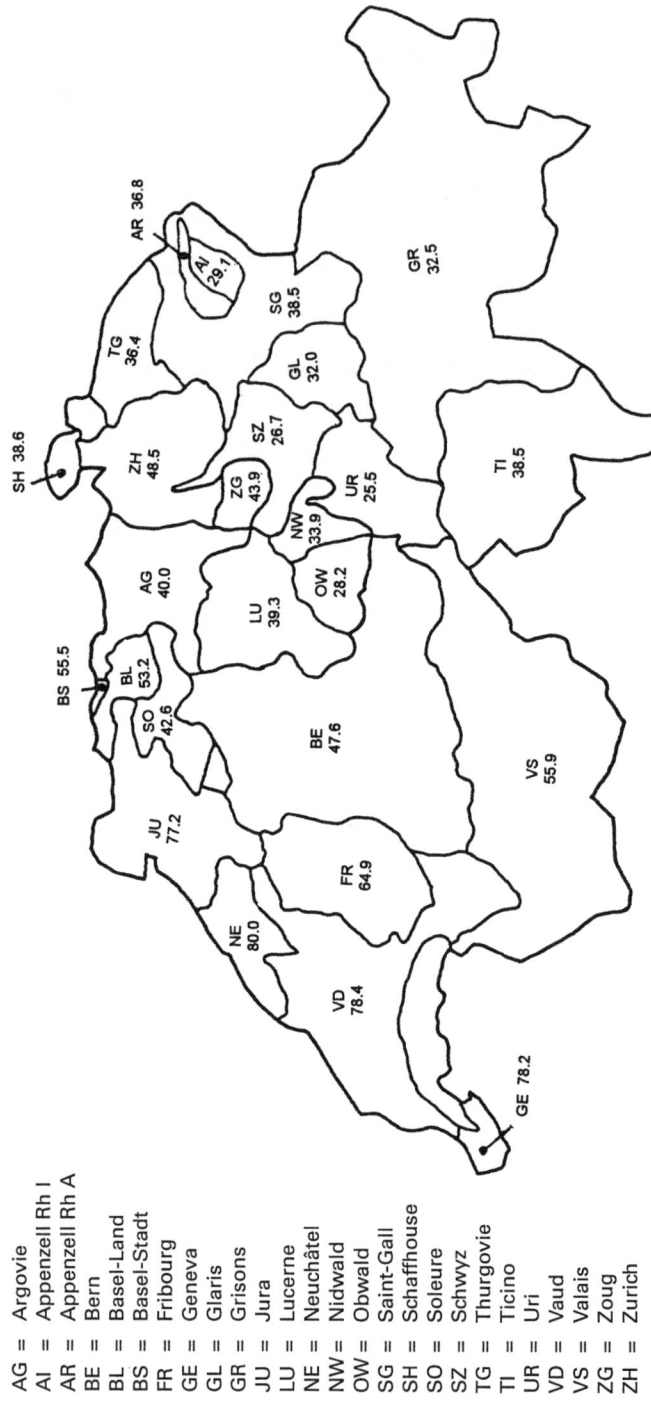

AG = Argovie
AI = Appenzell Rh I
AR = Appenzell Rh A
BE = Bern
BL = Basel-Land
BS = Basel-Stadt
FR = Fribourg
GE = Geneva
GL = Glaris
GR = Grisons
JU = Jura
LU = Lucerne
NE = Neuchâtel
NW = Nidwald
OW = Obwald
SG = Saint-Gall
SH = Schaffhouse
SO = Soleure
SZ = Schwyz
TG = Thurgovie
TI = Ticino
UR = Uri
VD = Vaud
VS = Valais
ZG = Zoug
ZH = Zurich

Fig. 9.1. The 26 cantons of Switzerland and the percentages that voted for EEA membership

Swiss independence and neutrality seemed to matter to many voters. Forty-one percent of eligible voters believed that membership would entail unacceptable losses in sovereignty. Among those who voted for membership, only 12 percent saw sovereignty as a problem, against 75 percent of those who voted no (Kriesi et al. 1993, 50). Similarly, 50 percent of eligible voters agreed that EEA membership would impair civil rights, with 27 percent of yes voters and 76 percent of no voters agreeing.

Fifty-five percent of eligible voters believed that EEA membership was vital for the Swiss economy. Among voters who favored membership, 92 percent held that view, against 6 percent among those who were opposed. Among yes voters, 81 percent accepted the argument that Switzerland had little choice but to seek integration with Europe, but only 31 percent of no voters did. Seventy percent of eligible voters believed that it was important for Swiss citizens to be able to study, work, or live anywhere in Europe.

Seventy-eight percent of eligible voters believed that Switzerland should show solidarity with Europe. Only a minority of eligible voters thought that EEA membership was an automatic first step toward EU membership.

Among economic arguments against membership, employment and wage issues appear to have played a role. While only 44 percent of eligible voters felt that EEA membership would bring an invasion of foreign workers, 73 percent of those opposed believed in that outcome. Similarly, only 43 percent of voters believed that membership would increase unemployment, but 71 percent of those opposed expected such an outcome. However, 52 percent of eligible voters believed that EEA membership would reduce wages in Switzerland, with 72 percent of no voters and 35 percent of yes voters sharing that view.

The overwhelming importance of language and location in explaining the cantonal vote is confirmed by the following regressions. The difference between the two regressions is that the second equation splits cantons composed of a mix of large city and surrounding countryside into two cantons, on the model of Basel, which is officially split into "Basel-Stadt" and "Basel-Land." This adjustment makes the urban-rural split significant in the second regression. Together, language and location explain 62 percent of the vote at the canton level.

$$\text{yes vote} = \underset{(5.82)}{.81} - \underset{(-5.04)}{.75} \text{ German speaking} + \underset{(.84)}{.13} \text{ urban} \qquad (1)$$
$$R^2 = .50$$

$$\text{yes vote} = \underset{(4.63)}{.59} - \underset{(-4.09)}{.55} \text{ German speaking} + \underset{(5.34)}{.63} \text{ urban} \tag{2}$$
$$R^2 = .62.$$

Concluding Remarks

When the European Union introduced the Single Market project, the over-whelming weight of informed opinion was that the EFTA countries had no choice but to join. The experts seemed to agree that the repercussions of Europe 1992 for nonmembers on the periphery would be negative in terms of competitiveness and growth. That pessimism was not shared by the bulk of studies in Austria and Switzerland, in the judgment of which the two countries would benefit from the completion of the Single Market with or without membership. Membership would simply make the gains somewhat larger.

The size of the gains expected from membership was sensitive to model specifications. Since economic integration in the EU and between the EU and EFTA nations had already reached an advanced stage, the gains from additional integration and policy harmonization would be small unless new and hitherto unexplored influences could be found. "New" sources of gains needed to be identified in order to make the "Single Market" package attractive within the EU and membership appealing to outsiders.

Most modelers, including the Commission, found those additional gains in scale economies, product variety, and endogenous growth. These "dynamic" effects bolstered the predicted benefits and made Europe 1992 look less anemic than would otherwise have been the case. But the models that generated these results were empirically largely untested, so that little can be said about the robustness of the forecasts. Not only may particular specifications and calibrations be questioned, but assumptions about adjustment speeds and the ability of European firms and workers to pull off structural change of the kind envisaged appear to have been rather optimistic.

If the forecasts are taken at face value, they represent a strong case for membership. Membership is also appealing to voters who worry about their country's isolation at the periphery of the ever expanding EU. On the other hand, the quantifiable results were not impressive and overwhelming enough to convince voters who worry about their country's neutrality, independence, and sovereignty and about constitutional processes such as direct democracy. In Austria, nonquantifiable considerations seem on balance to have favored membership in the eyes of voters, while in Switzerland the effect seems to have gone the other way.

So, Austria went one way and Switzerland the other. It is not clear that the latter made a mistake, nor that the former will gain all that was promised.

NOTES

I am indebted to F. Breuss, B. Eichengreen, H. Frisch, J. Frieden, H. Handler, H. Hauser, E. Hochreiter, E. Kitzmantel, H. Kramer, P. Moser, R. Rogowski, H. Ursprung, H. Weck-Hannemann, H. Wieser, G. Winkler, and A. Woergoetter for helpful discussions and comments on earlier drafts. Thanks to Terri Van Eaton for able assistance.

1. Legally, there is a European Community and a European Union, separated by differences in purview that are not important for present purposes. The two terms are used interchangeably in the text.

2. The results of these studies are conveniently summarized in Emerson et al. 1988.

3. See, for example, Krugman 1988; Baldwin 1989, 1992, 1993; Haaland and Norman 1992; Norman 1989; and Abrams et al. 1990. Krugman concluded that the EFTA countries would have to resort to large devaluations of their currencies in order to offset the effects of the Single Market on the competitiveness of their exporters. In an early study, Breuss and Schebeck (1989) concluded that the net effect on Austria of the Single Market would be positive but smaller than if Austria became a member. A major project led by Hauser and Bradke (1991) reached similar conclusions for Switzerland. The majority of outside experts, however, continued to be negative about the consequences of nonmembership for EFTA countries. For more recent examples, see Haaland 1993 and Keuschnigg and Kohler 1996. Also, more recently, see Breuss, Kratena, and Schebeck 1994, which continues to predict small but positive results for the case of nonmembership. Felderer et al. 1994, on the other hand, estimates that in the absence of EU membership Austria's labor market will stagnate, that unemployment will increase by 1.4 percent, and that real wages will decline by approximately 2.5 percent. See also Woergoetter 1994. A sample forecast for EFTA is given in table 9.1.

4. Trade costs were believed to run between 1 and 3 percent of the value of trade. See Baldwin et al. 1992, 11.

5. These approaches were questioned by Grossman (1990) in his review of Emerson et al. 1988.

6. See, for example, Breuss and Schebeck 1989 and Breuss 1992.

7. See note 3 for a selection of representative studies.

8. See, for example, Breuss and Schebeck 1989 for Austria and Hauser and Bradke 1991 for Switzerland.

9. See, for example, Breuss and Schebeck 1989 and Hauser and Bradke 1991. See also Baldwin et al. 1992, 9.

10. See Baldwin et al. 1992, 14.

11. See Schmitt 1990 for an assessment of these issues.

12. The importance of permanent growth is also cited in an International Monetary Fund (IMF) study by Abrams et al. (1990).

13. See, for example, Haaland and Norman 1992 and Haaland 1993. See also table 9.1.

14. Baldwin et al. (1992), p. 31.

15. The realization that real world adjustments are unlikely to follow model prescriptions may be starting to set in among observers. The president of the Austrian Institute of Economic Research (WIFO), Helmut Kramer, wrote in 1994 that the "cyclical and structural problems which have plagued the countries of the European Union since the Internal Market was completed have led to doubts as to whether the findings of integration theory are still valid and the hopes generated for the Internal Market are still realistic" (1994, S13). Kramer expresses the belief that these problems cannot be blamed on integration. But the complaints continue: in the introduction to their recent study, Keuschnigg and Kohler (1996) refer to popular unhappiness among Austrians with the results thus far of membership.

16. Indeed, a popular complaint about the EC's approach to product standardization was that it would replace the rich diversity of goods with a series of "Euro" products (see Flam 1992).

17. See Hauser and Bradke 1991, for example.

18. See M. Schneider 1994.

19. See, for example, Anderson and Reichert 1995 and Gabel and Palmer 1995.

20. See Rosam 1995 for an analysis.

21. As noted earlier, the exercise applies the alternative scenarios to the period 1982–87 and then compares the results with actual developments during that period. The deviations from the base scenario are thus deviations from realizations for that period. As discussed in an earlier section, this approach tends to bias the case against nonmembership because it does not allow for further bilateral integration and internal reforms of agricultural policies, technical standards, regulatory practices, and the like.

22. See, for example, Mueller 1995; Plasser, Sommer, and Ulram 1995; H. Schneider 1994; and Traxler 1992.

23. For these and the detailed results that follow, see Plasser, Sommer, and Ulram 1995.

24. Under 30, 55 percent; 30–44, 64 percent; 45–59, 68 percent; and 60 and older, 70 percent. See Plasser, Sommer, and Ulram 1995, 344.

25. Basic education (*Pflichtschule*), 60 percent; technical education (*Fachschule*), 65 percent; advanced education (*Maturanten/Akademiker*), 70 percent. See Plasser, Sommer, and Ulram 1995, 344.

REFERENCES

Abrams, R. K., P. K. Cornelius, P. L. Hedfors, and G. Tersman. 1990. *The Impact of the European Community's Internal Market on the EFTA.* Occasional Papers, no. 74. International Monetary Fund.

Anderson, C. J., and M. S. Reichert. 1995. "Economic Benefits and Support for Membership in the EU: A Cross-National Analysis." *Journal of Public Policy* 15 (September–December): 232–47.

Baldwin, R. E. 1989. "The Growth Effects of 1992." *Economic Policy* 9 (October): 248–81.

———. 1992. "Measurable Dynamic Gains from Trade." *Journal of Political Economy* 100 (January): 62–74.

———. 1993. "On the Measurement of Dynamic Effects of Integration." *Empirica* 20, no. 2: 129–46.

———. 1994. *Towards an Integrated Europe.* London: Centre for Economic Policy Research.

Baldwin, R., et al. 1992. *Monitoring European Integration: Is Bigger Better? The Economics of Enlargement.* London: Center for Economic Policy Research.

Breuss, F. 1992. "Was erwartet Oesterreich in der Wirtschafts- und Waehrungsunion der EG?" *Monatsberichte,* October, 536–48. Vienna: Austrian Institute of Economic Research (WIFO).

———. 1995. "Die vierte EU-Erweiterung—um Oesterreich, Finnland und Schweden." *Monatsberichte,* February, 105–25. Vienna: WIFO.

Breuss, F., K. Kratena, and F. Schebeck. 1994. "Effekte eines EU-Beitritts fuer die Gesamtwirtschaft und fuer die einzelnen Sektoren." *Monatsberichte—Sonderheft,* 518–33. Vienna: Austrian Institute of Economic Research (WIFO).

Breuss, F., and F. Schebeck. 1989. *Die Vollendung des EG-Binnenmarktes: Gesamtwirtschaftliche Auswirkungen fuer Oesterreich.* Vienna: WIFO.

Emerson, M., et al. 1988. *The Economics of 1992.* Oxford: Oxford University Press.

Felderer, B., R. Koman, K. Pichelmann, and A. Woergoetter. 1994. "Wirtschaftliche Folgen der Ausgrenzung Oesterreichs von der Europaeischen Union." Mimeo.

Flam, H. 1992. "Product Markets and 1992: Full Integration, Large Gains?" *Journal of Economic Perspectives* 6 (Fall): 7–30.

———. 1995. "From EEA to EU: Economic Consequences for the EFTA Countries." *European Economic Review* 39 (April): 457–66.

Gabel, M., and H. D. Palmer. 1995. "Understanding Variation in Public Support for European Integration." *European Journal of Political Research* 27, no. 1 (January): 3–19.

Gasiorek, M., A. Smith, and A. Venables. 1992. "1992: Trade and Welfare—A General Equilibrium Model." In *Trade Flows and Trade Policy after '1992',* edited by L. A. Winters. Cambridge: Cambridge University Press.

Grossman, G. M. 1990. Review of Emerson et al. 1988. *Journal of International Economics* 28:385–95.

Haaland, J. I. 1993. "Welfare Effects of 1992: A General Equilibrium Assessment for EC and EFTA Countries." *Empirica* 20, no. 2:107–27.

Haaland, J., and V. Norman. 1992. "Global Production Effects of European Integration." In Winters 1992.

Hauser, H., and S. Bradke. 1991. *EWR-Vertrag, EG-Beitritt, Alleingang.* Zurich: Ruegger.

Keuschnigg, C., and W. Kohler. 1996. "Austria in the European Union: Dynamic Gains from Integration and Distributional Implications." *Economic Policy* 22 (April): 155–211.

Kramer, H. 1994. "Austria in the European Union." *Monatsberichte—Sonderheft* (special issue), s5–s17. Vienna: WIFO.

Kriesi, H., C. Longchamp, F. Passy, and P. Sciarini. 1993. *Analyse der eidgenossischen Abstimmung vom 6. Dezember 1992.* Bern: Forschungsinstitut der Schweizerischen Gesellschaft fuer Sozialforschung.

Krugman, P. 1988. "EFTA and 1992." EFTA Occasional Papers, no. 23. Typescript.

Mueller, W. C. 1995. "Austria." *Political Data Yearbook, European Journal of Political Research* 28 (December): 93–106.

Norman, V. D. 1989. "EFTA and the Internal European Market." *Economic Policy* 4: 424–65.

OECD [Organization for Economic Cooperation and Development]. 1991. *Regional Problems and Policies in Switzerland.* Paris: OECD.

Plasser, F., F. Sommer, and P. A. Ulram. 1995. "Entscheidung fuer Europa: Analyse der Volksabstimmung ueber den EU-Beitritt Oesterreichs, 1994." In *Oesterreichisches Jahrbuch fuer Politik, 1994,* edited by A. Kohl, G. Ofner, and A. Stirnemann. Vienna: Verlag fuer Geschichte und Politik.

Rosam, W. M. 1995. "Die EU-Kampagne der Bundesregierung." In *Osterreichisches Jahrbuch fuer Politik, 1994,* edited by A. Kohl, G. Ofner, and A. Stirnemann. Vienna: Verlag fuer Geschichte und Politik.

Schmitt, N. 1990. "New International Trade Theories and Europe, 1992: Some Results Relevant for EFTA Countries." *Journal of Common Market Studies* 29 (September): 53–73.

Schneider, H. 1994. "Gerader Weg zum klaren Ziel? Die Republik Oesterreich auf dem Weg in die Europaeische Union." *Oesterreichische Zeitschrift fuer Politikwissenschaft* 23, no. 1: 58–73.

Schneider, M. 1994. "Chancen und Risken der Landwirtschaft im EU-Binnenmarkt." *Monatsberichte—Sonderheft* (special issue), s46–s61. Vienna: WIFO.

Schweizerischer Bundesrat. 1988. *Bericht ueber die Stellung der Schweiz im europaeischen Integrationsprozess.* Bern: Schweizerischer Bundesrat.

Traxler, F. 1992. "Interests, Politics, and European Integration." *European Journal of Political Research* 22, no. 2 (August): 193–217.

Weck-Hannemann, H. 1990. "Protectionism in Direct Democracy." *Journal of Institutional and Theoretical Economics* 146: 389–418.

Winters, L. A. 1992. *Trade Flows and Trade Policy after "1992."* New York: Cambridge University Press.

Woergoetter, A. 1994. "Empirische Evidenz der Integrations-wirkungen: Daenemark versus Schweiz." Mimeo.

CHAPTER 10

The Political Economy of Eastern Enlargement

Peter Bofinger

I. Introduction

When the countries of Central and Eastern Europe[1] started their transition to democracy and the market, they had very high expectations of support by the European Community. Indeed, the six Europe Agreements (EAs) that were concluded between 1991 and 1993 with Poland, Hungary, the Czech Republic, Slovakia, Bulgaria, and Romania soon provided a first step toward Eastern enlargement of the EU. And at the Copenhagen Summit (July 21–22, 1993) the heads of state and government made a first clear commitment to open the EU to the CEECs:

> The European Council today agreed that the associated countries in Central and Eastern Europe that so desire shall become members of the European Union. Accession will take place as soon as an associated country is able to assume the obligations of membership by satisfying the economic and political conditions required.
>
> Membership requires that the candidate country has achieved stability of institutions guaranteeing democracy, the rule of law, human rights and respect for and protection of minorities, the existence of functioning market economy as well as the capacity to cope with competitive pressure and market forces within the Union. Membership presupposes the candidate's ability to take on the obligations of membership including adherence to the aims of political, economic and monetary union.

The Union's capacity to absorb new members, while maintaining the momentum of European integration, is also an important consideration in the general interest of both the Union and the candidate countries.

In the last few years, however, the whole process has lost momentum.[2] The EU seems to be occupied mainly with its internal problems, above all the many unresolved issues that the Maastricht Treaty has created. As this chapter shows, there is a risk that the EU will adopt a "wait and see" approach, delaying a definitive schedule for the accession of Eastern Europe. At the same time, the initial EU enthusiasm in the East might cool so that it will become increasingly difficult to find the necessary political support in the CEECs for EU membership. But staying outside the EU would not only impair the transformation of political and economic structures in the East but would also have serious negative political and economic repercussions in the West. Hence, it is important to develop strategies that could overcome the present impediments for an accession of Eastern Europe.

The chapter is structured as follows: section 2 discusses the analytical problems that arise if one tries to apply the standard approaches of the theory of political economy to Eastern enlargement. Section 3 surveys the different dimensions of economic integration that are embedded in the Maastricht Treaty. It shows that with the focus of the academic debate on trade liberalization important political-economic aspects of EU membership are neglected. These concern above all the very stringent "hands-tying" of national governments by the regulations of the treaty. From this perspective, EU membership entails a major shift in the balance of power between national lobbies. Above all, it strengthens the relative power of lobbies (consumers, exporters) whose interests are neglected in political decisions on trade issues.

Section 4 analyzes how the incumbent members have so far responded to the situation in the East. Obviously, their actions have been guided by the imperative of a stringent EU budget constraint. As a consequence, all efforts were directed to the field of trade liberalization. Performance in the last five years has confirmed the prediction that increasing imports from the CEECs would have no major negative effects on EU producers even at the regional and sectoral levels. On the contrary, there are many areas where the EU producers have benefited from trade integration with the CEECs. Thus, the main political resistance comes not from manufacturing industries but from German taxpayers, the southern member states benefiting from structural funds, and the farmers' lobby. There is no doubt that the budgetary costs of including the

CEECs constitute the most important impediment for any major enlargement in the foreseeable future. An additional problem is posed by the inadequate political structures of the EU. Rapid enlargement would intensify the existing problems (disproportionately high representation of small countries, lack of parliamentary control, unclear allocation of powers) and make political reform more difficult.

Section 5 assesses EU enlargement from the perspective of the countries of the East. At the moment the CEECs clearly wish full membership as early as possible. Besides the stabilizing political effects, they expect participation in the transfer mechanisms of the EU and an improvement in their economic performance through unrestricted access to EU markets. As there is, so far, not very much literature on these issues, it is not easy to characterize the political economy process in the CEECs. On a general level, one can argue that far-reaching economic transformation together with strong output decline has temporarily weakened the power of existing lobbies. But, insofar as the overall political environment in the CEECs still favors rent-seeking processes, a strengthening of producers' lobbies over time is likely. These could become major opponents to EU membership once they realize how much the treaty reduces the supply of protection through its tying of national governments. Resistance to the EU might also come from the population, among which a growing nationalism can already be discerned, especially if it becomes obvious that net transfers from the EU will be limited.

Section 6 presents the main policy implications. Under present conditions, there is an obvious discrepancy between what the EU is willing to offer and what the CEECs are asking. This could lead to a complete standstill of the enlargement process. Baldwin's proposal of multilateralizing the EAs in the form of an "Association of the Association Agreements" is not very different from a "wait and see approach," as it only extends the limited trade liberalization of the EAs to trade relations among the CEECs. In order to avoid "hub and spoke bilateralism," EFTA membership would provide a more stringent framework. This solution has the additional advantage that its institutional setup already exists and could be transformed into the EEA arrangement.

As an alternative, this chapter develops a "comprehensive accession strategy" (CAS) for the countries of Central and Eastern Europe. It is characterized by the following elements that could be embedded in the treaty:

A common accession procedure for all CEECs and other Eastern European countries that are identified ex ante

A schedule for membership

A three-stage process toward full membership: stage 1, with the EAs (five years); stage 2, with far-reaching trade liberalization and the adoption of the treaty's regulations on subsidies, capital liberalization, fiscal policy surveillance, and the prohibition of central bank financed fiscal deficits (five years); and stage 3, with full membership, including the Single Market

2. Difficulties of Political Economy Analysis of the Eastern Enlargement

Analyses of political economy issues normally start from a well-defined economic framework. This applies above all to trade policy, one of the favorite playgrounds of political economy theory. In general, the models address a country where the relevant alternatives are clear and very limited (protectionism or free trade). They assume that the impact of political decisions on the relative incomes of specific industries, sectors, regions, or countries is well known. The interesting cases are situations in which solutions are rejected in the political process because they negatively affect some groups, although a country would be better off in general. Here political economy theory steps in and tries to detect the political and economic mechanisms that allow special interests to dominate the process of political decision making.[3]

Unfortunately, the topic of this chapter is complex. It has to deal not with one country but with the 15 EU member states and the up to 17 nations in Eastern Europe (table 10.1) that might join the EU at some future date.[4] There is not only a choice between two narrow alternatives for trade policy but between variable bundles of integration in many areas of economic policy (e.g., common agricultural policy, European monetary union, common social policy, and integrated labor markets). From this broader perspective, it becomes obvious how difficult it is to apply the standard tools of the theory of political economy, especially as many issues of economic integration have so far not been a preoccupation of this theory.

A comparison of the alternatives is also complicated by the fact that it is far from clear how the EU will look in the next decade, that is, when at least some CEECs might at last have a chance to become members. This confusion is due to the Single European Act (1987) and the Maastricht Treaty (1992), which assigned many new tasks to the Community. Unfortunately, this deepening was made without a clear concept of the overall structure of the Union. A major problem that has been created by this deepening is the unclear allocation of powers and functions compared with those in explicitly federal states. The *principle of subsidiarity* (Art. 3b), with its imprecise wording, did little to clarify these issues. As CEPR (1993, 22) mentions, the principle of subsidiarity is

> very general and open to many interpretations. The authors of the Maastricht Treaty did not clearly establish the principle as an instrument for the allocation as well as the excise of competences, and they choose not to give a list of particular areas where Community action was likely to be necessary and efficient. They did not put forward any guidelines for judging the effectiveness and necessity of a particular action. The principle of subsidiarity at the level of the Community therefore remains a general principle rather than a source of explicit guidance.

One can hope that a more structured treaty will emerge after the Maastricht II intergovernmental conference, but at the moment this is of little help.

Even if one could systematize all feasible political options, one would still be confronted with the problem that their specific impact on the individual countries, regions, sectors, and industries is far from clear. This applies above all to the CEECs. Although there is a rapidly growing literature that discusses trade patterns between East and West (CEPR 1995; Holzmann et al. 1994; Baldwin 1994; Anderson and Dittus 1994), its focus is on the short and medium term. But very little can be said about the structure of comparative advantage in the long term, which is the period that might become relevant to EU membership. In addition, while most calculations are for aggregate trade flows, there is less analysis on the structural effects, especially on wages, that are of main importance for political economy considerations in the West.

Thus, there is no clearly defined economic basis from which the chapter can start. This requires that consideration be given to the basic economic aspects of the Eastern enlargement. It also makes it necessary to focus on the main battlefields for political economic processes and to be less specific about how individual regions, sectors, or industries are affected by an enlargement and how they make their preferences felt in their respective national capitals.

TABLE 10.1. Possible Sizes of the EU and Population Shares

	Population in Millions, 1993	Percentage in EU–15	Population in Millions, 1993	Percentage in EU–20	Population in Millions, 1993	Percentage in EU–23	Population in Millions, 1993	Percentage in EU–28	Population in Millions, 1993	Percentage in EU–32
EU–12	**328**	**93.7**		**78.8**		**77.3**		**70.3**		**47.7**
Austria	8	1.9								
Finland	5	1.2								
Sweden	9	2.2								
EU–15	**350**	**100**		**84.1**		**82.5**		**75.1**		**50.9**
Czech Republic			10.3	2.5						
Hungary			10.3	2.5						
Poland			38.5	9.3						
Slovakia			5.3	1.3						
Slovenia			2.0	0.5						
EU–20			**416.4**	**100**		**98.1**		**89.3**		**60.6**
Estonia					1.6	0.4				
Latvia					2.7	0.6				

Lithuania	3.76	0.9		
EU–23	**424.5**	**100**	**91.0**	**61.7**
Albania	3.4		0.7	
Bulgaria	9.0		1.9	
Croatia	4.8		1.0	
Former Yugoslav Republic of Macedonia	2.19		0.5	
Romania	23		4.9	
EU–28	**466.9**		**100**	**68.9**
Belorussia	16.4			2.4
Moldova	4.3			0.6
Russia	148.3			21.6
Ukraine	52.1			7.6
EU–32	**687.6**			**100**

Source: EBRD 1994; CEPR 1992 (own calculation).
Note: Entries in boldface indicate the sum country groupings.

3. Economic Integration from a Political Economy Perspective

The present debate is not only very much focused on the effects of trade liberalization, but it also tends to neglect the political economy implications of different forms of economic integration. Thus, it seems necessary to begin the analysis with a short exposition of the main dimensions of economic integration that membership in the EU implies. As the chapter deals with economic integration only, it will not address the issues of political union (provisions of the common foreign and security policy, cooperation in the fields of justice and home affairs) that have also become a part of European integration with the Maastricht Treaty.

3.1. Market Integration versus Political Integration

The main dimensions of economic integration are traditionally described by differentiating between market and policy integration. In the Treaty of Rome (1957), *market integration* was at the center. It encompasses the four main liberties: free movement of goods (Arts. 9–37), persons (Arts. 48–58), services (Arts. 59–66), and capital (Arts. 67–73). *Policy integration* was originally limited to areas that were closely linked with market integration: common commercial policy (Arts. 110–16), common agricultural policy (Arts. 38–47), common transport policy (Art. 84), elements of a common development aid (Arts. 130u–y), and a common competition policy (Arts. 85–95; a council regulation regarding the control of concentrations was added in 1989). Social policy and industrial policy were included as early as in 1957, but with the exception of the coal and steel industries no common policies were established. As already mentioned, the Single European Act and the Maastricht Treaty transformed the relatively structured system of the Treaty of Rome into something that is quite complicated and increasingly opaque. The Single European Act aimed at perfecting market integration by establishing the *Single Market* by the end of 1992. But it also increased the structural funds. The Maastricht Treaty aimed at strengthening policy integration, above all by laying the groundwork for European monetary union (Arts. 105–9m). Other new issues in the treaty included consumer protection (Art. 129a), trans-European networks (Arts. 129b–d), regional policy aiming at economic and social cohesion (Arts. 130a–e), policies fostering research and technological development

(Arts. 130f–q), and environmental policy (Arts. 130r–t). In addition, existing regulations concerning social policy (Arts. 118a–b) and economic policy (Arts. 102a–104c) were extended. The latter considerably enhanced the surveillance of national economic polices by the Council and the Commission. Article 104 prohibits any central bank financing of public deficits for the member countries.

3.2. Obvious Implications of EU Membership

Taking into consideration the many areas of policy integration and the unclear allocation of responsibilities and functions, it is not easy to assess all implications of membership. Thus, it is necessary to concentrate on the core functions of the EU. These can be summarized as follows:

> Participation in the *Single Market* provides a country with the opportunity to reallocate its resources and improve its national welfare by realizing "gains from trade" with the EU. As basic trade theory demonstrates, these benefits depend on the magnitude of relative price changes at the national level and are therefore higher for small countries than for large ones.
>
> If a new member state is relatively poor, it can increase its welfare by participating in the *distributional mechanisms* of the treaty. These rest on the two pillars of the common agricultural policy and of the EU's structural funds, which together constitute about 85 percent of the EU's budget. As table 10.2 shows, the transfers that could be obtained are considerable, especially for the CEECs, with their relatively low per capita incomes (table 10.3).[5]
>
> If the principle of subsidiarity is applied, a country can benefit from the various forms of *policy integration*. This effect derives from the logic of this principle, according to which the tasks that "cannot be sufficiently achieved by the Member States can . . . by reason of the scale of the proposed action, be better achieved by the Community" (Art. 3b). An example is the common monetary policy that is scheduled for January 1, 1999. If a fully integrated European market for financial services will emerge, one can argue that a *European Central Bank* can provide more efficient monetary management than 15 (or more) independent national central banks (Bofinger 1994).

TABLE 10.2.   Projection of Income Transfers from the EU to the CEECs (ECU per capita)

	Gross Receipts	Gross Contribution	Net Transfers
Czech Republic	256	60	196
Hungary	271	48	223
Poland	209	37	172
Slovakia	211	31	180
V4	**227**	**42**	**185**
Slovenia	209	85	124
V4 + Slovenia	**226**	**43**	**183**
Estonia	428	64	364
Latvia	507	59	448
Lithuania	410	43	367
V4 + Slovenia + Baltics	**250**	**44**	**206**
Bulgaria	293	39	254
Romania	458	54	404
Total	**277**	**44**	**233**

Source: Baldwin 1994, 175 (own calculations); and Weltbank 1994.

Note: The averages for the country groupings were calculated using population data provided in Weltbank 1994. Entries in boldface indicate the averages for the country groupings.

3.3.   Political Economy Implications of EU Membership

From the perspective of political economy, the implications of EU membership clearly go beyond these three areas. Here the direct benefits that a country can obtain from entering the EU play only a secondary role. More interesting is the impact of membership on the power balance among national interest groups and the government. It seems obvious that the constraints under which a government operates are significantly altered by signing the treaty. In general, one can say that the discretion of national policymakers is considerably reduced, as membership implies a major transfer of national competences to the EU:

A country can no longer determine its own trade policy. It is obliged to keep its markets completely and irreversibly open vis-à-vis other members and can impose restrictions on nonmembers only as a part of the EU's overall trade policy.

It must refrain from all subsidies that are incompatible with the Common

TABLE 10.3. Per Capita Income Levels in the EU and the CEECs

	GNP per Capita, 1992 (in dollars)
EU–11[a]	**26,559**
Greece	7,290
Ireland	12,210
Portugal	7,450
Spain	13,970
Poor EUs	**11,755**
Czech Republic	2,450
Hungary	2,970
Poland	1,910
Slovakia	1,930
Slovenia	6,540
V4 + Slovenia	**2,299**
Estonia	2,760
Latvia	1,930
Lithuania	1,310
Baltics	**1,806**
Bulgaria	1,330
Croatia	1,685
Former Yugoslav Republic of Macedonia	1,685
Romania	1,130
Southern Group[b]	**1,276**
Belarus	2,930
Moldova	1,300
Russia	2,510
Ukraine	1,820
European Commonwealth of Independent States	**2,339**

Source: Weltbank 1994 (own calculations).

Note: Entries in boldface indicate the averages of the country groupings.

[a]Austria, Sweden, and Finland are included.

[b]Data for Albania were not available.

Market (Art. 92) and submit all state aids to review by the Commission (Art. 93), which acts as a sort of "anti-subsidy police force" (Stehn 1994).

It must renounce any central bank financing of public sector deficits (Art. 104).

It must abstain from all restrictions of capital movements vis-à-vis not only other member countries but also third countries (Art. 73b). Safeguard measures can only be decided by the Council (Art. 73e). Together with the prohibition of central bank financing of deficits, this regulation is especially important for disciplining fiscal policy, as it implies that national governments have to compete for funds in a completely integrated financial market. Thus, public debtors no longer possess monopsony position in the domestic national financial market.

It must avoid "excessive deficits" (Art. 104c) and submit its economic policies to the surveillance of the Council (Art. 103).

If a country qualifies for EMU, it must transfer all monetary policy competences to the European Central Bank and keep its exchange rate absolutely stable vis-à-vis the member countries. Thus, it can no longer use nominal depreciation as a means of providing protection to its producers.

By accepting these constraints, a country imports an economic constitution that corresponds in many respects with the German ideal of "*Ordnungspolitik*" that was developed by Eucken (1952): in the field of macropolicies, priority is given to the aim of price stability, while the room for maneuver of demand management is very limited. The efficiency of the market mechanism is guaranteed by an open trading system and the prohibition of subsidies. By embedding all of these regulations in the treaty, this framework provides what Eucken calls "*Konstanz der Wirtschaftspolitik*" (constancy of economic policy). This is due to the fact that the legal status of the constraints set by the treaty is much stronger than that of national laws or even a national constitution. Modifications of the treaty are only possible if they are ratified by all member states (Art. N of the Treaty of the European Union).

In terms of the *theory of political economy,* one can readily see how much EU membership affects the processes of internal income redistribution. It changes not only the balance of power between policymakers and lobbies but also that among the national interest groups. The government, for its part, becomes stronger by "tying its hands." After EU membership, the national *supply of protection* will decline, as there is much less that national politicians can offer to rent-seeking interest groups: the traditional tools of trade policy (global or selective) are no longer available at the national level. As the experience of incumbent members shows, some forms of subsidization will still be possible. But because of their greater transparency it will be more difficult to use this instrument for income redistribution (Baldwin 1989). In addition, the tighter restrictions on fiscal deficits will impose an overall constraint on government expenditure, thus limiting the potential for direct transfers to ailing industries. Finally, EU membership also has effects on the *demand for protection.* By entering the Single Market, competition in the hitherto sheltered national market increases. This reduces monopoly rents and prevents the emergence of future monopoly positions. As a result, the financial power of national lobbies, and thus their ability to influence the political process, is reduced.[6]

The new environment also affects the *relationship among different national interest groups*. It is well known that interest groups differ in their ability to organize themselves and exert political pressure. Successful lobbies are normally small and provide their members relatively large benefits from lobbying activity. Interest groups with many members (because of the "collective action problem" described in Olson 1965) and relatively small benefits per member are more difficult to organize. This explains why producer organizations are in general more effective in influencing the political process than consumer lobbies. Seen in this context, the decision about EU membership provides the traditionally weak interest groups a unique chance to improve their bargaining positions. As EU entry commits the government to adopting a restrictive position vis-à-vis the traditionally strong lobbies, the vote on membership bundles together the many future political decisions favoring either weak or strong lobbies. This effect could overcome the "low-benefit problem" which is regarded as a major impediment for organizing large groups, especially consumer lobbies.

The decision on EU membership also has an effect on the relative power of different national producer lobbies: above all, import-competing and exporting industries. If national tariffs and other trade restrictions are decided on a case by case basis, the national government does not have to take into account the interests of exporters. However, if a global decision on participating in the EU's Single Market has to be made, "the negotiations pit the export interests in a country directly against the import-competing interests in the same country" (Grossman and Helpman 1993, 2).

Of course, supranational institutions are not a panacea for the problems of special interest politics. At the European level, there are strong producer lobbies that try to influence the decisions of the EU bureaucracy. However, with its relatively small budget,[7] the potential of the EU to provide subsidies to specific industries is limited. In addition, in the special case of the CEECs one can assume that their industries will need some time before they can establish effective lobbies at the EU level. In the meantime, there is a chance for "unusual growth" (Olson 1987).[8]

Thus, for the CEECs membership in the EU has the important advantage of providing them with an economic constitution that is superior to any national framework for economic policy. By reducing the power of national producer lobbies and the potential for state intervention, it would create an economic environment that allows catch-up.

3.4. The Bargaining Process between the Community and the Aspirants

The classification of the advantages of EMU membership derived in the two preceding sections can be used to provide a first assessment of the bargaining process between the Community and the aspirants.

In dealing with a single country the gains from *market integration* are very unevenly distributed. This applies especially to trade liberalization. As table 10.4 shows, the share of exports to the Community in total exports is higher than 50 percent for the Czech Republic, Poland, and Romania and about one-third for the Slovak Republic and Bulgaria. With the exception of Bulgaria, the import shares are almost identical or somewhat lower. However, for the Community the share of imports from the CEEC–6 is only 3.3 percent of its total imports from third countries.

Participation in the Union's *distributional schemes* is a clear case of a zero-sum game. The incumbents lose what the new members gain. The bargaining power of the Community is strong if large transfers are involved, which is certainly the case with the Eastern enlargement: even the relatively advanced V4 are two and a half times more agricultural than the EU average and less than one-third as rich (Baldwin 1994, 165).

If the new members share *common policies* in cases in which the subsidiarity principle applies, this does not necessarily affect the incumbents. Thus, one can say that this part of the membership package has the character of a public good.[9] The same applies to *political economy effects* that are associated with adopting the regulations of the treaty as an implicit constitution for national economic policies. Thus, in both areas, the benefits of admitting a new member are unevenly distributed, as they only accrue to the entrant. For the incumbents, there are neither obvious costs nor obvious benefits.

This rough assessment shows that the EU has very strong bargaining power in negotiations with any single aspirant. This is even more so in the case of many countries in Eastern Europe that are relatively small, poor, and very agricultural. Under aspects of bargaining power, one can thus expect that the Community will wish to continue its traditional approach to accessions, negotiating each case individually. Seen from this perspective, it might be profitable for membership aspirants to unite and ask for a common accession procedure.

TABLE 10.4.   Percentage of Total CEEC Trade Accounted for by the EU

	Exports			Imports		
	1993	1994	1995	1993	1994	1995
Bulgaria	32.6	37.0	37.2	35.7	44.9	45.6
Czech Republic	49.4	54.1	55.2	52.3	55.7	56.4
Hungary	58.2	63.7	63.2	54.6	61.1	60.8
Poland	69.3	69.2	70.0	65.9	66.4	65.9
Romania	41.4	48.2	53.0	45.3	48.2	49.5
Slovak Republic	29.5	35.0	37.4	27.5	33.5	35.4

Source: WTO, Annual Report, 1996

4. The Position of the Incumbent Members

After the rapid breakdown of the socialist system at the end of the 1980s, the European Community had a strong political interest in supporting the newly emerging democracies. In some ways, the situation was similar to that of the 1970s when Spain, Portugal, and Greece restored democracy (Hamilton and Winters 1992). Notwithstanding the overall commitment to help the CEECs, the EU's response was very much shaped by the desire to avoid strains on the EU budget. Thus, most efforts focused on the area of trade integration, where relatively strong integration effects for the CEECs could be expected without major costs for the EU.

Because of the many issues raised by Eastern enlargement of the EU, the following section does not provide a comprehensive analysis of all areas that might be involved. Instead it focuses on topics that are regarded as "sensitive," as they might imply major adjustment problems in the EU.

4.1. Trade Integration

4.1.1. The Europe Agreements

The institutional framework for trade integration between the CEECs and the EU was laid with the so-called Europe Agreements, which were concluded in 1991 with Hungary and Poland and in 1993 with the Czech Republic, Slovakia, Romania, and Bulgaria.[10] These agreements cover many issues, but the most relevant parts concern trade policy, where they aim at creating bilateral free trade for nonagricultural products within a period of 10 years. For the EU, this will be achieved by means of the following schedule for the liberalization of imports from the CEEC–6:[11]

> For products amounting to about 50 percent of the value of total imports from the CEEC–6, all tariffs and quantitative restrictions were abolished when the EAs went into effect.
>
> Tariffs for certain *basic industrial products* (listed in the so-called Annexes 2a and 2b) were significantly reduced and had to be eliminated completely after two years. Thus, since 1996 such tariffs have no longer existed for the CEEC–6 countries.
>
> For "*sensitive products*" that are included in "Annex 3," all tariffs and quantitative restrictions were abolished immediately. However, these products remained subject to either tariff quotas (automatic reintroduction of tariffs once this level is breached) or tariff ceilings (the Commission retains discretion as regards the reimposition of tariffs). Three years after the Interim Agreements (IAs) took effect, all quotas and ceilings were removed. Thus, they no longer apply to the CEEC–6.
>
> For *steel imports*, all quantitative restrictions were removed immediately. Tariffs were reduced over a five-year[12] period and finally eliminated in January 1996 except for Romania, where they were phased out one year later. For coal products, all tariffs were abolished on January 1, 1996.
>
> For *textiles and clothing*, tariffs will have to be removed five years after the inception of the IAs, that is, in January 1997 for the V4 and in January 1998 for Bulgaria and Romania. Quotas will be abolished on January 1, 1998 (V4) and January 1, 1999 (Bulgaria and Romania).

Thus, at first sight one might come to the conclusion that the final aim of a bilateral free trade area has almost been achieved. However, the EAs still provide the EU with important weapons to protect its markets against CEEC imports:

> The EU (as well as its Eastern counterpart) is authorized to take appropriate *measures against dumping* in trade in accordance with the agreement relating to the application of Article 6 of the General Agreement on Tariffs and Trade (GATT). Before measures are taken, the Association Council must be supplied with all relevant information with a view toward seeking a solution acceptable to the two parties (Art. 33 of the

EA). Except for this mechanism, no framework for the settlement of disputes is specified in the EAs. A disguised form of antidumping measures are the informal price minimums for steel products that play an important role in the steel trade between the EU and the CEECs (Winters 1995).

The EU (as well as its Eastern counterpart) is authorized to take appropriate *safeguard actions* if imports from the other party cause "(a) serious injury to domestic producers of like or directly competitive products or (b) serious disturbances in any sector of the economy or difficulties which could bring about serious deterioration in the economic situation of a region" (Art. 30 of the EA).

The *rules of origin* in the EAs are extremely complicated and have a distortionary effect, as they favor goods using intermediate goods from EU countries that are not counted as a foreign input component (Drabek and Smith 1995, 10; EC 1994, 14).

Trade liberalization does not apply to *agricultural products,* for which the existing quotas and tariffs were left largely unchanged (Arts. 18–21 of the EA).

It is not easy to come to an overall assessment of the trade liberalization effect of the EAs. Several authors note that the CEECs received relatively little preferential treatment compared with other third countries. For instance, the liberalization in textiles and clothing is only five years ahead of the scheduled phasing out of the Multi Fibre Agreement (MFA), and many goods coming from the CEECs have already benefited from the General System of Preferences (Cadot and de Melo 1995).[13] Another major flaw is the lack of common enforcement procedures (Faini and Portes 1995, 3). In contrast to these arguments, the European Commission (1994, 2) states: "Overall, the Europe Agreements constitute a very substantial trade liberalisation package, the scale and pace of which is without precedent in the EU." The two sides of the debate are very clearly described by Winters (in CEPR 1992, 18): "The issue is not so much that the Agreements are directly restrictive . . . but that they leave a large number of opportunities for further restrictiveness in their implementation."

To establish bilateral free trade, the CEECs had to offer a gradual reduction of their trade restrictions for imports from the EU.[14] But this is achieved in an asymmetric way. Thus, the liberalization process in the CEECs started in 1995 only, and full elimination will have been reached at the latest by January 1, 2001. In addition to the antidumping measures and safeguard actions that are available to the EU, the CEECs are allowed "*exceptional measures*" in the form of reintroducing or increasing tariffs (Art. 28 of the EA).[15] The text leaves the CEECs ample room for introducing such measures, as it defines the conditions for their application in extremely vague terms: paragraph 2 refers to "infant industries, or certain sectors undergoing restructuring or facing serious difficulties, particularly where these difficulties produce important social problems." As most industries in the CEECs will be in the process of permanent restructuring in the next few years, this clause gives the CEEC governments almost unlimited discretion to introduce such measures.

4.1.2. Trade Performance

From a political economy perspective, the interesting question is how the increasing division of labor between Eastern and Western Europe has affected and will affect specific industries, sectors, regions, and countries. As tables 10.5 and 10.6 show, trade flows between the EU and the CEECs have increased considerably.

From 1989 to 1993, the average growth rate for imports from the CEECs to the EU was 15.9 percent, and EU exports to the CEECs increased even more, with an average rate of 23.6 percent. This overall pattern can be found in almost all sectors (Faini and Portes 1995, 5). It can also be seen in the trade patterns of Poland and Hungary and in the trade relations of all the transition countries in Europe (table 10.7).

There is much speculation about the determinants of these developments. In a period in which so many fundamental changes are occuring simultaneously, it is difficult to identify the impact of individual factors. It seems obvious that important catch-up effects have played a role. After the breakdown of the state monopoly in foreign trade, producers in the CEECs had a strong incentive to sell their goods for "hard currencies" in the West. One can assume that this was mainly possible in those areas where trade relations with the EU already existed. In fact, the strong expansion of trade flows left the commodity structure of trade flows between the EU and the CEECs almost unchanged. As table 10.8 shows, all five product categories that dominated EU imports from the CEECs in 1987–89 have maintained their leading positions. Given the limited production facilities for marketable goods, this diversion of trade to the West must have implied a decrease in trade with the East. Thus, at least for a certain amount of trade, the causation might have been different from what the literature assumes, that is, that the collapse of the CMEA has forced CEEC firms to sell their products in the West as a sort of "distress trade" (Halpern 1995, 64; Drabek and Smith 1995; Gacs 1995).

TABLE 10.5.   **Growth Rates of Imports from the CEECs to the EU–12 (percentages)**

	1989–90	1990–91	1991–92	1992–93	Average
Food and live animals	7.5	13.3	− 8.9	− 14.1	− 1.2
Beverages and tobacco	22.4	31.8	11.3	10.7	19.0
Crude materials, inedible, except fuel	− 1.2	13.0	17.9	− 11.0	4.7
Mineral fuels, lubricants, and related materials	− 27.8	− 12.3	− 23.9	12.8	− 12.8
Animal and vegetable oils, fats, and waxes	− 23.3	71.8	− 11.0	− 17.1	5.1
Chemicals and related products	20.4	31.7	0.6	− 11.6	10.3
Manufactured goods classified by material	15.2	23.0	28.4	− 2.5	16.0
Machinery and transport equipment	18.1	44.0	31.1	29.1	30.6
Miscellaneous manufactured articles	15.5	36.6	32.8	20.3	26.3
Other	4.7	43.1	4.0	6.9	14.7
Total	7.3	26.1	21.3	9.0	15.9

Source: Faini and Portes 1995, 4.

TABLE 10.6.   **Growth Rates of Exports to the CEECs from the EU–12**

	1989–90	1990–91	1991–92	1992–93	Average
Food and live animals	− 5.1	38.1	9.4	35.3	18.0
Beverages and tobacco	33.9	97.1	0.8	− 14.4	29.3
Crude materials, inedible, except fuel	− 3.1	15.6	9.7	− 0.6	5.4
Mineral fuels, lubricants, and related materials	261.3	152.5	40.7	− 2.8	112.9
Animal and vegetable oils, fats, and waxes	− 4.1	35.6	58.3	1.4	22.8
Chemicals and related products	− 11.9	22.1	23.5	23.5	14.3
Manufactured goods classified by material	2.6	34.7	32.5	29.7	24.9
Machinery and transport equipment	9.6	59.3	20.0	15.2	26.0
Miscellaneous manufactured articles	24.1	59.9	34.1	23.8	35.5
Other	− 9.3	13.5	− 5.9	13.7	3.0
Total	5.5	46.8	23.6	18.7	23.6

Source: Faini and Portes 1995, 5.

In spite of the impressive growth rates of imports from the CEECs, the effects on the EU remain very limited. As table 10.8 shows, the market shares of most CEEC products in EU markets have not changed very much and lie in many sectors in a range of less than half a percent. The major exceptions are "leather and leather goods" and "footwear and clothing." But here outward processing trade (OPT)[16] has played a predominant role (Corado 1995). Thus, there is no evidence that increasing trade with the CEECs has had a significant impact on the economies in the West.

However, this outcome might be due to the fact that the EAs have maintained restrictions for "sensitive goods." An indicator for the restrictiveness of

TABLE 10.7.   Trade of Eastern Europe with the EU (in million ecus)

	1989	1990	1991	1992	1993	1994	Percentage Change, 1989–94
Poland							
Exports to EU	3,862	3,156	6,212	7,081	7,581	9,106	136
Imports from EU	3,943	4,393	7,876	8,154	9,970	10,828	174
Trade balance	− 81	764	− 1,664	− 1,073	− 2,389	− 1,772	
Hungary							
Exports to EU	2,587	2,934	3,625	3,988	3,952	4,923	90
Imports from EU	2,990	2,876	3,486	4,061	4,966	6,152	105
Trade balance	− 403	58	139	− 73	− 1,014	− 1,229	
All former socialist countries[a]							
Exports to EU	27,359	29,219	34,660	36,627	39,456	49,289	80
Imports from EU	24,197	23,350	31,888	35,251	42,139	48,909	102
Trade balance	3,162	5,868	2,772	1,376	− 2,683	380	

Source: Eurostat (1996).
[a]Includes the Baltics, Russia, and the European Former Soviet Union countries.

the EAs is the quota utilization rate (QUR). For MFA clothing, this measure suggests that the restrictions have not been very binding. As Corado 1995 and EC 1994 show, QURs have declined substantially: for the CEEC–6 they decreased from 71 percent in 1986 to 34 percent in 1993. This can be explained by a combination of (1) rising quota levels due to the EAs, (2) weak EU demand in 1992–93, and (3) supply-side difficulties in the CEECs.

4.1.3   Trade Projections

Estimates of future trends in the trade between the CEECs and the EU are in line with what has been observed so far. Gravity models predict a considerable potential for further trade growth. Estimates by Baldwin (1994) based on 1989 income levels show that EU exports to the CEEC–12 in 1989 were about 50 percent of their potential level and that EU imports from the CEECs could increase by a factor of 1.2 (for Romania) to 5.2 (for Bulgaria). Assuming an income catch-up, the prospects for trade growth are considerably higher. Faini and Portes (1995, 8) present data for the gravity model which show that CEEC imports from the EU could still increase by a factor of 10, while their exports to the EU would increase by a factor of four. These projections also indicate that increasing trade relations between East and West will not lead to trade imbalances in the West.

The intuition for these results is as follows. So far, there has been little strategic adjustment in the CEECs (Grosfeld and Roland 1995). Instead of investing in new production structures, firms have behaved in a defensive way,

TABLE 10.8. Characteristics of EU Imports from the CEECs

Sectors	Nace[a]	Percentage Growth in Value of Imports		Share in Total Extra-EU Imports		Percentage in Total Exports to the EU		Market Share in the EU	
		1987–89	1989–92	1987–89	1990–92	1987	1992	1987–89	1990–92
Extract., prep. metal ores	21	16	20	0.4	0.5	0.2	0.2	0.4	0.5
Prod. process. metals	22	25	14	4.3	6.2	12.4	12.7	0.9	na
Extract. nonmet. en. min.	23	13	40	1.8	3.6	0.5	0.7	na	1.3
Manuf. nonmet. min. pro.	24	15	31	11.4	15.9	3.7	4.8	0.4	na
Chemical industry	25	10	14	4.0	4.7	11.6	9.2	0.4	0.7
Artificial fibers	26	12	16	4.5	5.6	0.8	0.6	0.0	0.0
Metal articles	31	19	49	4.1	8.1	2.9	5.9	0.2	0.4
Mechanical engineering	32	21	23	1.9	2.8	5.2	6.2	0.3	0.5
Office mach., data process.	33	-7	68	0.1	0.1	0.2	0.3	0.0	0.0
Electrical engineering	34	21	29	1.0	1.6	4.4	6.1	0.2	0.3
Motor vehicles, parts	35	12	39	1.6	2.2	3.2	4.7	0.1	0.2
Other means of transport	36	-18	44	0.7	0.7	1.2	1.1	0.1	0.2
Instrument engineering	37	2	33	0.4	0.5	0.4	0.5	0.1	0.2
Food, drink, tobacco	41	19	4	5.6	6.9	12.3	8.5	0.3	0.3
Textiles	43	-4	25	3.6	4.3	6.7	5.3	0.6	0.9
Leather, leather goods	44	8	32	2.3	3.9	0.9	1.1	0.7	1.3
Footwear, clothing	45	8	30	8.0	9.9	14.9	16.4	1.9	2.7
Timber, wooden furniture	46	7	17	8.3	9.8	11.3	8.8	1.3	1.5
Paper, paper prod., print	47	16	14	1.2	1.5	2.5	2.2	0.1	0.2
Rubber, plastics	48	16	26	2.8	3.6	2.0	2.3	0.2	0.3
Other manufacturing	49	5	24	1.4	1.7	2.7	2.5	2.1	2.5

Source: European Commission 1994, 5.
[a]Nomenclature generale des activites economique

taking measures to reduce costs and scale down enterprise activity (cutting obsolete production lines, shedding labor, and getting rid of nonproductive assets). The lack of strategic restructuring is reflected in disappointingly low levels of domestic investment. Although there is not much detailed information on investment activity, it is obvious that investment as a share of GDP has fallen in almost all transition countries since the introduction of reforms. This even applies to the Czech Republic, where the share of investment in GDP declined from 30 percent in 1991 to 17 percent in 1994. Thus, a major expansion of CEEC trade to the West, as predicted by the gravity model, would first require substantial investment.[17] This process provides a strong potential for EU exports to the CEECs.

Of course, the main concern of Western policymakers and interest groups is the *structural implications* of East-West trade. Cadot and de Melo (1995) have carefully analyzed the sectoral and regional adjustment effects for France, which because of its trade structure with the CEECs can be regarded as representative of an EU average. The main interest of this study is the employment impact at the regional level, as the literature expects a high demand for protection if trade causes strong local job destruction (Neven 1995). Cadot and de Melo use trade estimates provided by the gravity model and estimates derived by extrapolations of observed trade trends. In both cases, there is no evidence that increased trade with the CEECs would lead to major regional problems. The simulation based on the gravity model shows an upper-bound loss of roughly 13,000 jobs with a very low regional concentration; there is only one modest peak in the Lorraine, with about 850 job losses in the coal sector. The simulation using sectoral projections leads to the result that no net job losses will arise for the economy as a whole and not even for individual regions. A similarly positive assessment can also be found for Greece, one of the weakest EU economies. Dimelis and Gatsios (1995) report very strong export growth of Greek firms to the CEECs between 1989 and 1992, while CEEC exports to Greece remained rather mediocre. According to their estimates, this positive performance of Greek exports will continue, while they do not expect a competitive threat for Greek exports in the EU markets from CEEC products.

In spite of the popularity of all these approaches, one should not overestimate their predictive power. The gravity model provides no information on the commodity structure and the factor content of trade flows. Indices of revealed comparative advantage (RCA) are based on observed trade patterns that are still shaped by the legacies of the Communist regimes. Thus, they give some information on how trade will evolve over the short and medium term but say little about trade patterns for the time when CEEC capital stocks have become definitively obsolete and all trade restrictions between the EU and the CEECs have been removed. There are some indications that the comparative advantage of capital-intensive industries in the CEECs has already been reduced (Neven 1995, 43). Some observers expect that the CEECs will have a comparative advantage in goods that intensively use skilled labor (Hamilton and Winters 1992). However, this is not yet supported by actual trade flows. There are also doubts about the quality of the CEEC's "human capital," as the educational systems in the CEECs show obvious gaps in the fields of secondary and tertiary education (Halpern 1995, 76). A major flaw of all trade estimates based on revealed comparative advantage and the gravity model is that they are not able to incorporate the effects of relative prices and wages. There is no doubt that the trade performance of the East will very much depend on the development of its relative unit labor costs,[18] which may also influence the time required to reach the equilibria calculated by the gravity equations. The neglect of prices and wages might also tend to underestimate the adjustment effects for the West. Even with an equilibrium in the trade balance, increasing (labor-intensive) imports from the CEECs might exert a downward pressure on wages in the West, especially for low-skilled workers. With sticky wages, this could increase unemployment, which is already extremely high for workers with low skill levels. There is not too much evidence for such effects of the Heckscher-Ohlin-Samuelson-Stolper variety, but a recent article by Sachs and Shatz (1994) shows its implications very clearly in the trade relations between the United States and newly industrializing countries in Asia and Latin America.

4.1.4. Implications for the Political Economy of Eastern Enlargement

Nevertheless, it seems unikely that trade liberalization with CEECs will provoke major sectoral or regional disturbances in the West. This is also supported by the fact that one so far observes no initiatives by EU industries calling for safeguard or antidumping measures against CEEC imports. Thus, until now the EU seems to have coped well with competition from the East, even with the gradually increasing trade liberalization provided by the EAs. This applies also to textiles and clothing, one of the most sensitive industries, where one can observe that the net effect is clearly positive. The availability of OPT (which was exempted from EC tariffs when the Interim Agreements were implemented) has provided EU producers with "extended workbenches" in their neighborhood, which has helped them compete with low-wage producers from developing countries.[19] In the steel sector, Winters (1995) predicts a minor output loss in the EU due to the CEECs, but this is negligible compared with the overall need to slim down excess capacity.

Therefore, even if one takes into account the large margins of error that are associated with trade projections, it is obvious that EU-CEEC trade integration does not fit the textbook political economy case, in which the losers can clearly be identified. It also differs from these models in that it has implications for not only the import-competing sectors of the EU but also its export industries. As is mentioned by Grossman and Helpman (1993), the very nature of free trade agreements means that a government has to decide simultaneously on the interests of importers and exporters. In the case of the CEECs, exporting industries in the EU had a strong interest in entering markets in the East, where an immense unsatisfied demand for Western products was evident from the outset. In sum, from the available evidence it seems unlikely that trade issues will pose a major obstacle for EU membership of the CEECs. Or, at least, compared with the difficulties raised by other issues, they do not constitute a binding constraint.

4.2. Policy Integration

The more serious impediments for an Eastern enlargement concern above all issues of policy integration. They are related to the general problem that the political structures of the EU are already showing strains.[20] In particular, the common agricultural policy and the regional and cohesion policy pose almost insurmountable difficulties for EU membership of the CEECs.

4.2.1.   Inadequacy of the EU's Political Structures
It seems useful to enumerate briefly the main problems that are raised by an EU entry of the CEECs:

> Although the EEA has introduced majority voting for Single Market topics (Art. 100a), the *principle of unanimity* (Art. 100) still applies for many decisions. A comprehensive Eastern enlargement could increase the number of members substantially. As a consequence, this principle, which was originally designed for a Community with six members, could easily lead to a standstill in decision making in the EU or could require an increasing amount of financial compensation to overcome the resistance of countries to specific issues.
> The *votes* granted to large and small countries in the Council (Art. 148, sec. 2) and the European Parliament, as well as the representation of coun-

tries at the top of the Commission, clearly favor small countries. This problem has become acute since the accession of Austria, Finland, and Sweden. Thus, including the CEECs (with many small countries) would impair the position of large countries (table 10.9). In addition, even with V4 membership, the poor EU countries could easily block all Council decisions. [21]

With the unclear allocation of competences in the many areas that have been included in the treaty, the incumbents will be reluctant to accept new members, as this could it make even more complicated to agree on the necessary clarifications.

Then there is the problem that there is no effective parliamentary control of the Council that acts as a European government in areas where the EU has exclusive competences. Although the Maastricht Treaty has enhanced the power of the *European Parliament*,[22] there is still an obvious lack of democratic legitimacy. This will increase immensely if the tasks of the EU and the number of its members are growing simultaneously.

Thus, with the inadequate political structures of the EU the entry of new members could endanger not only the functioning but also the prospects for reform of the system. Major institutional changes are therefore a precondition for any enlargement of the EU.

4.2.2. *Insufficient Financial Means*

For many CEECs a main attraction of EU membership is the possibility of participating in the generous distribution schemes of the CAP and the structural funds. However, it is almost sure that this hope will never materialize. The budgetary effects of an Eastern enlargement have been intensively analyzed by Begg (in CEPR 1992), Courchene et al. (1993), Anderson and Tyers (1993), and Baldwin (1994). The results can be summarized as follows:

For budget expenditures associated with V4 membership in the year 2000, the most reliable estimates can be found in the work of Anderson and Tyers (1993), who calculated the costs to the CAP (ecu 37.6 billion), and Courchene et al. (1993), who estimated the impact on structural funds (ecu 26 billion). With budget contributions of the V4 of ecu 5.5 billion, as calculated by Baldwin (1994), the net costs of a V4 enlarge-

TABLE 10.9. Voting Shares in an Enlarged EU

	Percentage Votes in EU–15	Percentage Votes in EU–20	Percentage Votes in EU–23	Percentage Votes in EU–28	Percentage Votes in EU–32	Voting Shares of a Large Country (Germany) in an Enlarged EU (percentage)	Memorandum Item, Population Shares of Germany (percentage)
EU–12	87.4	68.5	63.3	54.3	42.7	13.2	23.2
Austria	4.6						
Finland	3.5						
Sweden	4.6						
EU–15	100	78.4	72.5	62.2	48.9	11.5	21.8
Czech Republic		4.5					
Hungary		4.5					
Poland		7.2					
Slovakia		2.7					
Slovenia		2.7					
EU–20		100	92.5	79.3	62.4	9.0	18.5
Estonia			2.5				

Latvia	2.5				
Lithuania	2.5				
EU–23	**100**	**85.7**	**67.4**	**8.3**	**18.2**
Albania		2.1			
Bulgaria		2.9			
Croatia		2.1			
Former Yugoslav Republic of Macedonia		2.1			
Romania		5.0			
EU–28		**100**	**78.7**	**7.1**	**16.6**
Belorussia			2.8		
Moldova			1.7		
Russia			11.2		
Ukraine			5.6		
EU–32			**100**	**5.6**	**11.5**

Source: Weltbank 1994 (own calculations).
Note: Entries in boldface indicate the sum of the country groupings.

TABLE 10.10.   Extent of Agriculture in the Six CEECs Relative to the EU–12, 1993

Indicator	CEEC–6 as Percentage of EU–12
Arable land	37.6
Employment	112.2
Cereals production	37.2
Pork production	31.0
Milk production	23.0
Beef production	15.4
Overall GDP	3.5

Source: Tangermann et al. 1994, 5.

ment total ecu 58.1 billion. Compared with a projected budget for the EU incumbents of ecu 84 billion in 1999 (Courchene et al. 1993,)[23] this amounts to 69 percent of the EU budget.

An enlargement by the CEEC–6 would certainly be more costly. Unfortunately, there are no detailed projections available for the CAP costs of the non-V4 countries. Using the methodology of Begg (in CEPR 1992), Baldwin (1994) estimates net costs for the CEEC–6 of ecu 21 billion. He states that these estimates are far too low and should be thought of as a lower bound.

To avoid these costs, one could think of admitting the CEECs only if their membership is budget neutral. According to Baldwin (1994), even under very optimistic assumptions concerning growth (6 percent per annum) and assuming a rapidly declining share of agriculture (see table 10.10 for current extent of agriculture), it would take 11 to 14 years for the CEECs to be admitted; in that period, they would have to at least double their real incomes.

With the huge costs of any major eastern enlargement, strong opposition can be expected, especially from Germany, which is the main net contributor to the EU. Especially since 1990, German net contributions have increased substantially (table 10.11). In 1994, payments to the EU (DM 32 billion) almost equaled the deficit in the German current account (DM 39 billion). If one assumes that the increase of net expenditures required for membership of the V4 would have to be financed according to the present structure of contributions, Germany would have to pay DM 22 billion per annum additionally in 1999. Such an increase in EU payments would hardly be accepted by German politicians. Presently, one of the main economic policy objectives of the Ger-

TABLE 10.11. EC Budget Transactions with the Federal Republic of Germany (in DM billions)

Item	1990	1991[a]	1992	1993	1994	1995
Payments to the EC general budget						
Agricultural levies, sugar levies	0.8	1.1	0.9	1.0	1.1	0.9
Customs duties	7.0	8.2	7.0	7.4	7.2	7.2
VAT, own resources	14.2	19.2	22.0	20.4	23.0	24.8
GNP, own resources	0.1	3.9	4.5	8.9	10.5	8.1
Other[b]	0.5	0.6	0.4	0.1	0.0	0.0
Total	22.5	33.0	35.7	37.9	41.8	41.0
Percentage change from previous year	−7.8	+46.7	+8.2	+6.2	+10.3	−1.9
	Payments from the EC general budget					
Agricultural market regulations of which	9.3	10.8	9.8	9.6	9.8	10.1
Interventions in the internal market	7.0	7.9	6.5	10.5	8.7	9.3
Refund of collection expenses	0.8	0.9	0.9	0.8	0.8	0.8
Refund of collection expenses	0.4	1.0	0.8	0.8	0.9	0.9
Total	10.9	14.0	13.6	14.3	14.2	15.1
Percentage change from previous year	−0.9	+28.4	−2.9	+5.1	−0.7	+6.3
Net contribution to EC general budget	−11.6	−19.1	−22.0	−23.6	−27.6	−25.9

Sources: Deutsche Bundesbank 1993, 66; Deutsche Bundesbank 1996, 36–37.
[a]Figures are from January 1991 and include payments relating to the new *Länder* and East Berlin.
[b]Figures include the coresponsibility levy and the superlevy for milk and grain.

man government is reduction of the high ratio of government expenditures in GDP and of the tax ratio, which both increased considerably after 1990. In addition, there is now the problem that Germany is still paying the highest EU contributions per capita, although after German unification it is only in the sixth rank in terms of GDP per capita (Deutsche Bundesbank 1993, 64).

As a costly enlargement would require a compromise between German taxpayers and the main EU beneficiaries, opposition to EU enlargement would be strengthened by those countries which receive substantial net transfers from the EU (Ireland, Portugal, Spain, Denmark, and Greece; see table 10.12) and

TABLE 10.12. Income Redistribution among EU Member Countries, 1994

	Belgium	Denmark	Germany	Greece	Spain	France	Ireland	Italy	Luxembourg	Netherlands	Portugal	United Kingdom	Other Expenditures	EU–12
Contributions to the EU (million ecu)	2,820.2	1,307.0	21,563.3	1,031.6	4,828.7	12,725.5	664.0	8,024.9	169.3	1,161.7	6,844.0	—	65,367.2	—
	4.1%	1.9%	31.4%	1.5%	7.0%	18.5%	1.0%	11.7%	0.2%	6.2%	1.7%	10.0%	—	95.3%
Funds received from the EU (million ecu)	2,512.8	1,495.1	7,729.2	4,844.2	7,834.7	9,924.5	2,390.0	5,219.2	419.1	2,416.0	3,042.6	5,258.6	7,217.7	60,304.8
	4.2%	2.5%	12.85%	8.0%	13.0%	16.5%	4.0%	8.7%	0.7%	4.0%	5.0%	8.7%	12.0%	100%
CAP (Mio ecu)	1,217.2	1,352.5	5,747.6	3,055.9	4,954.3	8,432.9	1,656.0	3,809.4	19.3	1,967.21	521.3	3,123.3	0.0	36,499.3
Structural- and Regional Fund (million ecu)	165.2	53.5	138.7	156.6	2,021.4	914.1	553.1	1,050.9	7.0	233.1	1,381.5	1,474.0	—	10,555.6
Net contribution (Mio ecu)	307.4	− 188.1	13,834.1	− 3,812.6	− 3,006.0	2,801.0	− 1,726.9	2,805.7	− 249.8	1,811.1	− 1,880.9	1,585.4	—	—
Net contribution per capita (ecu)	30.43	− 36.20	170.08	− 366.23	− 76.85	48.48	− 483.86	49.10	− 623.10	118.05	− 190.23	27.21	—	—
CAP payments per capita (ecu)	120.50	260.27	70.66	293.54	126.65	145.95	464.00	66.67	48.25	128.23	52.72	53.59	—	—

Sources: European Union 1995 (own calculations); Eurostate 1996.

from more wealthy countries, where the agricultural lobbies receive high CAP payments (above all France and the Netherlands).

Thus, given the interests of a Community that already included three relatively poor countries by the 1980s, the probability of full participation of the CEECs in the EU's distributional schemes is low. This leaves two alternatives: either the membership of the CEECs will have to be delayed for a long time or the CEECs will have to accept membership without major transfers. In any case, it becomes obvious that governments in Eastern Europe will have to acknowledge that the rationale joining the EU cannot be derived from the CAP and structural funds.

5.   The Position of the Aspirants

5.1.   The Impact of Transition on National Interest Groups

In the CEECs, political and economic transition has considerably changed the environment for the processes that are analyzed in the theory of political economy. The complete upheaval affecting all existing structures has above all reduced or even destroyed the power of those groups that had been dominant under the previous regime. Thus, after 1990 room was provided for political decision making relatively free from group interests. As Olson (1987, 251) emphasizes, this should have favored strong economic growth:

> In Germany, Japan and Italy after World War II, where totalitarianism and defeat in war had destroyed the organisations for collective action, we should expect exceptionally rapid growth. That is exactly what happened with the "economic miracles" after World War II in all three of these countries.[24]

While such growth effects did not materialize,[25] there is no doubt that the new economic and political environment confronted all interest groups with a loss of power. Thus, even if some of the dominant groups (above all, enterprise managers) remained the same, they had to reorganize and develop forms of political influence that were compatible with a market order and a democratic political system. But such a weakening is only temporary. More than half a decade has passed since the start of the transition process, and there are still no definitive prospects for accession negotiations with the EU. Thus, the national lobbies that opposed EU membership have had time to overcome the difficulties of collective action that were created with the transition process.

A gradual strengthening of lobby power can also be expected, as the CEEC economies overcome the economic crises that were created by the transition process. As Rodrik (1994, 40) puts it:

> a deep economic crisis relegates distributional considerations to the second place behind economy-wide concerns, and therefore allows an agenda-setting government to sneak in trade policy alongside macroeconomic reforms.[26]

According to Csaba (1995, 69), the effects mentioned by Olson and Rodrik did play a role in the CEECs:

> With the collapse of the Comecon and the one-party state, a peculiar situation emerged in Central and East Europe. Because of their strong integration into the ongoing power structures, priority areas and large firms often found themselves defenceless; subsidies were cut, trade regimes opened and their secure markets gone. In the first months of disarray, reformist governments could indeed make great advances in legislating market-conformable institutions and arrangements: structural adjustment had started.

But with a return to "normal conditions" politicians will become more open to demands for selective protection. The overall improvement of the economic situation is also important for the financial power of lobbies. The literature assumes that lobbies influence politicians by providing them with financial contributions, above all for election campaigns (Grosman and Helpman 1992). This requires that lobbies must be able to obtain financial support from their members. As long as many enterprises in the CEECs are loss making and in need of credits from the state-owned banking system, there is not much they can offer as compensation for political support. But this will change with time. Experience so far shows that governments in Eastern Europe are very much inclined to provide protection if it is demanded by groups that are in a strong financial position. From table 10.13 one can see that FDI-intensive sectors are sectors with high levels of import protection. EBRD (1994, 137) reports that in Poland FDI-intensive sectors have average tariffs on imports that are 66 percent higher than in manufacturing as whole. In Hungary, strong protection for foreign investors is mainly provided by nontariff barriers.

Thus, as the transition shock fades, one can expect that the strength of national interest groups will increase, especially as these countries provide favorable conditions for rent seeking. As Audretsch (1995) shows, there is still a strong concentration of economic activity with a small number of very large firms.[27] The same applies to the banking industry (Dittus 1994). The lobby power of the large firms is additionally enhanced by their high regional concentration (Pincus 1975). And, as employment in the state administration has hardly been reduced since 1990, there are many sympathetic civil servants in ministries looking for problems they can address (Csaba 1995, 70).

Compared with industry lobbies, which will become stronger over time, interest groups of consumers and taxpayers will remain in a relatively weak position. In most CEECs the general population is still not well informed about the new economic and political processes. There is no tradition of consumer and public-oriented groups with the financial resources and experience that are required to counteract the political pressure of industry lobbies (Audretsch 1995).

5.2. General Attitudes toward EU Membership

If one addresses the issue of EU membership at a more general level, one can find a positive attitude of the population in all CEECs. Opinion polls for the Czech Republic, Poland, and Romania show that a large majority of the population favors EU membership (table 10.14). Support is weakest in the Czech Republic, where the share of supporters has declined from 86 percent in 1992 to only 66 percent in 1993 (Handl et al. 1994). The overall assessment of the EU's targets and activities is on balance still somewhat positive, but the trend is declining and the positive opinion is shared by only little more than one-third of the population. Obviously, there must be many people in the CEECs who favor EU membership, although their assessment of the EU itself is not positive. Finally, few CEEC citizens expect rapid accession of their countries; the ratio is 37 percent for the Czech Republic and 26 percent for Poland. Although data are not available for all CEECs, an important finding is how much the commitment of the CEECs to the EU has weakened in only a few years.

This general trend, which confirms anecdotal evidence of a growing nationalism, indicates that if the decision on EU membership is delayed it might become increasingly difficult to find the necessary political support in the CEECs.

TABLE 10.13. FDI and Import Protection in Hungary and Poland

Products	Hungary[a]					Poland[b]			
	Average Tariff (%)[c]	Range of Tariffs (%) Min	Max	Nontariff Barriers[d]	FDI-Intensive Sectors	Average Tariff (%)[c]	Range of Tariffs (%) Min	Max	FDI-Intensive Sectors
1. Raw hides and skins	9.1	3	14	9		24.5	15	35	
2. Rubber	9.2	2	20	12		14.3	5	15	
3. Wood and cork	8.4	0	15	18		13.3	5	15	
4. Pulp and paper	7.6	0	40	12	yes	13.4	0	35	yes
5. Textiles and clothing	11.7	0	20	17		20.6	5	30	yes
6. Glass and chemicals	7.4	0	25	19	yes	13.0	3	40	yes
7. Precious stones	6.5	0	13	12		15.3	5	45	
8. Ores and metals[e]	7.7	0	50	5		14.1	5	35	yes
9. Coal and petroleum	6.3	0	30	30	yes	11.2	0	20	
10. Chemicals	9.9	0	40	7		14.3	5	45	
11. Nonelectrical machinery	18.7	0	50	28	yes	15.2	0	20	
12. Electrical machinery	26.2	0	50	13	yes	16.3	15	30	yes
13. Transport equipment	17.4	0	50	20	yes	20.1	0	35	yes
14. Scientific instruments	27.2	6	60	16		17.0	15	45	
15. Footwear and bags	10.1	9	12	7		22.4	15	35	
16. Photographic instruments	9.4	0	25	2		15.0	15	15	
17. Furniture	10.0	8	12	5		19.5	15	20	
18. Musical instruments	8.9	0	12	8		22.4	15	30	
19. Toys	11.2	0	13	3		20.2	20	35	
20. Works of art	0.0	0	0	4		0.0	0	0	
21. Firearms	8.5	0	13	5		34.4	15	35	
22. Office supplies	10.0	6	12	3		18.7	15	20	
23. Other manufactures	9.5	0	13	6		17.9	5	35	

24. Foodstuffs	28.1	0	80		29	27.4	10	45	yes
25. Grains	3.4	0	25		12	13.0	10	25	
26. Animals and produce	18.1	0	35		34	29.0	5	40	
27. Oil seeds	10.6	0	35		9	18.4	5	35	
28. Cut flowers	19.0	5	35						
29. Beverages	48.5	0	150	yes	17	45.8	20	145	yes
30. Dairy products	30.3	20	60	yes	28	35.1	10	40	
31. Fish	17.5	0	45		10	18.4	5	55	
32. Tobacco	58.3	10	90	yes	15	41.4	30	120	
33. Other animals	15.5	5	35						
34. Other vegetables	15.8	10	35						
All products[f]	16.0	0	150			18.4	0	145	
Computed figures[g]									
All sectors	15.0	2.1	35.8		13.4	19.8	9.1	37.6	
FDI-intensive sectors	24.9	3	62.5		21.1	21.3	7.3	49.4	

Source: EBRD 1994, 136.

[a] 1988 tariff schedule.
[b] 1992 tariff schedule.
[c] Simple average tariff rates.
[d] Numbers of nontariff barriers observed at two-digit level.
[e] Includes steel and aluminium.
[f] Simple average tariff rates for the whole economy.
[g] Simple averages based on rates by sector.

TABLE 10.14.   Results of Opinion Polls in the CEECs (percentages)

	Overall Assessment of the EU in the V4			
	Positive	Negative	Neutral	No Opinion
1990	49	26	2	23
1991	47	31	3	19
1992	44	33	5	18
1993	37	34	8	21

	Position on EU Membership (1993)		
	Czech Republic	Poland	Romania
Positive	66	70	88
Negative	12	7	10
Undecided	22	22	2

	Do You Expect That the EU Will Accept Your Country as a Member? (1993)	
	Czech Republic	Poland
Yes	37	26
No	44	26
Undecided	29	48

Source: Lamentowicz 1994; Gabanyi 1994; Handl et al. 1994.

5.3.   Specific Issues

This overall lack of enthusiasm concerning the EU will be considerably enhanced if people become aware of what they can really expect from the EU and
if the strengthened producer lobbies realize how much their environment will
be changed by European integration. In the following, the most important
economic issues are discussed using the classification developed in sections 3.2
and 3.3.

5.3.1.   Trade Liberalization
Since the EU enlargement in 1995, almost 60 percent of CEEC exports have
been sold to the EU. As already analyzed in section 4.1, trade liberalization is
the only area in which East-West integration is already relatively well
developed. Nevertheless, full EU membership would entail significant changes
for the producers in the CEECs:

Specific safeguard measures (Arts. 28 and 30 of the EAs) would no longer be available.

Antidumping and countervailing duties (Art. 29 of the EAs) would be excluded.

Single Market access would remove barriers created by spurious standards and norms. Application of the mutual recognition principle (resulting from the "Cassis de Dijon" ruling by the European Court of Justice in 1979) would require harmonization of minimum standards for health, safety, and the environment.

Simultaneous EU membership of several CEECs would automatically lead to full trade liberalization among the CEECs and avoid the "hub-and-spoke bilateralism" (Baldwin 1994) that is created by the bilateral character of the EAs.

It is not easy to assess the attitude of Eastern European producer lobbies toward trade liberalization with the EU. For *exporting industries* the abolition of safeguard and antidumping measures would constitute a major improvement. It removes the risk that the EU will impose trade restrictions as soon as Eastern enterprises become successful in Western markets.[28] Single Market access would additionally open EU markets, but there is also the risk that the EU could use minimum standards as a means of increasing the costs of CEEC producers. However, even if rapid enlargement were possible, longer transitional periods for Single Market access would be required in order to make regulations in the CEECs compatible with the EU laws concerning the Single Market. Thus, industries that export to the EU would certainly welcome further steps toward full trade integration.

Things would be different for industries that compete with imports not only from the EU but also from other CEECs. Already one can observe a strong inclination, especially in Hungary, to protect domestic producers against foreign competition. As Messerlin (1995, 51) reports, Hungary has since 1992 taken about 100 safeguard measures, which is more than twice the annual number of antidumping cases in the United States and the EU. So far, all these measures have been directed against imports from non-EU countries, mainly from other CEECs. But in Hungary there is also a strong demand for exceptional measures in accordance with Article 28 of the EA (Sapir 1995, 101). Thus, one can expect strong resistance against a complete and irreversible opening of domestic markets, especially if it includes trade liberalization vis-à-vis other CEECs.

So far, it has been assumed that export industries have different interests than import-competing industries. In reality, the dividing line is often unclear. As already mentioned, there is much uncertainty about the CEECs' comparative advantage in the longer term and about the prospective degree of intra-industry trade between the CEECs and the EU. It is not obvious which industries will become net exporters and which will become net importers from the EU. Such uncertainty could reduce the lobbies' resistance to free trade, since many industries might hope to be among the winners and it is not clear who will lose. But if risk-averse behavior prevails, the opposite could also be possible. As Rodrik (1993, 357) shows, uncertainty about the identity of gainers and losers from reform can block the adoption of efficiency-enhancing measures. With the predominance of defensive behavior among CEEC managers (Grosfeld and Roland 1995), the risk-averse strategy might be preferred over trade liberalization.

Thus, a move from the EAs to the Single Market might not be welcomed by all interest groups. Resistance could grow over time as industry lobbies become stronger and forms of contingent protection become more widespread.

5.3.2. Capital Market Liberalization

Citizens in the CEECs are generally concerned about a potential sell-off of their economies to investors from the West. Opinion polls in Poland show that only 28 percent of the population favors Polish EU membership if this will allow foreigners or Polish citizens living abroad to buy houses and real estate without restriction (Lamentowicz 1994). Especially in the Czech Republic, the population is afraid of Germans taking over industry. As a consequence, the EAs have done little to liberalize capital flows between the CEECs and the EU. Article 59 calls for current account convertibility, mainly to ensure free trade in goods and services, and is thus even more restrictive than the original Article 67 of the treaty, which calls for convertibility "to the extent necessary to ensure the functioning of the common market." A survey conducted by the OECD (1993, 7) summarizes the situation as follows:

> Although all countries have sectoral restrictions or barriers to FDI, more than one third (Bulgaria, the Czech and Slovak Republics, Hungary and Poland) have restricted foreign access in some areas, such as defence, public procurement, financial institutions, energy, aviation and shipping. Typically, the administrative procedures for registration and authorisation of FDI in these sectors are transparent, but in practice often remain cumbersome.

Under the conditions of the Single Market, the governments of the CEECs could no longer maintain restrictions on foreign investors acquiring domestic firms. Awareness of this specific implication of EU membership could raise public resistance considerably.

5.3.3.   Participation in the Distributional Mechanisms of the EU
(CAP and Structural Funds)

For the CEECs, participation in the EU's distributional schemes is certainly one of the main attractions of membership. It would boost the incomes of farmers and provide generous structural funds to "least-favoured regions, including rural areas" (Art. 130a of the treaty). In the political debate, the ability to obtain such funds would easily outweigh all other considerations.

However, as is explained in section 4.2.2, the prospects for such transfers from the EU to the CEECs are low. Thus, the CEECs will have to realize sooner or later that, no matter which form they choose for participation in the EU, it will not be possible to obtain the same treatment as other relatively poor countries have been offered in the past. This will considerably weaken political commitment to the EU. In addition, in the political debate on joining the EU the pro-European politicians cannot use the argument of huge transfers from the EU, which means that other obvious advantages have to be identified in order to overcome the resistance of anti-European interest groups.

5.3.4.   Participation in Other Fields of Policy Integration

As financial considerations will exclude the CEECs from the Common Agricultural Policy and policies strengthening economic and social cohesion, they will be excluded from the most important areas of the EU's policy integration. Of course, the CEECs could still share the many common policies that are envisaged in the treaty. But, because of the unclear allocation of powers (sec. 2), it is difficult to forecast whether the EU will develop strong common policies in such areas.

This even applies to European monetary union, for which the treaty includes very precise and detailed regulations (Arts. 105–109m). Especially in Germany, one can presently observe strong opposition to the mere idea of a European Central Bank. Together with the very restrictive set of criteria of convergence, the chances of the realization of EMU remain unclear.[29]

Thus, there are at the moment no other fields of policy integration that could make EU membership especially attractive for the CEECs. On the contrary, EU attempts to formulate common policies in the field of environmental and social policy (minimum requirements for labor law and working condi-

312 Forging an Integrated Europe

tions, social security, prevention of occupational accidents and diseases, the rights of association, and collective bargaining between employers and workers) could increase production costs for CEEC firms and thus impair their competitiveness in EU markets.

5.3.5. Aspects of Political Economy

The arguments presented in section 3.3 can be summarized with the following quote from Olson (1987, 250):

> So the theory leads to the prediction that the extent of damage done by organizations for collective action will be much smaller than usual after there has been a big freeing of trade, whether through national unification, a common market or unilateral action.

On economic grounds, there is no doubt that the CEEC economies would benefit from the restrictions that the treaty imposes on the discretion of national politicians. The installation of a credible policy framework according to the model of "*Ordnungspolitik*" could help to increase the amount of *foreign direct investment.* In the whole period from 1990 to 1993, cumulative FDI flows to all former socialist countries amounted to only US$ 12 billion.[30] The orders of magnitude become clear if one compares this area with other developing countries. EBRD (1994, 122) reports that "in 1992 China and Mexico each reported FDI inflows that were substantially higher than those recorded for eastern Europe and the former Soviet Union as a whole, and Argentina and Malaysia received comparable amounts." As the experience of Portugal and Spain shows, FDI from EU member states can increase substantially with EU membership (Gual and Martin 1995, 184; Cado and de Melo 1995, 139). This is also confirmed by surveys that conclude that the stability of the economic and political framework is the most decisive factor in FDI decisions (EBRD 1994, 130–31; OECD 1993).

In spite of its obvious economic merits, it is far from clear whether an externally imposed economic constitution would be accepted by a majority of the voters in the CEECs. Above all, the idea that a country can profit from giving up sovereignty in main areas of economic policy would be difficult to reconcile with growing nationalist feelings in many CEECs.

5.4. Prospects for EU Membership

Under present conditions, there is no doubt that all CEECs would favor immediate EU membership on economic as well as political grounds. But, if the decision is delayed, the outcome is much less certain. If people in the CEECs realize that transfers from the EU will be very modest, it is difficult to find convincing reasons for membership. The economic merits of a stable and open economic constitution that the treaty provides at the national level are difficult to understand outside the circle of economists. With relatively unclear benefits, the producer lobbies could use their growing strength for lobbying efforts against the EU. From their perspective, the "hands-tying" of national governments implied by EU membership could considerably threaten the long-standing relationship between industry and government that has managed to survive the transformation process. Thus, the longer accession negotiations are delayed, the less likely is acceptance of EU membership by the CEECs.

6. Policy Implications

Given the economic and political constraints, it seems obvious that there are major political risks for the process of eastern enlargement. On the basis of the analysis presented in this chapter, one comes to the conclusion that any sensible strategy for enlargement must entail the following "essentials":

> It should not substantially increase expenditures for the CAP or the structural funds. Thus, if the CEECs will receive any net transfers from the EU at all, this will require a reduction of transfers to the present recipients of EU money.
> It should create in the CEECs as soon as possible a stable and predictable economic policy framework that guarantees open markets, little government interference in the market process, and macroeconomic stability. As all this is achieved by the Treaty regulations mentioned in section 3.2, there should at least be a concrete schedule for the accession of the CEECs. This would also favor FDI in the CEECs.
> It should not proceed on a case by case basis. Each additional poor incumbent will increase the "lobby of the poor" which opposes the accession of other low-income countries. Already the poor member states account for about one-fifth of the EU's population, and they are very close to having a blocking minority in the Council of Ministers.

The following list enumerates the proposals that have been offered to date.

> A "wait and see" approach, which the EU countries seem to favor at the moment

The AAA proposal of Baldwin (1994)

EFTA and EEA membership

Early membership but long transition periods for participation in distribution schemes, a solution proposed in an article by CDU/CSU (1994)

A "comprehensive accession strategy" (CAS)

6.1. The "Wait and See" Approach

If one takes into account the constraint imposed by the EU budget and the problems associated with internal EU reforms, it seems likely that the EU will not actively pursue eastern enlargement for the time being. By delaying CEEC membership, it can hope to reduce the costs for the CAP and the Structural Funds. In the meantime, there is also a chance that the incumbents will find ways to reform the CAP, which would make participation of the CEECs less costly. A very slow eastern enlargement would be facilitated by the traditional procedure of negotiating accessions case by case. This is more time consuming and could retard a comprehensive enlargement, as the number of the poor insiders will grow over time.

For the CEECs, this approach would be dangerous in many respects that have been addressed in section 4.4. In the end, the "wait and see" approach might lead to a situation in which the dominant political forces in the CEECs are no longer interested in EU membership. Such an outcome would have very negative political and economic consequences not only for the East. It could also impair the EU, especially if the economic instability in the CEECs leads to strong migration to the West.

6.2. Baldwin's AAA Proposal

As neither immediate membership nor a wait and see approach is acceptable, it is obvious that some intermediate solution must be found.

A very detailed proposal is provided by Baldwin (1994, 207), who aims to redress "the current hub-and-spoke bilateralism by embedding the existing Europe Agreements into something that would be called an Association of Association Agreements (AAA)." The CEECs would be obliged to grant the liberalization of imports agreed upon with the EU to all other CEECs participating in the AAA. An AAA authority would play a surveillance and enforcement role.

Judged according to the "essentials" laid down at the beginning of this section, the AAA proposal is weak. If one takes into account the fact that the

EAs allow much discretion for safeguard measures of all kinds (sec. 4.1.1), they can contribute little to constraining the power of domestic lobbies. Especially in light of the many antidumping measures that are presently growing in intra-CEEC trade relations (sec. 5.3.1), it seems unlikely that the AAA could provide unrestricted trade relations between the "spokes." Thus, it is difficult to believe that the AAA solution would lead to a "heightened credibility, consistency and predictability of trade policy throughout the AAA region" (Baldwin 1994, xxi).

In terms of economic substance, the Baldwin proposal does not differ very much from the "wait and see" approach. From the perspective of the CEECs, the AAA model is especially unattractive for two reasons. First it would establish an identical status for all members of the CEEC–6, which would reduce the chances for single countries (e.g., the Czech Republic) to enter the EU before the door closes forever. Second, it could be used by the EU as evidence of further progress in the integration process with the East and thus support the EU's general strategy of delaying real enlargement.

6.3. EFTA Membership

Compared with the EAs, EFTA membership of the CEECs would entail:

> Abolition of the asymmetric exceptional measures granted to the CEECs (Art. 28a of the EA)
> Removal of the very broad safeguard actions provided by Article 30 of the EA
> Multilateralization of trade liberalization among all CEECs participating in EFTA

Thus, EFTA membership would restrict the discretion of national policy-makers considerably and would also remove the "hub and spoke bilateralism" of the EAs. It would have the additional advantage of requiring no new institutions or new negotiations with the EU. Since the EU membership of Austria, Finland, and Sweden, EFTA has become almost an empty shell, with only three members: Iceland, Norway, and Switzerland. Thus, this existing arrangement could be used as a sensible intermediate solution for the CEECs.

However, EFTA membership would still allow national governments to supply protectionist measures: antidumping actions would be still possible. There are no limitations on subsidies, and the restrictions on fiscal policy in the Maastricht Treaty would not apply. Finally, the CEECs would lack a definitive schedule for accession.

As the EU could still apply restrictive trade policies against the CEECs, this approach would also be suboptimal in terms of attracting FDI. The experience of Portugal and Spain shows that only full EU membership can overcome the obstacles to foreign investment.

From the perspective of the CEECs, adopting such an institutional solution also bears the risk that it could be regarded by the EU as a substitute for more comprehensive integration.

If the CEECs adopt EFTA membership, this approach could entail membership in the European Economic Area (EEA) as a next step. Under this arrangement, the main regulations of the Single Market would be applied to all trade with the CEECs. Baldwin (1994) proposes a similar procedure on the basis of his AAA model. But again he favors a completely new institution, the "Organisation for European Integration." Given the CEECs' biases against a "poor men's club" it is not obvious why such a new framework should be created instead of using the existing EEA arrangements.

6.4. Second-Class Membership and "Variable Geometry"

To avoid the budgetary consequences of the CAP and the structural funds, one might think of admitting the CEECs to EU relatively soon but excluding them from such programs, at least for a transitional period.[31] Here the accession of Spain and Portugal could serve as a precedent, since market access to the EU remained (and for some agricultural products will remain until 1996) restricted after full membership. However, as Baldwin (1994, 201) states, this was compensated for by "better than first-class treatment" in terms of the Structural Funds.

The problem with this approach is that it would grant the CEECs voting power on all issues, even on those from which they are temporarily excluded (Koop 1995). This would prevent the reforms that will be required to reduce the budgetary burden of such policies, as the CEECs would be tempted to maintain such distribution schemes as long as possible. They might also sell their votes on CAP reform in exchange for new funds supporting their economies (Baldwin 1994, 202).

It is obvious that this procedure is flawed, as it violates the fundamental principle that there should be a correspondence between competences in decision making and liability.

In this context it is also important to clarify the concept of "*variable geometry*" (VG). The main idea of VG is presented in this volume by von Hagen and Fratianni, as follows:

At the heart of VG lies the distinction between a core and a periphery of the EU. The core includes what all members have in common in European integration. The periphery contains those policies that are shared by some but not by all members of the EU. Thus, the principle of VG is that it does not require all members to participate in all areas of integration.

From this quote it becomes obvious that VG can not be applied to eastern enlargement. As this chapter shows, the main question for the CEECs is whether they will be allowed to participate in the core, while the policies of the periphery are not of immediate relevance for these countries. Thus, VG should not be confounded with the concept of restricted membership.[32]

6.5. A "Comprehensive Accession Strategy"

In order to meet all the requirements mentioned in section 6.1 simultaneously, this chapter proposes a comprehensive accession strategy (CAS). The CAS approach should be incorporated in the treaty as a general procedure that is open to any Eastern European country or a large list of CEECs that are enumerated explicitly. For each country, the CAS would prescribe a transition period of 10 years. It would be composed of two five-year stages:

> In *stage 1*, the EAs would be applied. In order to multilaterize the EAs, the CAS would prescribe the application of EA regulations in relation to all other CEECs participating in the CAS.
> In *stage 2*, trade liberalization would be enhanced by removing all safeguard clauses and antidumping measures on both sides. Thus, the EU would treat associate members in its trade policy like full members—with the exception of the Single Market regulations, which would be applied only after full accession. In addition, the CEECs would participate in the economic policy surveillance (Arts. 102–4c) laid down in the Maastricht Treaty and would accept all other rules enumerated in section 3.3.

If a CEEC is able to meet all obligations of stage 2 for five years, it would be automatically entitled to become a full member. To avoid the problems raised in the preceding section, during the CAS period the CEECs would have:

No voting power in the Council
No access to the CAP and the Structural Funds

Compared with other solutions, this approach has the advantage that it offers clear and not too distant prospects for accession[33] with a framework for economic policy that limits the power of domestic lobbies in the CEECs. Because a predictable accession path would attract much FDI, it would also lay the groundwork for growth in the CEECs. Thus, the budgetary costs at the date of full membership would be reduced.

A definitive schedule for CEEC membership would also help to set in motion far-reaching structural reforms on the side of the incumbents. As soon as the CAS is installed, it will create a momentum of reform similar to the 1992 deadline established with the Single European Act for the Single Market.

6.5. The Outlook

So far, it has been difficult to predict which of the different options will be implemented. In a recent article, Kornai (1995) suggested an approach along the lines of the CAS proposal. He argued that an intermediate stage between the association stage and full membership would help to maintain the political momentum in the CEECs in favor of the EU.

In the conclusions of the Madrid Summit adopted on December 15–16, 1995, the EU declared that it intends to start accession negotiations with the CEECs (CEEC–6 plus the Baltics and Slovenia) jointly with the accession negotiations of Cyprus and Malta. For the former, it has decided that they should begin six months after the end of the Maastricht II Inter-Governmental Conference. The conclusions of the Madrid Summit also mention that equal treatment of all CEECs that apply for membership should be sought. However, even if negotiations are opened simultaneously for a group of 10 CEECs, this will neither guarantee a clear schedule for definite membership nor avoid the problem that a few CEECs will become members ahead of the rest and a more comprehensive enlargement will be blocked.

ABBREVIATIONS

AAA	Association of Association Agreements
CAP	Common Agricultural Policy
CAS	Comprehensive Accession Strategy
CEEC	Central and Eastern European countries
CEPR	Centre of Economic Policy Research
CIS	Commonwealth of Independent States

CMEA   Council of Mutual Economic Assistance
EA   Europe Agreement
EBRD   European Bank for Reconstruction and Development
EC   European Commission
ECB   European Central Bank
ECU   European Currency Unit
EEA   European Economic Area
EFTA   European Free Trade Association
EMU   European monetary union
EU   European Union
FDI   foreign direct investment
GATT   General Agreement on Tariffs and Trade
GDP   gross domestic product
IA   Interim Agreements
IGC   Inter-Governmental Conference
MFA   Multi Fibre Agreement
OECD   Organisation of Economic Co-operation and Development
OPT   outward processing trade
QUR   quota utilization rates
RCA   revealed comparative advantage
VG   variable geometry
V4   Visegrad 4 (Czech Republic, Hungary, Poland, Slovakia)

NOTES

I thank Barry Eichengreen, Jeff Frieden, and Ronald McKinnon for helpful comments and Kathrin Berensmann for valuable research assistance.

1. In this chapter the following acronyms will be used: CEEC for all countries in Central and Eastern Europe; V4 for the four "Visegrad" countries (the Czech Republic, Hungary, Poland, and Slovakia); and CEEC–6 for the V4 plus Romania and Bulgaria.

2. A preaccession strategy was set out in the Essen conclusions (December 1994). However, it only added to the Europe Agreements the relatively noncommittal element of the "structured relationship" between the associated countries and the institutions of the European Union. In May 1995, a white paper was prepared by the Commission. It intends to provide "a guide to assist the associated countries in preparing themselves for operating under the requirements of the European Union's internal market" (European Commission 1995).

3. For surveys on the political economy of trade policy, see Baldwin 1989 and Rodrik 1994.

4. Article O of the treaty states that every European country may apply for EU membership.

5. However, as section 4 shows, it seems very unlikely that the CAP in its present form will ever be extended to the CEECs.

6. This important effect of an internationally open economic order is mentioned by Eucken (1952).

7. It amounts to only 1.2 percent of EU GDP compared with a ratio of 48 percent for the EU average of national budgets (Courchene et al. 1993, 3)

8. Olson (1987, 250) mentions that growth was very strong after the creation of the EC, the German Zollverein, the Meji Restoration, and the Dutch rebellion against the Spanish and after national unification in England and the United States.

9. This may not apply to all fields of policy integration. For instance, in the case of a common monetary policy, one could argue that with larger size the risk of asymmetric shocks increases and thus threatens the stability of the system (Bayoumi and Eichengreen 1993). For a discussion of the theory of "optimum currency areas," see Bofinger 1994.

10. As the Europe Agreements required time-consuming ratification by all EU parliaments and the parliament of the respective CEEC, so-called Interim Agreements (IAs) were concluded as an intermediate solution (in December 1991 with Poland, Hungary, and Czechoslovakia; in February 1993 with Romania; and in March 1993 with Bulgaria). Because of the Community's responsibility in foreign trade matters, it was possible to put into force the regulations concerning trade liberalization immediately.

11. For a comprehensive survey, see European Commission 1994.

12. In the case of Bulgaria, the transition period was four years.

13. However, as European Commission 1994 shows, the IA reduced the average tariff for imports from the CEECs by about 50 percent compared with the GDP rate.

14. For a detailed analysis, see Sapir 1995.

15. The additional tariffs may not exceed 25 percent ad valorem, nor can they cover more than 15 percent of the total imports of industrial products from the EU. They may not be applied for a period exceeding five years and cannot be levied on products that have been imported without restriction for more than three years.

16. EU firms send both the design and the fabrics ("textiles") to a CEEC, only to reimport the same "identifiable" products for final consumption (mainly clothing). Corado (1995, 247) reports that in 1992 OPT imports of clothing were 62 percent of EC imports of MFA clothing from the CEECs.

17. Thus, sending capital (import-led growth) and receiving goods (export-led growth) are not alternatives, as the article by Holzmann et al. (1994) suggests, but two sides of the same coin.

18. A striking example of how the adjustment process can be impaired by excessive wages is East Germany (Sinn 1994).

19. Of course, this positive effect is felt by the owners of capital only, while the owners of labor will be negatively affected. This shows that the identity of interests of

capital owners and workers in specific industries that the standard theory of political economy assumes (Frey 1985) is not applicable in the case of OPT.

20. See CDU/CSU 1994.

21. For detailed analysis of voting effects, see Baldwin 1994.

22. See the contribution of Lisa Martin in this volume.

23. This figure was decided upon the Edinburgh Summit on December 12, 1992, as a part of a medium-term financial assessment of the Community.

24. Olson explains the growth effects of such processes with the fact that for lobbies "it takes quite some time to overcome the difficulties of collective action, especially when the groups at issue are large ones" (1987, 251).

25. This can be explained by the fact that economic transition in the CEECs is a more complicated issue than those found in the historical examples mentioned by Olson (1987). The main difficulty in the East is the lack of private property rights and enterprise capital. In Olson's examples, these had existed from the beginning.

26. Rodrik (1994, 40) presents several examples of developing countries accomplishing "a dramatic turn-around by abandoning their protectionist trade regimes in favor of more open trade policies (Bolivia and Mexico since 1985, Argentina since 1987, Brazil since 1988, Peru since 1990)."

27. In Poland the mean number of employees per plant is 378. In the EU, the mean plant size is well under 100 employees per establishment (Audretsch 1995, 168).

28. As Stehn (1994, 206) notes, the EU's antidumping measures against CEECs are especially discriminating. They still treat the CEECs as "nonmarket economies," which means that domestic production costs cannot be applied as a criterion for defining dumping. Instead, prices of producers in comparable market economies will be used. This prevents the CEECs from profiting from their very low labor costs.

29. The importance of the convergence criteria was enhanced by a decision of the German Constitutional Court in 1993, which calls for a very strict interpretation of the criteria as a precondition for German membership.

30. This figure can also be compared with estimates of the annual investment required in the CEECs and the CIS to achieve an annual growth rate of 7 percent over 10 years; they range between U.S.$150 and U.S.$915 billion, depending on the methodology and the estimate of the region's GDP used in the calculation (EBRD 1994, 54).

31. A proposal along these lines was made in CDU/CDU 1994.

32. See Koop 1995, 26.

33. Koop (1995, 6) regards membership in 2005 as a "quick entry option."

REFERENCES

Anderson, K., and R. Tyers. 1993. Implications of EC expansion for European agricultural policies, trade and welfare, Discussion Papers no. 829. London, CEPR.

Andersen, P., and P. Dittus. 1994. Trade and employment: Can we afford better market access for Eastern Europe?, Working Papers, no. 17. Oesterreichische Nationalbank.

Audretsch, D. B. 1995. Industrial and trade policies for the emerging market economies. In CEPR, *Foundations of an open economy: Trade laws and institutions for Eastern Europe,* 155–77. London: CEPR.

Baldwin, R. E. 1989. The political economy of trade policy. *Journal of Economic Perspectives* 3 (Fall): 119–35.

———. 1994. *Towards an integrated Europe.* London: CEPR.

Bayoumi, T., and B. Eichengreen. 1992. Shocking aspects of European monetary integration. Discussion Papers no. 643. London: CEPR.

Bofinger, P. 1994. Is Europe an optimum currency area? In *Thirty years of European monetary integration: From the Werner Plan to EMU,* edited by A. Steinherr, 38–56. London and New York: Longman.

Cadot, O., and J. de Melo. 1995. France and the CEECs: Adjusting to another enlargement. In *European Union trade with Eastern Europe: Adjustment and opportunities,* edited by R. Faini and R. Portes, 86–122. London: CEPR.

CDU/CSU. 1994. Überlegungen zur europäischen Politik. Fraction of the CDU/CSU, Deutsche Bundestag. Mimeo.

CEPR. 1992. Is bigger better? The economics of EC enlargement. *Monitoring European Integration 3:* A CEPR Annual Report. London: CEPR.

———. 1993. Making sense of subsidiarity: How much centralization for Europe? *Monitoring European Integration 4:* A CEPR Annual Report. London: CEPR.

———. 1995. *Foundations of an open economy. Trade laws and institutions for Eastern Europe.* London: CEPR.

Corado, C. 1995. The textiles and clothing trade with Central and Eastern Europe: Impact on members of the EC. In *European Union trade with Eastern Europe: Adjustment and opportunities,* edited by R. Faini and R. Portes, 236–68. London: CEPR.

Courchene, T., et al. 1993. Stable money—sound finances. *European Economy,* no. 53.

Csaba, L. 1995. The political economy of trade regimes in Central Europe. In CEPR, *Foundations of an open economy: Trade laws and institutions for Eastern Europe,* 64–88. London: CEPR.

Deutsche Bundesbank. 1993. Die Finanzbeziehungen der Bundesrepublik Deutschland zu den Europäischen Gemeinschaften seit dem Jahr 1988. *Monthly Report* (November 1993), 61–78.

———. 1996. Balance of payments and statistics. *Statistical Supplement to the Monthly Report,* June.

Dimelis, S., and K. Gatsios. 1995. Trade with Central and Eastern Europe: The case of Greece. In *European Union trade with Eastern Europe: Adjustment and opportunities,* edited by R. Faini and R. Portes, 123–66. London: CEPR.

Dittus, P. 1994. Corporate governance in Central Europe: The role of banks. BIS Economic Papers, no. 42. Basle. Typescript.

Drabek, Z., and A. Smith. 1995. Trade performance and trade policy in Central and Eastern Europe. CEPR Discussion Papers, no. 1182. London: CEPR.

EBRD [European Bank for Reconstruction and Development]. 1994. *Transition report,* London.

Eucken, W. 1952. *Grundsätze der Wirtschaftspolitik.* Tübingen: Mohr (Siebeck).

European Commission. 1994. Trade liberalization with Central and Eastern Europe. *European Economy Supplement* A, no. 7.

———. 1995. White paper prepared by the associated countries of Central and Eastern Europe for integration into the Internal Market of the Union. Mimeo.

European Union. 1995. *Official gazette of the European Union, Communication and announcements of the European court of auditors,* vol. 38.

Eurostat. 1996. *External trade, Statistical yearbook retrospective.* Luxembourg.

Faini, R., and R. Portes. 1995. Opportunities outweigh adjustment: The political economy of trade with Central and Eastern Europe. In *European Union trade with Eastern Europe: Adjustment and opportunities,* edited by R. Faini and R. Portes, 1–18. London: CEPR.

Frey, B. S. 1985. *Internationale politische Ökonomie.* Munich: Vahlen.

Gabanyi, A. U. 1994. Länderbericht Rumänien. In *Mittel- und Osteuropa auf dem Weg in die Europäische Union,* edited by Bertelsmann Stiftung, 81–97. Gütersloh: Bertelsmann.

Gács, J. 1995. The effects of the demise of the CMEA and the USSR on output in Hungary. In *Output decline in Eastern Europe: Unavoidable, external influence, or homemade?* edited by R. Holzmann, J. Gács, and G. Winckler, 161–84. London: Kluwer Academic.

Grosfeld, I., and R. Gérard. 1995. Defensive and strategic restructuring in Central European enterprises. CEPR Discussion Papers, no. 1135. London: CEPR.

Grossman, Gene M., and Elhanan Helpman. 1992. Protection for sale. Princeton University. Typescript.

———. 1993. The politics of free trade agreements. NBER Working Papers, no. 4,597. Cambridge, Mass. Typescript.

Gual, J., and C. Martin. 1995. Trade and foreign direct investment with Central and Eastern Europe: Its impact on Spain. In *European Union trade with Eastern Europe: Adjustment and opportunities,* edited by R. Faini and R. Portes, 167–200. London: CEPR.

Halpern, L. 1995. Comparative advantage and likely trade pattern of the CEECs. In *European Union trade with Eastern Europe: Adjustment and opportunities,* edited by R. Faini and R. Portes, 61–85. London: CEPR.

Hamilton, C. B., and L. A. Winters. 1992. Opening up international trade with Eastern Europe. *Economic Policy,* no. 14: 77–104.

Handl, V., et al. 1994. Länderbericht Tschechische Republik. In *Mittel- und Osteuropa auf dem Weg in die Europäische Union,* edited by Bertelsmann Stiftung, 117–138. Gütersloh: Bertelsmann.

Holzmann, R., et al. 1994. Pressure to adjust: Consequences for the OECD countries from reforms in Eastern Europe. *Empirica,* 21:141–96.

Kornai, J. 1995. Der Beitritt in die Europäische Union: Implikationen für Mittel- und Osteuropa. Paper prepared for the conference, Vertiefung und Osterweiterung der Europäischen Union: Konflikt oder Kongruenz? November 14, Deutsches Institut für Wirtschaftsforschung, Berlin.

Koop, M. 1995. Joining the club: Options for the integration of Central and Eastern European countries into the European Union. Paper prepared for the conference, Europe's Economy Looks East: Implications for the EU and Germany, May 15–16, American Institute for Contemporary German Studies, Johns Hopkins University, Washington, D.C.

Lamentowicz, W. 1994. Länderbericht Polen. In Mittel- und Osteuropa auf dem Weg in die Europäische Union, edited by Bertelsmann Stiftung, 55–70.

Messerlin, P. A. 1995. Central and East European countries' trade laws in the light of international experience. In CEPR, Foundations of an open economy; Trade laws and institutions for Eastern Europe, 40–63. London: CEPR.

Neven, D. 1995. Trade liberalization with Eastern nations: How sensitive? In European Union trade with Eastern Europe: Adjustment and opportunities, edited by R. Faini and R. Portes, 19–60. London: CEPR.

Olson, M. 1965. The logic of collective action. Cambridge: Harvard University Press.

————. 1987. Economic nationalism and economic progress. World Economy, 10:241–64.

OECD. 1993. Foreign direct investment in selected Central and Eastern European countries and new independent states. OECD Working Papers, no. 11. Typescript.

Pincus, J. J. 1975. Pressure groups and the pattern of tariffs. Journal of Political Economy 83:757–78.

Rodrik, D. 1993. The positive economics of policy reform. American Economic Review 83, no. 2: 356–61.

————. 1994. What does the political economy literature on trade policy (not) tell us that we ought to know? NBER Working Papers, no. 4,870. Cambridge, Mass. Typescript.

Sachs, J. D., and H. J. Shatz. 1994. Trade and jobs in U.S. manufacturing. Brookings Papers on Economic Activity 1:1–84.

Sapir, A. 1995. The Europe Agreements: Implications for trade laws and institutions. In CEPR, Foundations of an open economy: Trade laws and institutions for Eastern Europe, 89–107. London: CEPR.

Sinn, H.-W. 1994. Schlingerkurs. CES Working Papers, no. 67. Munich. Typescript.

Stehn, J. 1994. Stufen einer Osterweiterung der Europäischen Union. Die Weltwirtschaft 2:194–219.

Tangermann, S., and T. E. Josling. 1994. Pre-accession agricultural policies for Central Europe and the European Union—final report. Bruxelles. Mimeo.

Weltbank. 1994. Weltentwicklungsbericht, Infrastruktur, und Entwicklung. Washington, D.C.: World Bank.

Winters, L. A. 1992. The Europe Agreements: With a little help from our friends. In *The association process, making it work: Central Europe and the European Community,* 17–28. CEPR Occasional Papers, no. 11. London: CEPR.

———. 1995. Liberalization of the European steel trade. In *European Union trade with Eastern Europe: Adjustment and opportunities,* edited by R. Faini and R. Portes, 201–35. London: CEPR.

Contributors

Sven W. Arndt
Claremont McKenna College

Peter Bofinger
University of Würzburg

Christian de Boissieu
University of Paris

Barry Eichengreen
University of California at Berkeley

Michele Fratianni
Indiana University

Jeffry Frieden
Harvard University

Geoffrey Garrett
Yale University

Anders Todal Jenssen
University of Trondheim

Kenneth M. Kletzer
University of California at Santa Cruz

Lisa L. Martin
Harvard University

Jonathon W. Moses
University of Trondheim

Jean Pisani-Ferry
CEPII

Michael Wallerstein
Northwestern University

Jürgen von Hagen
University of Bonn

Index

AAA. *See* Association of Association Agreements

abdication models, 145

accession to European Union. *See* Alpine case studies; comprehensive accession strategy (CAS); Nordic case studies

accountability

authority and, 8–9

of Council of Ministers, 132

democratic deficit and, 130, 152–53

in European Union institutions, 130–31, 136, 152–53

African countries, 10

agriculture, 256–57

à la carte form of variability, 170–72

Alpine case studies, 247–69

agriculture, 256–57

arguments, 250–51

Austria, 252, 257–63, 268–69

background, 247–48

competition, 251–54

factor market integration, 255–56

market segmentation, 251–54

options, 249–50

product variety, 254–55

Single Market program, predicting effects of, 248–49, 268

Switzerland, 263–69

trade diversion, 251

anticipated inflation tax, 95

aspirant members of European Union, 303–13

general attitude toward European Union membership, 305, 309

impact of transition on national interest groups, 303–5

prospects for European Union membership, 313

specific issues, 308–12

capital market liberalization, 310–11

distributional mechanisms, 311

policy integration, 311–12

political economy, 312

trade liberalization, 308–10

Association for the Monetary Union of Europe, 5

Association of Association Agreements (AAA), 314–15

Austria, 36–37

See also Alpine case studies

authority, accountability and, 8–9

Balladur, Eduard, 160

Banco Ambrosiano failure, 165

Bank for International Settlements (BIS), 79

banking regulation

beneficiaries of, 165

principles of, 162–69

competition, 162, 166

banking regulation (*continued*)
  European approach to, 166–69
  home-country rule, 169
  reasons for regulation, 162–66
  in variable geometry case study, 171–
    80
    application of, 177–79
    European Union enlargement, 179–
      80
    organization of periphery, 174–77
    placement in framework of variable
      geometry, 171–74
    reasons for studying, 161
banking sector, French, 80–83
bank panics, 162–65
bargaining, labor. *See* centralized
  bargaining
Barre, Raymond, 51, 53, 64
Belgium, 25, 39, 41–43
benefit-cost analysis of Economic and
  Monetary Union membership, 27,
  38–41
BIS. *See* Bank for International
  Settlements
bond rates, 59
Bretton-Woods system, 63, 65–66
Bundesbank, 24, 30, 42–43, 55, 60, 65,
  164

CAP. *See* Common Agricultural Policy
capital market liberalization, 310–11
CAS. *See* comprehensive accession
  strategy
CEECs. *See* Central and Eastern Euro-
  pean countries
Center for German and European Studies
  (University of California), 2
Central and Eastern European countries
  (CEECs)
  advantage of European Union mem-
    bership and, 286
  aspirant member's position

general attitude toward European
  Union membership, 305, 308
impact of transition on national interest groups, 304–5
prospects for European Union
  membership, 312–13
specific issues, 308–12
commitment to open European Union
  to, 273–74
comprehensive accession strategy for,
  275–76
European Economic Area membership
  and, 316
European Union enlargement and, 1, 14
imports, 287–89
incumbent member's position
  policy integration, 296–303
  trade integration, 287–96
interest groups and, 303–5
support of European Union membership by, 274
tariffs, 289–90
central bank independence (CBI), 29–30
centralized bargaining
  in Denmark, 186
  European economic integration and,
    199–202
  Katzenstein and, 190–91
  macroeconomic policy and, 202
  objective of, 13
  in Scandinavia, 193–94
  in Sweden, 185–86
  wage-setting institutions and, 185–86,
    199–202
Chirac administration, 51, 55–56, 64, 72,
  75
CNPF. *See* Conseil National du Patronat
  Français
codecision procedure, 140–44
collective action problem, 32, 285
Common Agricultural Policy (CAP), 66,
  75, 311

common currency
  benefits of, 68
  British participation in, 82
  budgetary consequences of, 94–96
  budget deficits and fiscal discipline un-
    der, 96–99
  debate over, 91–92
  seignorage revenues and, 94–96
company sector, French, 76–80
competition
  Alpine case studies, 251–54
  in banking regulation, 162, 166
  disinflation and, 59, 71
  unions and, 189–90
comprehensive accession strategy (CAS),
  275–76, 314, 317–18
concentric circles approach, 13, 161,
  174–77, 181
Conseil National du Crédit, 80
Conseil National du Patronat Français
  (CNPF), 76
convergence criteria, 21–22, 24, 40–41,
  43–44, 106, 216
cooperation procedure, 141–44
Copenhagen Summit (1993), 10, 273
corporatist argument, 187–88, 190, 194–
  99, 202
Council of Ministers
  accountability of, 132
  concerns about, 133–34
  convergence criteria and, 43–44
  democratic deficit and, 136–39
  national government influence and,
    5
  publicizing of proceedings of, 133
credibility approach, 29

defaults, 98–99, 117
de Gaulle government, 75
delegation models, 145–46
Delors, Jacques, 53, 67, 132–33, 257
Delors rule, 53

democratic deficit, 131–35
  accountability and, 130, 152–53
  analysis of, 129–30
  Council of Ministers and, 136–39
  European Union Commission and,
    136–39
  overview, 131–35
  representation issues and, 130, 152–53
  source of, 137
Denmark, 9, 39, 42, 146–48, 186
  See also Nordic case studies
dependence. *See* economic dependence of
  Nordic economy; trade,
  dependence
deposit insurance, 162, 164–69, 171, 173,
  178
d'Estaing presidency, 73–74
Deutscher Gewerkschaftsbund (DGB),
  192
devaluation, 67–68
DGB. *See* Deutscher Gewerkschaftsbund
Directive on Deposit Guarantee Schemes
  (1994), 167
disinflation
  Barre and, 51
  competition and, 59, 71
  Delors and, 53
  fiscal policy and, 58
  fixed exchange rates and, 57–58
  impact of, 74–75
  macroeconomic policy and, 49
  stability of exchange rates and, 65
  success of, in France, 57–59
distributional mechanisms, 281, 311
domestic interests, 2–3, 5–6

EAs. *See* European Agreements
eastern enlargement of European Union,
  273–318
  aspirant member's position, 303–13
    general attitude toward European
      Union membership, 305, 308

eastern enlargement of European Union
(*continued*)
  impact of transition on national in-
    terest groups, 303–5
  prospects for European Union
    membership, 312
  specific issues, 308–12
  background of, 273–76
  comprehensive accession strategy and,
    317–18
  difficulties in analyzing in political
    economy theory, 276–80
  economic integration from political
    economy perspective, 280–87
    bargaining process between the
      community and membership as-
      pirants, 286
    market integration versus political
      integration, 280–81
    obvious implications of European
      Union membership, 281
    political economy implications of
      European Union membership,
      282–86
  framework for assessing, 314–18
    Baldwin's AAA proposal, 314–15
    European Free Trade Area member-
      ship, 315–16
    second-class membership, 316–17
    variable geometry and, 316–17
    "wait and see" approach, 314
  incumbent member's position, 287–
    303
    policy integration, 296–303
    trade integration, 287–96
  variable geometry in, 316
EC. *See* European Community
ECOFIN. *See* Economy and Finance
Economic and Monetary Union (EMU)
  backdrop for discussions of, 1
  budgetary implications for members,
    93

  as coronation, 68–69, 83
  countries in, groups of, 177–80
  domestic impact of, 11
  European Union Commission and,
    25
  fiscal insurance and federalism and,
    91–121
    case of, 115–20
    monetary independence versus,
      105–15
    need for, 92
    with nominal rigidities, 99–105,
      113–14
    overview, 120–21
    political unions and, 115–20
    without nominal rigidities, 93–99,
      113–14
  fiscal policy and, 91–93, 120
  fragility of, 1
  French economic policy and, 49–84
    interest groups, 69–83
    interventionist powers and, 57
    logic behind, 63–69
    after Maastricht Treaty, 49–51
    monetary policy, 69–83
    since 1970s, 51–63
    overview, 83–84
  labor institutions and, 11
  membership, 10, 27, 38–41, 44, 93
  transition to, 21–44
    benefit-cost analysis of membership
      and, 27, 38–41
    convergence criteria, 21–22, 40–41,
      43–44
    costs of, 27–31, 36
    intra-European Union trade and,
      25–26
    labor market institutions and, 11,
      23, 31–38
    optimum currency area and, 26–
      28
    politicalization of, 41–44

price stability, 23–24
economic dependence of Nordic
    economy
    country level, 222–27, 240
        aggregate data, 224–26
        integration, 222–24
        national data, 226–27
    individual level, 228–40
        economic interests and consider-
            ations, 232–36
        issue salience, 236–40
        perceptions of personal and national
            economy, 228–32
    national level, 215–22, 240
        foreign direct investment, 216–19
        general economic well-being, 215–
            17
        trade exposure, 216, 220–22
economic integration. *See* European eco-
    nomic integration
economic openness, 189–94
Economy and Finance (ECOFIN), 68–69
EEA. *See* European Economic Agree-
    ment; European Economic Area
efficiency gains, 138–39
EFTA. *See* European Free Trade Area
electoral institutions, 3
EMS crisis (1992–93), 9
EMU. *See* Economic and Monetary
    Union
enlargement. *See* European Union (EU)
    enlargement
EP. *See* European Parliament
Ericcson Ltd., 217
ERM. *See* Exchange Rate Mechanism
ESCB. *See* European System of Central
    Banks
Essen Summit (1994), 159
EU. *See* European Union
Europe 1992. *See* Single Market program
Europe Agreements (EAs), 159, 273,
    287–91

European Central Bank, 11, 68, 91, 93,
    96–97, 311
European Coal and Steel Community,
    76–77
European Community (EC), 30, 53
European Council of Madrid, 82
European Court of Justice, 5–6
European Economic Agreement (EEA),
    214
European Economic Area (EEA)
    Austria in, 252, 257–63, 268–69
    Central and Eastern European Coun-
        tries membership and, 316
    as compromise, 250
    Switzerland in, 263–69
European economic integration
    agenda items, 1
    centralized bargaining and, 199–202
    conflicting forces facing, 159
    dynamics of, 5–10
        authority and accountability, ten-
            sions between, 8–9
        consolidation and extension, ten-
            sions between, 9–10
        deepening and widening, tensions
            between, 10
        domestic and international commit-
            ments, tensions between, 6–8
    features of, 180–81
    impetus to deepen, 160
    institutional challenge and response to,
        129–53
        Council of Ministers, 136–39
        democratic deficit and, 129–35
        European Parliament, 139–44
        European Union Commission, 136–
            39
        implications, 131, 151–52
        national parliaments, 145–48
        overview, 129–31, 152–53
        subsidiarity and, 148–50
    issues challenging process of, 1–2

European economic integration
   (*continued*)
   labor market institutions and, 13
   levels of analysis, 2–5
      domestic interests, 2–3, 5–6
      intergovernmentalism, 4
      national institutions, 3–4
      transnational institutions and inter-
         ests, 5
   Maastricht Treaty and, 15
   Monnet and, 134
   Nordic case studies and, 214–15
   wage-setting institutions and, 185–89
European Free Trade Area (EFTA), 247–
   53, 315–16
European Monetary System, 65
European Parliament (EP), 75, 132, 139–
   44, 297
European System of Central Banks
   (ESCB), 23–24, 30, 34, 42
European Union (EU)
   accountability of institutions in, 130–
      31, 152–53
   admission to, 21
   membership in
      aspirant's position, 303–13
      attitude toward, general, 305–8
      Central and Eastern European
         Countries, support for, 274
      Finland, 211
      incumbent's position, 287–303
      Norway, 212–13
      obvious implications of, 281–83
      opinions about, 213
      political economy implications of,
         283–87
      prospects for, 313
      second-class, 316–17
      Sweden, 211–12
   political institutions of, dissatisfaction
      with, 1
   public opinion of, 135
   regions in, role of, 148–50
   structure of, changes in, 151
   trade, 25–26
European Union (EU) Commission
   concerns about, 133
   democratic deficit and, 136–39
   Economic and Monetary Union and,
      25
   independence from member govern-
      ments of, 5
   representation on, 133
   role of, 132
European Union (EU) enlargement
   Alpine case studies, 247–69
      agriculture, 256–57
      arguments, 250–51
      Austria, 252, 257–63, 268–69
      background, 247–48
      competition, 251–54
      factor market integration, 255–56
      market segmentation, 251–54
      options, 249–50
      product variety, 254–55
      Single Market programs, predicting
         effects of, 248–49, 268
      Switzerland, 263–69
      trade diversion, 251
   Central and Eastern European Coun-
      tries and, 1, 14
   eastern, 273–80
      aspirant member's position, 303–13
      background, 273–76
      comprehensive accession strategy
         and, 317–18
      difficulties in analyzing via political
         economy theory, 276–80
      economic integration from political
         economy perspective, 280–87
      framework for assessing, 314–18
      incumbent member's position, 287–
         303
      policy implications, 313–18

variable geometry in, 316
impact of, 13, 160, 179–80
impetus for, 159
Nordic case studies, 211–41
  background, 211–14
  country level, 222–27, 240
  European economic integration,
    214–15
  individual level, 228–41
  national level, 215–22, 240
  opposition to, 159–60
  variable geometry and banking regula-
    tion, 179–80
excentric circles approach, 13, 161–62,
  174–77, 181
exchange market tensions, 55–56
Exchange Rate Mechanism (ERM), 53,
  55, 58–60, 65, 70–71
exchange rates
  fiscal policy and, 55
  fixed, 57–58, 99, 106
  flexibility, nominal, 93–94, 99–101,
    106–7
  floating, 66, 78
  inflation and, 59
  stability of, 30, 49–50, 65–67

factor market integration, 255–56
Federal Deposit Insurance Corporation
  (FDIC), 162
federalism, 91–121
  fiscal transfers and, 91–92
  political economy theory and, 119–20
  questions about, 115
Federal Regulatory Authority for Financial Institutions, 164
financial contagion, 162–63
financial markets, 98, 114
financial policy. *See* fiscal policy; *and specific types*
financial regulation. *See* banking regulation; *and specific types*

Finland, 211. *See also* Nordic case studies
fiscal crisis, 98
fiscal federalism. *See* federalism
fiscal insurance, 99–121
  case of, 115–20
  monetary independence versus, 105–
    15
    loss of fiscal instruments and, 114–
      15
    stabilizing fiscal policy and, 107–14
  need for, 92
  with nominal rigidities, 99–105, 113–
    14
  without nominal rigidities, 93–99,
    113–14
  overview, 120–21
  political unions and, 115–20
fiscal policy
  autonomous, 120
  disinflation and, 58
  Economic and Monetary Union and,
    91–93, 120
  exchange rates and, 55
  fiscal insurance in stabilizing, 107–14
  French, 55, 57–59, 61–63
  French macroeconomic policy and,
    11–12
  See also specific types
fiscal transfers
  autonomous fiscal policy and, 120
  in countries with economically diverse
    regions, 115
  federalism and, 91–92
  nominal exchange rate flexibility and,
    92, 107
  occurrence, in response to financial
    markets, 114
  regional purchasing power and, sta-
    bilizing, 105–6
  risk sharing and, 106
  schemes for international, 107–15
foreign direct investment, 216–19, 312

Foucauld, Jean-Baptiste de, 67
France, 10, 11, 39–41, 50, 59, 294
    See also French economic policy
franc fort policy, 60–61, 72
Franco-German alliance, 41, 43
French economic policy, 49–84
    interest groups and monetary policy,
        69–83
        agents' views, 69–71
        banking sector, 80–83
        company sector, 76–80
        debates, 71–72
        division among, 11
        public opinion, 72–76
    interventionist powers and, 57
    logic behind, 63–69
        Economic and Monetary Union as
            coronation, 68–69, 83
        European politics and domestic eco-
            nomic policy, 63–64
        price stability, 63, 65–68
    after Maastricht Treaty, 49–51
    macroeconomic, 11–12, 24, 64
    monetary policy, 69–83
    since 1970s, 51–63
        macroeconomic developments, ma-
            jor, 51–56
        results, assessing, 57–63
        structural changes, 56–57
    overview, 83–84
    Single Market program and, 57

G-7 countries, 61, 65
G-7 Louvre agreement (1987), 65
Gandois, Jean, 78
GDP. *See* gross domestic product
Germany, 25, 41, 43, 59, 149, 200–201
Governing Council, 42
Great Britain. *See* United Kingdom
gross domestic product (GDP), 21, 25,
    27, 63
gross settlement systems, 163–64

"hard" money policies, 22, 34, 43
Herstatt case, 165–66
home-country rule, 166–67, 169, 172

IGC. *See* Maastricht Intergovernmental
    Conference
imports, 288–289
incumbent members of European Union,
    287–303
    policy integration, 296–303
        inadequacy of political structures,
            296–297
        insufficient financial means, 297–
            303
    trade integration and, 287–96
        Europe Agreements, 287–90
        implications for political economy
            of Eastern European enlargement,
            295–96
        trade performance, 290–93
        trade projections, 293–95
inflation, 59, 94–96
inflation tax, 95–96, 98, 114
institutional challenge and response to
        European economic integration,
        129–53
    democratic deficit and, 129–35
    domestic level, 144–50
        national parliaments, 145–48
        subsidiarity and, 148–50
    European Union level, 135–44
        Council of Ministers, 136–39
        European Parliament, 139–44
        European Union Commission, 136–
            39
    implications of, 131, 152–53
    national parliaments, 145–48
    overview, 129–31, 152–53
    subsidiarity and, 148–50
integration
    deficit, 146
    "flexible architecture" for, 131

market, 280–81, 286
policy, 281, 311–12
political, 214, 280–81
trade, 288–96
See also European economic
    integration
interest-group model, 13–14
interest groups
    Central and Eastern European Coun-
        tries and, 303–5
    French economic policy and, 11, 69–
        83
        agents' views, 69–71
        banking sector, 80–83
        company sector, 76–80
        debates, 71–72
        division among, 11
        public opinion, 72–76
    national, 285, 303–5
    socioeconomic, 2–3
    transnational, 5
    See also specific types
interest rates, 33, 59, 72
intergovernmentalism, 4
Interparliamentary Conference, 148
Ireland, 39
Italy, 25

Kohl, Helmut, 24, 43–44, 159
Konstanz der Wirtschaftspolitik (constancy
    of economic policy), 284
labor market
    collective action problem and, 32
    immobility of, 101–2
    in Scandinavia, 193–94
    unemployment policies and, 3
    unions and, 187
labor market institutions (LMIs)
    British, 39
    Economic and Monetary Union and,
        11, 23, 31–38
    European economic integration and, 13

Lamers, Karl, 160
Länder, 101, 149
Large Exposure Directive, 167
l'autre politique, 50, 71–72
Laval government, 63
lender of last resort (LLR), 163, 165, 171,
    178
linkage politics, 6–7
LLR. *See* lender of last resort
LMIs. *See* labor market institutions

Maastricht Intergovernmental Con-
    ference (IGC), 129
Maastricht Treaty
    aim of, 280
    ambiguity of, 24
    centralized bank and, 42
    codecision procedure and, 140–44
    conception of, 83–84, 129
    confusion caused by, 276
    convergence criteria of, 21–22, 24, 40–
        41, 43–44, 106, 216
    cooperation procedure and, 141–44
    Danish rejection of, 135
    debate over, 10
    debt and deficits in, 93, 115
    declaration on transparency and, 137
    deepening of, problems caused by, 274
    European economic integration and, 15
    European Parliament and, 139–40
    fiscal criterion of, 72
    fiscal restraints prescribed by, 107
    French economic policy after, 49–51
    incomes and, stabilization of regional,
        105
    independence of central banks and, 30
    pivotal events after signing of, 3
    policy coordination and, 69
    policy integration and, 281
    public consensus and, 72–76, 134–35
    public sector deficits and, restrictions
        on, 120–21

Maastricht Treaty (*continued*)
  ratifying, 136
  strikes against, 56
  timetable of, 6–7
  United Kingdom's option and, 100
  variability in, 161
macroeconomic policy
  centralized bargaining and, 202
  corporatist argument and, 194–99
  disinflation and, 49
  Economic and Monetary Union mem-
    bership and, 27, 44
  French, 11–12, 24, 64
  optimum currency area perspective
    and, 27
  wage-setting institutions and, 188
Major (John) government, 138
market integration, 280–81, 286
Market Relations Committee (MRC), 147
market segmentation, 251–54
Mauroy government, 51, 71
Members of the European Parliament
  (MEPs), 140
MEPs. *See* Members of the European
  Parliament
MFA. *See* Multi-Fibre Agreement
Mitterrand presidency, 51, 64, 73, 160
monetary integration (MU), 170
Monnet, Jean, 134
MRC. *See* Market Relations Committee
MU. *See* monetary integration
Multi-Fibre Agreement (MFA), 289
mutual recognition, 167

national institutions, 3–4
  See also specific types
national interest groups, 285, 303–5
  See also specific types
national parliaments, 130, 132, 134, 139,
  145–48
net settlement systems, 163
New Zealand, 29

Nordic case studies, 211–41
  background, 211–14
  country level, 222–27, 240
    aggregate data, 224–26
    integration, 222–24
    national data, 226–27
  European economic integration and,
    214–15
  individual level, 228–41
    economic interests and consider-
      ations, 232–36
    issue salience, 236–40
    perceptions of personal and national
      economy, 228–32
  national level, 215–22, 240
    foreign direct investment, 216–19
    general economic well-being, 215–17
    trade exposure, 216, 220–22
Norway, 191, 212–13, 239
  See also Nordic case studies

OCA. *See* optimum currency area
OECD. *See* Organization for Economic
  Cooperation and Development
oil shocks, 51, 53, 66
open economies, 215
OPT. *See* outward processing trade
optimum currency area (OCA), 26–28,
  101
Ordnungspolitik, 284, 313
Organization for Economic Cooperation
  and Development (OECD), 21,
  195
outward processing trade (OPT), 290–91
Own Fund Directive, 167

payment-related lender of last resort
  (P-LLR), 164
payment systems, 163–69, 178
Plan Barre, 51
P-LLR. *See* payment-related lender
policy integration, 281, 311–12

political economy, 286, 312
political economy theory, 276–80, 284
political institutions, 1
    See also institutional challenge and response to European economic integration; *and specific types*
political integration, 214, 280–81
PPP. *See* purchasing power parity
price stability, 23–24, 59, 63, 65–68
product variety, 254–55
protection, supply and demand for, 284–85
prudential supervision, 166–69
public opinion, French, 72–76
public sector default, 98–99
purchasing power parity (PPP), 57–58

quota utilization rate (QUR), 292

RCA. *See* revealed comparative advantage
recession (1991–93), 55
recession (1992–96), 55–56
reflation program, 51, 53
regional asymmetric shocks, 101–5
related lender of last resort (R-LLR), 163, 169, 173–74
representation issues, 130, 133, 152–53
reunification shock, 53
revealed comparative advantage (RCA), 294–95

sacrifice ratios, 34
Schengen Group, 9
SEA. *See* Single European Act
Second Banking Directive (1989), 166
seignorage revenues, 94–96, 98
shocks
    oil, 51, 53, 66
    regional asymmetric, 101–5
    reunification, 53
single currency. *See* common currency
Single European Act (SEA), 3, 9, 15, 136, 139, 276, 280–81

Single Market program
    agriculture and, 256–57
    arguments, 250–51
    Austria and, 257–63, 268–69
    company sector and, 80
    consolidation needed for, 9
    creation of, 200
    economic times at launching of, 247, 268
    effects of, predicting, 248–49, 252–53, 268
    factor market integration and, 255–56
    floating exchange rates and, 78
    French economic policy and, 57
    implementation of, 146
    integration of, 170
    launching of, 77–78
    market segmentation and, 251–54
    options, 249–50
    product variety and, 254–55
    skepticism of, 75
    Switzerland and, 263–69
    trade diversion and, 251
SITC. *See* Standard International Trade Classification
small and medium-sized enterprises (SMEs), 78–79
social welfare gains, 106
socioeconomic interest groups, 2–3
sociopolitical institutions, 3–4
"soft money" policies, 22
Solvency Directive, 167
sovereign default, 98, 117
Spain, 25, 37–38
stability pact of Waigel, 24
Standard International Trade Classification (SITC), 221
structural funds, 311
subsidiarity, 137–39, 148–50, 277
Sweden, 185–86, 191–92, 201, 211–12
    See also Nordic case studies
Switzerland. *See* Alpine case studies

tariffs, 289–90
TEU. *See* Maastricht Treaty
"time inconsistency" problem, 29
trade
    dependence, 191, 216, 220–22
    diversion, 251
    foreign, 56
    integration, 287–96
    international, 2
    intra-European Union, 25–26
    liberalization, 308–10
    outward processing, 290–91
    performance, 290–92
    projections, 292–95
transnational institutions and interests, 5
Treaty of Maastricht. *See* Maastricht
    Treaty
Treaty of Rome, 280
Treaty on European Union (TEU). *See*
    Maastricht Treaty
Trichet, Jean-Claude, 67

unanimity, principle of, 297
unanticipated inflation tax, 95, 98, 114
unemployment, 3, 55, 59–60, 102
union monopoly argument, 187, 189–94,
    202
unions
    American, 193
    British, 185, 201
    competition and, 189–90
    disinflation and, 73–74
    labor market and, 187
    in Norway, 191
    Swedish, 191–92, 201–2
United Kingdom, 9, 39, 42, 79, 82, 100,
    138, 146, 185, 201

variable geometry (VG), 159–81
    banking regulation case study, 171–80
        application of, 177–79
        European Union enlargement and,
            179–80

organization of periphery, 174–77
        placement in framework of variable
            geometry, 171–74
        reasons for studying, 161
    conception of, 160–61
    concepts of, 170–71
    core integration, 170–74
    in eastern enlargement of European
        Union, 318
    French version of, 13, 161–62, 174–
        77, 181
    German version of, 13, 161, 174–77,
        181
    periphery integration, 174–77
    political economy of, 161
    second-class membership and, 316–17
    variants of, 174–77
        concentric circles approach, 13, 161,
            174–77, 181
        excentric circles approach, 13, 161–
            62, 174–77, 181

VG. *See* variable geometry
Visegrad 4 countries, 14, 159

wage compression, 201–2
wage-setting institutions, 185–203
    alternative view of, 199–202
    centralized bargaining and, 185–86,
        199–202
    change in, 185–86
    corporatist argument, 187–88, 190,
        194–99, 202
    European economic integration and,
        185–89
    macroeconomic policy and, 188
    union monopoly argument, 187, 189–
        94, 202
Waigel, Theo, 12, 24, 43
"wait and see" approach, 314
Working Group on EC Payment Systems,
    167